MW00606303

Daily Delight

*Meditations
from the Scriptures*

OTHER BOOKS BY P. G. MATHEW

The Normal Church Life:
An Exposition of the First Epistle of John

Victory in Jesus: A Feast from Joshua

The Wisdom of Jesus:
A Life Application of the Sermon on the Mount

Muscular Christianity:
Learning Endurance from the Book of Hebrews

The Joy of Christian Giving

Romans, Volume 1:
The Gospel Freedom (Romans 1–8)

Good News for All People

Power of the Holy Spirit: An Exposition of Acts

Romans, Volume 2:
The Gospel Life (Romans 9–16)

Daily Delight

Meditations from the Scriptures

P. G. Mathew

GRACE & GLORY MINISTRIES
MINISTRIES

GRACE & GLORY MINISTRIES
Davis, California

© 2015 by P. G. Mathew. Published by Grace and Glory Ministries, Davis, California. Printed in the United States of America. All rights reserved. No part of this book may be reproduced or transmitted in any form or by any means, electronic or mechanical, including photocopying, recording, or by an information storage and retrieval system—except by a reviewer who may quote brief passages in a review to be printed in a magazine, newspaper, or on the Web—without permission in writing from the publisher. For information, please contact Grace and Glory Ministries, gvcc@gracevalley.org.
ISBN: 978-0-9771149-9-3

All scripture quotations, unless otherwise indicated, are taken from the 1984 version of the Holy Bible, New International Version®, NIV®. Copyright ©1973, 1978, 1984, 2011 by Biblica, Inc.™ Used by permission of Zondervan. All rights reserved worldwide. www.zondervan.com [Occasionally wording has been modified without notation to reflect author's preference and emphasis.]

The "NIV" and "New International Version" are trademarks registered in the United States Patent and Trademark Office by Biblica, Inc.™

Contents

About the Author

The Reverend P. G. Mathew, who holds three graduate degrees in theology from Central and Westminster theological seminaries (USA), is the founder and senior minister of Grace Valley Christian Center in California. Originally a scientist from India, he is also a former professor of Greek and systematic theology and has traveled widely for Christian mission interests. He is the author of *The Normal Church Life* (1 John); *Victory in Jesus* (Joshua); *The Wisdom of Jesus* (the Sermon on the Mount); *Muscular Christianity* (Hebrews); *The Joy of Christian Giving; The Gospel Freedom* and *The Gospel Life* (Romans)*; Good News for All People;* and *Power of the Holy Spirit* (Acts). He is also the founder and president of Grace Valley Christian Academy and Grace and Glory Foundation. For more information, visit *www.gracevalley.org.*

Preface

As a young boy in India, I would go to bed hearing my parents' prayers. In the morning, I needed no alarm clock, for their early morning prayers would wake me up without fail. I still remember my entire family joining together at five o'clock to worship and then listen as my father taught us from the Scriptures. Whatever I am as a Christian and a minister of the gospel, and whatever success I have had, can be attributed to God's grace poured out on me through this priceless heritage of vibrant personal and family devotions.

Forty-two years ago, I arrived in Davis, California, with my family to teach New Testament Greek and systematic theology. In response to the requests of many university students, we founded Davis Evangelical Church (now Grace Valley Christian Center) in 1974. From its inception, this church has been committed to the authority of Christ and his infallible word. Accordingly, we soon began to follow a daily reading schedule which enables participants to read yearly through the Old Testament once and the New Testament twice. We have continued this spiritual discipline to this day and have been greatly blessed.

For the past four decades, our triune God has helped me to preach through the Bible, making clear to all the whole counsel of God. This daily devotional celebrates the powerful, life-changing ministry of God's word by taking excerpts from these sermons and applying them to a portion of the scripture reading for each day. Thus, the book is arranged in keeping with our daily reading schedule. However, it can be read with great profit by all who desire to be built up in our most holy faith.[1]

I would like to thank my wife Gladys, who has co-labored with me for Christ for almost fifty years, and my son Evan and

---

1   GVCC's reading schedule is included as an appendix. There are only two exceptions to the daily reading pattern: January 1 and December 25.

daughter Sharon and their families; Mr. Marc Roby, Dr. Lisa Case, Mr. Gregory Perry, and Mrs. Margaret Killeen, editing; Mr. Michael Ishii, formatting; Miss Jessica Blizard, cover design; Mr. Daniel Washabaugh, production; and Mrs. Sarah Trombly, whose idea it was to link my sermons to our daily reading schedule.

May God continue to bless the preaching and reading of his word for many generations to come, both at Grace Valley Christian Center and in every church that remains faithful to Jesus Christ and his word. *Soli Deo Gloria!*

P. G. MATHEW

I am a creature of a day, passing through life as an arrow through the air. I am a spirit come from God and returning to God; just hovering over the great gulf, till a few moments hence I am no more seen—I drop into an unchangeable eternity! I want to know one thing, the way to heaven—how to land safe on that happy shore. God himself has condescended to teach the way: for this very end he came from heaven. He hath written it down in a book. O give me that book! At any price give me the Book of God! I have it. Here is knowledge enough for me. Let me be homo unius libri *[a man of one book]. Here then I am, far from the busy ways of men. I sit down alone: only God is here. In his presence I open, I read his Book; for this end, to find the way to heaven.*

—John Wesley, *"Preface to Sermons on Several Occasions"*

January 1

Is it a time for you yourselves to be living in your paneled houses, while this house remains a ruin? —Haggai 1:4

ur New Year's resolution is to rise from our complacency and build God's house. We find encouragement to do this from the small book of Haggai. Fifty thousand Jews returned from the Babylonian exile to Judah in 538 BC under the decree and provision of King Cyrus. They wanted to rebuild the temple, and, soon after they came, they laid the foundation and built an altar for sacrifices. Yet within three years, they discontinued the project because of opposition from their enemies. They failed to trust in God to deliver them from all their foes.

Because they stopped building, the exiles became unclean and their sacrifices were unacceptable to God. They engaged in a life of self-sufficiency and independence. But such a life is cursed. God therefore brought charges against them through his prophet.

What is the word of the Lord to us today? "See to it that you complete the work you have received in the Lord" (Col. 4:17). Let us rise and build God's temple! Today we ourselves are that temple. God dwells, not in ornate buildings, but in his people, individually and corporately. The apostle Paul declares, "God's temple is sacred, and you are that temple" (1 Cor. 3:17). To rise and build, then, means to repent, turn to God, and live in obedience to his royal will.

In this new year, may God give us a new attitude toward doing good works that strengthen his church. Such works are holy and spiritual. Whenever we speak about Jesus and the gospel, we are doing God's work. Let us reach out to people and invite them to church or for a meal, and then share the gospel. God intends to build his church through each one of us.

God later told his people through Haggai, "From this day on I will bless you." Our day of blessing begins the day we repent. Beginning today, therefore, let us repent, and seek to be filled with the Holy Spirit. Let us strive earnestly to build ourselves up in the most holy faith. Let us work to build up our families in accordance with God's word. And let us build up our larger family, the church, by the grace God gives to each of us.

"All this I will give you," Satan said, "if you will bow down and worship me." —Matthew 4:9

atan's third temptation of our Lord exposed the devil's real goal in every temptation—that he be given the obedience and worship that is due to the triune God alone. Satan, in his opposition to the Most High, wants to be exalted above him. And so he craves the worship of God's creatures.

In Matthew 4 we read that the devil took Jesus to a very high mountain and showed him, in an instant, all the kingdoms of the world in all of their glory. Notice, he carefully hid the corruption of these kingdoms, and revealed only their external splendor. "All sovereignty, all glory, all authority, all power is mine," Satan told Jesus. "And I can give all of these to whomever I want."

What was Satan tempting Jesus to do? To avoid the cross. Implicit in Satan's promise was this: "Jesus, I can help you to avoid your messianic mission. I will keep you from having to suffer and die for the sins of the world. I can give you a shortcut to glory!"

What was the price? "You must bow down and worship me." This temptation was not unique to Jesus. We are all tempted to compromise with the devil. But Satan is a murderer and a liar and there is no truth in him. Jesus once asked his disciples, "What good will it be for a man if he gains the whole world, yet forfeits his soul?" (Matt. 16:26). Let me ask you the same question: What does sin profit, young man, young woman? That pleasure, that independence, that so-called freedom that you desire—they are, in reality, the devil's lies. You may gain the world for a season, but in the end you will lose your soul and experience eternal damnation.

In the power of the Spirit and by the word of God, Jesus defeated the devil and drove him away. And in due time, all authority in heaven and on earth was indeed given to Jesus—by his Father (Matt. 28:18). So I say to you: Hold fast to the path of obedience, be filled with the Spirit, and study and delight in the Holy Scriptures, so that you may recognize and resist Satan's lies. And God will enable you to stand victorious in temptation (1 Cor. 10:13).

JANUARY 3

The Lord God called to the man, "Where are you?" —Genesis 3:9

eminism is as old as the Fall recorded in Genesis 3. Feminism seeks the headship of woman over man and God. Feminism is a total reversal of the divine order God gives in his word—God is the head of man and man the head of woman (1 Cor. 11:3).

In Genesis 3 we see Satan deceiving Eve, and Adam passively following her leadership. Then God asked Adam, "Where are you?" That question should ring in the ears of every husband today. You are the God-appointed ruler for your family. Where are you? Adam became a rebel and an enemy of God in his failure to rule for God, and in his failure to love and shield his wife from the seduction of the devil.

God had been very generous with Adam and Eve; they could eat from any tree in the garden except one—the tree of the knowledge of good and evil. Adam was tested in the most favorable of circumstances, yet he failed. We do not hear his voice rebuking the serpent or reproving Eve. It was Adam who had named all the animals; he possessed authority to rule over all the living creatures, including this strange, speaking serpent. He was also the one who named Eve. Adam, therefore, had the primary responsibility to rule in behalf of God. It was his duty to confront the devil and cast him out of the garden. Adam was there, but he was silent and passive. He abandoned his post as ruler.

Adam's failure to rule brought death to all mankind. In Adam, all became sinners and all die. We are conceived in sin, born in sin, possess a sin nature, and daily practice sin. We are by nature enemies of God. The wrath of God abides upon every sinner.

Can sinners be saved from God's wrath? Yes! Where the first Adam failed, the second Adam—Jesus Christ, the Son of God, the Seed of the woman—succeeded. By his atoning death, Christ Jesus crushed the head of the devil, Satan, the ancient serpent, and nullified the effects of sin. In Christ, we are given eternal life. In Christ, we resist the devil, and he flees from us. In Christ, the pre-Fall order is restored.

3

Then the LORD said to Cain, . . . "If you do what is right, will you not be accepted?" —Genesis 4:6–7

od's word, not our hunches, regulates authentic, God-pleasing worship. In Genesis 4 we read that Cain was the first to bring an offering to the Lord. He did so from the fruits of the soil, for he was a farmer. Abel also brought an offering to the Lord. It consisted of the fat portions from some of the firstborn of his flock. Abel brought the prescribed offering to God. Cain knew what offering would be pleasing to God, but he followed his own ideas.

Cain failed to bring an acceptable sacrifice because he was an unbeliever. Hebrews 11:4 tells us that Abel by faith brought a more excellent sacrifice than Cain did. Without faith, it is impossible to please God, and such faith comes, not by listening to our hunches, but by hearing the word of God. So we read that God was pleased with Abel and his offering, but he was not pleased with Cain or his offering (Gen. 4:5). If God does not accept our person, he will not accept anything we do.

Yet then God in his great mercy came to Cain to counsel him so that he might repent and worship God in faith and in truth. God asked Cain: "Why are you angry? Why is your face fallen? Why are you depressed?" The cause of depression is guilt, and the cause of guilt is sin, which is transgression of God's law.

Then God counseled Cain, "Do what is right, and you will be accepted; your face will be lifted up." In other words, God was saying, "You know what is right. I revealed to you the acceptable way of approaching me—by blood sacrifice."

Sadly, Cain rejected God's divine counsel. He went away from God as a depressed man, to live evermore in misery (Gen. 4:13–16). Had he obeyed God, he would have enjoyed God's presence with a radiant face forever.

How can we avoid repeating Cain's tragic mistake? God told Cain, "Believe me and approach me with the prescribed sacrifice for a sinner." Today he says, "Repent and believe on the Lord Jesus Christ, and you will be saved. You will be happy forever; the guilt of sin shall not depress you." The obedience of faith in Christ is the cure of the sin that causes depression.

Therefore everyone who hears these words of mine and puts them into practice is like a wise man who built his house on the rock.
—Matthew 7:24

esus concluded the Sermon on the Mount by speaking of two kinds of builders and two kinds of foundations. First is the foundation of rock. The wise builders have to dig deep to find the bedrock and build upon it. The foolish build on a foundation of sand, and when the buildings of their lives are tested, they collapse.

What did Jesus mean when he spoke of the rock? In Psalm 18:2 we read, "The LORD is my rock, my fortress and my deliverer; my God is my rock, in whom I take refuge." God spoke through Isaiah, "See, I lay a stone in Zion, a tested stone, a precious cornerstone for a sure foundation; the one who trusts will never be dismayed" (Isa. 28:16).

Jesus Christ is the rock—tested by the Father, by the devil, by human authorities, and by saints throughout the ages—tested and approved. He is the only foundation that will stand firm in this world and the next. Therefore, we must build our lives upon the person and work of Christ alone. We must trust in Jesus alone for our salvation.

Jesus is not one of many possible foundations for our lives; he is the only foundation. The apostle Paul emphasizes this fact when he states, "Each one should be careful how he builds. For no one can lay any foundation other than the one already laid, which is Jesus Christ" (1 Cor. 3:10–11).

How, then, are you building? Let me assure you, everyone is building. Every day we build, and every decision we make is part of the building. Are you a wise or a foolish builder? A wise builder carefully studies Christ's instruction manual on how to build, and he will not add to or subtract from it. A foolish builder refuses to think and understand; he has a lazy mind. He is an emotional person, led by feelings rather than Scripture.

As you live your life, are you building to last? Or will your building collapse when it is tested? Are you building thoughtfully upon the foundation that is impregnable, the foundation of rock? The day of final judgment will reveal the foundation upon which we each have built.

Do you believe that I am able to do this? —Matthew 9:28

hristianity is the opposite of self-help. Christianity is God helping us, not you and I helping ourselves. God's plan has always been to take elect sinners and cause them to freely serve him, worship him, praise him, love him, and do his will. Throughout history there has always been a church that has been enabled by God to love and worship him wholeheartedly. Salvation is God's business, and God accomplishes this by grace. God is able to make us do his will on our own volition. This is the work of God, and if that is not happening to you, then you must question your salvation.

God is able to save us. But no one receives anything from him without first truly understanding the gospel that speaks of the person and work of God's Son, Jesus Christ. And so Jesus asked the blind men, "Do you believe that I am able to do this?" Jesus was asking these men if they really believed who he was and what he was able to do. Was he really able to save them? What did they reply? "Yes, Lord." Then he touched their eyes and said, "According to your faith will it be done to you," and their sight was restored. This is a picture of true, God-authored salvation.

We must make up our minds. We can rely on God, who is able, or rely on ourselves. How do you want to live? If you don't want Christ, you are left with self-help. Those who are into self-help don't read the Bible, the word of God's grace. They don't call on God in prayer. They believe they can look to themselves and their resources for help. But self will eventually fail us; self cannot save us from what really matters—sin, death, and judgment.

Salvation is not some form of self-help, or a little bit of Jesus and little bit of myself together doing something. No! It is my renouncing myself completely and entrusting everything to Jesus Christ for now and forever. Do you understand who Jesus is? He alone is able to save you from your sins. He alone is able to keep you from falling and present you before God without fault and with great joy.

The LORD then said to Noah, "Go into the ark, you and your whole family, because I have found you righteous in this generation." —Genesis 7:1

hat are family values? They are the things that you value most as a family. What does your family value most? Sports? Music? Money? Morality? Whatever it is, you will strive to see that your children have it. But if you are a Christian, you will treasure the gospel of our Lord and Savior Jesus Christ above all else. There is nothing more valuable than the gospel. If we truly understand this, we will do everything necessary to pass it on to our children.

Do you value the gospel above everything else? Have you realized that Jesus Christ is the most precious possession we can have? He is the hidden treasure, the pearl of great price, now revealed to us, and for whom we must sell all. As he himself asked, "What does it profit if you gain the whole world and lose your soul?" Are you making every effort to impart the wealth of the gospel to your children?

Noah taught his family to value God and his word. And the benefit to them was family salvation. When the great flood came, they alone—eight persons out of the vast multitude of people on the earth—did not perish.

One week after receiving God's invitation, Noah entered the ark. Praise be to God, this blameless preacher of righteousness did not enter the ark alone! As he went in, Noah looked behind him, and there was his wife, who had believed the gospel he preached to her. Then Noah and his wife looked, and there were their three sons, who also believed. Then the sons looked, and there were their wives, who believed as well.

If your greatest family value is not the gospel, then you are giving your loved ones something else. But how terrible it will be to come to the end of your life and realize that your family is not saved! How awful to know that those who lived closest to you do not possess the one thing needful!

Fathers and mothers, do you understand what God demands of you? You are to direct your entire household to walk in the way of the Lord (Gen. 18:19). You must strive to fulfill that obligation with everything that you have.

No one knows the Father except the Son and those to whom the Son chooses to reveal him. —Matthew 11:27

evelation of the Father, which is the essence of salvation, comes through Jesus Christ exclusively. Jesus prayed elsewhere, "This is eternal life: that they may know you, the only true God, and Jesus Christ, whom you have sent" (John 17:3). Jesus Christ was sent to reveal the Father. The world's greatest philosophers—Socrates, Aristotle, Plato, Thales—did not by their worldly wisdom find him. Jesus of Nazareth, the unique God/man, alone knows the Father.

Throughout the world people believe in many different gods. But saving knowledge of the one true and living God comes only through the Lord Jesus Christ. He proclaimed, "I am the way and the truth and the life. No one comes to the Father except through me" (John 14:6). We cannot know God without repenting of our sins and trusting in Jesus.

We must shout with great joy for this amazing revelation of the Father given to us through Jesus Christ. What mercy and grace! God said, "Let there be light," and light came into our dark and sinful minds. As a result, we repented of our sins and looked to Jesus with the understanding that he is not just a man, but the very Son of God who has come to make his Father known.

To all the elect of God, Jesus says, "Come!" He invites all who are weary and burdened by the crushing weight of their sin to come to him in faith. He invited us, and we came by his effectual call to receive his promised rest. Our guilt and depression and hell have been removed, and in their place we have joyfully received Jesus' yoke of ownership. It is the easy yoke that frees us from the slavery of sin by tying us to him. It is the yoke that gives us his righteousness and his rest.

All those whose eyes have been opened, those to whom the revelation of the Father is given, will surely come to Jesus, the Son of God. They will take up his yoke with great joy and walk with him all the days of their lives. The sovereign God who revealed himself to them in the gospel of his Son will himself enable them to do so.

He who is not with me is against me, and he who does not gather with me scatters. —*Matthew 12:30*

 crowd often followed Jesus. In Matthew 12 we read that they witnessed an amazing miracle—in one moment, a man who had been demonized, a man who was violent, deaf, blind, and mute, was saved and began to see and speak. What was this crowd's reaction? "All the people were astonished." They had been looking for just such a thrill, just such an astounding sight. And they exclaimed, "Could this be the Son of David?" But it was a question, not a statement or confession. These people were fascinated by Jesus, but they would not believe in him. They would not directly commit themselves and declare that Jesus is the Son of David.

The crowd did not want to decide. Having seen Jesus' miracles, and having heard Jesus' teaching, including his own statement that in him the kingdom of God had come, and having heard that Jesus was stronger than Satan, most in the crowd still preferred to remain uncommitted, to remain neutral. This is known as "sitting on the fence." For many of those Jews, it was a very comfortable stance. There are many, many people like this in the world today. They have been given sufficient understanding as to who Jesus is. Yet these people continue to be "fence-sitters." They may not act like enemies of Jesus Christ. They do not take up stones to kill him. They may not even mock him. But they will not confess. They will not repent. They will not trust him for their salvation. They will not follow him as their Lord.

All such people should realize, however, that when it comes to Jesus Christ, neutrality is, in fact, impossible. We must decide either for or against him. And not to decide for him is to decide against him. Such "fence-sitters" will soon die and enter into an eternity of doom, for they will die in their sins, under the rule of Satan. This day I say to you: Wake up! Realize that there is a stronger one who has come—Jesus Christ. He has bound Satan. He is even now freeing his captives. Now is the time when you must place your trust in this Christ. He is the Son of David, the Messiah, the only one who is able to save sinners.

The LORD had said to Abram, "Leave your country, your people and your father's household and go to the land I will show you. I will make you into a great nation and I will bless you." —Genesis 12:1–2

rials are ordained by God to purify our faith. No child of God is exempt. Abraham, the father of all believers, experienced many such tests. In Genesis 12 we read that God appeared to Abram, commanding him to leave Haran and go to the country God had in mind for him. This word of the Lord contained one condition and seven promises. The condition came as an imperative, for God always commands. "Leave your country," God said. In other words, "Leave the known and the familiar to go to the unknown and the unfamiliar." God was saying, "Deny yourself, take up the cross, and follow me."

This is the test God demands of us all: absolute faith and total obedience. Abram believed God's promises and obeyed his command. God said, "Leave!" and Abram left. God says the same to us. He demands that we separate from worldliness, from autonomy, from sin. God's people are a holy people. We must turn from sin and turn to God. We must repent and believe. We must live lives of separation, not compromise.

By faith, Abram obeyed God. His was the obedience of faith. So we read, "By faith Abraham, when called to go to a place he would later receive as his inheritance, obeyed and went, even though he did not know where he was going" (Heb. 11:8). Don't worry about where you are going; God leads his dear children along.

Faith without obedience is the devil's faith, not saving faith. Abram believed, and he obeyed. He left his country, his kindred, and his father's house. He took his wife Sarai, his nephew Lot, his servants, and all his property, including all his livestock. And in due time, the Lord brought him to Canaan and fulfilled his promises.

The Christian life is an exodus like that of Abram, and, later, like that of the Israelites from Egypt. God leads his dear children out of the land of slavery and into the land of liberty, a land flowing with milk and honey. He leads us through the wilderness of trials and testings. The Christian life is one test after another; we graduate only when we die. But in him, the elect will pass all the tests of faith.

Jesus immediately said to them: "Take courage! It is I. Don't be afraid."
—*Matthew 14:27*

n this passage Jesus commanded his disciples to get into a boat and cross the lake without him. This was a new experience for the disciples. They understood that Jesus would join them later, but they did not know how or when he would come. It was Jesus' intent that they grow in their faith.

When the disciples set out at Jesus' command, the weather was calm. Soon, though, it became stormy. Some Christians believe that if we are sent by God and we are walking in his paths, then everything will be smooth and easy. They think that no trouble or storm will ever face us, that no persecution will ever come our way, that we'll never have to endure sickness or poverty. This is a false view. The prophet Jonah faced a stormy sea because of his disobedience, but this does not mean that obedient Christians will never face trials. Even Christians who are led by the Spirit of God will encounter severe tests. The calm will change to a storm. It is life's storms that try our faith, not life's calms. These storms cause us to be aroused and awakened, so that we may trust in Jesus Christ alone.

And so we read that the wind rose up against the disciples. The sea became rough; the waves battered against their boat. The disciples were surely tempted to turn around and go back, yet they did not. Why? They were believers. Believers obey the commands of Jesus Christ. So they did not change their direction and instead strained at the oars. They worked hard as they endeavored to obey their Master in the face of adversity.

But notice and take heart: While the disciples were being buffeted by the waves, Jesus did not abandon them, nor were they hidden from his sight. He saw their struggle and interceded in private prayer for them.

What can we learn from this passage? Jesus is the omniscient God; he sees all things, and his eyes are especially on us, his disciples. He is interceding for us even now, and his prayer is always effectual. If Jesus sends us, no storm or enemy can defeat us; we will arrive at our destination.

Abram believed the LORD, and he credited it to him as righteousness.
—*Genesis 15:6*

n Genesis 15 Abram entered into a conversation for the first time with God. He asked, "Why am I without children? You promised me children. Yet my chief servant, Eliezer of Damascus, is going to inherit all my property."

God answered, "No, Abram, he is not going to be your heir; that is not my eternal plan. A son whom you father will be your heir, according to my plan for you. Come outside with me. Look at the clear night sky. Can you count all the stars?" Then God said, "So shall your offspring be."

Abram believed God's promise, and this was credited to him as righteousness. The Hebrew can be translated, "Abram said, 'Amen,' to his promise," or, "Abram rested upon God himself, and he was justified." Abram was clothed with divine righteousness because he believed in the promised Messiah, the Son of Abraham. "Abraham believed God" means he believed in his own distant offspring—the Lord Jesus Christ. What must we do to be saved? "Believe on the Lord Jesus Christ, and you will be saved."

Then Abram expressed a second concern to God: "You have not given me any land, as you promised." In loving response, God reassured him by making a covenant with him. Abram brought a heifer, a goat, and a ram. He cut them in half and arranged the halves opposite each other. In a typical covenant, both Abram and God would have passed between the pieces to seal covenant between the two parties. But God was not making a bilateral treaty; he was making an unconditional, unilateral covenant with Abram. God alone was taking a self-maledictory oath, saying, "If I do not fulfill my promises to you, let me be destroyed like these animals." God alone passed through the divided animals. And all the promises God made to Abraham were fulfilled in due time.

God fulfills his promises in his time, not ours. And his timing is always perfect. The promise of the Messiah was fulfilled after two thousand years, in the fullness of time. True believers wait in expectation for God to fulfill his promises: "I wait for the LORD, my soul waits, and in his word I put my hope" (Ps. 130:5).

She said to Abram, "The LORD has kept me from having children. Go, sleep with my maidservant; perhaps I can build a family through her." Abram agreed to what Sarai said. —Genesis 16:2

enesis 15 records one of the high points in the life of Abraham. There we read one of the most important verses in all of Scripture: "Abram believed the LORD, and he credited it to him as righteousness." But Genesis 16 speaks of one of Abraham's lowest points. This warns us that right after a mountaintop experience, we can make the most terrible mistakes. A tremendous spiritual victory does not guarantee our avoiding a grievous error the next day. How careful we must be as we make decisions, and how important it is to learn from this chapter in Abram's life.

The Christian life entails a series of tests that help us to grow in our faith in God. Abram passed several such tests of faith in Genesis 12 through 15. He earned an "A." But now he faced a trial of patience: Could he be patient and wait on God's perfect timing for a son, or would he try to solve the problem in his own way by leaning on his own understanding? Here Abram failed terribly. At his wife's leading, he who had risen to the zenith of faith now descended to the Dead Sea of self-reliance. Abram meekly obeyed Sarai's carnal instructions, and Hagar, her Egyptian maidservant, conceived a son, Ishmael.

God allowed Abram and Sarai to carry out their plan in opposition to his will, but he would never add his blessing. The consequences proved to be devastating, both at that time and for generations to come. As soon as Hagar knew she was pregnant, there was bitter strife in the household. Fourteen years later, when God appeared to Abraham to renew his promise of a son to be conceived through Sarai, Abraham pleaded with God, "If only Ishmael might live under your blessing!" (Gen. 17:18). But it would never be. We can never manipulate God's will to make it conform to our own. God will never bless our Ishmaels. Eventually, Abraham and Sarah would have to send him away, which "distressed Abraham greatly because it concerned his son" (Gen. 21:11). Not only so, but the descendants of Ishmael also became archenemies of the future nation of Israel. How bitter is the fruit of self-will!

Lord, how many times shall I forgive my brother when he sins against me? —Matthew 18:21

od desires that we live healthy lives. In Exodus 15:26, God told his people, "I am the LORD, who heals you," and in 1 Peter 2:24 we read, "By his wounds you have been healed." But no one can live a truly healthy life unless he first repents, puts his faith in Jesus Christ, and then begins to forgive others. When we receive forgiveness from God for our infinite sin against him and then practice a life of forgiveness toward our fellow believers, including our spouse and children, then we will enjoy health of body and soul.

In ancient Judaism there was a limit placed on the number of times a person had to forgive another. In fact, the rabbis taught that God would forgive his people only up to three times. Peter came to Jesus with this idea that there is a limit to forgiveness. How did Jesus respond? He rejected outright the idea of putting any limits on forgiveness. "Not seven times, but seventy-seven times," Jesus replied. Jesus' answer spoke to the core issue behind Peter's question, which is man's basic unwillingness to forgive others.

Man needs forgiveness continuously from God, and I am sure none of us wants to put any limits on the forgiveness we receive. But we often want to place constraints when it comes to our forgiving those who have sinned against us. Jesus insists, however, that we forgive without limit, just as God forgives us. If we have experienced the infinite forgiveness of God for our infinite sin, then forgiveness will be a way of life for us. Just as we receive forgiveness from God for the sins we commit daily, so we must daily forgive those who sin against us. If we refuse to do so, we will experience divine chastisement in this life.

I believe that some Christians are ill because they will not forgive their husbands or wives or others in the church. Perhaps you are currently experiencing such sickness in your spirit, mind, or body. Have you ever considered that your malady may be the result of your unwillingness to forgive someone? If you are so convicted, I urge you to repent of this serious sin today and begin to live a healthy life of unlimited forgiveness.

JANUARY 15

For I have chosen him, so that he will direct his children and his household after him to keep the way of the LORD by doing what is just and right. —Genesis 18:19

or I have chosen him." The Lord's statement speaks of election. We are not our own; we are chosen of God, and we have certain God-given responsibilities. What does Genesis 18 tell us about God's purposes in choosing Abraham? First, God says, "so that he will direct his children." This statement of purpose runs completely counter to the modern idea of childraising. The Bible, however, says that parents are God's delegated authorities; we must not allow our children to walk in the way of folly. If we fail to restrain them, we are not rendering obedience to the God who has chosen us. We are not autonomous, but under the authority of the eternal Jehovah. His will is that we command, direct, and govern our households so that our children may bring glory to God throughout their lives.

To honor God in this high calling, the father must read and teach the Bible daily. We are told in Deuteronomy 6 to talk about the Book when we walk and when we sit down, when we get up and when we lie down. We must give this training and instruction more importance than chemistry, physics, mathematics, or ballet lessons. We must train each child in godly wisdom. And we must practice what we preach by saying goodbye to worldliness.

What is God's second purpose in election? "So that the LORD will bring about for Abraham what he has promised." The Lord committed himself by a covenant to bless Abraham and all his descendants. And what greater blessing is there than to see our children walking in the truth! When we see that a child has internalized the gospel and is living for God, living in wisdom and making godly decisions, then we will not be worried about what he will do as he gets older.

"I have chosen him," God said of Abraham. We also are chosen for the same purpose, that we may impart wisdom to our households. Then surely the blessing that Abraham received—a child of promise who served the Lord throughout his entire life—will be ours as well. God in covenant faithfulness will come and bless our entire family.

Hurry and get out of this place, because the LORD is about to destroy the city! —Genesis 19:14

W e read in Genesis 13 that Abraham had generously given his nephew Lot the first choice of land. Abraham was called by God and therefore lived by faith in God; he let God choose for him. Lot, however, was a person who lived by sight and not by faith. What he desired was independence from Abraham and Abraham's God. He was not seeking the kingdom of God and his righteousness; his choice was based on what was good for his animals, not what was good for his soul.

And so Lot chose and pitched his tent near Sodom. He knew Sodom's people were extremely wicked, known for their homosexuality. But he ignored the dangers. It was not the God of Abraham who formed his value system; it was the pagan world. Soon he moved into the city itself and began to enjoy great success. No more tents. No more moving from here to there. Now he lived in a large house in the highly cultured city of Sodom. Not only that, he had climbed the social ladder and was now a judge, a figure of great prominence.

What a terrible choice Lot had made. "Lot chose for himself" (Gen. 13:11). He did not look to God to direct him. He did not ask his uncle to help him. He was independent and self-sufficient. But in relying on his own wisdom, Lot chose what the Lord would eventually completely destroy. At the height of his success, Lot lost everything to God's fiery judgment—his property, his security, his wife, his Sodomite sons-in-law, and the spiritual blessings he could have enjoyed had he stayed with Abraham. What tragedy!

Lot went away from God's prophet, God's people, and God's presence, to a city that was destined to be destroyed. And all along he thought he had made the right decision. He went away to seek worldly success, and he achieved it all, only to lose it all. You and I can make the same mistake if we are not careful. We can move towards and settle in something that God has determined to judge by fire. We can fall in love with a doomed world. How we play the fool if we choose for ourselves and ignore the plan of God!

Abraham said of his wife Sarah, "She is my sister." —Genesis 20:2

ll who truly believe in Christ will undergo God-ordained trials that test their faith. These tests end finally when we die in faith. Abraham, who is described as the father of all believers, had to go through many tests.

In Genesis 20, we find Abraham and Sarah living in the Philistine territory of Gerar, which was ruled by a powerful king named Abimelech. Abraham had not sought direction from God to go to Gerar, just as he had not sought direction when he went to Egypt twenty-five years earlier (Gen. 12:10–20). Abraham and Sarah were not progressing in their spiritual lives; rather, they were regressing. So when King Abimelech asked about the beautiful Sarah, Abraham and Sarah both lied to him about their marriage covenant.

Abraham was by nature very fearful. Thus, he and Sarah had entered into an agreement years before to lie about their marriage wherever they encountered danger. In this way, if Sarah was taken as a wife by a ruler, she could save both Abraham's life and her own. So they used the lie in Gerar that they had used in Egypt twenty-five years earlier. They never canceled this covenant of lie, this insurance policy, even though they were following the God of truth. In Gerar, Abraham once again was reverting to fear, even though he had previously fought against four mighty kings and won (Gen. 14). He was afraid now, even though God had told him, "Fear not; I am your shield and very great reward. I am El Shaddai. Walk before me and be blameless" (Gen. 15).

Thanks be to God, he kept the morally upright Abimelech from sinning! Yet consider this: he did not prevent Abraham and Sarah from sinning. God allows his people to sin. Abraham and Sarah failed miserably, and their failure must serve as a warning to keep us humble also. We learn from this episode that sin will still dwell in us until the day we die.

Nevertheless, God in his faithfulness did not abandon Abraham. God surely comes to deliver his servants even when they sin. God must chasten us for our sins; yet not even our sins can separate us from his love. Our God remains faithful to his covenant of love throughout all generations.

Love the Lord your God with all your heart and with all your soul and with all your mind. —Matthew 22:37

he will of God for us is to love him without limit and to love our neighbors as ourselves. But what does it really mean to love God with all our heart, mind, soul, and strength?

Biblical love is not an unpredictable feeling that just comes over us. If it were, how could God command us to love him? Biblical love means action. Jesus taught his disciples, "If you love me, you will obey what I command" (John 14:15). If we say we love God but do not obey him, we are lying. When a child says, "I love my father and mother," but refuses to do what they say, that child is not telling the truth. Love for God means total obedience to him.

First John 5:3 says, "This is love for God: to obey his commands. And his commands are not burdensome." If we complain to God, "Your yoke is heavy and your commands are grievous," then the love of God is not animating us. When God's love truly fills our hearts, we will agree with the Bible that his yoke is easy, his burden is light, and his commands are a joy.

In 1 John 4:19 we read, "We love because he first loved us," and in 1 John 4:11 we read, "Dear friends, since God so loved us, we also ought to love one another." God's love for us comes first, and it is the basis for our love for him. Does this love mean that we are promised a non-stop emotional high? Not at all! But Jesus did promise, "If anyone loves me, he will obey my teaching. My Father will love him, and we will come to him and make our home with him" (John 14:23). When God the Father and God the Son come and make their home with us, we discover that his commands truly are liberating. We are filled with joy unspeakable, and we will be full of glory when God manifests himself to us.

To love God with all our heart, mind, soul, and strength thus means that we must surrender ourselves entirely to him and obey him completely with all the strength and joy he provides. If we do not obey God in this way, then we do not love him as we ought.

God said, "Take your son, your only son, Isaac, whom you love, and go to the region of Moriah. Sacrifice him there." —Genesis 22:2

his command from God was the hardest test Abraham ever faced. It is the hardest test that any human father could face. Yet Abraham obeyed God without wavering. With his servants and Isaac and the wood, he set out for Mount Moriah, a journey of three days. Abraham was resolute to obey God's command. We must ask, "How could he do this?" The answer is found in Hebrews 11:17–19, where we read: "By faith Abraham, when God tested him, offered Isaac as a sacrifice. He who had received the promises was about to sacrifice his one and only son, even though God had said to him, 'It is through Isaac that your offspring will be reckoned.' Abraham reasoned that God could raise the dead, and figuratively speaking, he did receive Isaac back from death."

Abraham exercised his spiritual reasoning capacity. There is a right way of reasoning and there is a wrong way. Only a true Christian who believes in the God of glory, the God of miracles, can reason correctly and consistently. Divine reasoning places the God of the Scriptures at the center—the God of truth, the God who cannot lie, the God for whom all things are possible. Those who reason falsely refuse to believe in this God.

Authentic Christianity is the only reasonable faith in the whole world. The fear of God is the beginning of wisdom. So Abraham reasoned based on God's word to him: "The Lord promised me a son when I was seventy-five. And God promised that it is through this son that the Messiah, the Savior of the world, will come. God is truth; he has never lied to me. God is now demanding that I must kill Isaac and sacrifice him in worship, a demand that seems to contradict his promise. But there can be no real contradiction in the true and living God; therefore, I am sure this apparent inconsistency can be resolved when thought through correctly."

What was Abraham's final line of reasoning? He concluded that God must raise Isaac up from his ashes. So he told his two servants, "We will go up the mountain, we will worship God, and then we will come back to you." We too must exercise our God-given faith, and God will bless us.

And he will send his angels with a loud trumpet call, and they will gather his elect from the four winds, from one end of the heavens to the other. —Matthew 24:31

hat is the blessed hope of the church? It is the glorious return of our God and Savior, Jesus Christ. Why does this give us hope? Because when Jesus comes again, Christians will receive glorious bodies like his glorious body, and we will be united with Christ forever. If this is not our desire, then we are living substandard Christian lives. As the bride of Christ, we should be ever looking forward to that day when we shall see him, and keeping ourselves pure from every defilement.

When Jesus Christ returns, he will descend personally, visibly, powerfully, gloriously, and audibly. He will be accompanied by his holy angels and the spirits of those who died in faith. He will commission his angels to gather the elect from throughout the world. The bodies of those who died in Christ will be raised from the dead, while the elect who are living will be transformed. Together, both groups will be raptured, caught up in the clouds to meet the Lord.

Jesus' second advent will not be secret. There will be lightning from one end of the earth to the other, followed by total blackness, and then brightness and glory as the Son of Man descends with power and authority. There will be great mourning among the unbelievers of the earth when they see this Christ, whom they mocked, cursed, and treated with contempt and total unbelief, coming in great glory and power. His enemies will experience anguish, perplexity, and faintness of heart. They will mourn, weep, and even cry to the mountains, "Fall on us! Hide us!" (Rev. 6:16).

How will those who believe in Christ respond when they see him? It is stated very clearly in Luke 21:28: "When these things begin to take place," Jesus counseled his people, "stand up and lift up your heads, because your redemption is drawing near." At Christ's second coming, all who trusted in him will receive their glorious spiritual physical bodies, engineered to exist in the presence of God—their redemption will be fully consummated. So Jesus encourages his people to lift up their heads, stand up, and rejoice, knowing that when they see these events of his coming, their longed-for redemption is close at hand.

Here is Rebekah; take her and go, and let her become the wife of your master's son, as the LORD has directed. —Genesis 24:51

od is the believer's guide, and every person in Genesis 24 was led by him. Unlike unbelievers, Christians are not free to marry just anyone. We are to marry only true believers of the opposite sex. God ordains a godly woman for every godly man. For Adam, God provided Eve. For Isaac, God ordained Rebekah.

Abraham believed that God would choose a godly wife for Isaac to fulfill God's eternal purpose for him. He therefore instructed his most trusted servant to go to his country and kindred to find a God-chosen wife for Isaac. He wanted no ungodly, Canaanite woman for his believing son. It is in God's church, not the surrounding world, where we also should look for a godly spouse, chosen by God from all eternity for us.

Isaac, in turn, feared God and trusted him for the provision of a godly spouse. He stayed in Canaan and waited for God's provision to come to him.

Abraham's servant also was assured of God's presence to guide him every step of the way. The Lord was the one who would find the girl for Isaac and oversee the servant's quest from beginning to end. The servant was led by God in devising a test to identify the future wife of Isaac: she must be a servant at heart—not a self-centered person who demanded that others serve her, but one who sacrificially ministered to others. Rebekah was pure, humble, gracious, hospitable, industrious, and godly. And so she passed the divine test—she gave water to the servant, and then she watered the camels.

When Rebekah was asked if she would go with the servant to be Isaac's wife, the Holy Spirit came upon the girl and she replied, "I will go." In other words, "I will go right now, without delay. I will unite with this man, whether in sickness or in health, in plenty or in want, in joy or in sorrow. I will go, as God wills."

The God who saved us will also guide our lives every step of the way, whether we are trying to find a church, a career, or a godly spouse. Our job is to trust him, and carefully and gratefully follow his leading.

Then Jesus told them, "This very night you will all fall away on account of me." —Matthew 26:31

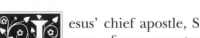

Jesus' chief apostle, Simon Peter, was a weak man, a man of many contradictions. He had faith enough to walk on water, then he sank because he doubted. He was the first to confess by divine revelation that Jesus is "the Christ, the Son of the living God," but immediately after his confession, he rebuked Jesus for speaking about the cross. On the Mount of Transfiguration, he blurted out many things, even though he did not know what he was talking about. In Gethsemane, Jesus asked Peter to watch and pray, and yet he slept. In Matthew 26, Peter promised to follow Jesus all the way to prison and death, yet he denied him three times later that night.

How could Jesus choose such an emotional, impetuous, contradictory person to be his chief apostle? In choosing Simon, and in choosing us, we see the marvelous, inscrutable wisdom of God. Paul spoke about such divine choosing: "Brothers, think of what you were when you were called. Not many of you were wise by human standards; not many were influential; not many were of noble birth. But God chose the foolish things of the world to shame the wise; God chose the weak things of the world to shame the strong. He chose the lowly things of this world and the despised things—and the things that are not—to nullify the things that are, so that no one may boast before him" (1 Cor. 1:26–29).

Peter failed many times, but he did not fall away forever. Why? He was chosen by God unto eternal salvation. Though Satan asked to sift Peter as wheat, Jesus prayed for Peter, that his faith would not fail. In the same way, Jesus intercedes for every one of his elect.

Like Peter, we may have partial eclipses of faith, times when we demonstrate very little faith, times when we doubt God. But just as Peter's faith in Christ did not suffer total eclipse, neither will ours. Faith is a gift of the Holy Spirit, which he produces in every elect person who has been effectually called. And so we may stumble, we may fail, we may doubt, we may backslide, yet we are preserved by God. By his mighty grace we shall persevere to the very end.

Stay in this land for a while, and I will be with you and will bless you.
—Genesis 26:3

enesis 26 begins, "Now there was a famine in the land." That speaks of a trial of faith. There was a famine in the land, the land that God promised to his own people. It was not Babylon or Egypt, it was the Promised Land that was experiencing famine. The Sovereign Lord himself sent it to test Isaac.

So also it is by divine ordination that trials enter our lives. God's purpose is to test us to see whether we will persevere by faith despite difficult circumstances. We are to live not by sight but by faith—faith in the God who called us to this land.

Initially, though, "Isaac went to Abimelech king of the Philistines in Gerar." Why? Isaac was en route to Egypt, just like everybody else, to solve his problem. His thinking seemed so logical, so correct, so obvious, that he felt no need for prayer. Why should he pray when the answer is so evident? And so this man did not pray, just like his father did not pray in Genesis 12.

Isaac did not ask God for guidance in this matter. Nevertheless, God, who is rich in mercy, came to him and said, "Don't do it." He encouraged Isaac, "Live in the land where I tell you to live. Stay in this land, and I will be with you and will bless you."

There are times when we think that the answer to our problem is very clear, but God's perfect will may be the exact opposite of what we are proposing. That is why we must not rely on our own understanding, but seek God's guidance.

Notice, though, that to embrace God's will and stay in the land requires greater faith. Going to Egypt did not require any faith; it was the natural thing to do, and all the pagans were headed there. But God strengthened Isaac in his faith, saying, "Trust me. Remember the covenant. Remember the promise. I will do everything for the fulfillment of that promise. Exercise faith in me." What was the outcome? Isaac obeyed, settled down, planted crops, and harvested one hundredfold.

He is not here; he has risen, just as he said. Come and see the place where he lay. —Matthew 28:6

od blessed the two Marys for their loyal devotion to Jesus, allowing them to become the first witnesses of the resurrection. The angel encouraged them to remember what Jesus had told them earlier. Five times in this gospel Jesus had told his disciples that he would be killed and then be raised to life on the third day. "Come and see," commanded the angel. He was saying, in essence, "Open your eyes to the evidence. Understand the truth. Only Jesus who rose from the dead is mighty to save."

Come and see! God is telling us today to read the Scriptures and understand the gospel. Open the Bible and see Christ. Come to church and listen to what God is speaking. Jesus was crucified and buried, but on the third day, God raised him from the dead because it was impossible for death to keep him who was without sin in the grave. The sinless Son of God made atonement for all the sins of his people by his death. The resurrection was God's "Amen" to Jesus' cry, "It is finished!" The work of atonement is now finished; no more sacrifices are required. No longer do sinners need to be separated from God. The veil has been torn away, and God now welcomes penitent sinners to come to him in peace.

Come and see, so that you may go and tell. The women were to tell the disciples so that they, in turn, could believe the gospel. The women saw the folded grave clothes and heard that Jesus had been raised. They believed and went out, and as they did, Jesus himself came to meet them. The women came seeking a dead Jesus, and Jesus the risen One came to meet them.

As they fell before him, Christ comforted the women, saying, "Do not be afraid." Fear is due to sin, but Christ's death atoned for all of our sins forever. All fear stems from fear of death, which is the wages of sin. But if we have trusted in Christ, our sins are gone forever. Therefore, Christians, stop fearing! Come and see, go and tell. Come to the Bible and see the irrefutable evidence of Christ's resurrection. Then go and tell others about the risen Lord.

In these last days he has spoken to us by his Son. —Hebrews 1:2

The book of Hebrews establishes the finality of the gospel by demonstrating the supremacy of Jesus Christ. He is God's perfect word to man and man's perfect representative before God. The entire book is an exhortation to us that we should not give up, but continually press forward along the trail blazed by the pioneer of our faith, Jesus Christ.

In Hebrews 1 we are unequivocally told, "God has spoken." We do not worship a god who is shrouded in mystery, who does not reveal himself to us, who must be sought by groping in the dark. We do not worship the unknown god of the Athenians. God has revealed himself in his creation and in our consciences. More importantly, he has revealed himself in his Son, as revealed in the Scriptures. God has spoken to us that we may understand, believe, and obey his words. This special, redemptive revelation saves all who receive it with faith. Alternatively, anyone who searches for a way of salvation outside of biblical revelation stands condemned by this Book.

God has spoken to us "by his Son." Who is Jesus Christ? He is God's only-begotten Son, "the radiance of God's glory and the exact representation of his being," who created and sustains all things by his powerful word. This One provided purification for sins by his death on the cross, and then sat down at the right hand of the Majesty in heaven. He has completed his work and now sits at the most exalted place of honor as King of kings and Lord of lords. Jesus is now interceding on behalf of his children who cry out to him. And he is preparing to judge all of his enemies, who are but a footstool for his feet.

In Jesus Christ, God has spoken the final word, a word that fulfills all of the Old Testament messianic promises. We thus make a fatal error if we become dissatisfied with this revelation and look for another to replace or augment what we have received in the Bible. Anyone who hears the gospel and rejects it rejects God's final word to man. The wise man combines this word with saving faith and obeys it. God has spoken!

In bringing many sons to glory, it was fitting that God, for whom and through whom everything exists, should make the author of their salvation perfect through suffering. —Hebrews 2:10

n this verse we are given the plan of the triune God for our lives. His design for our lives is nothing less than our everlasting glory and splendor! From all eternity it has been the Father's intention to bring a miserable, sin-infested, inglorious people to himself. The Son freely agreed to come down from glory to bring his people to that same glory. And the Holy Spirit is now engaged in his work of sanctification in us so that we will emerge as a people who are fit to dwell in the presence of the holy, glorious God.

Not only is God's plan astounding, but so also is his method. Here we are told that it was fitting for God the Father to make his Son, Jesus Christ, perfect through suffering, so that he might accomplish God's plan and purpose. Substitutionary atonement—Jesus' suffering and death on the cross on behalf of sinners—was entirely in keeping with God's character. Man may dislike and even mock the bloody cross, but God himself says that Calvary is the ultimate display of his love, wisdom, holiness, and grace.

God's way of redeeming a people was not arbitrary—there *is* no other way of salvation. Sinful man needed a kinsman-redeemer, a nearest relative who belonged to our family and who was willing and able to pay the redemption price. Thus, because we his children have flesh and blood, the eternal Son of God voluntarily became a man in order to make atonement for the sins of his people by shedding his own most precious blood (Rom. 6:23).

As a result, Jesus, who was temporarily made a little lower than the angels, has now been crowned with glory and honor by his Father. This exalted Savior is ours! And even now he is ministering to us his perfect salvation. Because he is our older brother, his victory and honor guarantee our future dignity and honor. He is the trailblazer, the firstfruits, our forerunner. When he returns, we shall all be changed. We will be given bodies without sin and will be ushered into a world without sin. And we shall see him as he is, face to face. That, indeed, will be glory.

Encourage one another daily . . . so that none of you may be hardened by sin's deceitfulness. —Hebrews 3:13

The Hebrews writer warns, "See to it, brothers, that none of you has a sinful, unbelieving heart that turns away from the living God" (Heb. 3:12). The Greek word translated as "turns away" actually means to actively revolt against God; such people are called apostates, those who stand away from God. How can we guard our own souls and help others to avoid this deadly heart condition? In verse 13 he gives one chief imperative: "Encourage one another daily."

What does this call to encourage entail? First, we have a responsibility to quickly recognize and respond in love when a brother or sister begins to turn away. We must say with great compassion, "Stop, friend! Remember what God has done for you. He has given you his word; he has forgiven your sins. Don't turn back to the way of rebellion, for the end thereof is destruction." Our goal is to win that person back, so that we can continue to walk together on the narrow way that leads to heaven. And we, too, must respond in humble repentance when a brother or sister comes to us with a similar exhortation.

It is the responsibility of each church member to engage in this ministry. The church is necessarily a community where people are vitally connected. That implies close relationships, not a "Don't ask, don't tell" attitude. We are to spur one another on to love and good works. Notice that such close fellowship is wonderfully therapeutic. It prevents hard-heartedness, which ultimately damns.

Why is this exhortation so important? The writer explains, "We have come to share in Christ if we hold firmly till the end the confidence we had at first" (Heb. 3:14). Perseverance in the faith is one mark of a genuine Christian. If we do not persevere, if we apostatize, we are not children of God. The Israelites began well, but they did not continue in obedience and faith, and their bodies fell in the desert. By way of contrast, in Hebrews 3 we read that Moses was faithful as a servant in all God's house, and Jesus was faithful as a son over God's house. If we would be his house, we must together walk faithfully before God, encouraging one another daily until we each arrive safely in heaven.

So Jacob was left alone, and a man wrestled with him till daybreak.
—*Genesis 32:24*

his man who wrestled with Jacob was not just a man; this was the angel of the Lord, the pre-incarnate Christ, the second Person of the Trinity. What did he want from Jacob? He came to bring Jacob to a genuine realization of his nothingness, to make him see what a poor, helpless creature he was, to defeat and conquer his willfulness, and to teach him that in acknowledged weakness lay his strength.

If God has ordained us to salvation, he will see to it that our rebellion and resistance are subdued. He will reduce us to utter nothingness. And he never loses a battle. He touches the sockets of our hips and dislocates our plans. He touches us with disease and disaster. He wrestles with us until we surrender ourselves to his supreme rulership as King of kings and Lord of lords. Wisdom is always to surrender early.

In his stubbornness and self-will, however, Jacob wrestled with God Almighty for a long time, until daybreak. In the end, who won Jacob's wrestling match? Christ. And so, at daybreak, fallen Jacob was clinging to the angel of the Lord and praying. Jacob had given up his rebellion, stubbornness, and resistance. He realized that his opponent was superior in strength. His power and self-reliance had vanished. Oh, the blessed loss of human strength! Now Jacob was clinging to, leaning on, and trusting in the Lord.

And then he prayed. Let me assure you, if we do not feel the need to pray, God has a way of bringing us to our knees. We do not pray, because we feel strong. We have tactics to solve our problems. Our strength and arrogance say, "Don't pray," and God must break our strength until we cry out to him. So Jacob prayed, "You alone can help me. I am not going to let you go until you bless me!" God heard his prayer and delivered him from all his troubles.

Notice, only after total surrender to God was Jacob told, "You have overcome." In other words, our surrender is our triumph, for "God's power is made perfect in weakness." Jacob, like Paul, learned, "When I am weak, then I am strong" (2 Cor. 12:9–10). That is winning by losing.

We have this hope as an anchor for the soul, firm and secure.
—*Hebrews 6:19*

ebrews 6:13–20 introduces us to the anchor of the Christian's life. An anchor stabilizes a ship by sinking into the water until it finally grips the solid ground. The people of the world have no such anchor. In the ocean of relativism, they have no mooring, no stabilizer when the storm and waves threaten to overwhelm their vessel. What is our anchor? It is God's sworn promise to each of his children: "I will surely bless you" (v. 14).

Abraham himself received this gracious promise from God and believed it, and it was credited to him as righteousness. Although he had to wait patiently for twenty-five years for its fulfillment, Abraham "did not waver through unbelief regarding the promise of God" (Rom. 4:20). The recipients of the Epistle to the Hebrews needed this reminder, and so do we. Trouble, problems, and delay are part and parcel of the Christian pilgrimage. Each of us is called to "imitate those [like Abraham] who through faith and patience inherit what has been promised" (Heb. 6:12).

This divine promise is not the equivalent of the world's "hope-so" that so often disappoints. Rather, God provided Abraham, and us today, with a sure guarantee by adding his oath to the promise. God, who cannot lie, intends for his people to be greatly encouraged so that they will persevere and trust in him, despite troubles, persecutions, and setbacks. His gracious purpose for us who live in a world of ceaseless flux remains fixed and unchangeable, because he is the immutable God.

God's promise to bless us is ultimately fulfilled in Jesus Christ. He is our true hope, the true anchor for our souls. Every Christian is united to the risen Christ by faith, and this Christ has entered into the very presence of God as a high priest forever on our behalf. We are completely secure!

Notice, though, that such encouragement is only for those who "have fled to take hold of the hope offered to us" (v. 18). The imperative of the gospel is this: to run from destruction to safety, to come and surrender to Jesus Christ and find refuge from the wrath of God. He himself enables us to run, that we may flee to Christ in accordance with his gracious promise.

The time is coming, declares the Lord, when I will make a new covenant with the house of Israel. —Hebrews 8:8

n Hebrews 8 we learn that the old Sinaitic covenant was faulty, imperfect, and temporary, though God himself had instituted it. The fault, however, lay not in God, but in his people. The old covenant placed the emphasis on Israel's obligation. God established his covenant with Israel on Mount Sinai, and they agreed to keep it, declaring, "We will do everything the LORD has said; we will obey" (Exod. 24:7). But notice what God says about his people: "They did not remain faithful to my covenant" (Heb. 8:9). During the forty years in the wilderness, most of the Israelites were killed by God because of their unbelief and disobedience. After the next generation entered Canaan, they too proved to be unfaithful to their covenant Lord. And to a large extent, this remained the story of Israel.

Yet thanks be to God, it has always been his plan to bring about a new covenant and a new priesthood after the order of Melchizedek, as we read in Psalm 110 and Jeremiah 31. By design, then, the Aaronic priesthood and the law were temporary. The purpose of this temporary Sinaitic covenant was to bring home to our consciences a heightened awareness of our sin and moral inability, so that we would see clearly our need for the promised Savior.

In the seventh century BC, God declared through Jeremiah his intent to bring about this new covenant that would be permanent, effectual, and final. In the verses quoted from Jeremiah by the Hebrews writer, three times we see the words, "declares the LORD," and seven times God says, "I will," indicating that he would surely bring it about. In the fullness of time, this covenant was ratified by our mediator, Jesus Christ. He solved our sin problem once for all and now enables us to enter the presence of God so that we may worship him in spirit and in truth, and fellowship with him forever.

What, then, shall we do? Let us consider Jesus, the apostle and high priest of the new covenant. Let us consider him who lives forever to intercede for us before the Father. Let us consider him, our guarantor and mediator. Then we will be filled with all hope, power, and peace to live for God's glory in joy inexpressible, here and hereafter.

Get rid of the foreign gods you have with you, and purify yourselves. . . .
Then come, let us go up to Bethel. —Genesis 35:2–3

enesis 35 continues the story of Jacob and his family. Earlier, God had told him to go to Bethel, but Jacob preferred to pitch his tent on the outskirts. Bethel means "house of God." For some Christians, Bethel is too close to God's holy presence. Some of us, too, have been pitching our tents away from Bethel. We do not want to be so close to the light. We want to be at the back of the church, in the shadows, where we imagine God will not confront us. We want to be able to indulge in a little sin.

Why didn't Jacob go to Bethel the first time? He did not go because his family was sinning—they had idols, and he knew it. Jacob had lost control of his family. He told himself, "I think we can work out a deal, a negotiated arrangement with the Almighty." But God always demands exclusive worship. Jesus Christ said that no man can serve two masters. It is an utter impossibility. Yet in every generation, the children of God try to do it.

At first, Jacob deliberately chose to disobey God's word and settled somewhere else. As a result, God made his life extremely difficult. Because Jacob was God's elect, he experienced the Lord's fiery discipline: his daughter Dinah went out to visit the pagans and was raped. She, and Jacob's whole family, experienced a great tragedy. God has a way of making us conform to his will. How much better it is to move in obedience the first time we are told to do so!

God will bring serious pain to us as well if we are not walking in holiness. So my counsel is to move now, move willingly, and move unconditionally. God will not put up with our stubbornness and rebellion forever.

Verse 2 begins, "Jacob said to his household." He finally mustered his strength, after discovering that he could not live any longer in the shadows. All of a sudden, the father Jacob, the patriarch, found the courage to say to his family, "Get rid of the foreign gods you have with you." Fathers, husbands, you must do what Jacob did. Eliminate every idol of sin and rebellion in your home, and move to Bethel.

FEBRUARY 1

Therefore, brothers, . . . we have confidence to enter the Most Holy Place by the blood of Jesus. —Hebrews 10:19

 hy is man in his sin restless, miserable, and fearful? His access to the true and living God has been cut off; he is like a fish thrown out of the water and gasping for oxygen. We can trace the root of this problem back to Genesis 3, which relates the history of our first parents' sin against God in the garden. They and their offspring were punished with death, banishment from the very presence of God.

Thanks be to God, that is not the final word. In Hebrews 10, we read that access has been restored; thus, we have confidence to enter God's presence. The Greek word used describes the exclusive right of a Greek citizen to come into the council and speak freely. A slave had no such right. Such confidence is ours through Jesus Christ, who has changed our status from a slave of sin to a citizen of heaven, an adopted son of God himself.

Jesus, our great high priest, is far superior to the Old Testament high priests. They made sure that the worshippers did not enter the Holy of Holies. The thick curtain that separated the people from God remained intact. Only once a year, on the Day of Atonement, could the high priest enter God's presence for a brief moment with blood and incense. But now Jesus has appeared once for all at the end of the ages to do away with sin by the sacrifice of himself, and we have been made holy through the sacrifice of the body of Jesus Christ once for all (Heb. 9:26; 10:10). We cannot go to God on any other basis. We cannot come into his presence by claiming that we have been good people. God is looking for only one thing—the sprinkled blood of Christ.

According to some, confidence is a subjective feeling—some days we have it, other days we don't. But the confidence we read about in Hebrews 10 has nothing to do with how we feel on any given day; it is based, rather, on the objective reality of Christ and his sacrifice. Therefore, "let us hold unswervingly to the hope we profess, for he who promised is faithful" (v. 23). God, who does not change, welcomes all who come by this new and living way.

When his brothers saw that their father loved him more than any of them,
they hated him and could not speak a kind word to him. —Genesis 37:4

 itterness, envy, and jealousy are infectious diseases of our spirit, and can go on to infect the entire church. When we harbor negative thoughts towards a brother, we cannot pray for him and will not fellowship with him. This sin is extremely evil, for it is ultimately against God and his sovereign decrees. Bitter Christians have, in effect, lodged a serious accusation against their Lord, complaining that the place and calling God has assigned them is unfair and wrong.

Joseph's brothers were envious of his purity, possessions, and position. They resented the fact that Jacob had given him preeminence. And they kicked against God's plan, revealed in two dreams, to make him the head. As their hatred grew, the root of bitterness manifested in the fruit of murderous intent. So they said, "Here comes that dreamer! Come now, let's kill him" (Gen. 37:19–20). This is nothing less than demon possession—the thief comes to steal, kill, and destroy.

By God's amazing grace, the one who had been truly wronged by so many people—Joseph—was the one who remained free of such crippling passions throughout his life. What was the key to his spiritual success? "The LORD was with him." We read in Genesis 49 concerning Joseph: "With bitterness archers attacked him . . . but his bow remained steady . . . because of the hand of the Mighty One of Jacob." Joseph understood in the core of his being that the God who was for him would help and sustain him, and that he therefore did not need to take matters into his own hands by resorting to devilish revenge.

Joseph grew up without an iota of bitterness. Later, as vice-regent of Egypt, he embraced his trembling brothers. He is perhaps the foremost Old Testament example of grace. But there is one who is greater than Joseph—the Lord Jesus Christ. We are told, "Christ suffered for you, leaving you an example, that you should follow in his steps. . . . When they hurled their insults at him, he did not retaliate. . . . Instead, he entrusted himself to him who judges justly" (1 Pet. 2:21–23). The Holy Spirit will help us to do this too. We need not construct a prison cell of lifelong bitterness. Instead, may we entrust ourselves to our faithful God.

Can you pull in the leviathan with a fishhook? —Job 41:1

he first thirty-seven chapters of Job are filled with human speech, much of it tinged with sin and serious accusations made against the justice of God. This was not solely Job's problem; it is every believer's problem. We easily fall into thinking that God is not fair, that we deserve better treatment, especially when we are undergoing trials. In Job's case, God himself showed up and confronted him, commanding, "Be quiet!" By means of a series of rhetorical questions he silenced Job's arguments and brought him to sobriety. "Brace yourself like a man, I will question you, and you shall answer me."

In Job 38 and 39, the Lord revealed himself as the awesome, transcendent Creator and Sustainer of the universe. Job responded, "I am unworthy—how can I reply to you?" In Job 40 and 41, the Lord reveals himself as the moral governor of history and the one who alone is able to defeat sin and Satan. In these chapters, the great and mighty Satan is symbolized by two mythological figures, the behemoth and the leviathan. Man cannot prevail against such evil creatures, but the sovereign Lord can and shall!

The message of these chapters is both a great comfort and a reminder to us, especially when we are suffering and evil seems to be prevailing. We must never forget that God is completely in control. We do not and cannot know all things; it is enough that God knows. And so we must trust in him completely. All things work together for good to those who love God and are called according to his purpose (Rom. 8:28).

Our suffering is not like the suffering of Jesus Christ. God, in his wise ordination, permits each of us to experience grief for our ultimate good—to remove the dross of sin. But there is One who suffered who was entirely without sin—the perfectly innocent Jesus of Nazareth. He was crucified in our place to defeat the behemoth and leviathan and accuser of the brethren. So we must keep our eyes focused on him, not on ourselves. May God help each of us to do so even this day.

FEBRUARY 4

od was with Joseph, not only throughout his life, but also specifically when he was tempted by Potiphar's wife. God was with Joseph and gave him a way out. Joseph employed a sanctified mind and will to avoid sin in a highly difficult situation. He was not ruled by passion, but rather by the fear of God.

First, Joseph refused the woman's invitation with intense conviction. He said, "My master trusts me with everything. I cannot violate his trust." Joseph remained a covenant-keeper and a highly honorable man, despite the immensity of his suffering.

Then Joseph said, "How can I do this wicked thing?" Adultery is a hugely wicked sin. Joseph was saying, "My God, who is holy, wise, and most powerful, and who gave me being, is watching me. He is with me. How can I sin so greatly against him?" If Joseph had succumbed, he would have been sinning against Potiphar and his wife. But, ultimately, he would have been sinning against God himself.

So Joseph fled the scene of danger, not as a coward, but as a triumphant covenant-keeper. Sometimes fleeing is the way of wisdom. It can be a sign of strength and victory. Joseph lived out the truth of 1 Corinthians 10:13: "No temptation has seized you except what is common to man. And God is faithful; he will not let you be tempted beyond what you can bear. But when you are tempted, he will also provide a way out so that you can stand up under it."

This understanding that God is with us must regulate our ethics. When we face serious temptation, we should recite with the psalmist, "Where can I go from your Spirit? Where can I flee from your presence? If I go up to the heavens, you are there; if I make my bed in the depths, you are there. If I rise on the wings of the dawn, if I settle on the far side of the sea, even there your hand will guide me, your right hand will hold me fast" (Ps. 139:7–10). When temptation comes, God is not far from us. He is with us to help us to stand and to show us the way out.

Blessed is the man who does not walk in the counsel of the wicked . . . but his delight is in the law of the LORD. —Psalm 1:1–2

salm 1 is the gateway to all wisdom psalms. All other psalms are in turn an exposition of the first. In it is revealed the profound cleavage that marks the lives and destinies of the righteous and the wicked. There is a most radical division, and it begins with two completely different words.

There was a time when there was only one word—God's word. God counseled our first parents, Adam and Eve, to trust him and live by his word. Adam was to rule the world for his God, who, in turn, would fellowship with him face to face. If our first parents had obeyed that gracious word, they and their posterity would have lived in a blessed state of everlasting happiness—no death, no war, no disease, no tears.

But then a different word entered the world. The serpent, speaking for the devil, contradicted the word of God. He counseled Eve to pursue happiness through disobedience. This anti-word proved disastrous; Adam and Eve did not become gods, but rather children of the devil. And all their offspring are born into the world in the same condition—sinners needing salvation.

When God saves such a sinner through new birth, that man or woman immediately discovers a new and great love for the once-despised word of God. If anyone loves God out of a converted heart, he becomes a man of one Book. He studies God's word, meditates upon it, and applies the law of God to every situation in his life. Because the law of the Lord is upon his heart, he impresses it upon his children at every opportunity.

This psalm makes it abundantly clear that the way of blessing in this life and the life to come is through fidelity to God's word. Those who walk in God's ways shall prosper in everything they do, and, most importantly, they shall stand on the day of judgment. But not so the wicked.

Let us listen to the counsel of God's word! Let us meditate on, love, and apply the wisdom of God as we make decisions throughout our lives. Then we too shall know the psalmist's joy: "O the happinesses of the man whose delight is in the law of the LORD."

So Pharaoh said to Joseph, "I hereby put you in charge of the whole land of Egypt." —Genesis 41:41

hat was the reason why God sent Joseph to Egypt? God foresaw the needs of his people. Soon there would be a seven-year famine throughout the entire world, and those living in Canaan would lack food. In God's providence, the only place with provisions was Egypt, and Joseph was now in charge of those vital supplies.

In his common grace, God cares for all people, including the unbelieving world. And yet he takes a special, primary interest in his chosen people. The covenant Lord is interested in our eating and drinking. He is interested in our children's welfare. We see in Genesis 41 that he was also interested in Jacob's family, despite the grievous sins committed earlier by Joseph's brothers. Their intent had been to send Joseph to a life of slavery; God's overruling intent was to send a man ahead so that there would be plenty in the time of crisis for Jacob's descendants. Joseph came to understand this, saying, "God sent me ahead of you to preserve for you a remnant on earth and to save your lives by a great deliverance" (Gen. 45:7).

Joseph is a type of the Lord Jesus Christ. Just as Joseph gladly brought his family to a land of plenty, so Jesus tells us to come. In Isaiah 55 we read, "Come, all you who are thirsty, come to the waters; and you who have no money, come, buy and eat! . . . Your soul will delight in the richest of fare." Note that it is those who have no money—those who recognize their utter unworthiness—who are summoned. God is interested in meeting the needs of every sinner who will humble himself and say, "Lord, have mercy upon me!"

The New Testament amplifies this theme. We are invited to "approach the throne of grace with confidence, so that we may receive mercy and find grace to help us in our time of need" (Heb. 4:16). The throne of judgment has been changed to a throne of grace because of the person and work of the Lord Jesus Christ. All who repent of their sins and place their faith in Christ are now invited to come with confidence, so that they may find their every need met by our sovereign God.

In the morning, O LORD, you hear my voice. —Psalm 5:3

salm 5 is a psalm of lament. David's enemies are attacking him, and David goes to the Lord, pleading for help. His prayer teaches us how to pray in times of great trouble.

"Listen to my cry for help, my King and my God" (v. 2). An unbeliever cannot pray in this manner, for this is a prayer based on intimate relationship. God hears only the prayers of his elect, the people he has brought near to himself in his covenant of love.

"Give ear to my words, O LORD, consider my sighing" (v. 1). David's prayer is earnest, born out of great need and great confidence in his God. Note the imperatives: Give ear! Consider! Listen! We are reminded of Psalm 143:7: "Do not hide your face from me or I will be like those who go down to the pit."

David prays with words, articulating his praise and his needs. Our God is personal and infinitely wise, and we must address him in an orderly, thought-through manner. We must not rush into his presence mumbling nonsensical statements.

David also prays with sighing. Here is groaning that cannot be expressed in mere words, because the issue is so urgent. Such also was the prayer of the barren Hannah as she prayed for a son. Such was the prayer of blind Bartimaeus as Jesus approached.

David also prays with persistence: "In the morning I lay my requests before you and wait in expectation" (v. 3). He does not simply utter a brief prayer and then walk away, as do the vast majority of people in affluent countries. Most people who have houses, cars, and food do not really pray with persistence, for they already possess what they think they need. Prayer for them is a mere ritual.

Not so David. He waits in expectation, as a watchman in his watchtower looks out, straining to see what help will come. He has no Plan B. The prophet Micah said, "As for me, I watch in hope for the LORD, I wait for God my Savior; my God will hear me" (Micah 7:7).

This ought to be our daily devotion. Morning by morning, our first thoughts should be directed to God and him alone. With praise and supplication, with great earnestness, let us exercise this priceless privilege of prayer.

Humble yourselves, therefore, under God's mighty hand, that he may lift you up in due time. —1 Peter 5:6

he way to true prosperity is the way of submitting to God under his mighty hand. In the light of this letter as a whole, this verse should be understood to say that success, defined biblically, results when we embrace God's divine dealings in our lives. This is the chief topic of 1 Peter—the sufferings, persecutions, and fiery trials that fall upon God's people in his providence. We must never lose sight of the fact that God has an ultimate purpose that is good.

What is the purpose of Christian suffering? To purify us. In 1 Peter 4:19 we read, "So then, those who suffer according to God's will should commit themselves to their faithful Creator and continue to do good." This word "commit" means to deposit ourselves into God's hand. We are to trust God to take care of us, even in suffering. In Romans 5, Paul tells us to rejoice in suffering "because we know suffering produces perseverance; perseverance, character; and character, hope," which is hope of the glory of God. Do you see the connection? First comes suffering; then, in the end, glory.

When we go through pain, troubles, and problems, we should not murmur. Instead, we should humbly submit to God's dealings and receive the variegated grace offered to us by him. We must persevere by this grace, knowing all things work together for good to those who love God and are called according to his purpose, and that in due time he will reach down and lift us up even as he lifted up Joseph in Egypt. Joseph suffered unjustly for years, and everyone forgot about him. But God had not forgotten. In due time, in the course of a single day, Joseph was lifted up from his dungeon and placed on the throne of Egypt, to be second only to Pharaoh himself. He and his entire household were saved in God's sovereign plan and purpose.

Christians are promised suffering in this life, but eternal glory in the life to come. The God who delivered Joseph will, at just the right moment, use his mighty hand to save us and lead us into everlasting glory. He is a trustworthy Savior.

To those who through the righteousness of our God and Savior Jesus Christ have received a faith as precious as ours. —2 Peter 1:1

he apostle Peter is writing this epistle to a select group of people, to those who have received a most precious faith from God himself. Note Peter's theology: This faith, which has been given to God's people, does not leave us tied to our own merit or righteousness, but rather unites us with the Lord Jesus Christ, whose perfect righteousness is imputed to us. We do not have any righteousness of our own; we cannot perform any works that God will accept, for everything we do is corrupted by sin. God's righteousness alone avails with him.

The word *received* is very important. It was the word used by Greek historians when they wrote of a king freely granting gifts to his noblemen. We who were once God's enemies, dead in our trespasses and sins, have now been invested with marvelous dignity! But dead men must first be raised to life before they can receive and exercise faith.

Christianity begins with God putting his life into the soul of a man. God, who is rich in mercy, first makes us alive in him as we hear the gospel preached. Concomitantly, he gives us the exceedingly precious gift of faith by which we savingly trust in the Lord Jesus Christ, who is offered in that gospel. May we never underestimate or devalue what God has bestowed upon us! This gift of faith is most precious, and we must consider it as such, value it as such, and proclaim it as such.

Those who have received this blessing go on to enjoy his grace and peace in abundance. We know that peace reigns only after one of the combatants has won the war. Even so, Jesus has conquered us, and hostilities have ceased. "Therefore, there is now no condemnation for those who are in Christ Jesus" (Rom. 8:1). Not only so, but he is also committed to helping us rebuild our lives. Repairs are being made, reconstruction is proceeding, roads are being made straight, and our fields are beginning to bring forth a harvest of righteousness. Even now, we, in an ever-increasing measure, are enjoying fellowship with him. Thanks be to God! By giving us saving faith, he has given us everything we need for life and godliness.

Why, O LORD, do you stand far off? Why do you hide yourself in times of trouble? —Psalm 10:1

he psalmist here wrestles with a question, a riddle, that has concerned God's people throughout the ages: Why do the righteous suffer and the wicked prosper? Where is the justice of God when practicing atheists are enjoying life while true believers are languishing? It seems at times to believers that God is far away, having forgotten about his people's plight and their prayers.

What should we do when we feel this way? This psalm teaches us that we ought first to come to God in prayer with our questions. The Bible does not forbid us, but rather encourages us to bring all such concerns to our covenant Lord. But we must come to him in humility and faith, trusting ultimately in the sovereign and good God revealed to us in the Scriptures. The Holy Spirit will then strengthen us in our spirits so that we can join with the psalmist and confess, "But you, O God, do see trouble and grief; you consider it to take it in hand."

We must affirm and rest in our knowledge of God's unchanging character. He is true, omniscient and almighty. When he appears to be indifferent, it may be a trial of our faith. Such tribulations produce patience. Thus, God does allow us to suffer for our good, but in his perfect time he will encourage and defend the fatherless and the oppressed. A Christian can therefore rejoice even in the midst of tribulations, for he knows that all things must be subservient to his salvation.

A godly person is interested in the glory of God. Therefore, when God is mocked and reviled by unbelievers, the Christian prays, "Arise, LORD! Lift up your hand" (v. 12). At the same time, the believer rests in God's rulership: "The LORD is King for ever and ever; the nations will perish from his land" (v. 16). God is the great King who is interested in the affairs of this world, and his kingdom is an eternal one. Wicked unbelievers will not reign forever. The secure, arrogant atheist will be shocked when Christ returns as Judge, and the Day of Judgment is surely coming. Every knee shall bow and every tongue shall confess that Jesus Christ is Lord, to the glory of God the Father (Phil. 2:10–11).

Then [Jacob] blessed Joseph and said, "May the God before whom my fathers Abraham and Isaac walked, the God who has been my shepherd all my life to this day . . . may he bless these boys." —Genesis 48:15–16

hen you are about to die, what will be your last words? Will you be confused and afraid? Or will you bless God and the people around you? When the time came for Jacob to die, he was a saint of God, hoping and trusting not in anything in this world, but only in his God and Savior.

Jacob was born a sinner. His name in Hebrew means "deceiver." When Jacob became a believer, this sin nature was still in him. Would he continue to live in his sin, or would the God who saved him also make him holy?

The Bible clearly teaches us that the justified will be sanctified. Jacob experienced a life filled with God's corrections, which finally produced in him holiness. By the end of his life, Jacob wholly leaned on the God who had been with him in the past, who was with him in the present, and who would be with him in the future.

God had been with Jacob, not only in saving and justifying him, but also in sanctifying him. In the same way, the God who saved us will also purify us through discipline. If we are crooked, like Jacob, God will use a Laban to straighten us out. If we are self-confident, God will use an Esau to teach us to pray and look to him. If we are still clinging to something in this life, God will take away a Joseph and a Benjamin until our faith is purified.

After surrendering Benjamin to God, Jacob was completely stripped of his own strength. Jacob's eyes now looked to God and his promises alone. Though an aged, blind man, his spiritual vision was perfect. "I am about to die," he told his son Joseph, "but God will be with you" (v. 21). How could Jacob tell Joseph that God would be with him and the other children of Israel? He could do so because he himself had experienced God in his life for one hundred and forty-seven years. He was speaking from his own experience, not from some theoretical belief.

I pray that God will help us to say this to those around us when our time comes to die. To do so, we must first experience God, as Jacob did.

You intended to harm me, but God intended it for good to accomplish what is now being done, the saving of many lives. —Genesis 50:20

ere, in Joseph's words to his brothers, we are introduced to a profound perspective on the events of our lives. We see two intentions, two plans, two purposes that are mutually opposed. One is man's plan inspired and fueled by Satan. The other is God's eternal plan. In Joseph's recounting of his life, we see who triumphs.

Joseph's brothers hated him because of his upright conduct. They had every intention of killing him, but they could not, for God's plan was different. God is the all-wise, almighty, sovereign Lord who allowed the brothers to exercise their free agency without coercion. Yet he brought to pass his ultimate purpose through them. The same is true for each of the billions of people now alive. Truly our God is an awesome God!

The unbeliever is like a fish swimming within the confines of a large net. The net is the sovereignty of God. The fish thinks he is free to swim wherever he wills, but, in reality, he can only move from one side of the net to the other. Just so, when the sinner tries to run away from God, he runs toward him. And after a few short years he will meet him face to face. All of life is lived *coram Deo*.

In the New Testament, we find the most amazing working out of this mysterious principle. In Peter's Pentecostal sermon, he declared to his Jewish listeners, "[Jesus] was handed over to you by God's set purpose and foreknowledge; and you, with the help of wicked men, put him to death by nailing him to the cross" (Acts 2:23). Peter understood the two intentions. From all eternity it was God's sovereign intention to send his Son into the world to be crucified for the sins of his people. And yet, in handing Jesus over to Pilate, the religious leaders acted in complete accordance with their sinful malice, and they will be held responsible for history's most heinous murder.

What shall we conclude? Nothing happens outside of God's providence. Satan intends to harm us, but he will not succeed. God's people are indestructible. God has a plan, and every aspect of that plan will be fulfilled until the kingdoms of this world become the kingdom of our God and Christ.

LORD, who may dwell in your sanctuary? —Psalm 15:1

salm 15 begins with a wonderful, profound question addressed to Yahweh, the covenant Lord. It is not a question of how to make more money or how to make friends and influence people. Rather, the heart of the inquiry is: "Lord, who may sojourn in your tent, who may dwell with you?" We are shocked by the sublimity, transcendence, and greatness of this request, for such a concern is often far from our thoughts.

David is passionately asking God, "What sort of man can dwell with you?" Why is he asking? He greatly desires communion with his Savior God. Nothing else in all the world will satisfy him. Apart from God's redeeming grace, no sinner will ask such a question, for he comes into the world alienated from God and hating him. But David has been born again, he has been justified by faith, and he is now concerned about having fellowship with the Most High.

The Lord's answer to David in verses 2 through 5 puts a dagger in the hearts of both legalism and antinomianism. It is not those who rely on daily sacrifices, who are ceremonially or ritually pure, who can live with the thrice-holy God. Nor can those who continue to lead immoral lives. We are told that only those who are ethically pure and keep God's commandments may dwell with him. Fellowship with God demands moral purity. "Blessed are the pure in heart, for they will see God." Jesus told his disciples, "If you love me, keep my commands." And the essence of his commandments is, "Love the Lord your God with all your heart, soul, mind, and strength, and your neighbor as yourself."

This answer is the same as that given centuries earlier by God to Abraham: "Walk before me and be blameless." Blamelessness does not mean perfection; rather, it speaks about a person's basic character. A blameless person's heart attitude is to please the God who has saved him. God has chosen us in Christ before the creation of the world to be holy and blameless before him. He who justified us will therefore help us to live this life of holiness so that we may enjoy him forever.

Dear friends . . . I felt I had to write and urge you to contend for the faith that was once for all entrusted to the saints. —Jude 3

he Greek word for "contend" means to fight fiercely, to exert oneself maximally, like a champion athlete who trains without distraction in order to attain the gold medal. Jude here urges us to vigorously fight for a far more glorious cause—the faith once for all entrusted to the saints.

Christians are not to be spectators seeking entertainment when they come to church. We are to fight for truth. We are to fight against our enemies—the world, the flesh, the devil, and the false church. Why? Because these enemies of the gospel are secretly trying to slip into the church. Antinomians and libertines will not endure the true gospel or the holy life it enjoins. In fact, it is their aim to change the gospel of grace into a license for immorality. But the truth is fixed; we have no authority to alter it. Orthodox Christians are to know the gospel, live the gospel, proclaim and defend the gospel, suffer for the gospel and, if needs be, die for the gospel, because it alone is the power of God unto salvation for everyone who believes. Therefore, it is the responsibility of every believer—not just of ministers—to fight fiercely for this unchangeable message, the very word of God.

In verse 17, Jude calls us to remember "what the apostles of our Lord Jesus Christ foretold." Specifically, we are to remember the predictions of Jesus and his apostles concerning the coming of heretics into his holy church. "Many false prophets will appear and deceive many people," Jesus cautioned (Matt. 24:11). And Paul warned, "Even from your own number men will arise and distort the truth in order to draw away disciples after them. So be on your guard!" (Acts 20:30–31).

It is essential that we remember the apostolic teaching. But how can we remember unless we study carefully the Scriptures? To "remember" in the Scripture means "to take thoughtful action." The enemies of the true gospel target those whose minds are empty. They know such people are not praying and not reading and believing the Scriptures. They know such people like to sin, and therefore want a gospel that permits them to sin. Therefore I exhort you: Be a knowing Christian, a remembering Christian, and a fighting Christian.

The LORD is my rock, my fortress and my deliverer; my God is my rock, in whom I take refuge. —Psalm 18:2

salm 18 is a royal psalm wherein King David, the vassal, celebrates with great thanksgiving the salvation brought about on his behalf by his Lord, the suzerain. It was this psalm that inspired Augustus Toplady to write the hymn "Rock of Ages" as he hid in the cleft of a rock during a severe storm.

David's gratitude issues from his love for his Savior. He exclaims, "I love you, O LORD, my strength." The Hebrew speaks of intense, earnest, emotional love that fills a man's entire being. This is a love based on relationship, a wholehearted love that answers to the first commandment.

Here the king's term of endearment for the covenant Lord is "my rock." To call God a rock is to speak of his immutability, the fact that he is the same yesterday, today, and forever, and that his promises can be trusted.

This rock is the believer's strength. The apostle Paul writes, "I can do all things through him who gives me strength" (Phil. 4:13). The rock is the believer's foundation. It cannot be washed away; it will hold us up forever. God took us out of the miry clay and set our feet upon a rock. The rock is also the believer's protection, a fortress that is high and inaccessible to our enemies. Our life is hid with Christ in God, and nothing can destroy those who have taken refuge in him.

Most importantly, as our rock, God is our salvation. We recall that Moses was told to strike the rock in the wilderness, and the water of life gushed forth. This historical event points to the Messiah, Jesus Christ, who himself issued a gracious offer to all, saying, "If anyone is thirsty, let him come to me and drink." He, the true rock, was stricken on the cross for our sake; at Calvary, blood and water flowed from his side for our salvation.

God became man in Christ Jesus to save King David and every child of God throughout the ages. He reached down from on high to rescue us from death. Jesus Christ is the rock that was cleft for all the elect. We are invited this day to take refuge and hide ourselves in him.

The law of the LORD is perfect. —Psalm 19:7

salm 19 speaks of the living and true God's self-disclosure in natural and special revelation. The natural revelation of God given us in the creation itself is continuous, abundant, universal, and illustrative of divine purpose. "Since the creation of the world God's invisible qualities—his eternal power and divine nature—have been clearly seen, being understood from what has been made, so that men are without excuse" (Rom. 1:20). The sun, moon, and stars thus protest against creature worship. They point away from themselves to their powerful and glorious Creator God. No one can say that he does not know this God; atheism is impossible in light of the revelation around and inside man.

Nevertheless, natural revelation alone cannot save a man, for the sinner suppresses the truth about God and refuses to thank and serve him. While people respect and even worship birds, bees, and trees, they continue to treat their Creator with utter contempt. The special revelation of Scripture alone reveals a God who is able to save such rebellious creatures. Neither sun nor moon can tell you how to be saved from guilt and eternal judgment; such revelation is given solely in the Son of God in the Holy Bible.

So we read in this psalm, "The law of the LORD is perfect, reviving the soul" (v. 7). God's word is perfect, complete, lacking nothing. And as we internalize it, we are transformed by it. "All Scripture is God-breathed and is useful for teaching, rebuking, correcting and training in righteousness, so that the man of God may be thoroughly equipped for every good work" (2 Tim. 3:16–17). The word of God alone raises the dead and nourishes the living. It alone heals us and cleanses us from all our filth. Man can indeed live by every word that proceeds from the mouth of God.

No wonder the psalmist concludes by affirming that the word of God is the believer's greatest treasure, more precious than pure gold, and the believer's greatest pleasure, more delightful than the finest honey. And keeping God's law leads to life's greatest reward—fellowship with the Creator himself. May God help us to add faith to his word and so be saved, sanctified, and made fit to enjoy him forever.

For the king trusts in the LORD; through the unfailing love of the Most High he will not be shaken. —Psalm 21:7

salm 21 is another royal psalm; King David is giving thanks to his covenant Lord for granting him victory over his enemies in answer to his prayers. God helps us before we pray, because we pray, and even when we do not pray. He is always for his covenant people. Do we join with David in giving thanks to the Lord who always gives us victory and daily blesses us with good things? The people of God should be a praising people.

Thanksgiving demonstrates that we have trusted God in the past. David trusted in God, not in horses and chariots. He therefore sought God urgently in his distress, and God in great mercy heard his cry. The first six verses thus speak the language of grace, placing the emphasis on God's unmerited favor poured out in the past: "You gave . . . you granted . . . you bestowed." Answer to prayer is a gift. God does not have to answer us, but he always does. He grants us eternal blessings. Some people think of blessings solely in terms of the gifts, not in terms of the Giver. But the highest form of blessing and the Christian's greatest joy is the presence of God himself.

Thanksgiving also reveals our trust in God in the present (v. 7). The basis for the psalmist's present confidence is God's own character—his unfailing, everlasting, covenant-keeping love. Our faith may waver and even seem to expire at times, but God's love for us is unchanging. Peter, for example, denied the Lord three times, yet Jesus promised him, "I have prayed for you, that your faith may not fail." And Peter was restored.

What about our future? We are promised, "He will not be shaken" (v. 7). Ultimately, all shaking is the result of sin. But the future cannot shake a child of God, for Jesus took away the guilt of our sin when he died on the cross. We may live in grateful confidence, rejoicing in the hope of the glory of God. Let us therefore say "Thank you" to him from the depths of our hearts for the grace we have received and will continue to receive, for this is the will of God for us in Christ Jesus.

For he has not despised or disdained the suffering of the afflicted one;
he has not hidden his face from him but has listened to his cry for help.
—Psalm 22:24

salm 22 is quoted often in the New Testament. It is a messianic psalm that Jesus Christ himself meditated on as he endured the agony of the cross. It is a song that begins with a lament and concludes with triumph, that begins with God's abandonment yet ends with a glorious answer to prayer.

The psalmist begins with the silence of God in prayer; he is groaning and crying out to his God, and he will not stop until he is heard. Despite his distress, he addresses God as "my God"; he continues to trust in him who is faithful and can do no wrong. He reposes his confidence in the character and perfections of God. The sufferer also recounts God's past mercies to his people and to him. As he passes through the dark tunnel of divine silence, he meditates on the goodness of the Lord. He understands that his suffering is God's will; thus, he harbors no bitterness or self-pity.

In the perfect will of God, Jesus Christ was put to death for our sins. God the Father abandoned his only begotten Son. Jesus meditated on these verses as he hung on the cross and experienced the outpoured wrath of God on Good Friday. Jesus, the innocent One, suffered as no man has suffered or could suffer. Then, having drunk the cup of God's wrath to the full, Christ emerged once again into the sunlight of God's favor.

The psalmist finally affirms that God has not forsaken him, but that he has, in fact, listened to his cries. In the same way, Jesus prayed, "Father, into your hands I commit my spirit." The face of God had turned towards him again.

In Hebrews 5 we read, "During the days of Jesus' life, he offered up prayers and petitions with loud cries and tears to the one who could save him from death, and he was heard because of his reverent submission." God did indeed hear Jesus' prayer and answered him. How? By raising him from the dead! May God help us to place our trust in this Jesus who was raised for our justification. And when we ourselves pass through suffering, may we move from lament to thanksgiving through prayer and trust in our faithful Lord.

The LORD is my shepherd, I shall not be in want. —Psalm 23:1

 salm 23 is still the most well known and most loved of all the psalms. Every day chaplains are called to the hospital to visit the dying, and many read this psalm to comfort them. Nevertheless, the sobering truth is that the majority of those to whom this psalm is read go on to die without ever having known the Good Shepherd. The comfort and blessings we read about here are, in fact, for Jesus' sheep alone.

Psalm 23 is born out of Psalm 22, which speaks of the shepherd laying down his life for his sheep. That psalm began with a cry of abandonment: "My God, my God, why hast thou forsaken me?" This psalm begins with a confident affirmation: "The LORD is my shepherd." Jesus accomplished redemption for his people by suffering the wrath of God in our stead on the cross. As a result, all who put their faith in him, who hear his voice and follow him, may legitimately say, "I shall not be in want."

Our Lord is truly our Good Shepherd, who is with us always, and who meets our needs, both spiritual and physical. The guilt of sin causes the wicked to be restless, but Jesus grants rest to his sheep. Those who come to him shall never hunger or thirst. Sheep are foolish and tend to stray from the shepherd, but Jesus goes after them and restores them, forgiving their sins. Sheep are prone to wander, but Jesus faithfully guides them in paths of righteousness and good works.

Not only so, but the Good Shepherd will be with us in the hour of our greatest need—when we walk through the valley of the shadow of death. Notice, the preposition is *through*, not *in*. We will surely face death, but we will be ushered through death unto resurrection life because he is walking alongside, holding our hand. No one, not even our loved ones, can travel with us through that valley; Jesus alone will go with us. The sheep of his pasture, the people of God, may therefore joyfully acclaim, "I will fear no evil, for thou art with me." Finally, when our journey ends, we will arrive in our heavenly home to dwell with him forever.

You have let go of the commands of God and are holding on to the traditions of men. —Mark 7:8

he word *tradition* appears six times in Mark 7. The scribes and Pharisees of Jesus' day held to a large number of oral laws—rules of men—that were later codified and became the basis for the Talmud. Mark introduces us to two of these traditions: ceremonial washings and Corban. The denunciation of such practices often brought Jesus into fierce conflict with the Jewish religious leaders.

Note Jesus' sharp response when his opponents accused him of not living according to the tradition of the elders. He rebuked the Pharisees, saying, "Isaiah was right when he prophesied about you hypocrites. You nullify the word of God by your tradition." Jesus understood this multiplication of rules to be an ancient problem, one that involves damnable hypocrisy and, at its core, insidiously negates the very word of God.

All of which confronts us with a question: Do we also nullify the Scriptures with our own ideas? We too have our own ways of annulling the Bible and rendering it powerless in our lives. Some in the church today utilize psychology to trump the clear teaching of the Bible. As a result of the prevailing medical model, for example, sins are now excused and explained away as simply due to illness. Other people are continually looking for a new idea, a new revelation that goes beyond the once-for-all message entrusted to the saints in the Scriptures. Perhaps most commonly, we are tempted to allow our ever-changing feelings to invalidate the written word of God. How I feel becomes more important than what God has said.

Jesus' stance reminds us of the prophet Jeremiah, who told the Israelites, "Stand at the crossroads and look; ask for the ancient paths, ask where the good way is, and walk in it, and you will find rest for your souls" (Jer. 6:16). We too must return to the ancient paths by exalting the word of God in our lives and allowing it to function powerfully as God intends. We must say good-bye to every tactic we have used to hinder the effectiveness of God's word as it convicts, rebukes, corrects, and instructs us. As we do so, we shall surely find great blessing, even rest for our weary souls.

By day the LORD went ahead of them in a pillar of cloud to guide them on their way and by night in a pillar of fire to give them light.
—*Exodus 13:21*

xodus 12 spoke of the Passover—how the blood of the sacrificial lamb sprinkled on the doorway spared the believing Israelite household. This points to the sacrifice of the Lamb of God, the Lord Jesus Christ, whose blood was outpoured for the sins of his people. Exodus 13 now alerts us to what follows the Passover, namely, Pentecost. Here, for the first time, we read of the pillar of cloud and the pillar of fire—symbolic of the presence of God—which led the Lord's redeemed people through the wilderness to the Promised Land.

God's leading and government immediately follow God's salvation. God does not redeem a sinner only to let him pursue his own agenda. Instead, a born-again Christian comes under the command and government of the indwelling Holy Spirit. God then directs every aspect of the believer's life for the entirety of his life.

The Holy Spirit is the gift of God to his children. Jesus promised his disciples, "I will ask the Father and he will give you another Counselor to be with you forever. When he comes, he will guide you into all truth." He guides us through the wilderness of a very dark and perverse world. His way is not always the easiest nor the quickest way, but it is the right way that leads to the Celestial City. No matter how complicated your problem, if you come to God in humility, he will provide a clear answer by means of the infinite personal Holy Spirit speaking in the Scriptures.

What must we do to enjoy the guidance and protection of the pillar of cloud and of fire? Jesus put it very clearly: "If anyone would come after me, he must deny himself, take up his cross, and follow me." We are not called to deny our individuality or our minds; rather, we are to bring our thoughts into conformity with the Holy Scriptures. We must understand and obey God's will, loving what he loves and hating what he hates. We are to follow the guidance of the Holy Spirit, for he will not take us back to the slavery of Egypt. Instead, he leads us into the kingdom of God where there is righteousness, peace, and joy.

When they came to Marah, they could not drink its water because it was bitter. . . . So the people grumbled against Moses. —Exodus 15:23–24

xodus 15 begins with great worship and ends with great sin—the sin of murmuring. Murmuring expresses the heart's discontent, not with ourselves, but with God and his delegated authorities. Those who grumble are treating God with contempt and accusing him of incompetence. This sin came to be the dominant theme of Israel's life in the wilderness, especially in times of crisis.

Murmuring turns everything upside down. First, it puts the covenant structure on its head. The Lord told the people that they must "listen carefully to the voice of the LORD your God and do what is right in his eyes" in order to enjoy his covenant blessings. The grumbler, however, demands that God serve him and make him happy. This is sheer arrogance and self-centeredness.

Second, grumbling turns our view of reality upside down. The Israelites actually claimed that their life under the bondage of slavery to Pharaoh was preferable to the beneficent rule of Yahweh. This was a horrible distortion of the truth. Murmuring springs from a dark heart, and it darkens the heart. The grumbler misinterprets and misrepresents reality.

Third, grumbling results from an attitude that is the exact opposite of the Christian mindset. We are to live by faith, not by sight. The complainer, however, is focused solely on the problem that can be seen and felt, not on the invisible God who is in the midst of our problems to deliver the humble believer. The grumbler does not live by faith in God's word; therefore, he gives way to anxiety and fear when life's storms come. He questions God's justice, goodness, power, and leading.

Finally, murmuring controverts the command to build each other up. Grumblers want company; they campaign relentlessly to influence others, dragging them down to destruction. Everyone associated with Korah was killed by God. Grumbling is a highly contagious sin.

We are all prone to murmur when we face trials and difficulties. Let us instead come with an attitude of prayer and praise, saying with Moses, "In your unfailing love you will lead the people you have redeemed; . . . you will guide them to your holy dwelling" (v. 13).

Strike the rock, and water will come out of it for the people to drink.
—*Exodus 17:6*

xodus 17 records yet another one of the many instances when the Israelites sinned grievously against their covenant Lord. They did so through murmuring and rank unbelief, though God had performed many glorious miracles on their behalf in bringing them out of Egypt through the Red Sea and providing for them in the fiery wilderness. Faced with this new trial, they quarreled, grumbled, and questioned whether the Lord was even among them. Such distrust and murmuring is a great offense against Almighty God.

Moses' response was the correct one—he cried out to the Lord. We, too, should go first to our great God in believing prayer when we face serious trials and troubles. Our God hears the prayers of his people.

We do well to give careful attention to the way in which the Lord answered Moses' cry of distress. He commanded Moses to take his staff and approach the rock of Horeb. The Lord promised to stand before him as he struck the rock and to perform a miracle by bringing water from the stricken stone. Moses obeyed in faith, and the people's thirst was quenched.

Herein is an Old Testament story that points to the substitutionary atonement that would be accomplished in the fullness of time at Calvary for God's covenant people by the Savior, the Lord Jesus Christ. He is the true, spiritual rock that was stricken for our sake. We, like the Israelites of old, have sinned and deserve to be struck with the rod of God's just punishment. Yet it was God's eternal will to punish his Son in our place. He did not spare his Son but gave him up for us all. The prophet Isaiah writes, "For the transgressions of my people he was stricken" (Isa. 53:8, KJV). As a result, we who come to him in faith may drink freely from the water of life.

Let us never grow cold in our love and appreciation for the marvelous salvation accomplished by Jesus, the Suffering Servant who came to give his life a ransom for many. Let us appreciate the gospel. Let us appreciate mercy. We must never give in to murmuring, but instead should rejoice in God our Savior, who is just and the one who justifies those who have faith in Jesus.

When I felt secure, I said, "I shall never be shaken." —Psalm 30:6

 hen God in his mercy grants us abundance of material blessings and physical health, we are prone to become arrogant, self-reliant, and boastful. We are tempted to congratulate ourselves rather than acknowledging and thanking God. We conveniently forget him, neglecting prayer and worship. The history of the Bible and the church confirm that we are never at greater risk of falling than when we are basking in the sunshine of prosperity.

This is what happened to David. When he felt secure, when life was prosperous and everything was going his way, he said, "I'll never be shaken." This is the language of arrogance.

The Bible is replete with warnings about the deceitfulness of riches. God told his covenant people, "When you have eaten and are satisfied, praise the LORD your God. . . . Otherwise, . . . your heart will become proud and you will forget the LORD" (Deut. 8:10, 12). Jesus himself taught his disciples, "The deceitfulness of wealth chokes the word, making it unfruitful" (Matt. 13:22).

When one of his believing children becomes self-deluded and self-reliant, God's anger is aroused. He will not share his glory with another; therefore, he will discipline his proud people. The Lord hid his face from David, which brought terror and dismay (v. 7). David was also chastised with a severe illness that brought him to the brink of death.

As a result, David engaged in self-examination and repented of his sin. He prayed with great earnestness, not on the basis of his own merit, but on the basis of God's mercy. This is the type of prayer that God hears. He not only forgave David his sins, but also healed him completely.

Is God hiding his face from you? Has he ordained suffering for you or your family? It is wise to examine yourself and see whether you have strayed from the way of trust, humility, and dependence on God. More importantly, are you instead presently enjoying prosperity? If so, now is the time to make sure that you are not beginning to boast and trust in your success and wealth. Let us join with the apostle Paul and say, "What do we have that we did not receive?" And let us praise God, especially for his unspeakable gift to us, the Lord Jesus Christ.

And God spoke all these words. —Exodus 20:1

oday we live in a corrupt culture that is anti-law. Christians too, though they have been redeemed from sin, must be ever vigilant lest they fall back into antinomian thinking and living. Such lawlessness destroys the very heart of the covenant we see unfolded in Exodus 20.

Throughout the history of redemption, the covenants God establishes with fallen man have always had this essential form: the great King tells us what to do if we want to be saved. He remains the King forever, and we remain sinners saved by grace, bound to keep his stipulations. To pretend that we are above law is simply a delusion. This is why in the New Testament no one becomes a Christian without making the good confession, "Jesus is Lord."

It does not matter how long we have claimed to be Christians or how long we have attended church. If we do not take delight in God's laws and practice them on a consistent basis, we simply are not Christians.

The Ten Commandments are the heart of the covenant stipulations; they are words spoken by the mouth of God himself and written in stone by the finger of God himself. The number ten stands for completeness; all other laws and stipulations come from these. Their inscription in stone means that they cannot be erased; they have abiding relevancy and validity for mankind. They stand forever as the perfect expression of God's character and God's will for us.

The Ten Commandments convict the sinner by exposing the sinfulness of his sin. They point to the cross where Jesus Christ, the One who never sinned, died on behalf of those who would repent and believe on his name. And they are the believer's unfailing moral guide. Because we have been born again, the Holy Spirit has written these laws afresh, not on tablets of stone, but upon our very hearts. He is in us, helping us to understand and fulfill his word, though we remain imperfect in this life. This progressive work of sanctification wrought in us by God's Spirit is the sure sign that we are genuine Christians. May God help us to shine as stars in this corrupt culture as we obey his word.

I will extol the LORD at all times; his praise will always be on my lips.
—*Psalm 34:1*

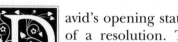

avid's opening statement in Psalm 34 takes the form
of a resolution. The making and keeping of this
resolution reveals King David's moral strength and
Christian character. Holy character is typically forged
in the furnace of fiery trial, however, and David's life was no
exception.

We are told that this psalm was penned just after David's sinful
flight to King Achish in Gath. Instead of trusting in God and his
promises, David leaned on his own understanding and fled in
fear of Saul to the land of the Philistines. Soon, fear of Achish
took hold, and David resorted to a ruse—feigning madness in the
king's presence. Surely David's own folly had brought him to one
of the lowest points in his tumultuous life.

In God's covenant mercies, David was freed and released to
the Judean wilderness. God spared David, and then restored him
by bringing him back to his senses. As a result of the Holy Spirit's
ministry, David realized that he had been foolishly trusting in his
own wisdom and schemes to solve his problems. This self-reliance
had served only to deepen the pit. Now David repented and began
to chart a new course.

To declare, "I will bless the Lord at all times," is to first
acknowledge that it is God who helps us at all times. It is to align
ourselves with the Scriptures, which proclaim that all things work
together for the good of those who love him. This is genuine
faith—to trust God even in the midst of bitter circumstances.

David's resolution also meant that he would now look to God
alone to direct his paths. He would no longer lean on his own
understanding. We too may find ourselves in a low place, but we
need never resort to feigning madness! When we cry to him for
help, we will hear his voice saying, "This is the way, walk in it."

David concludes his statement by resolving to ever praise the
One who had delivered him, and his gratitude reverberates down
through today. As a result, we too are encouraged to worship him
who has done great things for us. And as we ourselves discover
God to be truly great, we in turn encourage others to join us in
glorifying him.

Do not follow the crowd in doing wrong. —Exodus 23:2

he directive of Exodus 23:2 speaks against following the majority view in the realm of truth, lifestyle, morals, behavior, and philosophy. This imperative, given to God's people at Sinai, remains relevant for the church today. The crowd has always done and will always do wrong, for the world lies under the control of the devil. But those who have been born of God and redeemed from bondage now belong to the Lord. We are his treasured possession; therefore, we are to obey him fully and keep his covenant. We are to be holy because our Savior God is holy.

The crowd's worldview is always wrong. For example, the very first line of Scripture affirms the infinite, personal Creator God; yet the crowd believes the evolutionary hypothesis. The Bible affirms the transcendent importance of what is unseen; the crowd says that this life and its pleasures are what matters. Jesus well summarized the antithesis when he declared, "What is highly valued among men is detestable in God's sight" (Luke 16:15).

Sadly, though, we find members of the crowd even in God's church. Many modern Christians reject the Scriptures and instead blend in with the world. They have absorbed the crowd's philosophy, especially as it is piped into our homes through the television and Internet. How many churches preach against sexual immorality today? How many speak against the materialism and greed that typify American culture? Truly we are living in an age when most call evil good and good evil.

We must, therefore, redouble our resolve to follow Christ, not the crowd. We must conform no longer to the pattern of this world, but be transformed by the renewing of our minds. We must store God's word in our hearts and then view all of life through the lens of Scripture. While others fornicate, we must live disciplined, holy lives as virgins until we are married. While others lie, we must tell the truth. While others hoard wealth, we must share and serve others.

Let us be glad members of the glorious minority who are regulated by the Bible and the awesome presence of our God. Let us daily affirm the words we declared at our baptism: "Though none go with me, still I will follow where Jesus leads me."

Do not fret. . . . Trust in the LORD. . . . Delight yourself in the LORD. . . .
Commit your way to the LORD. —Psalm 37:1–5

hese four imperatives that we read in the first verses of Psalm 37 sum up the way of peace and joy for the Christian. They are words of life for us, which we must understand, believe, and obey. If we do so, we can triumph in the face of our trials and tribulations.

Fretting is the opposite of trusting in God, and it is expressly forbidden here by the covenant Lord. The same prohibition is articulated in the New Testament: "Do not be anxious for anything" (Phil. 4:6). We may paraphrase the Hebrew "Do not fret" by saying, "Don't be a hothead; don't lose your head." The believer should not allow circumstances to cause him to abandon his rationality and self-control. We must remind ourselves that evil shall not ultimately prevail; our almighty God will win! Therefore, we need never behave like an unbeliever who has neither hope nor anchor nor foundation to stabilize him in the storm.

The heart of saving faith is trust. The believer wholeheartedly embraces God as Savior, Father, and King. Such faith manifests in a day-by-day trust in God. "Abram believed the LORD" is one of the most important Old Testament verses (Gen. 15:6). The language means that Abram cast himself on God who, like a sure foundation, was able to bear his weight. Joshua and Caleb exhibited the same trust when they rejected the majority report (Num. 14).

What does it mean to delight in the Lord? One translation reads, "Make Yahweh your only joy." The first and greatest commandment is to love the Lord our God with all our heart, mind, soul, and strength. We tend to love something in creation first, whether self, spouse, or child. Godly delight therefore involves a redirecting of our emotions. As we delight in God with a first love, he delights in us.

When we trust and delight in God, commitment follows. The Hebrew means to roll one's entire life—our past, our present, and our future—onto another for safekeeping. Christians may roll their burdens and cast their cares onto Jesus Christ, who alone is capable of carrying us on his mighty shoulders. When we do so, peace will flood our souls and he will make our righteousness shine like the dawn.

There is no difference, for all have sinned and fall short of the glory of God. —Romans 3:22–23

omans 3:22 concludes by asserting, "There is no difference." At the most fundamental level of analysis, all men are the same—all are moral agents, created by God, and all have sinned against their Creator. We tend to exclude ourselves when we speak about sin and sinners, but God puts every person within that circle. All have sinned, this passage maintains, and fall short of the glory of God.

What does it mean to lack the glory of God? First, it signifies that sinful man lacks God's approbation. Man was to glorify God in everything and, in turn, be glorified and approved by his Creator. Now, however, the sinner is under the wrath of God. This statement also speaks to the fact that the perfect image and likeness of God in which man was originally created has been horribly marred by the Fall. Additionally, to lack the glory of God is to lack the presence of God. Sinful man cannot enjoy fellowship with God; it takes holiness to fellowship with the thrice-holy God. It takes glory to fellowship with glory.

Thanks be to God, his plan of redemption remedied this terrible lack. At the moment God regenerated us and we repented and placed our faith in Jesus Christ, we who never had glory were given glory. God made his light shine in our hearts to give us the light of the knowledge of the glory of God in the face of Jesus Christ. Not only so, but we as Christians now can go on to experience an ever increasing measure of glory. The apostle Paul declares, "We, who with unveiled faces all reflect the Lord's glory, are being transformed into his likeness with ever-increasing glory" (2 Cor. 3:18).

The Christian's final destination is glory. When Christ returns, we will receive a final installment of glory, and so we who once fell short may now rejoice in the hope of the glory of God. Our future is so certain that Paul can state it as an already-accomplished fact in Romans 8. We cannot see him now, but on that day he shall banish sin forever and qualify us to see him as he is. That will be glory!

This is what you are to do to consecrate them, so they may serve me as priests. —Exodus 29:1

xodus 29 speaks about the consecration, the setting apart, of the house of Aaron to serve the Lord as priests in the Old Testament theocracy. Today, in the New Testament era, we know that every believer is a priest in Jesus Christ, as Peter explains in his first epistle. Accordingly, the principles enunciated here in Exodus pertain to each and every one of us.

We notice that the priests were first washed with water; they could not approach God as unclean people. This points to the washing accomplished in us by the Holy Spirit when he regenerated us through the word of God. Next, the priests were clothed with holy garments. So too, each Christian is clothed with the glorious, everlasting robe of Christ's own righteousness. The priest was then anointed with the sacred anointing oil. We also are anointed with the Holy Spirit himself to guide and empower us to perform the tasks we are called to complete.

Finally, the blood of the ram of ordination was applied to the right ear lobe, the right thumb, and the right big toe of Aaron and his sons. What does this mean for us who are priests today? First, our ears are to be consecrated to hear and understand the will of God alone. Others can live for themselves, but we cannot. The thumb speaks about our hands—hands that are to do the will of God alone. We are set apart for his service. Finally, we are to walk in the will of God throughout all of life. We are God's workmanship, created in Christ Jesus unto good works that God has foreordained that we should walk in them. We have no right to go wherever we want and do whatever we want. We are not like the world; we are a royal priesthood, a holy nation, a people belonging to God.

The Aaronic priests had prescribed offerings to present to God. Likewise, God's word instructs Christians what offerings are acceptable to him in our day. Through Jesus, we are to continually offer to God a sacrifice of praise, and we are to continue to do good and share with others. May our lives be a pleasing aroma to him!

If by the Spirit you put to death the misdeeds of the body, you will live.
—Romans 8:13

erses 12–13 reveal to us the heart of progressive sanctification—how we can defeat the sin that remains in us as believers. Here the apostle Paul moves from exposition to exhortation, from the indicative to the imperative. In other words, in light of what God has done for us, let us live for him. Let us put to death the sin in us by the power of the mighty Holy Spirit. Progressive sanctification is not accomplished through our passivity, nor through sheer self-effort, but rather by our taking action in the might and direction of the Spirit who dwells in us.

Christians are a set-free people—set free from slavery to sin, Satan, and death. As emancipated slaves, we are no longer obligated to obey sin as our master; instead, we are now glad debtors to our triune God. God the Father planned redemption from all eternity; God the Son accomplished redemption; and God the Holy Spirit applies that redemption to each of the elect. We owe everything to our Redeemer.

Our life of progressive sanctification consists in two elements: mortification and conformation. Mortification speaks of putting sin to death. If we live by the Spirit, we will not gratify the desires of the flesh (Gal. 5:16). Conformation speaks of our being gradually conformed to the image of Jesus Christ (Rom. 8:29). As believers in Christ, we now have real freedom not to sin.

Though sin still dwells in us, so does the Holy Spirit, who is infinitely greater. By his mighty power, we can say "No" to sin and make it stick. Now, in the strength of Christ we can wrestle against the devil and cause him to flee. Like David of old, we can strike down Goliath and enjoy the victory. But make no mistake; this is a battle unto death. We must daily kill our enemy, for his intent is to destroy us. We must reject sinful thoughts and temptations at their very inception. Be ruthless. Be violent. Be angry, hating sin enough to kill it. Neutrality and negotiation are not options.

Holiness is essential to our eternal fellowship with God. It is our present delightful obedience—our progressive sanctification—that proves our past justification and assures us of our future glorification.

Come, make us gods who will go before us. —Exodus 32:1

 n the chapters leading up to Exodus 32, we have learned much about the one living and true God, Yahweh. We saw his mighty acts of judgment and redemption as he delivered the Israelites out of Egypt. We saw how the people trembled with fear as he came down to meet with Moses on Mount Sinai. Now, however, we are introduced to a new god, a rival god, the bull god. He is the product of man's imagination, an idol reduced to man's size, a dumb domesticated god who will let the people follow their lusts. In less than four months, the Israelites forgot the mighty God who saved them and exchanged their Glory for an image of a bull.

Since the Fall, there have been two kinds of religions in the world. One is God-centered, giving him the glory; the other is man-centered, with the worshipper's intent being the pursuit of happiness through personal pleasure, power, and pride. This is what we see in Exodus 32: "They sat down to eat and drink and got up to indulge in revelry." Such religion remains very popular today, and many so-called evangelists promote it by emphasizing entertainment, avoiding the topics of sin and holiness, and promoting what religion can do for people. This is nothing less than idol worship in the name of Yahweh. Exodus 32 teaches us that the true and living God's anger is aroused whenever and wherever this occurs, and his wrath will surely issue in judgment.

As in Exodus 32, we are also called to make a choice: "Who is on the LORD's side?" Either we shall serve Yahweh with fear and trembling, or we shall act corruptly and demand a bull god who never restrains or rebukes sin. We must be extremely careful and guard our hearts, for we live in a horribly corrupt culture that constantly tempts us to turn away from the living and true God who alone is worthy of our worship. We ought to emulate the Levites, who separated themselves and were zealous for God's glory. And we should reflect on the respective outcomes seen in this chapter: the bull god was pulverized and his followers struck down by the sword and plague; Yahweh's worshippers received his divine approval and blessing.

My Presence will go with you, and I will give you rest. —*Exodus 33:14*

e read in Exodus 33 that the Israelites were distressed when they heard that, though the Promised Land would be theirs, the God of Israel would not go with them. Their reaction may surprise us, because many in the modern-day church would be quite pleased with such an arrangement. This is just the message for today's evangelical churchgoers: you can have all of God's blessings without the constraint imposed by his holy presence. You can do whatever you want and still call yourself a Christian!

Why, then, were the people distressed? Sobriety had hit them. They had come to their senses and realized that their Redeemer God might not be present with them; the pillar of fire and cloud may not guide them. Their sins had separated them from God, and his wrath alone remained. "If I were to go with you even for a moment, I might destroy you," the covenant Lord solemnly warned. The people suddenly understood that to have riches but lack God is an abomination, a tragedy. Such an awareness ought to lead to a true revival.

And so we find the people who had been happily indulging in revelry now weeping as a result of their acute pain and sense of loss. Not only so, but they also were beginning to repent of their sins. The Israelites stripped off their ornaments at Mount Horeb in response to the Lord's explicit command, for the detestable bull god fashioned by Aaron had been made from such jewelry. These ornaments stand for anything that comes between us and God; anything that prevents us from worshiping God with wholehearted devotion; anything that has become an idol. The people counted the cost and willingly gave up their precious jewelry.

What was Jehovah's response to Moses' prayer and the people's repentance? We read his glorious promise in verse 14: "My Presence will go with you, and I will give you rest." Undoubtedly the Israelites shouted for joy at these comforting words. Do you want the joy of your salvation restored? Do you want the assurance that God is with you? The moment we obey God and strip off our ornaments, he will fill us with the unspeakable joy of his presence.

Everyone must submit himself to the governing authorities, for there is no authority except that which God has established. —Romans 13:1

he Bible declares that God is sovereign over the kingdoms of men and gives them to anyone he wishes. He sets up kings and deposes them. This absolute, sovereign God has chosen to rule his world through his delegated authorities, who are given power to minister in his behalf for the good of the governed and to restrain evil in a fallen world. God is not the God of confusion, but of order.

The authority of the state is addressed specifically in Romans 13. Her authority is not inherent in herself, but is given to her by God. Because the state is a delegated authority, her right to command is a limited one; she may not legitimately tell us to disobey God's laws. The state is explicitly granted the power of the sword. When faithfully executed, capital punishment curbs evil and promotes the sanctity of life.

What is the responsibility of the people towards their government? They are to be subject to God-ordained authorities and render obedience for the sake of conscience. We all are to pay our taxes, obey just laws, and respect those who govern. We also are to pray for our leaders. And if we are permitted, we should participate in the political process, especially by informed voting.

We are not told to submit only to a Christian government; in fact, no Christian government existed when Paul wrote his letter. However, we are to submit to our leaders only up to the point where obedience to them would entail disobedience to the sovereign Lord. We must disobey Caesar when he insists that he be worshiped, even if it costs us our lives.

Finally, we must avoid the trap of an illegitimate appeal to conscience to justify disobedience. Conscience can be the final refuge of an autonomous "Christian" scoundrel. History is littered with examples of those who flouted civil or church government based on an argument involving liberty of conscience. Yet conscience is never absolute nor the final authority, for it is fallen and fallible. When a Christian knows the word of God, is led by the Spirit, and is living a holy life, he will enjoy a good conscience that leads him to submit to God and to all his delegated authorities.

MARCH 7

I myself am convinced, my brothers, that you yourselves are full of goodness, complete in knowledge and competent to instruct one another.
—Romans 15:14

e all need godly counsel. Only the foolish and arrogant pretend otherwise. The Bible warns us, "There is a way that seems right to a man, but in the end it leads to death" (Prov. 14:12). God has met our need for life-giving counsel first by providing parents for their children, and pastors for their flock. And this verse tells us that certain Christians are able to counsel others. What are the qualifications for such counselors?

First, Paul describes such Christians as "full of goodness." This fact testifies to God's marvelous grace, for we all have sinned and fall short of the glory of God; we all come into the world as bad trees bearing bad fruit. But God is able to make bad trees good by regeneration, by the word, and by the Holy Spirit. He takes away our stony, wicked, stubborn, rebellious, sinful hearts and gives us hearts that think God's thoughts, will his holy will, and feel the way God feels, loving the good and hating the evil.

Second, competent counselors must be "filled with all knowledge," meaning they must have relational knowledge of God through regeneration and the diligent study of the Bible. They are not dull in their minds, but are actively growing in the grace and knowledge of our Lord and Savior Jesus Christ (2 Pet. 3:18). This knowledge of God that leads to salvation does not come from science, psychology, or hollow philosophy, but from the revelation of Jesus Christ in the Holy Scriptures by the Holy Spirit.

Only those who are filled with the goodness and knowledge of God are competent to counsel. The Greek for "counsel" means to put the word of God into one's mind so that it brings about a fundamental change in attitude and actions. Under the guidance of a God-called pastor, mature Christians are to warn and admonish their brothers and sisters by bringing the truth of God's word to bear on their minds and consciences. They do so in keeping with the moral model of the Scriptures, not the medical model of secularism. And what is the promised outcome? As the counselee understands and humbly obeys the word, he will enjoy an ever-increasing harvest of righteousness and peace.

We preach Christ crucified: a stumbling block to Jews and foolishness to Gentiles, but to those whom God has called, both Jews and Greeks, Christ the power of God and the wisdom of God. —1 Corinthians 1:23–24

hat is wisdom? J. I. Packer says, "Wisdom is the power to see, and the inclination to choose, the best and highest goal, together with the surest means of achieving it."[1]

We see the wisdom of God in creation, as well as in God's providential care and governing of that creation. But the highest wisdom of God is demonstrated in redemption. All creation, all providence, and the entire history of the world are for the singular divine purpose of creating a people for God. It is in the forming of the church of Jesus Christ that we find the maximum display of divine wisdom—and that goal could only be accomplished through the cross.

What is wisdom for man, the highest goal to which we can aspire? It is to be connected with God, to have fellowship with him. And the means for achieving that is the cross of Christ. God solved our insoluble problem by punishing his Son in our place on Calvary. He can now justly forgive our sins and grant us his Son's perfect righteousness. All the wisdom of the world cannot give meaning to man. It cannot save a single person from sin, death, judgment, and hell. We need the wisdom that is from above; we need Jesus Christ, who is wisdom incarnate, our righteousness, holiness, and redemption.

How do we obtain such wisdom? God must reveal it to us by his Spirit. Unbelievers may scoff at a dying Savior, but we whose eyes have been opened see in the cross the most marvelous display of God's love and wisdom. By this wisdom, the elect sinners of this world will be converted to glory. The work of Jesus Christ on the cross alone procures glory for sinners who have fallen short of the glory of God. Not only so, but we who believe are also indwelt by the mighty Holy Spirit, who enables us to walk in that holiness which fits us for fellowship with God. A life of wisdom is one in which we live a holy life by the power of the Holy Spirit, communing with Jesus, who qualifies us to dwell with him in eternal glory.

---

1   J. I. Packer, *Knowing God* (Downers Grove, IL: InterVarsity, 1973), 80.

For who makes you different from anyone else? What do you have that you did not receive? —1 Corinthians 4:7

ome in the Corinthian church had evidently become worldly, self-satisfied, and proud. This had led to divisions in the church, boasting about men, and criticism of the apostle Paul himself. In response, Paul pointedly declared that all we are and have is the result not of our native abilities but of God's munificent grace in our lives.

Paul began this letter by reminding the Corinthians of their status when they first heard the gospel and became Christians. "Not many of you were wise," he wrote, "Not many were influential, not many were of noble birth" (1 Cor. 1:26). The Corinthian Christians had no reason to take pride in their background or social standing. They were really nothings. Paul reminded them that he who boasts should boast in the Lord alone.

Now, in 1 Corinthians 4, Paul gives another powerful argument to demonstrate the absurdity of man's pride. The Corinthians, who had once been among the lowly and despised, had been recently congratulating themselves on their attainments, as if the blessings they now enjoyed were self-generated. The apostle brings their pretensions to an abrupt end by the use of rhetorical questions and irony. "What do you have that you did not receive?" he asks. The answer is: Nothing. No man can boast in himself as if he did not depend on God's merciful providence for his very existence.

Paul then engages in sarcasm. "You have become kings—and that without us!" Some in the church, it seems, even felt as though they were now superior to the apostle himself. That church's true spiritual father, the very man God had marvelously used in bringing them the gospel, was now subject to their criticism.

This shameful state of affairs highlights an ever-present danger when we begin to enjoy God-given success. We are tempted not only to credit ourselves for our achievements, but also to begin to judge our superiors—fathers, pastors, bosses—who have enabled us to advance in life. We begin to think of ourselves as indispensable to God, as though the church could not go on without us. May God help us, whenever we are given various gifts of grace, to walk in greater thanksgiving, faithfulness, and humility rather than in pride.

Moses did everything just as the LORD commanded him. —Exodus 40:16

he last chapter of Exodus is also the climactic chapter of the book. Three times Moses had been solemnly told by God to build the tabernacle according to the pattern shown to him on the mountain (Exod. 25:40; 26:30; 27:8). Moses had, in turn, instructed the Israelites, and they had done all the work just as the Lord had commanded (Exod. 39:42). Now Aaron and his sons were anointed and the tabernacle was set up for the first time. Would God be pleased? Would his blessing rest upon their labors?

The covenant Lord's benediction did indeed rest upon the Israelites' work. We read that the cloud covered the Tent of Meeting and the glory of the Lord filled the tabernacle. God came down in blessing, and the Israelites were filled with joy.

We, the people belonging to God, are his tabernacle in these latter days. Just as Moses had to build according to the pattern, so we also must build our lives according to our pattern, which is the Lord Jesus Christ. How can we know the correct standard? Left to our own devices, we will concoct our own view of Jesus. God therefore has seen to it that we have the written, infallible Scriptures, translated into our language, to reveal Christ to us. Our pattern for living is not our subjective feelings, nor what is culturally popular; it is what we read in the objective, immutable word of God.

Christians are not at liberty to edit this divine pattern. We cannot carve out exceptions to God's covenant rules. God will not bless a rebel who picks and chooses what he will obey. If we want to experience God's approval, we must be cultural contrarians, Christ-conformists who do all things for the glory of God.

What blessing will we enjoy as we obey God's commands? Jesus promised, "If anyone loves me, he will obey my teaching. My Father will love him, and we will come to him and make our home with him" (John 14:23). The more we love and obey God, the more we will enjoy his presence with us, and the more we will be satisfied. This is the creature's highest blessing and greatest delight—holy communion with the infinite, personal God, his Creator and Redeemer.

Wash away all my iniquity and cleanse me from my sin. —Psalm 51:2

salm 51 follows King David's heinous sins of adultery and murder, subsequent cover-up, and ultimate conviction of sin when the prophet Nathan confronted him. Here we learn what constitutes authentic, God-authored repentance.

David begins with honest, forthright confession. He had been hard-hearted and duplicitous for nearly a year, but now by the mercy of God he owns his many sins. Moreover, he understands and acknowledges that his problem is not simply his sinful behavior, but rather his whole sinful nature. He recognizes his total depravity, that he has been a perverse sinner from birth.

He therefore cries out to God for cleansing and forgiveness. He is not asking for justice, but for mercy on the basis of God's covenant love. Notice the language used in verse 7: "Cleanse me with hyssop." We read in Exodus 12 that this plant, dipped in the blood of the sacrificial lamb, was used to sprinkle the doorframes of the Israelite homes at Passover. The king is thus speaking of substitutionary atonement; there is no cleansing possible apart from the blood of Jesus Christ.

David, however, is spurred on to ask God for more than forgiveness; the king also wants a pure heart. He uses a Hebrew word for *create* that is only used in reference to God. David is asking God for nothing less than a new creation so that he might love, worship, and obey him out of a converted heart. He will not be satisfied with some sort of reformation; he sees the need for an entirely new heart.

Finally, the king prays that God will open his mouth and enable him to declare the Lord's praises. Sin stops our mouths and prevents us from worshiping God in an acceptable manner until proper confession and repentance occurs. Now, though, the king desires to sing God's glories and to teach others his ways. Glorious fellowship with God has been restored.

These elements—confession, cleansing, creation, and communication—are always present when God the Holy Spirit has worked repentance in our hearts. May God have mercy upon us, that we might not resist him as David did for a year, but rather be quick to repent and be restored.

Do you not know that in a race all the runners run, but only one gets the prize? Run in such a way as to get the prize. —1 Corinthians 9:24

e are surrounded by advertising slogans such as "Eat all you want and still lose weight!" or "Get fit without exercising!" We know better, and will even acknowledge the importance of physical and spiritual discipline. Yet we are still tempted to believe that we can enjoy the benefits without the struggle and pain. The truth is, there is no gain without pain, and no crown without the cross.

In 1 Corinthians 9, Paul uses the imagery of a footrace and a boxing match to picture the Christian's life. The Isthmian games, held in Corinth every two years, required the competitors to abstain from wine and other indulgences, and to work strenuously under a trainer's supervision for ten months prior to the games. In the end, though, only one contestant would win the victor's wreath.

The Christian engages in a far more serious fight and contemplates a far better prize than these Grecian athletes. Spiritual self-discipline is much more difficult than physical exercise, for sin, Satan, and the world are opposed to our spiritual success. How often we fail in the duty of prayer! But thanks be to God, he assists us by the indwelling Holy Spirit. In fact, the Greek word for discipline means "in strength." We can govern our bodies and make them our slaves only with the strength our Lord supplies.

Paul exhorts, "Run in such a way as to get the prize." This means we must not only work with all our energy, but also compete according to the rules. This principle holds true in every area of life. Yet many so-called Christians do not like rules; they view Christ's salvation as a release from rules. This antinomian outlook is anti-Christian and results in failure and loss. We have an unchanging rulebook that must be understood and carefully obeyed—the Holy Bible. Only those who obey the Father enter the kingdom of heaven (Matt. 7:21).

In the ancient Greek games, only one runner received the prize, a wreath made of leaves. But every Christian who disciplines himself and lives according to the Bible's rules wins the race of the Christian life. And every victorious Christian will receive a crown—an incorruptible and everlasting crown of righteousness, life, and glory—from the Lord himself.

No temptation has seized you except what is common to man. And God is faithful; he will not let you be tempted beyond what you can bear. But when you are tempted, he will also provide a way out so that you can stand up under it. —1 Corinthians 10:13

emptation is personified in 1 Corinthians 10 as an enemy who, whenever possible, pursues and seizes the Christian. No believer is exempt. Satan is a prowling lion, we are told elsewhere, looking for someone to devour, especially those who live carelessly. Temptation itself, though, is not sin, and its ubiquity certainly does not mean that we have to give in and do Satan's bidding. Rather, we should look upon every temptation as an opportunity to demonstrate our strength in God and our love for God by saying "No" to sin's allure. When we resist the devil, he will flee from us.

God's faithfulness to us is emphasized in this verse. He can be trusted, for he cannot lie; all his promises are sure. Here we are guaranteed that he will not let us be tempted beyond what we are able to bear. We may have tried to excuse ourselves when we failed in the past, but God's word declares that none of our temptations is unique, and none is too powerful to resist. There is no excuse for a Christian sinning. If the Son has set you free, then you are free indeed—free not to sin.

We are promised that, when we are tempted, God will provide the way out. The Lord God Almighty, who made the universe out of nothing, will make the specific way out for us in our specific trial. Our responsibility is to trust him, fight the good fight, and take the exit he shows.

Why then the testing? We read in 1 Corinthians 1 that God has called us into fellowship with his Son, Jesus Christ our Lord. His grand purpose is to fit sinners for this fellowship with a thrice-holy God through justification, sanctification, and glorification. He is therefore committed to doing everything necessary to clean us up. To this end, he is at work in us to make us stronger and stronger in our Christian walk. As we successfully bear up under temptation, looking for and acting on the way out that God graciously provides, we become daily overcomers in the Lord's mighty power, and God is glorified in our moral strength. Let us then glorify our God who gives us the victory through Christ Jesus our Lord!

But in fact God has arranged the parts in the body, every one of them,
just as he wanted them to be. —1 Corinthians 12:18

n 1 Corinthians 12 we learn that God the Father
through his Son gives the Holy Spirit to those who ask
him. The Spirit, in turn, distributes spiritual gifts—
gifts of grace—to each believer according to his own
sovereign will for the common good and edification of the church.
The context for this instruction about gifts is the body of Christ.
God's gifts to his people are meant to produce not independence
or autonomy but interdependence in love for one another.

Two common mindsets distort and disrupt the proper use of
God's spiritual gifts in his church: the inferiority complex and the
superiority complex. Both are ruled out in this chapter.

In verse 15 we read, "If the foot should say, 'Because I am not
a hand, I do not belong to the body.'" This sentiment springs from
a false humility, which is actually self-pity. In reality, the individual
is saying that he wants to be the hand, that as a foot he does not
feel important enough to the body, and that he therefore wants
to leave the body. This rebellious, "poor me" attitude is an utter
defiance of God, who in his providence placed us in the body in
accordance with his sovereign good pleasure.

Alternatively, we read in verse 21, "The head cannot say to
the feet, 'I don't need you!'" This prideful mindset also harms
Christ's church and arises from ignorance and arrogance. No one
member of the body is self-sufficient; each believer depends on
every other member for his own health and ministry. Not only so,
but we each also are who we are solely by the grace of God; we
have no reason to look down on others.

Elsewhere Paul exhorts, "Do not think of yourself more highly
than you ought" (Rom. 12:3). Western man glories in self-esteem;
it is in the culture and in us. But we must remember Korah
(Num. 16), who, dissatisfied with his office, coveted what was not
his to have. Korah's superiority complex resulted in his and his
followers' swift destruction. Therefore, we ought to take warning,
and embrace the position and calling God has assigned to each
of us, faithfully utilizing the gifts we have received to build up the
body of Christ.

But Christ has indeed been raised from the dead, the firstfruits of those who have fallen asleep. —1 Corinthians 15:20

hen the enemies of Jesus asked for a miraculous sign so that they might believe in him, Jesus gave them the greatest sign: his resurrection from the dead. The truth of the Christian message is inextricably linked to the historical reality of the life, death, and resurrection of Christ, for by his incarnational life and death Jesus fully accomplished redemption for all who believe. Jesus declared, "Because I live, you also will live" (John 14:19).

The resurrection of Christ verified his claim to be the Son of God, the promised Messiah, and demonstrated his power over death. The Jewish Sanhedrin knew that he had predicted his resurrection on the third day. Therefore, the authorities sealed his tomb and posted guards to keep him there. But Jesus rose indeed! The leaders could not stop the apostles' preaching and the growth of the church, because they had no body to produce.

Many witnesses saw the risen Lord. In 1 Corinthians 15, Paul cites six appearances: first to Peter; then to the twelve apostles; then to more than five hundred brothers at one time; then to James, the Lord's brother; then to all the apostles; and last of all, to Paul himself. The risen Christ ate and drank with his disciples for forty days after his resurrection.

Jesus does not make such appearances anymore to satisfy unbelievers' curiosity and demands. We are expected to trust the written account in the Bible given by those eyewitnesses chosen by God. The apostle Peter could therefore write to believers who had never met Jesus in the flesh, "Though you have not seen him, you love him . . . and are filled with an inexpressible and glorious joy" (1 Pet. 1:8).

God has indeed given us many infallible proofs of Christ's resurrection. He is not asking us to take a leap in the dark. He is insisting, rather, that we believe in his gospel that is grounded in historical facts divinely interpreted. As we exercise such wholehearted faith, we will be filled with confidence and hope, for the certainty of Christ's resurrection guarantees our own. He is the firstfruits of all who have fallen asleep in him. Our hope therefore is not a hope-so; it is absolutely sure!

*This is what the L*ORD* has commanded you to do, so that the glory of the* L*ORD* may appear to you. —Leviticus 9:6*

n Leviticus 9, Aaron and his sons, who were called and ordained by God to be priests, began their ministry on behalf of the Israelites. They were coming to the thrice-holy God in worship, and such an approach must always be by means of a sacrifice. Herein is the grace of God displayed. Sinners have no access to God on their own, but he in mercy has given us an acceptable way of approaching him through substitutionary atonement.

We must note how careful Moses and Aaron were in Leviticus 8 and 9 to do everything in the prescribed way: "as the LORD commanded." Undoubtedly they were thinking of the solemn warning, "Do what the LORD requires, so you will not die" (Lev. 8:35). And having offered the prescribed sacrifices to the Lord with fear and trembling, they received his approbation. The God of glory appeared in the midst of the gathered people, not in judgment, but in blessing, and fire consumed the burnt offering.

God's remarkable act conveyed to his people that he was pleased with them, that their sins had been forgiven, and that they could enjoy covenant fellowship with him. What was the people's response? They shouted for joy and fell facedown. Now, through the person and work of Jesus Christ, God has come to meet with us, and we bow down, worship, and shout for joy. Christians have confidence to enter the Most Holy Place by the blood of Jesus.

All of this highlights the starkly different outcome we will encounter in Leviticus 10. Two of Aaron's sons were not careful to come into God's presence in the authorized way, and they paid with their lives for their irreverence. Their end foreshadows what will surely happen to all who refuse to repent and believe on the Lord Jesus Christ. If we do not take refuge in Christ today by a living, obedient faith, we will stand naked before God and be subject to his fiery wrath on the last day.

The prescribed way for sinners to approach Almighty God remains by means of a sacrifice. Christ was sacrificed once to take away the sins of his people. In him and through faith in him we may now approach God with freedom and confidence.

March 17

For just as the sufferings of Christ flow over into our lives, so also through Christ our comfort overflows. —2 Corinthians 1:5

t is no surprise that misery and troubles—wars, catastrophes, illnesses, injustices—abound in a fallen, sinful world. Many are surprised, though, that Christians must face even more difficulties. They ought not to be, though, for the devil is now their bitter enemy. They no longer conform to the world, and are therefore persecuted by the world. So we will encounter much trouble in our Christian life, but we also will receive much comfort from the God of all comfort.

The word *comfort* appears ten times in 2 Corinthians 1. The Holy Spirit makes this emphasis to encourage us and keep us from complaining in our trials. We are told that God is the God of *all* comfort—he gives us every kind of comfort for every kind of challenge. We are told that God comforts—the verb is in the present tense. Now is the time of encouragement! We are also told that he is the Father of mercies—the plural indicates rich abundance.

How does our heavenly Father provide us with the strength we need for each new day? First, he does so directly through the indwelling Holy Spirit. Jesus promised his disciples, "I will ask the Father, and he will give you another Counselor to be with you forever" (John 14:16). Second, he encourages us through the reading of his word. We are told in Romans 15:4 that all Scripture "was written to teach us, so that through endurance and the comfort of the Scriptures we might have hope." It is the Bible that convinces us that God works all things together for our good, for our sanctification.

Finally, the saints themselves are vessels of God's grace to us when we need help. Paul alludes to this when he writes, "[God] comforts us in all our troubles, so that we can comfort those in any trouble with the comfort we ourselves have received from God" (v. 4).

Therefore, we need not give way to fear, misery, and complaining. There is no need to be graceless. God delights to give us the strength and comfort we need as we humbly make use of the many means of grace available to his children. Let us then join with Paul and exclaim, "Praise be to the Father of compassion and the God of all comfort!"

My soul finds rest in God alone; my salvation comes from him.
—*Psalm 62:1*

his psalm of David is without petition; the king has poured out his heart before God and is now completely at rest. The original language reads, "My soul is silent before God alone." David is like an infant who was distraught but is now held and comforted by his mother. He trusts solely in God, and teaches us to do the same.

Note the word "alone"; it appears six times in the Hebrew. The unbeliever by nature trusts in this world, in created things. Double-minded Christians unwittingly rely on God plus something else. But if we place our final and ultimate trust in our country, our money, our spouse, our intellect, or anything other than Jesus Christ alone, we are fools and will be sorely disappointed. As David observes, "Lowborn men are but a breath, the highborn are but a lie" (v. 9).

David then points us to God and gives us two mighty reasons to trust him exclusively. First, "to God belongs power" (v. 11). He is the omnipotent God who created the universe *ex nihilo*, who raised Jesus Christ from the dead, and who redeems sinners from the bondage of sin, Satan, and death. Such invincible power does not reside in us—it belongs to our awesome God alone.

Second, "to God belongs *chesed* [Heb.]"—imperishable, everlasting, loyal, covenant-keeping love (v. 12). He has promised never to leave or forsake his believing children, and he can be trusted to keep his word. When we sin, he will chastise us accordingly, but he will not abandon us.

How can we know that we have placed our trust in this loving, almighty Lord? We enjoy rest. Worry, fear, and anxiety are the opposites of trust. "Let not your hearts be troubled," said Jesus, "Believe in God; believe also in me. In this world you will have trouble. But take heart! I have overcome the world."

King David, having entered this rest that results from trusting in God alone, could therefore encourage and exhort others to do the same: "Trust in him at all times, O people; pour out your hearts to him." The apostle Paul concurs: "We can comfort those in any trouble with the comfort we ourselves have received from God" (2 Cor. 1:4).

MARCH 19

We are hard pressed on every side, but not crushed; perplexed, but not in despair; persecuted, but not abandoned; struck down, but not destroyed.
—*2 Corinthians 4:8–9*

n November 1999, a 72-year old, 30-year veteran of the mission field in India was brutally murdered as he went to work. His martyrdom reminds us that the Christian life includes sufferings for the sake of Jesus Christ. Second Corinthians 4 teaches us how to respond properly when sufferings spill over into our lives.

The key is found in verse 18: "So we fix our eyes not on what is seen, but on what is not seen." The Greek word translated as "fix our eyes" is *skopeō,* from which we derive the word "telescope." The word also means "goal." The picture is one of an athlete who concentrates on the goal and continues to do so as he strains for the prize. Paul thus describes his daily practice—he continually fixed his eyes on the invisible, eternal realities of the kingdom of God.

We each come into the world, however, lacking this ability to see what is truly real. The god of this age, the devil, has blinded the minds of all men everywhere so that they cannot see. We each labor under a deep, incurable spiritual blindness.

Thanks be to God, what is impossible with man is possible with him. As the gospel is preached, God performs the miracle of regeneration in the hearts of the elect. He makes his light shine into our hearts to give us knowledge of him. As a result, we are given the scope of faith by which we see heavenly glories and live the Christian life. The Christian can thus honestly say, "I walk by faith, not by sight."

By faith, we study and understand the Bible; thus, we do not think it strange when we experience troubles. By faith, we are consoled with the knowledge that, in God's will, our sufferings are producing an eternal weight of glory. By faith, we daily focus our eyes on God and his heavenly kingdom.

Do your problems loom large, and does God appear small? You have not been exercising the faith given you by Christ. You are focusing on what is seen, rather than on eternal, invisible truths. May God help us instead to fix our eyes daily on the author and perfecter of our faith, the Lord Jesus Christ!

MARCH 20

Godly sorrow brings repentance that leads to salvation and leaves no regret, but worldly sorrow brings death. —2 Corinthians 7:10

hat is the full-orbed biblical understanding of repentance? First, we come to our senses and begin to view reality, including sin, from God's point of view. Second, we feel grief, pain, and detestation for our sins. Finally, we forsake our sins and start doing what is right. Each of these elements is illustrated in this passage.

The apostle's earlier letter to the Corinthians, in which he had rebuked them sharply for their toleration of sin in the church, had been used by the Holy Spirit to open their eyes and cause them to think correctly. They were now gripped by divine truth and their point of view had changed entirely.

This intellectual awakening inevitably led to the deep, godly sorrow that accompanies repentance and leads to salvation. Their grief centered not on themselves or their consequent troubles, but rather on the fact that they had grieved the apostle and, most importantly, the Lord himself. Sin is ultimately against God, and this is what most pains a repentant sinner.

Paul compares godly sorrow with the all too common worldly sorrow that brings death. The Bible is filled with examples of such phony repentance, the classic case being Pharaoh's. His acknowledgments of sin (Exod. 9:27; 10:16) were elicited by external pressure, not internal renewal. Consequently, we do not see any lasting change in his attitude or behavior.

In contrast, the Corinthians' Spirit-given understanding and sorrow over sin led to fundamental change in their lives. We know from what we read elsewhere that they obeyed Paul's directive and excommunicated the offending member in the congregation (see 1 Cor. 5 and 2 Cor. 2). And they did not do so half-heartedly, but with earnestness, eagerness, indignation, alarm, and concern (v. 11). Titus could therefore report that they had obeyed and honored the apostle as Christ's delegated authority. This is the type of repentance that heaven demands.

What is the end result of authentic repentance? God sends his blessing and approbation. Let us therefore follow the Corinthians' example by acknowledging our sin, repenting truly, and trusting in our Lord and Savior Jesus Christ.

80

Thanks be to God for his indescribable gift! —2 Corinthians 9:15

od's gift, the Lord Jesus Christ, cannot be fully comprehended or understood, but we can discover what we need to know by learning what the Holy Scriptures have to say about him.

We first discover that Jesus Christ is God. John's gospel begins, "In the beginning was the Word, and the Word was with God, and the Word was God." We read elsewhere, "The Son is the radiance of God's glory and the exact representation of his being, sustaining all things by his powerful word" (Heb. 1:3). He who is the Father's gift is the eternal Son of God, the very One through whom the universe was created and by whom the universe is sustained.

Jesus is fully God, but he also became a man. The virgin Mary was overshadowed by the Holy Spirit and conceived the baby Jesus. John Murray writes, "The infinite became finite, . . . the immutable became mutable, the invisible became visible, the Creator became the created, the sustainer of all became dependent." Then he says that there is a "conjunction in one person of all that belongs to Godhead and all that belongs to manhood."[1] In the incarnation, Jesus did not surrender his divine attributes.

This supreme gift is our Savior, the only Redeemer of God's elect sinners. Joseph was told, "Mary will give birth to a son, and you are to give him the name Jesus, because he will save his people from their sins." At his birth the angel proclaimed, "Today in the town of David a Savior has been born to you; he is Christ the Lord." There is no other savior; Jesus, by his death and resurrection, brought his people out of slavery to sin, law, death, Satan, and hell.

Jesus is the Father's merciful gift to sinners. Have you understood and marveled at God's indescribable gift? More importantly, have you opened the gift? We do so by repenting of our sins and believing on the Lord Jesus Christ for our eternal salvation. We have received sufficient revelation about this Savior to be held accountable if we reject him. To refuse to trust in Jesus is to despise the gift and show contempt for the Giver. May God help us to receive his gift with great thanksgiving today!

---

1   John Murray, *Collected Writings:* Volume Two, *Systematic Theology* (Edinburgh: Banner of Truth, 1977), 132, 133.

MARCH 22

The weapons we fight with are not the weapons of the world. On the contrary, they have divine power to demolish strongholds.
—2 Corinthians 10:4

ach of us is born a sinner. Consequently, we grow up with wrong ideas about the world, ourselves, and God. These false notions develop into a fortification that we often stubbornly fight to preserve. God, however, has declared war on such fortresses, and he will tear them down, in due course, in the life of each of his elect. God is committed to rebuilding the lives of his children, not on the basis of their own treasured ideas, but on the solid foundation of his sacred truth.

In light of these facts, we who love the Lord ought to join with him and begin to wage war against the ungodly thoughts in our minds. We do so by first realizing that we are combatants in a mighty spiritual war, a battle against evil spiritual forces that typically begins in the mind. As soon as a sinner becomes a Christian, he is on God's side, and the devil, whom he once served, is against him. Satanic thoughts straight from hell are brought to his mind on a daily basis, and must be defeated.

Thanks be to God, the weapons we fight with have divine power to enable us to stand against the enemy and demolish the strongholds he has helped us to erect. We have taken our stand with God and with the indwelling Holy Spirit. Thus, we are furnished with all the weapons we need, including the belt of truth, the breastplate of righteousness, the shield of faith, the helmet of salvation, and the sword of the Spirit (Eph. 6).

God intends for us to use these armaments to demolish arguments and everything that sets itself up against the knowledge of God. He intends that we begin by acknowledging and forsaking the self-justifying rationale we have used to reject the words of rebuke and correction brought to us in the past. Such resistance constitutes disobedience, and our Lord insists that every thought and act of ours be an obedient one. He will not make an exception for any of us.

God has given us a new nature, and he indwells us by his mighty Holy Spirit. Let us therefore walk in the Spirit, fight the good fight, and enjoy the victory he has secured!

For if someone comes to you and preaches a Jesus other than the Jesus we preached, or if you receive a different spirit from the one you received, or a different gospel from the one you accepted, you put up with it easily enough. —2 Corinthians 11:4

n a true revival, people's false views of God are exposed so that they may confess their sin of idolatry and then worship the true and living God in spirit and in truth. Sadly, most Christians today cling to their own unbiblical ideas about the thrice-holy God of the Scriptures. They believe God is only love and not also a holy Judge who is wrathful towards sinners. They think, "God always forgives. When we sin, God will forgive, even without our true and holy repentance. God wants us above all to have fun and enjoyment. In fact, he gives us health and wealth so that we might enjoy all the good things of this present life."

Such people say that a person can become a Christian by merely deciding to accept the facts about Jesus in the Bible. To them, there is no need for regeneration or saving faith; mere mental assent to certain biblical propositions is all that is required. Then that "believer" can continue in his sins. He does not need to produce any fruit of the Holy Spirit in his life. In fact, he can sin even more than before he became a Christian. Such a person is called a "carnal Christian." According to today's most popular theology, a carnal Christian is truly saved and on his way to heaven. He can enjoy the pleasures of many sins here and the pleasures of eternal life in heaven. He can live the life of the rich man here and yet have the good life of Lazarus in heaven. The carnal Christian says, "Let us sin more so that grace may abound."

Such a person embraces pluralism, saying that there are many ways to be saved and that Jesus is not the only way. He says the Bible is only one of many holy books, and many parts are no longer culturally relevant. He opposes the old-fashioned ideas of cross-bearing, self-denial, and holy living. His Jesus always loves, always forgives, and never judges. Eventually, he will deny hell and eternal judgment altogether.

This is not Christianity. This is a different gospel, one that leads to eternal death. May God help us to follow the real Jesus, and be saved.

Though you have made me see troubles, many and bitter, you will restore my life again; from the depths of the earth you will again bring me up.
—Psalm 71:20

salm 71 unabashedly informs us that we will have troubles all of life, for we live in a fallen, sinful world. Yet we know that God uses these troubles to bring about our spiritual maturity and endurance. As the Heidelberg Catechism says, all things must contribute to our salvation, especially things that we do not like.

God uses trials to draw us to himself. The psalmist declares, "In you, O Lord, I have taken refuge; let me never be put to shame" (v. 1). That is what faith is—taking refuge in God all of life. There is no other Savior.

Both young and old can take this psalm to heart. Verse 5 says, "For you have been my hope, O Sovereign Lord, my confidence since my youth." Young people, understand that you can live in this world with complete confidence because God is your hope. You do not have to walk about with your head hanging down. I am not promoting self-esteem. Rather, my confidence is in my God, who loved me from all eternity and sent his Son, Jesus Christ, to die on the cross for my salvation.

"Since my youth, O God, you have taught me" (v. 17). Youth is the best time to learn. That is why young people should open the Bible and study, and come to church and listen to God's people. These declare God's gospel to build us up in our faith.

Older saints should also look to the Lord. "Do not cast me away when I am old" (vv. 9, 18). He who has helped us all our lives, every step of the way, will not abandon us when we are gray and infirm. He who loved us when we were sinners and rebels and prodigals will not later reject us.

Thus, young and old alike can face the trials and tribulations of this life with a sure, triumphant hope. We can assert with the psalmist, "But as for me, I will always have hope" (v. 14). When you give birth, when you are fired, when people speak evil of you for preaching the gospel, and when you become infirm, God will be with you. "Behold, I am with you always," he promised, "even unto the end of the ages."

If anybody is preaching to you a gospel other than what you accepted, let him be eternally condemned. —Galatians 1:9

e are living at a time when the vast majority of "Christians" believe in a false gospel, a different Jesus, and an unholy spirit. They worship a god who loves unconditionally and never judges sin in holy wrath. Their motto is, "We sin, and God forgives." Many such churchgoers have come to deny the very idea of hell and eternal judgment. Their Jesus is simply one of many ways to arrive in heaven.

We must be on our guard at such a time of great apostasy and ask whether we ourselves believe in the true and living Jesus Christ or a different Jesus of our own creation. Are we filled with the Holy Spirit or a different spirit, an evil one?

The importance of honestly facing these questions is highlighted by the shocking language we encounter here. The apostle Paul invokes a curse upon all who preach a different gospel which offers a different Jesus. By necessary implication, all who embrace such a false message will find themselves under the same condemnation. If those who heard the apostle himself were capable of being misled at this point, surely we ourselves are at risk as well. How carefully we should examine ourselves in the light of God's holy word!

How can we know which Jesus we are serving? When we know and worship the true and living God, our lives will show forth the corresponding fruit of holiness. Paul wrote to the Corinthian church, "I promised you to one husband, to Christ, so that I might present you as a pure virgin to him" (2 Cor. 11:2). Jesus Christ is the eternal Son of God who became man, and who is now reigning in heaven. He is pure, and his bride will be spotless.

Authentic Christians are humble, penitent, obedient people who are being transformed into Christ's likeness by the Holy Spirit. They have seen themselves and their sin in the light of the glory of God, and are forever changed. If our experience of God has not resulted in such radical conversion, then we must face the fact that we too have fallen prey to a false gospel. Only by renouncing such a gospel and embracing the real Jesus can we be saved.

So the law was put in charge to lead us to Christ that we might be justified by faith. —Galatians 3:24

alatians 3 is one of the marvelous New Testament passages that sounds the glorious theme of redemption in Christ. Here once and for all the pernicious notion of salvation by works, or merit, is defeated.

The apostle Paul writes, "All who rely on observing the law are under a curse" (v. 10). Paul is referring to the moral law—the Ten Commandments—and is addressing everyone who thinks that he can be right with God on the basis of his own righteousness or lawkeeping. The apostle categorically asserts that all such people are actually cursed, not saved. Why? Because all the law hangs together. If we do not steal, but we lie, we have broken God's commandments. Not only so, but we must keep the law perfectly every moment of our lives. One infraction spells destruction.

Clearly, no one can bear such a burden successfully. We are all born sinners; we have all sinned and fallen short of the glory of God. We must abandon every thought of self-righteousness.

Thanks be to God, the passage does not end there. In God's mercy, he has made a way for sinners to be justified. "Christ redeemed us from the curse of the law by becoming a curse for us" (v. 13). In Christ Jesus, we are granted forgiveness of sins and Christ's own perfect righteousness. In other words, every believer is justified by faith.

Why then was the moral law given? First, it is meant to convict us of our utter sinfulness. We read in Romans 3:20, "Through the law we become conscious of sin." In fact, the law aggravates and stimulates our flesh to sin all the more. Consequently, the law's second purpose is to convince us of our utter need for a Savior and Redeemer. As Paul says, "The law was put in charge to lead us to Christ."

Justification by faith in Christ is the glorious chorus of our redemption. No wonder Paul gave his life for this truth. No wonder Martin Luther's rediscovery of this truth sparked the mighty Reformation. Let us wonder and rejoice at God's great love and mercy shown to hell-deserving sinners. We are all sons of God through faith in Christ Jesus.

Do not be deceived: God cannot be mocked. A man reaps what he sows.
—Galatians 6:7

 ur verse begins with an imperative, "Do not be deceived!" Why this directive? Because even as Christians we can be deceived, and especially so in our culture today. Lying is now the norm, and gradually we can lose sight of the importance of truth.

What was the lie that the apostle Paul particularly opposed here? That God can be mocked and we can sin without consequence. This deception is perennially attractive because it appeals to our flesh. By nature we are prone to wish it is true.

This lie can only be exposed and overcome by biblical truth, which Paul presents in the next verse. If we would be overcomers, we must therefore be students of the Scriptures. To recognize the counterfeit, we must become experts in the authentic. To this end, God has also graciously provided us with pastors and teachers in the local church to instruct and disciple us in his word.

In our present passage, Paul emphasizes the truth of the inviolability of the law that what a man sows, so shall he reap. Delegated authorities may at times be ignorant or impotent, but God is sovereign, omnipresent, and omniscient. Thus, this God-authored principle will inexorably work itself out in one of two ways. The one who sows to please his flesh will from the flesh reap destruction, and this reaping will be thirty, sixty, or one hundredfold. We cannot break God's moral law and go unpunished in this life or in the one to come. We may not remember the sins committed twenty years ago, but God cannot and does not forget. Ultimately, the impenitent will experience eternal hell.

Thanks be to God, he enables the Christian to choose another way: the one who sows to please the Spirit will from the Spirit reap eternal life. Paul means that God will richly bless those who daily make decisions to please God. They live by the principle of love—love for God and neighbor—rather than the principle of lust, which is love for self. Such people will enjoy a life of righteousness, peace, and joy in the Holy Spirit in this age, and unending glory in the next.

The choice is clear: flesh or Spirit, destruction or life. May each of us this day see clearly and choose life.

I pray also that the eyes of your heart may be enlightened in order that you may know . . . his incomparably great power for us who believe.
—*Ephesians 1:18–19*

n August 2003, the northeastern part of North America experienced a massive power failure. Fifty million people from Ohio to Ontario, Canada, were suddenly plunged into darkness. Nothing worked. Without power, life as we know it came to a standstill.

Christians too need power, the power of God, to live the Christian life. Without God's power, we cannot love God with all our heart, mind, soul and strength, nor can we love our neighbor as ourselves. Without God's power, we cannot obey his moral law. A weak Christian falls prey to many deadly enemies, including the world, the devil, and the sin that remains within.

Accordingly, in Ephesians 1, Paul encourages us to understand and appropriate God's incomparably great power for us who believe. It is a power that we experienced when God made us alive with Christ. As a result, this power is not only available to us, but it is also in us in the person of the indwelling Holy Spirit—he himself gives us the strength to endure hardship, perform good works, resist temptation, and die in faith.

The greatest demonstration of God's marvelous power is not creation *ex nihilo,* but rather the mighty, objective resurrection of Jesus Christ from the dead. In this act, God the Father declared his approval of the Son and displayed his victorious power over all evil. The risen Christ is now seated at the right hand of the Father, exercising sovereign dominion over his universe as the Lord of lords on behalf of his church.

Because Jesus rules over all, his church has nothing to fear. As Head, he daily sustains and protects every one of the members of his body. Every branch receives the nourishment necessary for life and fruitfulness from the true vine, Jesus Christ.

What then can possibly keep us from experiencing this power on a moment-by-moment basis? Sin, especially the sin of unbelief. It is by faith in God that we appropriate his mighty power. Jesus taught, "All things are possible for those who believe." In contrast, unbelief cuts us off and leaves us powerless. Let us therefore trust in God and enjoy the power-filled life of victory he intends for us.

[I pray that you] may have power, together with all the saints, to grasp how wide and long and high and deep is the love of Christ. —Ephesians 3:18

he Christian life is utterly impossible for those who have not experienced the miracle of spiritual resurrection. Many who profess to be Christians find themselves continuing to live in sin because they have not been truly born of God. They are trying to do the impossible—live victorious, obedient lives in their own strength. We who are Christians are different; God's mighty, marvelous, limitless love has been poured out into our hearts by the Holy Spirit, and so we are fortified with supernatural strength.

In Ephesians 3:16–19, Paul places particular emphasis on the power of this divine love. God's love is very potent, highly energizing and invigorating, enabling us to do his will in his strength for his glory. Here the apostle prays that the Father would strengthen us in our inner man through the Holy Spirit so that we may grasp the divine geometry of Christ's love for us.

We are exhorted to know the love of Christ even though we can never comprehend it fully. But, notice, Paul says that this love *surpasses*, not *bypasses*, human knowledge. We must therefore keep on grasping, learning experimentally, and growing in the love of Christ for us. Why make such an unstinting effort? Because such knowledge alone will motivate us to live and even die for God. Paul exclaims elsewhere, "The life I live in the body, I live by faith in the Son of God, who loved me and gave himself for me" (Gal. 2:20).

Love is power. The apostle John writes, "We love because he first loved us" (1 John 4:19). And in 2 Corinthians 5:14 Paul asserts, "Christ's love compels us." Christ's love motivates us, impels us, and keeps us going even in the face of adversity. If we have received the love of God outpoured into our hearts, then we will have sufficient power to obey his will.

May God help us to reverently meditate on the width, length, height, and depth of Christ's everlasting love for his people, especially as it is demonstrated in the awesome dimensions of the cross. As we do, we shall increasingly share in what the apostle prayed for the Ephesians: we shall be filled to the measure of all the fullness of God.

Put on the new self, created to be like God in true righteousness and holiness. —Ephesians 4:24

phesians 4 makes clear in the strongest terms the utter contrast between the pagan way of life and the Christian. The saints of God cannot think or behave like unbelievers; they are to live an entirely different life. Yet the vast majority of evangelicals, who claim to believe in the Bible, now embrace the view that Christians may live like the world as long as they have in the past "received Jesus." This view is manifestly demonic and has nothing to do with New Testament teaching.

In verses 20–24, the apostle Paul uses three verbs to describe how the life of every born-again Christian has been radically changed. We read, "You did not so learn Christ." Unlike pagans, Christians are not ignorant of God. Paul utilizes the image of an academy where believers learn from Christ himself. We read in the Gospel of Mark, "[Jesus] appointed twelve, designating them apostles, that they might be with him." The apostles were learning Christ. Later we are told, "When [the Sanhedrin] saw the courage of Peter and John, they were astonished and took note that these men had been with Jesus." So, too, we want to know Christ personally through Bible study, prayer, and obedience to his commands.

Paul continues, "Surely you heard him." The Ephesians had not simply heard about Christ; they had heard him. How so? The risen Christ had spoken to them through his chosen servant, the apostle Paul. When the preacher preaches, we are to hear Christ himself. When we do so, Jesus and his gospel become our chief concern, the pearl of great of price, the treasure hidden in the field.

Finally, Paul writes, "You were taught in him." Believers learn God's truth in a certain environment—in union with the Lord Jesus Christ himself. We are united with Christ and we therefore have the mind of Christ. The pagan's mind is empty and darkened; our thoughts are filled with God and his word.

All those who have so learned Christ, heard him, and been taught in him are nothing less than new creations. They have put off the old man and put on the new, created to be like God. And they will by necessary consequence lead holy, God-pleasing lives.

MARCH 31

If you follow my decrees and are careful to obey my commands . . .
—Leviticus 26:3

od's deliverance of the Israelites from slavery in Egypt is a picture of the spiritual redemption accomplished in Jesus Christ for the people of God. In Leviticus 26, we read the Lord's own description of his gracious accomplishment: "I broke the bars of your yoke and enabled you to walk with heads held high" (v. 13).

What are God's people to do in view of this great salvation? The simple answer is that we ought to lovingly obey the One who redeemed us. Anyone who considers obedience to be optional has not yet been delivered from the power of the devil. Our Redeemer God has given us clear instructions in his covenant book about what he hates and what he loves. As his people, we are obligated to follow his decrees and obey his commands. If we do, God promises to look on us with favor and keep his covenant with us.

The tragic history of Israel is that most of God's people went on to experience covenant curses rather than covenant blessings. He warns, "But if you will not listen to me . . . then I will do this to you" (vv. 14–16). God cannot be mocked. His promises are true and his threatenings are sure. He will apply increasing pressure and pain to his recalcitrant people until their stubborn pride is broken down. The covenant Lord will not allow a proud man to stand against him.

This passage is not historical fiction. Every warning set out here came to pass in the life of the nation of Israel. And the same God is Lord of the New Testament church. He is the one who struck down Ananias and Sapphira. He is the one who brought weakness, illness, and death to the sinning Corinthian church members. It remains a fearful thing to fall into the hands of the living God.

Thanks be to God, there is a glimmer of hope found in verses 40–45. The Lord promises, "But if they will confess their sins, I will remember my covenant. They will pay for their sins, yet I will not reject them." Let us, then, keep covenant with God, and when we fail, let us be quick to confess and forsake our sins.

If anyone makes a special vow . . . to the LORD . . . —Leviticus 27:2

eviticus 27 speaks about the importance of making and fulfilling vows to the covenant Lord. The subject may seem irrelevant to us today, but such a conclusion is misguided. In fact, we as Christians have made many vows to God, beginning with the fundamental, all-encompassing confession, "Jesus is Lord."

The summary teaching of the Scriptures regarding vows is found in Ecclesiastes 5:4: "When you make a vow to God, do not delay in fulfilling it. He has no pleasure in fools; fulfill your vow." This solemn message is also the theme of Leviticus 27. We dedicated ourselves to the Lord when we confessed our faith, were baptized, and joined the church. At that time, we made vows in the presence of God and other witnesses. From that point on, we are obligated to serve our covenant-keeping Lord with all of our strength for all of our days. We may say we changed our minds or we may forget what we promised. But Almighty God does not change or forget, and he will hold us accountable.

Many of us have made other vows also. Christian marriage begins with vows of lifelong fidelity to one's spouse. Child dedication entails a vow on the part of both parents to raise their children in the fear and admonition of the Lord. We may have made additional promises to God: to pray regularly, to have morning and evening devotions, to tithe, to evangelize, or to perform certain acts of service. In light of this chapter, we must consider whether we are keeping our promises to God.

Thanks be to God, there was one who dedicated himself to the Lord's service and did not shrink back—the Lord Jesus Christ. We read in Psalm 40, "Here I am, I have come—it is written about me in the scroll. I desire to do your will, O my God." This was Jesus' vow of dedication, and he lived a perfect life in fulfillment of that promise. Additionally, he died the horrible death of the cross as a ransom for many in keeping with his vow. Christ died for us so that we should no longer live for ourselves, but for him. Let us then with great gratitude keep our vows, especially, "Jesus is Lord."

Make my joy complete by being like-minded, having the same love, being one in spirit and purpose. —Philippians 2:2

nity belongs to the very essence of the Christian life. It is an imperative that rests firmly on the indicative of what God has done for us in Jesus Christ. Every born-again Christian is united with Christ and has become an adopted child of the King of kings. And if we are born of God, we necessarily enjoy unity with our brothers and sisters, for we are all members of the same family.

Our heavenly Father's will is that we live out the implications of this call to unity. He who began a good work in us continues to work in our hearts so that we will and act according to his good purpose. And so the apostle says, "If you have any encouragement from being united with Christ" (Phil. 2:1). The thought in the original language is better stated, "*Since* you have encouragement." By faith we are united with Christ as a branch is united to the vine, from which flows life, comfort, love, fellowship, tenderness, and compassion. Christians are people who share in the Holy Spirit—we are daily provided with all that is necessary for us to obey God and live a life of love and unity.

In view of these rich blessings that flow to us as a result of the redemption accomplished by Christ, we are exhorted to conduct ourselves "in a manner worthy of the gospel" (Phil. 1:27). Our daily lives should reflect the worth of this priceless gospel. What dignified status we have as members of God's family! Not only so, in 1 Thessalonians 2:12 we are also urged to "live lives worthy of God." The world is watching how we treat one another—children of God ought to bring honor, not shame, to their glorious, loving heavenly Father.

Paul gives one further reason why the Philippians should zealously maintain the unity of the Spirit when he implores, "Make my joy complete" (Phil. 2:2). Paul is writing this epistle from prison, yet his concern is not for himself, but for the church. Just as loving, unselfish children bring joy to their parents, so too the members of the church can and ought to give their pastor encouragement by walking in peace and humility.

April 3

And my God will meet all your needs according to his glorious riches in Christ Jesus. —Philippians 4:19

hilippians 4:19 can be translated, "My God will fill to the full the empty vessels of all your needs according to his riches in glory in Christ Jesus." The imprisoned apostle had received a much appreciated care package from the Philippian church which, though poor, had helped him since its founding. Though Paul had nothing by way of material wealth to give in return, he was able to give them a priceless promise in view of their sacrificial giving: the assurance that God would supply all their needs.

This promise is not for every religious person. It is given only to those who are in Christ Jesus. Paul says, "*My* God," meaning the God of the Bible, the only true and living God, who is known through faith in Jesus Christ alone. The popular notion that the three great monotheistic religions are essentially the same is a lie that damns.

It is the God of the Bible who meets all our needs. And these begin with our need for grace, forgiveness, justification, and the presence of the Holy Spirit. This rich salvation is for those who will repent of their sins and place their trust in the person and work of Jesus Christ. Those who are united with Christ by faith discover him to be their righteousness, holiness, and redemption. Not only so, they are also given all grace so that at all times they may abound in every good work. God fills us to the full!

God's riches are infinite and inexhaustible. The old hymn puts it well: "His love has no limit, his grace has no measure, his power no boundary known unto men. For out of his infinite riches in Jesus he giveth and giveth and giveth again."

It is not true that we will only have health, plenty, and joy in life. There will be joy *and* sorrow; plenty *and* want; health *and* death. Life is full of change. But one certainty will never change: Christ is with us and will give us grace sufficient for the hour. He promised, "I have come that [you] may have life, and have it to the full. . . . In this world you will have trouble. But take heart! I have overcome the world" (John 10:10; 16:33).

Since the day we heard about you, we have not stopped praying for you.
—Colossians 1:9

 majority of evangelical churches today want a Jesus who will make them rich, guarantee them good health, and provide them with power and fame. But the apostles' prayers recorded in the Scriptures rarely have to do with money, health, or things temporal. As we look at Paul's prayer for the Colossians, we ought to examine our own prayers and see how they compare.

The prayer we find in Colossians 1 can be condensed to two chief points: God's holy will and our holy lives. Churches that focus on other matters are wandering off course.

Paul begins by praying that God may fill the church with the knowledge of his will through the enlightenment of the Holy Spirit. The apostle is concerned that the Colossians have been contaminated with the poison of human philosophy (Col. 2:8). The antidote is to be filled with the word of God. We must be constantly growing in the knowledge of God as objectively revealed in the Bible, especially as it is exposited by God-ordained pastors.

Paul continues with several requests that help us to further understand why we should hear, comprehend, and then do God's good and perfect will. First, we obey in order to please God himself. He, not our spouse, children, or career, must be first in our lives. Second, we do so in order to bear much fruit to his glory. What is Christian fruit? The good works which God has foreordained for us to perform.

When we look at the Christian's high calling, we feel our own utter inadequacy. We are weak, but he is strong! God promises to strengthen us so that we can do all his holy will with the power he supplies. The result is great endurance—not obedience for a day, but for a lifetime of service to the King of kings.

Paul's prayer concludes with a call to give thanks to our heavenly Father, who has qualified us to receive an eternal inheritance. Nothing can separate us from the mighty, effectual love of God.

Holy doctrine and a holy life lived for the glory of God—may God help us to pursue these ends with holy zeal, and pray this apostolic prayer for the church in our day.

For the LORD God is a sun and shield; the LORD will give grace and glory;
no good thing will he withhold from them that walk uprightly.
—*Psalm 84:11, KJV*

salm 84 gives expression to the believer's intense
delight in and longing for the presence of the true
and living God. Every Christian is a happy pilgrim
journeying to the Celestial City where God dwells.
Many so-called Christians believe in a Christianity that promises
escape from suffering. Such faith is nominal, not saving, faith.
Every true pilgrim will pass through the Valley of Baca. This valley
is a metaphor for the hardships, trials, and persecution a Christian
will experience as he goes to meet with God in heavenly Zion. The
apostle Paul said, "We must go through many hardships to enter
the kingdom of God" (Acts 14:22). None of us can circumvent the
Valley of Baca.

This valley notwithstanding, the believing pilgrim continues
on with great hope, for the Lord his God bestows grace and glory
on his people. Grace transforms the Valley of Baca into a valley
that receives showers of blessings, for our God is with us. He never
leaves nor forsakes his pilgrim child.

Our hope is not found in riches, fame, or political power in
this world. What does it profit to gain the whole world and lose
one's soul? Our hope is in God alone. The Lord God is our sun—
the source of all our light and life. Life is not possible without
the sun! He is also our shield—he guards and defends his people
from all harm. Nothing in all creation is able to separate us from
his love.

There is no end to the grace which God gives us. Grace is all
the benefits that come to us from the life, death, and resurrection
of Jesus Christ. Grace is heaven for hell-deserving sinners. Such
divine grace is sufficient for all our needs. God also gives us glory.
Satan dragged us into the mud and mire, but God's eternal plan is
to bring many sons to glory (Heb. 2:10). Every recipient of grace
shall in due course be glorified. We will see the glorified Christ
and we shall be made like him.

No wonder the psalmist can exclaim, "No good thing will he
withhold from those whose walk is blameless." God will give us
everything we need to ensure our safe arrival in heaven.

And so you became a model to all the believers. —1 Thessalonians 1:7

irst Thessalonians 1 is the only place in the entire New Testament where the apostle Paul says a church became a model to other believers. What a commendation! We must immediately ask ourselves: Am I a good role model for others? The fact is, each of us is a model, whether for better or worse.

The Thessalonian church could be so designated because she became an imitator of the apostle in terms of Christian life and proclamation. Paul notes the abundance of good fruit—their work of faith, labor of love, and patience of hope—produced in the setting of severe suffering.

A true Christian is always busy doing good works, which simply means obedience to God's will. We are God's workmanship, created in Christ Jesus for this very purpose. Such labor is prompted by love—love toward God and toward his people. And we persevere in these good works, inspired by our hope in the Lord Jesus.

Our continuance in faith and obedience to Christ in the face of sustained persecution is sure proof that the gospel came to us not only in word, but also in power and full assurance. This is the overcoming life that the gospel invariably produces in true saints.

By contrast, a nominal Christian will leave Christ and his church when troubles come, for nominalism does not have the power to endure persecution and hardship. Jesus himself warned of such wholesale apostasy in the end times, and Paul spoke similarly in his second epistle to the Thessalonian church.

The apostle also commends this young, faithful church because they continually communicated the gospel. He writes, "The Lord's message rang out from you" (1 Thess. 1:8). Not only were the Thessalonians living holy lives while facing adversity, but they were also proclaiming the truth with the courage given by the Holy Spirit.

All of this ought to convict us of our shortcomings. We must ask: Am I a Christian of proper character—full of faith, hope, and love? Can I tell others, "Follow me as I follow Christ"? Do I share the gospel with those I meet? Is my witness characterized by holiness, power, deep conviction, and the indwelling Holy Spirit? These are the marks of a true Christian.

Brothers, we do not want you to be ignorant about those who fall asleep.
—1 Thessalonians 4:13

he great hope of the church, the second coming *(parousia)* of our Lord Jesus Christ, is mentioned in each chapter of Paul's first letter to the Thessalonians. The return of Jesus was of immense importance to these believers, who were particularly concerned about those who died before Christ's return. The apostle assuages their concerns with that which must fortify our own souls today: divine doctrine.

Paul does not want the church to be ignorant of spiritual realities. And so he begins with the incontrovertible fact that Christ is coming again: "You turned from idols to serve the living and true God," he reminds them, "and to wait for his Son from heaven" (1 Thess. 1:9–10). The Old Testament predicted this coming, and Jesus promised it to his disciples. The angels reminded the disciples of it at Jesus' ascension, and the apostles preached this truth wherever they ministered. Jesus' return is certain, and it shall be personal, public, powerful, and glorious.

The apostle then comforts the church by revealing that, according to the Lord's own word, those who have fallen asleep in Christ will be resurrected first. On that day, the Lord who created the universe by his word will give a great shout, and the dead in Christ shall rise with a glorified spiritual body. Not only so, but those believers who are alive at Christ's *parousia* will also be changed in the twinkling of an eye and be raptured—we shall all be caught up to meet the Lord in the air.

What is the purpose for rapture? To unite the bride with her glorious Bridegroom! This is the biblical definition of blessing—to see God face to face and enjoy him forever. This communion with God, which Adam forfeited in the garden, is restored in Jesus Christ. And this communion is without end; it is the everlasting Sabbath rest promised to the people of God.

The preeminent hope of the first-century church was the second coming of Christ. So, too, we ought to have this in the forefront of our thoughts. We need not fear death; we are waiting expectantly for our Lord's return. This is our sure hope, a hope that will not make us ashamed.

So then, let us not be like others, who are asleep. —1 Thessalonians 5:6

irst Thessalonians 5:1–11 highlights the utter contrast between the Christian and the unbeliever. It is a total difference involving status, ethics, and destiny. Unbelievers are asleep. They live in the closed universe of their own imaginations and show complete disregard for the spiritual dimension. God has been excommunicated from their thoughts; the true and living God, their Creator and Sustainer, has been rejected.

As a result, unbelievers live in moral darkness. Paul uses the terms "night" and "drunk" to summarize their ethical lives. They hate the light and are afraid to come into it, for they are pregnant with evil. They are also darkened in their understanding and cannot see the horror of the sudden future judgment that awaits them.

By contrast, the apostle reassures the Thessalonians that they "know very well" that the day of the Lord is coming; the Greek can be translated, "know correctly." How could this church, so small and young, have such spiritual wisdom? It is because God translates all believers from the dominion of darkness into the kingdom of light through the miracle of regeneration. Christians are by nature alive and awake; they are sons of the day. We are told elsewhere that we have the mind of Christ. As a result, the day of Christ's return will not surprise us like a thief.

This day of the Lord, which spells inescapable destruction for the unbeliever, will bring uninterrupted joy for those who are waiting for Christ. God has not appointed us to suffer wrath, but to receive salvation through Jesus. Our blessed future is certain, for it rests upon God's plan, purpose, and immutable determination.

These are the glorious indicatives that are true of Christians. The apostle then enumerates the imperatives that necessarily follow. "Since we belong to the day," he writes, "let us be self-controlled, putting on faith and love as a breastplate" (1 Thess. 5:8). We must understand who we are and be what we are, so that others may come to know our great Savior. Let us not be like unbelievers. We are Christ's faithful witnesses only when we live differently than those in the world. It is the contrast that will attract God's elect sinners to the light.

We hear that some among you are idle. —2 Thessalonians 3:11

 weat is very spiritual. We pray, "Give us this day our daily bread," and our heavenly Father answers by giving us wisdom, health, and the opportunity to work, to sweat. Our daily bread is earned through labor. Even students must study six days a week to prepare themselves for a life of productive work.

Paul and Silas had to address the Thessalonian church several times on this issue. They had noticed on their initial visit that some people, perhaps out of the misconception that Jesus' return was imminent, had stopped working and started depending on others for food. Such laziness is so antithetical to the Christian life that Paul sternly rebuked them, saying "If a man will not work, he shall not eat." The idlers did not heed the apostle's injunction, however, so he was compelled to speak to this serious issue in his first epistle. "Work with your hands," Paul insisted, "just as we told you" (1 Thess. 4:11). Yet the offenders remained recalcitrant, and the apostle now writes more emphatically in his second letter.

Notice what the apostle commands the church by the authority of the sovereign Lord Jesus Christ. First, the officers of the church are to mark out the disobedient and warn the guilty. The Greek word used for "warning" here means to place the word of God into the counselee's mind. Second, other church members are to withdraw from having intimate fellowship with the persistently idle. The goal of this discipline is redemptive, so that the offender might become ashamed of his ungodly behavior and repent of his disorderly life.

Why this sustained emphasis on living a productive life as a Christian? In his first epistle Paul explained, "[It is] so that your daily life might win the respect of outsiders" (1 Thess. 4:12). The gospel is at stake! When we have earned others' respect, we can then credibly share the gospel with them. A second reason to work hard is so that we will not be a burden to anyone else. Additionally, by working hard, we become proper godly models for others in the church to follow. Let us then heed the apostle's admonition and be hardworking, industrious people who "never tire of doing what is right."

Even though I was once a blasphemer and a persecutor and a violent man, I was shown mercy. —1 Timothy 1:13

n the course of his pastoral life a minister often hears members of his congregation say, "I am what I am. I've been this way for many, many years. Please just accept me." This line of argumentation is ultimately a denial of God's plan to save us and then conform us to the image of his Son. The angel said, "His name is Jesus, for he will save his people from their sins." We come to the Savior as we are, but we are not to continue as we were. If we are not being sanctified by the Holy Spirit, we are not Christians.

In 1 Timothy, we are given a brief before-and-after portrait of the apostle Paul. Here Paul confesses that he was once a vile blasphemer who tried to force others to blaspheme Jesus too. He admits that he was filled with hatred and arrogance and enjoyed humiliating his opponents. His anger gave way to such violence that he persecuted Christians even unto death. No wonder he could say without exaggeration, "I am the worst of sinners."

This was the man who wrote this apostolic epistle to Timothy. What happened? Paul tells us succinctly, "The grace of our Lord was poured out on me abundantly" (1 Tim. 1:14). The apostle is here describing what happened at his conversion on the road to Damascus. His words evoke an image of the Nile River overflowing its banks, soaking the dry land and bringing forth crops all over Egypt. Abundant grace, like a mighty river, flowed into the persecutor's heart and produced a hundredfold crop of faith and love. Elsewhere Paul writes, "And his grace to me was not without effect. I worked harder than all of the apostles" (1 Cor. 15:10).

Real Christianity transforms. When the gospel comes to us with Holy Spirit power, our arrogance, enmity, and unbelief depart as we are suffused with the grace of God. The self-righteous Pharisee becomes the sin-conscious publican when God is at work in his heart. The sinner who once murmured and complained now overflows with praise and thanksgiving to his Savior. He gladly and spontaneously joins with the apostle, singing, "Now unto the King eternal, immortal, invisible, the only God, be honor and glory forever!"

APRIL 11

Who knows the power of your anger? For your wrath is as great as the fear that is due you. —Psalm 90:11

salm 90 reminds us that while the great theme of the Bible is the love of God for elect sinners, it remains true that he is angry with sinners every day. Unrepentant man finds himself in the hands of an angry God; at any moment his wrath can be aroused and the sinner destroyed.

This is the only psalm Moses wrote. He knew firsthand something of the power of God's righteous indignation against sin. He saw Pharaoh and the Egyptian army drowned in the Red Sea. He watched the earth swallow Korah and his family in the time of rebellion. He led the Israelites in the wilderness for forty years until that entire generation, over 600,000 men, had been killed because of their unbelief and disobedience. And he knew that he himself was prohibited from entering the Promised Land because he had failed to honor God as holy at the waters of Meribah.

Yet this same Moses wrote, "Who knows the power of your anger?" (v. 11). No man has yet experienced the full extent of God's wrath, except the Son of Man, Jesus Christ, who cried out from the cross, "My God, my God, why hast thou forsaken me?" Jesus, who committed no sin, experienced the full impact of his Father's wrath on Calvary so that his people will never have to know the fire of eternal hell.

A story is told about a farmer who lost his wheat field to a fire started by a stray spark. As he walked through the smoldering stubble, he came across the burned-out carcass of a mother hen. Gingerly touching it with his foot, he was astonished to see several chicks emerge from underneath, unscathed by the inferno.

The farmer's discovery pictures what happened at the cross. Everyone who repents and believes on Jesus Christ will be shielded from the consuming fire that is God's holy wrath against sin. But those who stubbornly refuse to repent must experience the unmitigated anger of God in all its intensity in hell throughout all eternity.

Verse 12 says, "Teach us to number our days aright, that we may gain a heart of wisdom." May God grant us a heart of wisdom to flee to Jesus for our eternal salvation.

APRIL 12

Fight the good fight of the faith. —1 Timothy 6:12

urveyors of a "seeker-friendly" gospel give their listeners the impression that Jesus Christ wants to relieve us of all our struggles and troubles and replace them with uninterrupted pleasures. The apostle Paul taught otherwise. Here he insists that his young lieutenant, Timothy, fight the good fight of faith. The Greek word means to agonize—to engage in an intense, protracted struggle against very strong enemies. Fight! Struggle! Agonize! Take hold! There is a real, lifelong battle to be fought by you and me.

Our first enemy is the flesh—the sin that still dwells in us even though we are redeemed Christians. We must personally wage war with the help of the mighty Holy Spirit against the sin that is inside us. We receive great encouragement from the promise, "If by the Spirit you put to death the misdeeds of the body, you will live" (Rom. 8:13). With the Spirit's help, we can say "No" to sin and make it stick.

Our second enemy is the world around us. The unbelieving world is under the dominion of Satan. We are called to vigorously oppose the wicked culture in which we live—its immorality, atheism, materialism, and rationalism. When the church is revived, she influences the culture; when we are lukewarm, the world begins to corrupt us. There can be no compromise; friendship with the world is hatred towards God.

Finally, we have a supernatural enemy, a created spirit being of very great ability, the devil. The moment we become Christians we become targets of Satan. Defeated at the cross, he still prowls around like a roaring lion. He is more powerful than we are, but the Holy Spirit, who is in us, is greater than all. With the Spirit's help, we can wrestle against the spiritual forces of evil in the heavenly realms—and win.

Onward, then, Christians soldiers! Paul later exhorted Timothy, "Endure hardship with us like a good soldier of Jesus Christ" (2 Tim. 2:3). We too must live to please our commanding officer. Do not relax. Rather, be vigilant, alert, and sober. Look into the Book, be filled with the Spirit, and pray zealously. As we fight the good fight, we will be bolstered by the knowledge that Jesus has already won the war at the cross.

APRIL 13

But because my servant Caleb has a different spirit and follows me wholeheartedly, I will bring him into the land. —Numbers 14:24

n Numbers 13 and 14 we are introduced to two behaviors of the Israelite majority: paralysis and convulsion. We see spiritual paralysis when they failed to trust in God and refused to go up and take possession of the Promised Land. Spiritual convulsion followed God's subsequent prohibition and resulted in defeat. Both behaviors are the result of unbelief. In the end, most of the Israelites died in their sins.

Two men, however, shine as stars in the midst of this crooked generation—Joshua and Caleb. Unlike the others, they did cross the Jordan to enjoy a land flowing with milk and honey. We are told four times in the Bible that they "followed the Lord wholeheartedly." What does this commendation mean?

First, they exercised saving faith in the covenant-keeping, Redeemer Lord who had brought them out of Egypt and had promised to bring them into Canaan. This faith necessarily issued in complete obedience, the very opposite of paralysis and convulsion. Obedience is ridiculed in today's society, yet it alone receives God's commendation. We tend to look upon one hundred percent obedience as an unattainable ideal. But God says that it is his unchangeable requirement.

Mature faith also bears the good fruit of hope and confidence in God and his promises. The majority report emphasized the size of the Anakites and concluded with the counsel of despair. Joshua and Caleb, however, encouraged the people: "We should go up and take possession of the land, for we can certainly do it" (Num. 13:30). They looked to the Lord while the others looked around. A child of God is eager to solve problems, while the unbelieving and the timid retreat from problems.

Joshua and Caleb went on to cross the Jordan, fight their enemies, and triumph. They and their families each inherited a portion of the Promised Land. Caleb's daughter married a proven man of God who had a lively faith. At the end of his life, Joshua could say, "As for me and my household, we will serve the Lord."

The choice is clear. We can die in our unbelief and disobedience, or we can choose to follow the Lord wholeheartedly and enjoy covenant life and blessings. May God help us to choose life!

In the presence of God and of Christ Jesus, who will judge the living and the dead . . . I give you this charge: Preach the Word. —2 *Timothy 4:1*

hat which gripped Paul's heart in 2 Timothy, his final epistle before his death, was God's infallible word. Scripture alone is God-breathed and able to make us wise unto salvation. When God revives his people by the Holy Spirit, he always leads us back to the Bible, the book of life. The Bible is what makes the difference in our lives. Accordingly, Paul places great emphasis on three admonitions to Timothy in this last letter: preach the word, guard the word, and prepare to suffer for the word.

How can we give hope to a world of misery, sin, and death? Dead orthodoxy is not the answer. The antinomianism found in modern evangelicalism is not the answer. The mysticism of the charismatic world is not the answer, nor is sacramentalism. Instead, we must preach God's word in the power of the Holy Spirit.

Without the Holy Spirit we are afraid, apologetic, and ashamed of the gospel. Timothy was afraid, too, so Paul told him to fan into flame the gift—the anointing of the Holy Spirit—he had received when Paul laid hands on him. The Holy Spirit gives us power, love, and a sound mind that thinks God's thoughts after him. Empowered by the Spirit, we can boldly preach the gospel that brings eternal life, for no one else will.

As a pastor, it was Timothy's responsibility to guard this precious treasure of the gospel. He could not add to, subtract from, or twist God's word. He must turn away from every heresy and oppose all perversions of the only true gospel. He must carefully preserve the gospel as the most precious entrustment from Christ himself.

The church's failure to guard this deposit resulted in the Dark Ages, when the Bible was, in essence, lost until the Reformation brought the truth of God's word back to light. Today we are experiencing another dark age; so we too are called to guard the truth by the Holy Spirit's help.

Finally, Timothy must be willing to suffer for the gospel like a good soldier of Christ Jesus. Paul, who would soon suffer martyrdom by beheading, knew that a preacher must be willing to die for Christ and his message of salvation. May God grant us each a fresh anointing of the Holy Spirit!

April 15

The Lord will show who belongs to him and who is holy. —Numbers 16:5

he kingdom of God is the rule of God. This rule and order extends over the family, the church, and the state. To this end, the Lord commissions delegated authorities to govern on his behalf and in his name. Those who despise and disobey duly established authorities therefore despise the sovereign God who ordained them. Numbers 16 graphically illustrates God's response to such insolence.

Ambition, arrogance, insolence, jealousy, and rebellion—these words describe the heart of Korah, a Kohathite. Not satisfied with his God-given station in the Levitical system, Korah coveted the priesthood. His complaint, though cloaked in the politically correct argument that all God's people are holy, was really an accusation against God. Korah challenged God's appointing Aaron and Moses over himself. He would pay a very high price for his self-centered ambition.

We read that Moses became very angry at Korah and his followers. But we do well to note who else became hot with righteous indignation: the Lord God Almighty himself. Those who murmur and rebel against delegated authorities, whether they are fathers or pastors or teachers or elders, are, in fact, guilty of treating God himself with contempt. But he will not let us shame him or despise his authority and glory.

The glory of the Lord appeared to the entire assembly (v. 42). In a dramatic, miraculous fashion, divine judgment was meted out to Korah and all his co-conspirators. The earth swallowed Korah and his household, and fire consumed the 250 rebels. In fact, if not for the mediatorial intercession of Moses and Aaron, the entire Israelite congregation would have been destroyed.

Let us not think we can play games with the living, almighty, all-holy God. He is the same yesterday, today, and forever. He is ever-present in the midst of his church, and he opposes those who dishonor him. Korah did not care for his wife, family, and fellow Israelites, and they all suffered terribly for his arrogance. So, too, our sins bring harm to our community, beginning with our family. Let us therefore fear God, walk humbly with him, and show proper respect to God's delegated authorities.

If he has done you any wrong or owes you anything, charge it to me.
—Philemon 18

n this short letter about a runaway slave we find a beautiful picture of the glorious gospel of our Lord Jesus Christ. Philemon, apparently a wealthy believer, had a slave named Onesimus. This slave ran away from his master and, in God's providence, became a Christian through the ministry of Paul in Rome. Paul was now sending Onesimus back to his owner in Colosse.

In Philemon 17–19, Paul makes three important assertions: Onesimus had, in fact, done wrong in illegally leaving; Philemon nonetheless should welcome him as he would the apostle himself; and Paul would make things right by assuming Onesimus' debt and paying back anything owed to Philemon.

In this, we see the gospel. Paul's benevolence to Onesimus points to the much greater mercy and love demonstrated by God in our salvation. We, like Onesimus, have done wrong; we have sinned against our infinite, thrice-holy Creator. As a result, we owe him an infinite debt that cannot be excused and that we can never pay. We read in Psalm 49, "No man can redeem the life of another or give to God a ransom for him—the ransom for a life is costly, no payment is ever enough."

Yet from all eternity God planned a way to justly forgive our debt. Just as Paul took the place of the guilty slave and paid his debt, so we too have a merciful benefactor in the Lord Jesus Christ. He, being the eternal Son of God, became man so that he could suffer on the cross the penalty due us for our sins. The apostle explains elsewhere, "God made him who had no sin to be sin for us, so that in him we might become the righteousness of God" (2 Cor. 5:21).

We are never told whether Paul in the end had the opportunity to repay Philemon. It is a historical fact, however, that Jesus Christ came in the fullness of time and paid our debt in full at Calvary. "It is finished," he cried out on that terrible cross, and the elect of all ages were delivered from eternal condemnation. Jesus paid it all; there is no debt—past, present, or future—that remains.

My soul glorifies the Lord and my spirit rejoices in God my Savior.
—Luke 1:46–47

he first two chapters of Luke's gospel are filled with music—five hymns of praise to God are sung, with perhaps the most magnificent being Mary's Magnificat. Although she was a poor peasant girl, Mary had been brought up in a godly home where she was thoroughly versed in the Holy Scriptures. Along with other pious Jews of that day, she was looking forward to God's redemption of Israel. Accordingly, when she was told the astounding news that she, a virgin, would conceive and give birth to a baby who would be the promised Messiah, she believed God's word to her.

Mary's Magnificat (Luke 1:46–55) adores God's person and his promises. Mary recognized him as the Almighty One, the Creator of the ends of the earth, whose strength is exercised on behalf of his people: "The Mighty One has done great things for me" (v. 49). She also understood that this holy God is the sovereign Judge of all. He scatters those who are arrogant in the thoughts of their hearts and sends the rich away empty.

Mary rejoiced, moreover, that God is at the same time a merciful Savior who had come to seek not the self-righteous, but sinners: "His mercy extends to those who fear him" (v. 50). Mercy is God's love shown to those sinners who are convinced of their sin and misery and come to him in reverent humility. This love is bestowed in keeping with the Lord's covenant faithfulness promised to Mary's forefathers. She now understood that the promise given to Abraham two thousand years prior was being fulfilled in her womb. She would be the mother of her own Lord and Savior, Jesus Christ.

Can you join in Mary's song of praise and worship? Do you understand yourself to be the chief of sinners, in need of the salvation accomplished by Jesus Christ, the Son of God and the son of Mary? Have you come to him in humility, repentance, and faith? If so, then you also can rejoice in God and glorify the Lord our Savior with your praise and your life.

But the LORD said to Moses and Aaron, "Because you did not trust in me enough to honor me as holy in the sight of the Israelites, you will not bring this community into the land I give them." —Numbers 20:12

umbers 20 is filled with misery, the misery that ensues when God's people are stubborn and rebellious. It relates a most shocking and poignant instance of God's covenant sanctions, which fell upon the one who gave Israel the law and spoke with God face to face—Moses himself. God's promises, as well as his threatenings, are true, and God is no respecter of persons.

The context is, once again, murmuring on the part of the Israelites. Moses wisely went to the Lord and, falling facedown, sought guidance. He was told to take his staff and speak to the rock, and God in mercy would miraculously pour forth water for a complaining nation. How longsuffering is our covenant Lord!

We are told elsewhere that this rock is a metaphor for Jesus Christ. Moses had been told in Exodus 17 to strike the rock—a foreshadowing of what would later take place once for all at the cross of Calvary. But Jesus is not to be re-crucified; his people should now speak to the risen, reigning Christ in humble, submissive petition. The rock must not be struck again.

Moses, however, lost patience with the people. It may even be that he was frustrated with God himself for moving in mercy rather than judgment. Tragically, Moses became a rebel too. He had been instructed to speak to the rock; instead he lashed out at the people, shouting, "You rebels! Must we fetch water for you?" Then, in a continuing fit of anger, he struck the rock twice.

In God's marvelous grace, water gushed forth and the community drank their fill. Yet we must note with great sobriety the loss incurred by Moses: He was denied his greatest desire— to lead the people into the Promised Land. Disobedience always brings great loss and regret.

We must each learn this lesson. It does not matter how many years we have attended church. It does not matter how long we have been faithful Christians. We can lose our heads in an instant and behave wickedly. How we need to walk humbly and receive daily God's keeping grace! He alone can say, "I AM." We must continually say, "I am what I am only by the grace of God."

The LORD said to Moses, "Make a snake and put it up on a pole; anyone who is bitten can look at it and live." —Numbers 21:8

 umbers 21 presents God's promise of and prescription for salvation. His solution is at once simple, yet profound: "Look and live!" When faced with hardship, the Israelites once again sinned by murmuring. "We detest this miserable food," they protested, thus treating God and his gifts with remarkable contempt. Where there is sin, there follows the wrath of God. And wrath must manifest in judgment and punishment. This time God sent venomous snakes among them to inflict pain and death.

While many died, other Israelites came to Moses and said, "We have sinned." In response to their confession and repentance, and to Moses' mediatorial prayer, the merciful covenant Lord provided his divine solution.

Moses was to make a replica out of metal of a poisonous serpent and place it high on a pole in the midst of the camp. Any Israelite who had been bitten by a snake but who trusted in this God-appointed means of salvation could look to the bronze serpent and live.

Jesus himself gave us the definitive interpretation of this Old Testament history in the third chapter of John's gospel. "Just as Moses lifted up the snake in the desert," he taught Nicodemus, "so the Son of Man must be lifted up, that everyone who believes in him may have eternal life" (John 3:14). This is the simple, wonderful gospel! Just as the bronze serpent represented the sinner and sin's punishment, so Christ came into the world to be our representative sin-bearer. Just as the serpent was lifted up on a pole, so Jesus was lifted up on a cross so that he might suffer as our substitute the punishment due us for our sin. And just as the dying Israelites must look at the serpent in order to escape death, so we sinners must look to Jesus by faith in order to be eternally saved.

What a marvelous, merciful gospel! Its very simplicity is foolishness to the Greeks and a stumbling block to the Jews. But for us, thank God, it is nothing less than the power of God unto salvation. Let us then be filled with the Spirit and tell others who are dying this simple truth: Look to Jesus Christ alone in faith and live!

God said to Balaam, "Do not go with them." —Numbers 22:12

uthentic Christianity, a life of discipleship, is in its essence simple: Hear and do. Those who are truly born of God want to know and perform the will of God. Those, however, who are nominal Christians argue, debate, and become angry when the word is brought to them.

The original word from God to Balaam was "No." That is all a child of God needs to know; no further explanation is needed. But Balaam, whose name means "glutton," was a double-minded man who ultimately loved money.

God's proscription derived from his eternal purpose and covenant made with Abraham to redeem and bless a people to be his very own. The "No" depended on the immutable plan of God, yet Balaam hated it. The same man who prophesied, "God is not a man that he should lie," convinced himself that God might change his mind after all. Surely, the heart is deceitful above all things!

God had not changed his mind; yet he then gave Balaam the answer he wanted. When we secretly hope to change God's "No" to "Yes," he may, in fact, give us over to the desires of our sinful hearts. This is nothing less than divine abandonment, judgment, and curse. Such abandoned people are committed to carrying out their reckless plans despite the warning given by the angel of the Lord with an outstretched sword.

Balaam's tragic end is a sobering warning to us. He himself expressed the wish, "Let me die the death of the righteous," but he could not and would not. As a result of his ultimate allegiance to money and materialism, the prophet devised a plan to secure Balak's reward and, unwittingly, his own destruction (Num. 31). He gained the gold and lost his soul.

The Lord's unchangeable character and commitment to his covenant promises brings terror to the unrepentant, but great comfort to his humble, obedient children. God has determined from all eternity to bless his elect, and they shall indeed be blessed. No Balak or Balaam can finally destroy the people of God. We may count on our faithful God whose word is immutable, not "Yes" and "No" (2 Cor. 1:17). Let us be very careful then to hear and obey his voice.

April 21

When Jesus saw their faith, he said, "Friend, your sins are forgiven."
—Luke 5:20

 e read in Luke 5 that a crowd had gathered around Jesus and "the power of the Lord was present for him to heal the sick" (v. 17). This is just what you and I need—to experience the mighty, healing touch of Jesus in our souls, bodies, and families. And this is what the paralytic in our story needed as well. But how could he make his way to the Savior for deliverance?

The paralytic was helpless in himself, but he had four remarkable friends who were filled with the love of God. These friends had already experienced the power of Jesus Christ in their lives and so they knew that the long-promised Messiah was in their midst. They had heard Jesus preach and seen him perform miracles. Thus, they were convinced that he could also heal their paralyzed friend; they had only to bring him to Jesus. This is faith expressing itself through love.

Whenever we resolve to draw close to Christ, there will be hindrances, even opposition. These friends had to carry the paralytic a distance, only to discover an overflowing crowd blocking their way to Jesus. Active faith, however, will find a way. They were not deterred, but used Spirit-given creativity to solve the problem. They carried him to the roof, dug by hand through the straw and mud, and slowly lowered the mat to the ground with ropes. In this way they brought their friend to Jesus.

We are told that Jesus "saw their faith." Faith is internal, but is made visible by our deeds. Faith is what avails with God. Immediately Jesus forgave the man's sins and made his body whole. He and his friends went home praising God.

Jesus is present in his church today with power to heal, forgive, and bless us. Have we come to him in humility and faith? Or are we like the Pharisees and teachers of the law, filled with pride, unbelief, and criticism? Have we loved others enough to overcome all obstacles and bring them to the One who alone can forgive sins? May God work by his Spirit once again in our midst, that all may shout, "We have seen remarkable things today!"

Give, and it will be given to you. —Luke 6:38

eople worry. Even Christians worry. Even in the middle of a worship service, some are anxious. But the Bible from beginning to end tells us not to be afraid. "Trust me!" says the Lord.

There is an old saying, "All the water in the world, no matter how turbulent, cannot sink a ship unless it gets inside." Problems can sink us only when they get inside. The remedy? We must learn to trust God by taking him at his word and believing his promises. At the same time, we have to understand that all of God's promises are conditional.

Money issues are no exception. In Luke 6, Jesus gives a wonderful, conditional promise to his disciples about personal finances: "Give, and it will be given to you." We are reassured that our needs will be met as we give to others, beginning with God and his church. This has particular application in today's church world with respect to tithing.

Many today no longer feel it is necessary to obey the biblical command to tithe regularly. God addressed a similar situation when he rebuked the post-exilic Jews through the prophet Malachi: "You are under a curse because you are robbing me. Bring the whole tithe into the storehouse." Christians who experience financial distress typically are not givers, especially when it comes to obeying this injunction. Relief, both material and spiritual, can only be had when God's conditions are met. The covenant Lord then promised, "I will pour out so much blessing that you will not have room enough for it" (Mal. 3:9–10).

No one has ever outgiven God. Jesus put it this way: "A good measure, pressed down, shaken together and running over, will be poured into your lap." This is true financial freedom, and freedom from anxiety and worry. We cannot afford not to give!

Let us understand and believe God's promises for his people, and obey the conditions that are inextricably attached. Specifically, we ought to be liberal with our tithes and gifts; then we need never worry about having food and clothing for tomorrow.

Neither of them had the money to pay him back, so he canceled the debts of both. Now which of them will love him more? —Luke 7:42

esus is the friend of sinners. He did not come to condone sin, but to save us from it. Luke 7 gives us a beautiful account of what such saved sinners are motivated to do in return for rich mercies received.

Simon the Pharisee had invited Jesus to his home, not out of a Spirit-given conviction of sin, but out of curiosity. He enjoyed a self-righteous complacency. How different was the woman with the alabaster jar of perfume! She had already met Jesus and responded to his gracious summons, "Come unto me, all you who are weary and burdened, and I will give you rest." At that moment, she had repented of her sins and placed her trust in Jesus Christ, her Savior and Lord. Now, having been forgiven of all her sins, she was seeking Jesus again to express her gratitude in worship and praise.

This once-notorious prostitute came, uninvited, to the Pharisee's banquet. Her shame is gone, for she is now dressed in the righteousness of Christ. She has God-given courage and boldness to approach him, for perfect love casts out all fear.

We do well to take note of her attitude and actions as she approaches Jesus. She knows well the depth of her sins. So out of deep humility and gratitude, she begins to weep in remembrance of what Jesus has done for her. Then she worships the Savior with all her heart, mind, soul, and strength by pouring costly perfume on Jesus' feet. He who has been forgiven much loves much.

By contrast, Simon, in smug self-righteousness, passes judgment on both the woman and Jesus. He is completely wrong on both accounts. Such is the blindness of unrepentant sinners! As a result, he neither gives Jesus the honor that is due him, nor shares in Jesus' benediction given to the pardoned sinner: "Your faith has saved you; go in peace."

If our love for God has grown cold, if we have forgotten the depth of the sin from which we have been delivered, we must remember it anew. May we then go on to live a new life, a life filled with true humility, great thankfulness, and sacrificial love for the One who forgave us.

They found the man from whom the demons had gone out, sitting at Jesus' feet, dressed and in his right mind. —Luke 8:35

hat is a sound mind? It is one that believes in God, thinks his thoughts after him, and does that which is pleasing to him. Adam and Eve, prior to their fall, had sound minds with which they communed with their Creator. Now, after the Fall, none of us comes into the world with a right mind. The only way back is through God's monergistic work of regeneration.

The story of the demoniac illustrates what Jesus does for a man with a sinful, depraved mind when he saves him. His story is our story.

The Bible teaches us that the entire world is under the control of the evil one. Some are demon-possessed; all are subject to his will. The result is what we see in Luke 8—alienation from self, family, society, and, most importantly, from the Creator God himself. No one could or wanted to help such a man, yet Jesus loved him and traveled across a stormy lake to save him.

When Jesus shows up, things happen. The demons trembled and cowered before Deity. They were sent out of the man and into a herd of pigs at Jesus' word. And the demoniac was gloriously delivered. What does this salvation look like?

The first thing we see is that this once-restless, self-destructive man was now sitting quietly at Jesus' feet. He was at peace, completely taken up with the person of Christ. The second thing we notice is that this once-naked man was now clothed. We are reminded of the clothing provided by God to Adam and Eve to cover their nakedness. And just as their animal skins pointed to the coming Messiah who would lay down his life for the elect, so the demoniac was dressed not only in a robe but also with the very righteousness of Christ.

Finally, we are told that this former schizophrenic was "in his right mind." Hallelujah! He was free from the control of demons and free to worship God with all his heart and mind. What had been disintegrated was fully integrated under the lordship of Christ. The man's one request was the one that everyone with a sound mind makes: "Lord, I want to follow you the rest of my life."

They all ate and were satisfied. —Luke 9:17

he feeding of the five thousand is the only miracle recorded in all four gospels; thus, we do well to pay close attention. Every miracle is a sign that points to the fact that Jesus is not just a man, nor even just a messiah, but the eternal Son of God.

We read that Jesus and his exhausted disciples withdrew by themselves, yet they could not escape the crowds who were eagerly seeking him. We read in the parallel account that when Jesus saw the people, he had compassion on them. What divine condescension! Jesus welcomed them, spoke to them about the kingdom of God, and healed their sick. He spent hours ministering to the spiritual and physical needs of many thousands of men, women, and children. Then, instead of sending them away, he elected to reveal his glory by relieving their hunger in a miraculous manner. But first the disciples must be called up in their faith.

These disciples, like us, were often guilty of "little faith." Here they reasoned on the basis of sight—the area was remote, the hour late, the crowd too large, and their resources too meager. Jesus, however, wanted them to learn to solve seemingly insoluble problems by looking solely to him in simple trust. In fact, he sovereignly arranged this very situation to help his disciples to mature in their faith (cf. John 6:6). The key insight? That Jesus of Nazareth is not just a man; he is God himself. He is the one who called the universe into being out of nothing. He is the one who fed the two million in the desert with manna. Surely he could feed the crowds now.

In the same way, we are called to look to the risen Lord Jesus Christ in simple, complete faith. We are called to do that which seems impossible—to feed and care for the spiritually hungry. We must come to God, admitting that in ourselves we are nothing and can do nothing. Then we must see Jesus in the pages of Scripture, and in humble dependence on him, obey his command. Whether our problem is big or small, Jesus is bigger. We are weak, but he is strong!

*You are worried and upset about many things, but only one thing is
needed. —Luke 10:41–42*

esus taught his disciples, "Do not worry, but seek first
his kingdom and his righteousness, and all these
things will be given to you as well." This imperative
and promise are wonderfully illustrated in Luke 10 in
the story of Mary and her sister Martha.

On this occasion, Martha was upset and anxious, distracted
by her many duties, while Mary sat riveted at Jesus' feet, focusing
on every word of him who said, "My word is spirit and my word
is life." We can sympathize with Martha, for she was distracted
by a legitimate concern—finishing preparations for the meal.
Nevertheless, Jesus gave her a gentle admonishment, for she failed
to prioritize correctly. Work and service are good and proper, but
worship and adoration must have first claim on our time. Mary
chose what is better.

If we find ourselves beset with anxiety, it is because we have
become distracted by our cares and have lost sight of our great
God and Savior, Jesus Christ. When we daily spend time with
him and hear his voice by reading, studying, meditating on, and
memorizing his word, we will enjoy the peace of God that passes
human understanding. We cannot sit at the feet of Jesus as his
disciple and be upset. Anxiety and Jesus are mutually exclusive.

We ought also to take notice of Jesus' surprising, gracious
commendation and be encouraged. No woman would have dared
on her own to sit at the feet of a rabbi in those days. Yet Jesus
welcomed Mary to come and listen to his words of life. Not only
so, but he also insisted that she be allowed to stay and bask in his
presence. The eternal Son of God was pleased with her single-
hearted devotion.

Jesus is not endorsing laziness or passivity. We do have to work,
serve, and lay down our lives for others. But first things first. When
our duties distract us from communing with our God, then we
have lost sight of what is most important in life. The Lord of the
universe, the incarnate Word of God, is present in our home by
his Spirit. Daily he welcomes us to join with Mary and choose what
is best—worshiping him and hearing his voice.

The LORD says to my Lord: "Sit at my right hand until I make your enemies a footstool for your feet." —Psalm 110:1

salm 110 could readily be entitled, "Thy God Reigneth." It is a messianic psalm that speaks of the present, powerful reign of the exalted Son of God. His kingdom, his rule, is sovereign. This is good news for his people, and the guarantee of utter defeat for his enemies.

So much is taught here in seven verses; no wonder it is one of the most quoted messianic psalms in the New Testament. "The LORD says to my Lord"—Jesus Christ's divine nature is stated in this short statement. God the Father is speaking to his co-equal, his Son, who is King David's Lord. The psalm also speaks of Christ's incarnational life: he is the son of David who grew weary, who became our great high priest and offered himself as a sacrifice, who was raised from the dead and now is ascended, and who shall judge the nations. He has been declared the Son of God with power.

Jesus is now the reigning Christ; the days of weakness and humiliation are over. After finishing his work of redemption, he ascended to heaven and was told by the Father, "Sit at my right hand." To do so is to occupy a seat of great honor; just as the Son glorified the Father in accomplishing redemption, so now the Father is honoring the Son. The right hand is also a place of great power and authority. The Israelites sang the Song of Moses: "Your right hand, O LORD, was majestic in power. Your right hand, O LORD, shattered the enemy" (Exod. 15:6). Finally, the right hand is a place of great blessing: "You will fill me with joy in your presence, with eternal pleasures at your right hand" (Ps. 16:11). Truly God has exalted Jesus to the highest place.

Jesus' present reign has profound consequences for both his people and his enemies. When we said, "Jesus is Lord," we came under his beneficent rule as a result of our unconditional surrender. If we stray from that good confession, he has ways and means to bring us back to the way of obedience. Alternatively, if someone chooses to remain his enemy, he will in due course be defeated and destroyed. His enemies shall be made a footstool for his feet. May God give us sobriety.

*Praise the LORD. I will extol the LORD with all my heart in the council of
the upright and in the assembly. —Psalm 111:1*

raise the Lord! This is an exhortation to everybody by
the writer. In fact, *hallelujah* is actually a command.
It is an imperative. So, if I say, "Hallelujah," then you
respond, "Praise the Lord." The psalmist is filled with
thankfulness for what God has done in his life, and he is asking
everyone to praise the Lord with him.

Then the psalmist says, "I will extol the LORD." If we want to
get others to do what is pleasing to God, we must show them by
example. If we want our children to do what is right, then we must
be a role model. We cannot say, "Do what I say, not what I do." The
psalmist himself is setting the example and is exhorting everyone
to join with him.

How should we praise the Lord? The psalmist does not do so
in a half-hearted, superficial, sleepy way. The first commandment
is to love the Lord with all our heart, mind, soul, and strength.
When we worship him, we must do so with total focus, complete
commitment, and intelligent understanding of the truth. If we
come to church in a sleepy, distracted way, we are dishonoring
God. So the psalmist says, "I will extol the LORD with all my heart."

Why should we praise the Lord? The psalmist points us to
God's marvelous works, which include his creation—the universe
that he made and the people he placed on this small, blue planet.
A Christian is fascinated by the universe and its Creator: "Great
are the works of the LORD; they are pondered by all who delight
in them" (v. 2). Here is the basis for the scientific enterprise—the
believer studies, observes, and thinks about God's works. In fact,
this verse is inscribed over the entrance to the famous Cavendish
Laboratory at Cambridge University.

Unbelievers do not praise God at all. In fact, the more they
study science, the more they hate and deny God, and they praise
themselves. But we must join the psalmist in giving our Creator
God the praise due his name. And as we study creation, whether
macrocosm or microcosm, our hearts will be filled with wonder,
and we will join the chorus, "Hallelujah!"

APRIL 29

We would like to build pens here for our livestock and cities for our women and children. —Numbers 32:16

euben, Gad, and the half-tribe of Manasseh met with Moses and asserted, "We are sick and tired of wandering. We are a cattle-centered people and would like to stay in this wonderful cattle country." Then they pleaded, "Do not make us cross the Jordan." It is a sad story. I feel sorry for "Christians" who make decisions based on "cattle," whether money, careers, or houses.

Their request, in effect, was, "Don't make us follow the ark." But friends, we must follow the ark, for the ark represents the presence of God. We must go where God is going because that is where blessing resides. Our heart's desire must always be to move, move, move with God!

Let us stop and consider what great losses these Israelite wives and children incurred by choosing to remain on the far side of the Jordan. When the ark crossed the Jordan, God caused the waters to miraculously part; these families missed it. Then the community held a great Passover celebration; these families lost out. The walls of Jericho fell down without a fight; these families did not get to see this mighty miracle. Victory after victory took place without these families being aware of a single one.

Yes, they enjoyed a prosperous, comfortable, predictable life on the far side of the river. They enjoyed their cattle. The ark, however, remained far away, and eventually they slipped into a pagan, godless lifestyle. At first, their consciences were unsettled, and they built an imposing altar to assuage their misgivings (Josh. 22). Nevertheless, we do not read much that is encouraging concerning these tribes in the subsequent history of Israel. Later, when the other Israelites joined forces to fight the enemy in Deborah's time, we read this indictment: "Why did [Reuben] stay among the campfires? Gilead stayed beyond the Jordan" (Judg. 5). Eventually, they became the first to fall to conquest by Syria and then Assyria (2 Kings 10 and 15).

The warning is clear. We cannot afford to be like Reuben and Gad, making decisions based on money, power, and position. The world and its desires are passing away. We are on a journey to the city of the living God. Let us follow the ark!

121

In hell, where he was in torment, he looked up and saw Abraham far away, with Lazarus by his side. —Luke 16:23

uring the past few centuries, people have been sanitizing the Scriptures—removing from them doctrines they do not like, especially God's revelation of hell. Jesus, however, spoke about hell more often than any other prophet. For our eternal benefit, he unveiled in Luke 16 what awaits every person at his death—heaven or hell. There is no third option.

The rich man in Jesus' account, like most of the Pharisees of that day, took heaven for granted. He assumed he enjoyed God's favor because he was a descendant of Abraham, went to the temple regularly, and had become wealthy, a supposed confirmation of divine blessing. Like Saul of Tarsus, he boasted in his self-righteousness. No doubt he looked at the stinking Lazarus with contempt, certain that his poverty indicated God's curse on his life. In the rich man's view, he would, after many good years on earth, enter heaven, while Lazarus would experience hell.

In stark contrast, Lazarus—the only person identified by name in all of Jesus' teachings—had nothing. He was a cripple, homeless, and despised by his contemporaries. We have no doubt, though, that this poor outcast trusted in God and endured his life without murmuring. He committed his grievous trials to God without ever questioning God's goodness or sovereignty. All this is sure evidence of a heart made new by God's divine regeneration; Lazarus was saved by grace, and heaven became his glorious inheritance and future hope. We are told that as soon as he died, angels were dispatched by God Almighty to carry his soul to paradise with great celebration.

The rich man also died—and was surprised by hell. His funeral was no doubt splendid, but Jesus says his soul entered immediately into everlasting torment. Jesus' teaching makes it clear that everyone in hell remains fully conscious, with an intact memory, and able to see the bliss out of reach on the other side of the chasm that no one can cross.

Do not presume to be a Christian, or you too may be surprised. This rich man was not a pagan; he was a religious person. But he was not rich toward God. May God help us to take warning and fear him.

When he saw them, he said, "Go, show yourselves to the priests." And as they went, they were cleansed. —Luke 17:14

s Jesus was on his way to Jerusalem, ten lepers met him. They stood at a distance because they were the untouchables, the pariahs of Jewish society. But they had heard that Jesus cleanses lepers, and here was their opportunity—Jesus, who cleansed lepers, was right there! They called out in a loud voice, just like Bartimaeus had on another occasion, "Jesus, Master, have pity on us!"

Now, that is the proper way to come to Jesus. We cannot demand anything of God, for we are all sinners under his wrath. Nevertheless, we are invited to pray this sort of prayer with great humility. It is like the prayer of the publican: "Lord, have mercy upon me, a sinner." Though we are undeserving, God promises to hear the penitent pleas of humble sinners.

It is good for us to remember that God does not have to hear anyone's prayer. There is no law that says God must listen to our petitions or forgive our sins. Justice simply dictates that God pour out his wrath on all peoples of the world, for all have sinned.

Nevertheless, in great compassion, Jesus did hear the lepers' cries. And in response he said, "Go, show yourselves to the priest," which means, "I say to you that you are healed. Take me at my word and obey my instructions." The lepers had no proof of the miracle; they simply had Jesus' word. Would they trust and obey?

Note well what we read next: "As they went, they were healed." We too have God's promises and directives found in the Bible; we must not wait for some kind of feeling or experience to take place before we believe his word and act upon it. God spoke to the Israelites in the wilderness: "I took you out of Egypt to bring you into the Promised Land." But we are told they did not combine the word with faith. They did not act upon God's promise. And they all died except Joshua and Caleb.

If we are calling out to God to help us and heal us, we must believe his promises and obey whatever he tells us to do. Only then will we experience his saving grace.

But you were unwilling to go up; you rebelled against the command of the LORD your God. —Deuteronomy 1:26

n the first chapter of Deuteronomy, Moses recalls what God told the Israelites at Mount Sinai in the second year of their exodus: "You have stayed long enough at this mountain. . . . See, I have given you this land. Go in and take possession of the land that the LORD swore he would give to your fathers . . . and to their descendants after them" (vv. 6, 8). The time had come. The iniquity of the Canaanites was now full, and God's judgment was ready. The Israelites were to advance and take the land at the Lord's command.

The Lord's command was for his people's good. In effect, he was saying, "I want to bless you. I came and delivered you from the Egyptians, and I have a great purpose for you. My plan is to prosper and not to harm you. My plan is to save you and bring you into a land that flows with milk and honey. The time has now come. Go, break camp, and take possession of the Promised Land." Moreover, God specifically encouraged them, "Do not be afraid; do not be discouraged."

But they would not go. Moses says, "But you were unwilling to go up; you rebelled against the command of the LORD your God." Then they also proceeded to grumble against God.

Let us be clear: God is always interested in blessing his people. The problem is never that God is unwilling to help us; the problem is always that we are unwilling to hear and obey his voice. So let us not complain and murmur. It is not God who is unfaithful. We are disobedient, stubborn, and unwilling. We create our own hell and our own troubles. We create our own misery, and then we blame God, as we read in Proverbs 19:3: "A man's own folly ruins his life, yet his heart rages against the LORD."

When we maximize our problems, we minimize God, and the outcome is fear, anxiety, and failure. But those who truly believe in God will maximize God, and their problems will take on the proper proportions. Those who believe will obey the Lord's commands and will go on to defeat every enemy in the land with the strength he supplies.

Blessed is the king who comes in the name of the Lord! —Luke 19:38

osanna to the Son of David! Blessed is the king who comes in the name of the Lord!" the pilgrims cried out, and what they were proclaiming was absolutely true. Jesus is the King of Israel and the Son of David. But the pilgrims' expectations of Jesus were absolutely false. In first-century Israel, there was a common misunderstanding about what the Messiah was coming to do for his people. Not one person in this crowd, even Jesus' own disciples, fully understood the real purpose of Jesus' royal entrance, even though Jesus had disclosed that purpose several times to them.

Those gathered to view the triumphal entry believed what their flesh wanted to believe, and so they stubbornly held on to their wrong-headed view of the Messiah. Luke 19:37 tells us that they were quite aware of the miracles Jesus had performed, especially the miracle of raising Lazarus from the dead. I am sure they were thinking, "Finally, we have a Messiah who has supernatural powers. Hasn't he fed the multitudes, healed the sick, cleansed lepers, and raised a dead man to life? We can't wait to see what this Messiah will do next for us."

Sadly, two thousand years later there continues to be the same mass misunderstanding about Christianity. Many modern evangelicals are, in effect, looking only for a political and economic Messiah. They are not interested in the greater freedom from sin and Satan that Jesus promises to his people. They are happy and satisfied as long as the stock market is up and their wallets are overflowing. In fact, many so-called Christians follow Jesus only as long their notion of freedom is promoted, especially the "freedom" of wealth and health.

But this one riding on a donkey—Jesus of Nazareth, the King of Israel, the Messiah—was coming into the city to secure a different kind of freedom for us. His purpose was to bring his chosen people freedom from sin, death, Satan, hell, and the curse of the law. Jesus said that everyone who sins is a slave to sin. Have you trusted in this Jesus, the only one who can free us from our sore bondage? May God help us to receive this greater freedom that only the Messiah can give!

"Tell us by what authority you are doing these things," they said. "Who gave you this authority?" —Luke 20:2

lways question authority. I am not endorsing rebellion. Nevertheless, I say that we must learn to question authority. If God were the only ruler operating in the world, we would not have to be concerned. But at present there is more than one authority in the world. While God is sovereign, he permits Satan to rule in this fallen world within God's constraints.

Therefore we must question authority in order to determine its source. If it comes from God, we delight in submitting to it and gladly obey it. If, however, we find that it does not come from God, we must reject and oppose it with all our might.

Question authority. Now, if you think that you can live in this world without any authority, you are a fool. There is no blessing possible in this world or in the world to come without our recognizing the central importance of authority. It is the very air that we breathe. The man who walks in righteousness lives under the beneficent rule of God. Conversely, the man who does wicked things is also living by authority—the rule of the kingdom of darkness.

In order to question authority properly, we have to know the Bible. When Satan tempted Jesus in the desert, Jesus did not quote Aristotle, Plato, or the Stoics. He quoted the Scripture. "It is written" means that the Bible is the final authority for doctrine and life. Whenever we determine that a delegated authority is speaking in line with the Scriptures, we must come under and obey that authority. We say, "The Bible is the very word of God; therefore I believe it, I obey it, and that settles it."

Learn to question authority and, in so doing, oppose Satan and his kingdom. Learn to argue from the Bible, to take every thought captive to the obedience of Christ, and you will be blessed. Blessed is the man whose delight is in the law of the Lord.

Question authority in the university, in the high school, in the workplace, and in the public square. Question it, and learn to discern truth from lie. Then stand for truth without wavering, and God's blessings will come upon you and accompany you all the days of your life.

MAY 5

But if from there you seek the LORD your God, you will find him if you look for him with all your heart and with all your soul.
—*Deuteronomy 4:29*

od cannot be found by man on his own because man is finite and God is infinite. Moreover, man is sinful and God is all-holy. It is an absolute impossibility for a sinner to find God on his own. Yet Deuteronomy 4:29 says that if we seek God with all our heart, we will find him. How can that be? God must reveal himself to us. There is no way we can find God unless God first comes down from heaven.

Thanks be to God, he has indeed come down from heaven. He sent his Son into this world so that the Son may reveal God to us. Jesus lived among us and became the atoning sacrifice for our sins on the cross. Surely the triune God is very much interested in being found by us!

The Lord himself promises in his word, "If you seek me, you shall find me." How should we seek him, according to this verse? With all our heart. Someone might say, "Pastor, I have sought him, but it feels like the heavens are brass. There is nothing happening. I haven't found him." My question to such a person would be, "Did you seek him with all your heart?"

If I hear in response, "Yes, I have sought him with all my heart, and yet I have not found him," then I know there is a problem. That person is, in effect, saying that God has lied. But we read in the Bible, "Let God be true and all men liars." We know that God cannot lie; he is truth. So who is lying? Man is lying. We have not fulfilled the condition that governs the promise.

God wants to be found by us. But we have to seek him in the way he has prescribed. If we are serious about seeking God, we must first come to him in his word. He has revealed himself to sinners primarily in the Holy Scriptures. We must also come to church and listen to the gospel as it is preached by God-appointed ministers. Finally, we must get on our knees and pray. As we do these things with all our strength, we will seek God and be found by him.

127

Honor your father and your mother, as the LORD your God has commanded you, so that you may live long and that it may go well with you.
—*Deuteronomy 5:16*

hat it may go well with you" means simply "that you may be blessed." What is blessing? It is more than experiencing good health, earning a large salary, and enjoying a long life on earth. The Lord may indeed bless us in these ways, but this commandment is promising something that is much more profound. It is saying, "that you may enjoy salvation."

There is no greater blessing than to be saved. Our prayers for our children should be that they may grow up in wisdom, that they may grow up strong in their spirit, and that they may grow up, as Jesus did, having favor with God and man. There is no greater joy for a spiritual father than to know that his sons and daughters are saved and love God.

Nothing in the world, however, will save our family. Only the word of God will. It is therefore our responsibility to teach our children this gospel that will make them wise unto salvation. We have to speak and emphasize that the blessing of the gospel is not a lot of money and things. "That it may go well with you" means "that you may be saved, that you may have knowledge of God, that you may have eternal life."

This eternal life comes through the teaching of fathers and mothers. Saving faith comes by hearing—hearing the message spoken in the home. Very early in life, a child who is eagerly listening to his mother and father can be saved. What a joy it is to see a child growing up, loving God, loving the word of God, rejoicing in God, and worshiping God. The child who embraces the gospel, and who loves and fears God, is blessed in every way. Truly it shall go well with him.

But a child who grows up despising his father and mother grows up to despise the greatest message that a father and mother can give—the gospel message of repentance and faith in Jesus Christ. See the serious problem when God's delegated authorities are not obeyed or respected. Those who live this way are cutting themselves off from that testimony, teaching, and instruction which alone is able to save them.

These commandments that I give you today are to be upon your hearts. Impress them on your children. Talk about them when you sit at home and when you walk along the road, when you lie down and when you get up. —Deuteronomy 6:6–7

hildren of believers are covenant children. I did not say they are born-again children; they are covenant children, though they are conceived in sin, born in sin, and practice sin daily. Yet the promise of salvation remains for us and our children (Acts 2:38). So we have the solemn responsibility of teaching and training our children in the knowledge of the true and living God. Our prayer is that each child will grow up to confess Jesus Christ as Lord and Savior.

We must train them up in the way of the Lord, not in the way they naturally choose. As sinners, they naturally choose the way of the world, the flesh, and the devil. Therefore we have to impress upon them the way of the Bible, the way of salvation, the straight and narrow way of everlasting life. We train them to say "No" to sin and "Yes" to righteousness. We must train them to love and choose the way that glorifies God and results in their eternal happiness. And if we do not train them in the way of godliness and morality, the world will surely train them in ungodliness and immorality.

We must teach and then train, instruct and then practice. It is like training a child to ride a bicycle. He will fall down, but keep at it until he takes off, thoroughly trained.

The world tells us that we should let children choose their own lifestyle. The way of secularism is sheer moral relativism and a denial of the Scriptural revelation. But, praise God, Christian parents are in charge of the education of their children, not the state.

Notice, "These commandments are to be upon *your* hearts." This word is addressed to parents. Before we can tell our children how they should live, we ourselves must love the word of God, not money, power, or more stuff. We must know the Bible and practice its truth to be able to teach and train our children. Otherwise, we will be guilty of hypocrisy. Inevitably, we will pass along to our children what we truly love. May the Holy Spirit fill our hearts and cause us to love the Lord our God with all our heart, soul, strength, and mind.

Make no treaty with them, and show them no mercy.
                                          —*Deuteronomy 7:2*

he book of Deuteronomy is a covenant document issued by the great Suzerain, the King of kings and Lord of lords. This covenant, like other treaties of that era, has a certain well-defined structure. Chapter 7 belongs to the treaty component known as covenant stipulations. It is here we learn what we must do to please our great King, the Lord God Almighty. He is not one king among many—he is the only King and he has all authority to tell us how to live.

When we read the Pentateuch, we notice that the Lord clearly tells his people how he wants them to live. Every aspect of our lives is under divine regulation. He tells us what to eat. He governs our sexual life. His word regulates everything. This is the high and comprehensive view of the Holy Scriptures that we should have.

Notice that the text says, "When the LORD your God brings you." It is not a matter of if, but when. In other words, it was God's eternal, divine determination to bring the Israelites into the Promised Land. He made this promise to Abraham in Genesis 15 and he does not change his mind. Thus, the Israelites' sure hope lay not in their own abilities, but in God's immutable word of promise. Their success would be the Lord's doing.

We also read about "nations larger and stronger than you." Salvation is divinely accomplished. We must never think that we have somehow saved ourselves. Salvation is of God and through God from beginning to end. He is the one who drives out nations stronger than us.

Yet we go on to read, "And when you have defeated them." We have something to do! God has delivered us, but we also have to defeat our foes. The Christian life is not one of passivity, but of vigorous, Holy Spirit-empowered activity.

Finally, the Israelites are commanded, "You must destroy them totally. Make no treaty with them." Why? Because the Israelites are the Lord's own possession—they are already in an exclusive covenant with Almighty God. Therefore they must not make a covenant with the sinful nations around them. We also are set apart exclusively for our covenant Lord. The thrice-holy God demands holiness from his covenant people.

And you will be my witnesses. —Acts 1:8

he greatest need of the modern world is to have the gospel proclaimed in the power and demonstration of the Holy Spirit. In fact, the final command the Lord Jesus Christ gave to his disciples before he ascended into heaven was that they should declare the kingdom of God to all nations. To do so, they, and we, must know the person and work of the Master.

The hopes of Jesus' followers had been dashed through unbelief when he was crucified. But later his disciples became convinced of his resurrection. After he rose from the dead, he showed himself to the apostles with many infallible proofs. He appeared regularly to his disciples during this forty day period following Easter Sunday. Now they had the responsibility of bearing witness to his resurrection, the fact on which Christianity rests.

After teaching his disciples about the kingdom of God, Jesus took them to the Mount of Olives and blessed them. Then, while the apostles watched, the cloud of shekinah glory enveloped Jesus and he was taken up and received into the heavens by the Father. That cloud was the manifestation of the divine presence; it symbolized the Father's embrace of his Son, who had pleased him by accomplishing the work of redemption for our salvation.

Thus, Jesus' apostles were eyewitnesses of both the resurrection and the ascension of Christ. They now fully understood who Jesus was, and we must understand as well. He is the one who died on the cross for our sins, who was raised from the dead, and who destroyed death for us. He is the one who has defeated every power that is against us. He is the one who is the Judge of all the earth, and who is coming again according to his own promise. He is the one who received the Holy Spirit and who now sends him to be our Counselor, Guide, and Lord. And he has commanded us to share this good news with all people everywhere.

Our Master is the glorious Lord Jesus Christ. Therefore, we must not be ashamed, but proclaim to all the world that Jesus is Lord. All authority and power have been given to him! How can we be silent?

Salvation is found in no one else, for there is no other name under heaven given to men by which we must be saved. —Acts 4:12

hen a minister preaches about this verse, people generally respond, "This view is too absolute; anyone who believes it is a narrow-minded exclusivist. Do you really think Jesus Christ is the only Savior of the Jews as well as the Gentiles?" Let me tell you, the word of God clearly teaches that there are only two paths for a man to take in life: the broad way, which goes to hell, and the narrow way, which leads to heaven.

Go ahead, then, and call me an extremist, an exclusivist, and a narrow-minded preacher. Accuse me of believing in this absolute truth that Jesus is the only Savior of the whole world. I do not mind, because the apostle Peter's statement remains true for all time: "There is no other name under heaven by which we must be saved."

Suppose a doctor discovers a sure cure for AIDS. He tells his patients, "You cannot be saved by anything else. But if you come to me and take this medicine, you will be healed. In fact, I can show you many others who have been cured already. Not only that, this treatment is free. All are welcome." If you were suffering from this debilitating disease, would you call this doctor an extremist, an exclusivist, and a narrow-minded person? Would you refuse his cure because it was the only effective remedy? Of course not!

Jesus Christ is the only Savior of the whole world; therefore, as a minister of the gospel, I must preach Jesus and him crucified. Though the Bible may be narrow-minded and extremist by your standards, it is the truth, and, thus, I must declare it. Can you show me anyone else who can give sinners true salvation? We need a Savior who can identify both with God and with us. The only such Savior is the God/man Jesus Christ, true God and true man. He died for our sins, rose from the dead, is seated as King on the throne, and is even now ruling the universe and his church. May we therefore join with Peter and boldly declare that it is in Jesus' name alone that we are saved from the wrath of God, from death, and from hell.

MAY 11

Great fear seized the whole church and all who heard about these events.
—*Acts 5:11*

re you naturally arrogant and argumentative? Do you claim to know more than your pastor, your parents, or your boss? Are you characterized by pride rather than humility? If so, you have not yet seen God. That was the problem of Ananias and Sapphira: they did not see God. And as a result, they thought they could hide their sin from him. But we do well to note that their deception was exposed and punished publicly by the omniscient, eternal God himself. And what was the outcome of his judgment? Great fear came upon the whole church.

Why do we sin? We do not fear God. True fear of God is not some meaningless shaking and trembling. True fear of God is a potent, powerful reverence for him that will keep us from sinning. When God came down on Mount Sinai, the people were filled with this holy fear. Quaking in terror, they pleaded with Moses, "Speak to us yourself and we will listen. But do not have God speak to us or we will die" (Exod. 20:19). Moses instructed them that God had come to them this way so that the fear of God would keep them from sinning.

What was the result of this fear in the early church? Unity was restored. The church had originally been characterized by such love, but Ananias and Sapphira, acting under the influence of Satan, introduced disunity. After God's summary judgment, however, the people again lived in one accord, in all honesty, purity, and holiness.

No doubt some people were surprised by God's swift judgment upon this couple. But we must understand that the God of the New Testament does in fact act in this way to keep his church holy. Dr. Martyn Lloyd-Jones once said that churchgoers often come on Sundays to receive some sweet syrup so they can feel good. This frame of mind represents a fatal misunderstanding of Christianity. We must change our view of God to align with the view that is revealed in the Scriptures. Hebrews 12:28–29 warns us to worship God acceptably with reverence and awe, "for our 'God is a consuming fire'." When we see God as he truly is, then we will fear him and live holy, humble lives.

MAY 12

But Stephen, full of the Holy Spirit, looked up to heaven and saw the glory of God, and Jesus standing at the right hand of God. —Acts 7:55

 e read in Acts 7 that Stephen "looked up to heaven" (v. 55). Let me assure you, there is a heaven. We tend to focus on that which can be touched, felt, analyzed, and measured—the created visible world, in other words. That is all an unbeliever sees—the world of money, power, and position. But there is a real heaven and a real hell, and at just the right moment heaven opened to encourage Stephen. The Holy Spirit and the Lord Jesus Christ came to Stephen's aid.

Heaven opened, and Stephen saw the glory of God. With face glowing, he exclaimed to his hearers, "Look at this! What I have been preaching is not false. It is the truth. Look, I can see heaven and the Lord Jesus Christ standing at the right hand of God. You murdered him, but he is risen, exalted, and ascended into the heavens. And I see him now!"

Stephen also told the Sanhedrin, "I see the Son of Man" (v. 56). Stephen was the only person in the New Testament, besides Jesus himself, to use this title to refer to Christ. This title hearkens back to the book of Daniel, where the prophet declares, "In my vision at night I looked, and there before me was one like a son of man, coming with the clouds of heaven. He approached the Ancient of Days and was led into his presence. He was given authority, glory and sovereign power; all peoples, nations and men of every language worshiped him. His dominion is an everlasting dominion that will not pass away, and his kingdom is one that will never be destroyed" (Dan. 7:13–14). Thus, Stephen strikingly affirmed to the Jewish leaders that Jesus Christ is the Son of Man described in Daniel. He is God, and he has all authority in heaven and on earth.

Heaven opened! This passage confirms that there is a heaven, and there is a God in heaven. And the Son of Man has received all authority in heaven and on earth, and now is at the right hand of God the Father in heaven. May God fill us with the Holy Spirit, so that we may see heaven as Stephen did and testify about the glorious Son of Man.

MAY 13

The Spirit told Philip, "Go to that chariot and stay near it." —Acts 8:29

he angel told Philip, "Arise and go," and Philip went. That is one way we know that Philip was a true Christian. A Christian does not negotiate or argue; he simply obeys God. If you are a true Christian, filled with the Spirit of the living God, you will submit and yield to him, and you will obey his word.

The angel told Philip, "Arise and go," and Philip rose up and went. Philip did not say to the angel, "Not now; I have something more important to do." He took the road God said to take and left at the time God told him to leave. And as he went, he saw a man in his chariot, reading the book of Isaiah. God specified the exact route and time for Philip because an elect sinner, the Ethiopian eunuch, must hear the gospel and be saved that day.

Then the Holy Spirit began to speak to Philip. I believe in the guidance of the Holy Spirit. The Holy Spirit told Philip, "Go to that chariot and stay near it." How did Philip respond? He ran. He had already responded quickly when the angel said, "Arise and go." Now the Holy Spirit said, "Go near," and Philip ran.

Philip's response reminds us of Abraham's when he was told to sacrifice his son Isaac. The Bible tells us that Abraham got up early the next morning to obey this command of God (Gen. 22:3). May God help us to be so quick to do his will! Such obedience characterizes authentic Christianity—it is the lifeblood of one who is a new creation in Christ. If we delay, argue, or refuse to do the will of God, it proves that we are not Christians.

Philip ran to the chariot, eager to obey God and zealous to do his will. Why? Philip was full of the Holy Spirit. To be filled with the Holy Spirit means to be led by him and by the Holy Scriptures. As a result, Philip played a part in the great miracle of the salvation of the Ethiopian eunuch. May God fill us with his Spirit and his word, so that we too may serve God in our generation, and, by our witness, save the elect.

As he neared Damascus on his journey, suddenly a light from heaven flashed around him. —Acts 9:3

ent by the authority of the Sanhedrin, Saul traveled to Damascus to extradite Christians from there and bring them to Jerusalem. There he would put them in prison to be tried, beaten, forced to blaspheme, and even killed. Acts 9 tells us that as he traveled, Saul was breathing out threatenings like a wild beast. Confident that his mission would succeed, Saul drew near Damascus with papers from the temple authorities in his hand and the temple police as his escort.

There was only one problem with Saul's plan: it clashed with the plan of Jesus, the Sovereign Lord of the universe, the conquering One under whose feet the Father has put all things. No arrogance of man, no arrogance of a nation, and no arrogance of Satan can prevent Jesus from accomplishing what he has purposed, which is to subjugate all things and put them under his feet. Jesus Christ is the King of kings and Lord of lords, full of power and authority. This same Jesus Christ is the One who said, "I will build my church," and as the head of his church, he builds and protects it.

Saul of Tarsus was coming to destroy the church of Jesus Christ. The early church was known as the Way because Jesus had once said, "I am the way, the truth and the life; no one comes to the Father but by me." Saul hated the people of the Way because he was convinced that Jesus was a cursed blasphemer. In Saul's thinking, God was pleased with his zeal in hunting down Jesus' disciples. In his ignorant arrogance, he did not recognize God's way of salvation in Jesus Christ.

Saul's mission was to destroy the people of the Way. As he neared the city of Damascus, success was in sight. But then something happened. Man proposes, God disposes. "Suddenly a light from heaven flashed around him" (v. 3). What was this light? It was the almighty power of God, the shekinah glory, the glory of the Lord Jesus Christ. Saul saw the light, was blinded by it, and fell to the ground. The conqueror was conquered.

May we, like Saul, fall prostrate before this glorious Lord Jesus Christ and so be saved.

On the testimony of two or three witnesses a man shall be put to death.
—Deuteronomy 17:6

e read in the Lord's covenant law book given to theocratic Israel, "If a man or a woman living among you is found doing evil in the eyes of the LORD your God in violation of his covenant . . . then you must investigate it thoroughly" (Deut. 17:2–4). God gives his leaders the important task of investigating. They are not to just believe rumors. They are to conduct interviews and ask questions in order to establish truth. And they must speak with two or three witnesses, not just one.

When the authorities have done everything correctly and established guilt, what are they to do next? "Stone that person to death" (Deut. 17:5). We are not told to arrange for a prison sentence where the person can be rehabilitated and reformed at $50,000 a year. In the case of a capital offense, God says, "Put him to death." He cannot be rehabilitated. Do not be more merciful than God.

God's church is not given the sword to punish offenders. Yet we are given a crucial mandate: "You must purge the evil from among you" (Deut. 17:7). What are church leaders to do? They are commanded to give church members the opportunity to repent. But if someone refuses to do so, the church must eventually do the maximum it can, which is to release the stubborn rebel to the custody of Satan.

We all have a duty to keep the church pure because the church is where the Holy Spirit dwells. The people of God are holy people. Every person and every family should be holy to the Lord. And it is the responsibility of ministers to observe the flock and protect the sheep from those who are not. If someone wants to join the church, the leaders must find out whether that person is a predator who wants to destroy the flock.

We read in Acts that when God put Ananias and Sapphira to death, great fear came upon the early church. In fact, others did not dare to join the church because they knew of God's holy judgment. This is in keeping with God's word to the Israelites: "All the people will hear and be afraid, and will not be contemptuous again" (Deut. 17:13).

So for a whole year Barnabas and Saul met with the church and taught great numbers of people. —Acts 11:26

hen Barnabas arrived in Antioch, he encouraged the young church to "remain true to the Lord with all their hearts" (Acts 11:23). As he spent more time with them, he concluded that what they needed above anything else was sound biblical teaching. A large number of people had recently been converted to the Lord, and they needed to be taught how to live according to God's word.

Here we see God's sovereign leading. No doubt Barnabas prayed, and God reminded him of Saul, who earlier had been sent to Tarsus by the brothers (Acts 9:30). "Go to Tarsus of Cilicia," God spoke, "where you will find the great biblical scholar Saul, the former student of the renowned Gamaliel. You know how he was gloriously saved, and he continues to preach that Jesus Christ is Lord." So Barnabas went to Tarsus to find Saul and bring him back to Antioch. We read that for a year Barnabas and Saul taught God's word to great numbers in the church.

The need of every church is the word of God. Yet, unfortunately, the modern church does not know or care much about the Bible. We seem more interested in emotionally satisfying experiences than in studying the Scriptures. People come to church and say, "Uplift me, Pastor. Say something that will make me feel good!" But this is not true Christianity. The great need of the church is the word of God.

The Bible is our true soul food. If you are converted, you will love this book. If you do not love the Bible, you are not saved. We are to read and study the Scriptures and then put them into practice. We are to make disciples of all nations, teaching them to obey everything God has commanded (Matt. 28:19–20).

A mature church is one that is steeped in the word of God, which alone causes Christians to grow strong and mighty in the Lord. Biblical teaching is so important that the Holy Spirit led Barnabas to go all the way to Tarsus from Antioch to find Saul. Sound biblical teaching is our great need as well. If we are not taught well, we will not be fed; and if we are not fed, we will surely become weak and sick, and remain infants.

If a man has a stubborn and rebellious son who does not obey his father and mother . . . his father and mother shall take hold of him and bring him to the elders at the gate of his town. —Deuteronomy 21:18–19

euteronomy 21 brings home to us the solemn, abiding truth that the Lord of the covenant must be obeyed. The Lord of the covenant is Yahweh, the self-existing, self-sufficient, almighty God. Just as he led his people out of Egypt, so our Lord has done a great saving work in bringing us out of slavery to sin into God's glorious kingdom. Consequently, we are no longer under Satan's harsh rule. Instead, we are under the rule of our mighty Lord, who delivered us out of our spiritual bondage and gave us his laws—laws that are for our eternal good, that it may go well with us and our children and our children's children.

God calls us to "observe the LORD's commands and decrees that I am giving you today for your own good" (Deut. 10:13). We should note that these laws are for our welfare, not God's. God is self-existing and self-sufficient; he has no need of anything in his creation. He insists that we love and obey him, not because he needs us, but because we need him.

Parents are responsible to instill in their children from a very early age reverence and love for God. There can be no room for disobedience. Parents are under divine authority to enforce the law of the Lord, especially the fifth commandment. Thus, a disobedient child must be confronted with all seriousness.

Parents are called to raise their children in the fear and admonition of the Lord by reproving them, correcting them, training them in righteousness, and punishing them when necessary through the proper use of the rod. We must do this so that all our children, very early on, will learn what it means to respect their father and mother and so respect the Lord of the covenant.

We must not fail in carrying out this most important job. If we are lax, our children will in due time surely be destroyed. What a tragedy that would be! We must not let our children treat God or his delegated authorities with contempt. Instead, they must understand that keeping God's law is for their own good and their children's good. There is no greater inheritance that we can bequeath than this: the fear of the Lord and love for God.

MAY 18

If you, O LORD, kept a record of sins, O Lord, who could stand? But with you there is forgiveness; therefore you are feared. —Psalm 130:3–4

 he psalmist asks, "If God kept a record of sins, who could stand?" The unequivocal answer is "No one!" But praise be to God, when he forgives our sins, our record is wiped completely clean. No guilt remains, for Christ has blotted out our transgressions by his own death on the cross. In Jeremiah 50:20 we read, "'In those days, at that time,' declares the LORD, 'search will be made for Israel's guilt, but there will be none.'"

Someone may ask, "If this is so, why not continue to sin?" The apostle Paul answers, "Shall we go on sinning that grace may increase? God forbid!" How can we dishonor God by turning our back on his moral commandments? True forgiveness from God can never result in a Christian living as an antinomian. If you see a "Christian" who is careless in his walk and practices sin, then you must draw the conclusion that he is not forgiven and that he is not saved. A truly born again person, one who has received God's amazing grace and complete forgiveness, will be careful to follow the guidance of God's moral law.

In this verse, the psalmist goes on to make this vital connection explicit—God forgives sinners so they may fear him. Those who are authentic Christians, those who have truly been forgiven of their sins, will revere God by keeping his commandments. People sin because they do not fear God. Conversely, no one who truly fears God will sin, for the Bible clearly affirms that the fear of God will keep us from sinning.

If we have been saved, we are now new creations in Christ. We have new natures and new capacities. When John Newton experienced God's free forgiveness of all his sins, he wrote, "'Twas grace that taught my heart to fear and grace my fears relieved." We who have been forgiven by Christ are freed from the guilt, the penalty, and the power of sin. We are freed from death, hell, and Satan. We are freed to do good works, which is simply obedience to God's moral law. We are freed to walk in wisdom, and the fear of God is the beginning of this wisdom. How, then, can we continue in sin? God forbid!

140

The jailer called for lights, rushed in and fell trembling before Paul and Silas. He then brought them out and asked, "Sirs, what must I do to be saved?" —Acts 16:29–30

 hat must I do to be saved?" This is the most important question any one of us can ask, no matter who we are. We are not told how this jailer first heard of Jesus. Perhaps he knew of the slave girl's declaration, "These men are servants of the Most High God, who are telling you the way to be saved." Perhaps he had heard others in Philippi discussing the gospel, especially after the conversion of Lydia and her household. Now God was drawing this hardened Roman soldier to himself with a mighty, effectual call, and for the first time the jailer began to realize, "I am doomed! I am lost! I am under the wrath of God. What must I do to be saved?"

Paul gave the warden a clear, direct answer: "Believe in the Lord Jesus and you will be saved—you and your household." I am sure Paul told him about Jesus, the Son of God who became flesh and lived a perfect life. Undoubtedly he explained that Christ was crucified for our sins, on the third day was raised from the dead for our justification, and is now ascended into the heavens as Lord of all. He would have concluded with the fact that this Jesus will return to judge all who refuse to believe and obey him, and to bring salvation to those who have trusted in him.

As the apostle declared these gospel truths, God graciously gave the jailer the gifts of repentance and saving faith. He and his family experienced true salvation by Christ alone through faith alone by grace alone plus nothing. All the members of his household were saved instantly and they were saved forever. Such is the wonder of eternal salvation.

How do we know he was saved? The love of the Spirit of God was shed abroad in the jailer's heart and he brought Paul and Silas out from prison and washed their wounds. We are told that he also rejoiced with exceeding joy, a joy which proceeds from the Holy Spirit. Salvation is a marvelous miracle—the miracle of miracles!

Have you asked the most important question? Money, power, wisdom, fame—none of these can save you. Jesus Christ alone saves sinners from their sins.

In the past God overlooked such ignorance, but now he commands all people everywhere to repent. —Acts 17:30

n Acts 17, we see Paul condemning the idolatry of the Athenians in the meeting of the Areopagus. Then he declared, "In the past God overlooked such ignorance." What was the problem of these sophisticated, intellectual Athenians? Ignorance!

The apostle was not implying that man cannot make calculations and say that four plus three is seven. Nor was he asserting that man cannot learn philosophy or achieve great technological advances. What Paul was declaring is that in the fundamental arena of knowing God, the Athenians had failed. When it came to knowing ultimate truth, they were ignorant.

Moreover, Paul's statement asserts that such ignorance is culpable. In a certain sense, God had overlooked this failure in the past. But now that time was over. Paul told his audience, "In the past God overlooked such ignorance, but now . . . ." "Now" is defined by the incarnation of Jesus Christ. No longer can anyone say, "I am ignorant of God," because Christ has come and explained the Father to all mankind.

"The time has come," Paul was saying to these intellectuals, "to decide whom you are going to worship—idols or the true and living God." The God of the Bible is not only Creator, but he is also Judge of all people. So Paul warned the Athenians that God "has set a day when he will judge the world with justice by the man he has appointed" (Acts 17:31).

In a word, Paul was telling the intellectuals of the Areopagus to repent. He boldly confronted them: "Your thinking about God is false. You pretend that you know the truth, but you are ignorant. God demands that you forsake your old way of thinking and turn away from idols to serve him who created and sustains all things. This same God is Lord and Judge. Change your mind!"

God "commands all people everywhere to repent." This command to repent is universal because God's judgment is going to be universal. The Lord of the whole earth commands us to change our minds. He is not suggesting, requesting, or pleading with us. He is commanding us, as Creator, Sustainer, Lord, and Judge. We shall not escape if we ignore such a great salvation.

Cursed is the man who carves an image or casts an idol—a thing detestable to the LORD, the work of the craftsman's hands—and sets it up in secret. —Deuteronomy 27:15

ne of the Israelites' first duties upon entering the Promised Land was to pronounce covenant blessings and curses in the hearing of the assembled people. Thus in Deuteronomy 27 we read a dodecalogue—twelve curses to be recited on that day by the Levites. Each of these curses concerns secret sins.

Anyone who thinks he can sin secretly has a problem of theology. His god is like a mere man. But if our God is the God of the Scriptures, we know that no one can sin secretly. God's word tells us, "Nothing in all creation is hidden from God's sight. Everything is uncovered and laid bare before the eyes of him to whom we must give account" (Heb. 4:13). The infinite, omniscient, almighty God is everywhere present in his creation. He knows our thoughts before we think them. Men may fail to discover and punish our sins, but God sees them all, and God will judge them both here and hereafter.

So we read, "Cursed is the man who carves an image or casts an idol . . . and sets it up in secret" (v. 15). The offender is one who rejects the true God, who rejects the theology of revelation, and secretly creates his own theology and his own god. He thinks no one cares or pays attention. This rejection of God is at the heart of all philosophies, idolatries, and manmade religions. Aristotle taught about a god, for instance, but he spoke of a thinking "it," not the infinite, personal God who sees and judges every person.

People like to be religious, as long as their god can remain the creation of their own minds, the postulation of their own intellects. They become very comfortable with their manufactured god who tolerates sin. Little do they realize that the honor of the true and living God is at stake, and he does not tolerate this behavior.

Such idolatry can take place even in the church. A preacher can be declaring the truth about the God of the Scriptures, yet some of his hearers will be busy creating their own secret gods in their heads. But the true and living God sees all things, and he has already pronounced a curse on those who make idols. The God of the Bible demands that we honor him alone.

If you fully obey the LORD your God and carefully follow all his commands I give you today . . . all these blessings will come upon you.
—Deuteronomy 28:1–2

he first two verses of Deuteronomy 28 speak about the fundamental importance of God's word in the life of the Christian. God's words are spirit and life; therefore we must read them, meditate on them, delight in them, and obey them. Our philosophy of life—what we really think—dictates whether or not we will obey God's commands and be blessed. The Bible says, "As a man thinketh in his heart, so is he" (Prov. 23:7, KJV). How vital it is, then, for our thinking to be shaped by the Holy Scriptures.

Accordingly, we are exhorted in the New Testament, "Let the word of Christ dwell in you richly" (Col. 3:16). And in Deuteronomy 11 we were commanded, "Fix these words of mine in your hearts and minds; tie them as symbols on your hands and bind them on your foreheads. Teach them to your children, talking about them when you sit at home and when you walk along the road" (Deut. 11:18–19). The Bible emphasizes throughout how essential it is that we are guided, not by our lusts or emotions, but by the word of God as we daily make decisions.

We will read in Deuteronomy 32, "When Moses finished reciting all these words to all Israel, he said to them, 'Take to heart all the words I have solemnly declared to you this day, so that you may command your children to obey carefully all the words of this law. They are not just idle words for you—they are your life'" (Deut. 32:45–47). We can hear idle words twenty-four hours a day, seven days a week, if we watch television and surf the Internet. Our media outlets are by and large filled with ethical garbage, empty chatter, and human philosophy. Not so the words of God! They are not just idle words; they are our very life.

To neglect God's words is therefore to neglect life and blessing, and to court disaster. The God of heaven wants us to be blessed. He tells us in Deuteronomy 30:19: "I have set before you life and death, blessings and curses." Then he implores us, "Choose life!" May God help us to do so by daily choosing to obey his words.

Make sure there is no man or woman, clan or tribe among you today whose heart turns away from the LORD our God to go and worship the gods of those nations; make sure there is no root among you that produces such bitter poison. —Deuteronomy 29:18

n Deuteronomy 29 we read about a "root of poison." The covenant Lord is warning his people about those who join the visible church, God's covenant community, but who, in fact, are insincere professors of faith.

A local covenant community is always a mixture, consisting of the true people of God and those who are false—roots of poison. The term *root* points to something that is hidden. Both true and false believers come to church. They both smile and appear to be very nice. But the root-of-poison person knows in his heart that his covenant vows are not sincere.

We may not recognize at first who these people are. But God has news for all hidden roots: though the pastor may not find you out, God will. He warns in Numbers 32:23, "You may be sure that your sin will find you out." We all stand naked before God. He sees us and hears us when we think to ourselves, "I will be safe, even though I persist in going my own way." Why do false believers invariably leave a true church? They leave to commit immorality. They were hidden roots of poison for a season, pretending to be loyal covenant-keepers. In due time, however, they will be exposed by the Lord of the covenant and evicted.

What about you? What are you doing in the night? Do you think that no one knows? There is One who knows, and he will expose your sins in broad daylight. What you whisper in the chamber will be proclaimed from the housetops. That is the way it is going to be.

True believers are called to be their brother's keepers. We read in Hebrews 12:15, "See to it that no one misses the grace of God and that no bitter root grows up to cause trouble and defile many." Every member of the family of God has a responsibility to all other members to see that they are loving God and one another. And if we see someone sinning, it is our job to confront that person and say in love, "You must stop doing evil; you are disrupting the life of the community. Repent! For you are behaving as a root of poison."

The LORD your God will circumcise your hearts and the hearts of your descendants, so that you may love him with all your heart and with all your soul, and live. —Deuteronomy 30:6

n Deuteronomy 30, the tragic future of Israel is revealed to Moses. It is as if he already sees the coming Assyrian and Babylonian captivities. Moses prophesies, "When all these blessings and curses I have set before you come upon you and you take them to heart wherever the LORD your God disperses you among the nations . . ." (v. 1). But in this chapter he also sees God's great compassion revealed, for the next verse describes the Israelites' subsequent repentance. This does not mean that everyone is going to return. In fact, very few people—only a remnant—ever do.

Nevertheless, in God's mercy a remnant will repent. But notice, the standard of God never changes. So we read, "And when you and your children return to the LORD your God and obey him with all your heart and with all your soul according to everything I command you today . . ." (v. 2). A repentance that does not require us to love God and obey his commands is false and damnable.

We cannot repent conditionally and say, "I want to return to God, but I want to sin." It does not work that way. When we return in true repentance, we will love the Lord and keep his covenant word.

How can anyone truly repent in this manner? After all, we read, "The heart is deceitful above all things, and desperately wicked: who can know it?" (Jer. 17:9, KJV). We need a change of heart! We need a clean heart, a new heart, but we cannot change ourselves. Thanks be to God, then we are told: "The LORD your God will circumcise your hearts" (v. 6). No one can return from the far country unless God first comes to him and works in his heart. We must be born again, born of the Spirit. God himself must give us a heart of flesh, pour out his Spirit upon us, and change our thinking.

Here is the great key. It is God who, in his distinguishing mercy, will grant us repentance and faith. When he does so, we will love God and delight in him. And this glorious promise will be true of us: "The LORD will again delight in you" (v. 9).

MAY 25

King Agrippa, do you believe the prophets? I know you do. —Acts 26:27

n Acts 26, we find the longest and most important of the five recorded speeches that the apostle Paul gave in defense of the gospel and his innocence. Many charges were leveled against Paul by the Jewish people, including allegations that he was against the law, against the temple, and against Caesar. None of these charges was ever proven; yet, because of politics and self-interest, the Roman governors Felix and Festus did not set Paul free.

Paul's defense was not primarily self-defense. When Paul finished preaching to this regal crowd, he made a bold evangelistic appeal. Paul challenged King Agrippa to testify to the truth before Festus and the others. "King Agrippa," Paul was saying, "you know these things. You are an authority in Jewish affairs and the Jewish scriptures. You know that Jesus' life, death, and resurrection are historical facts that did not take place in a corner. For about three decades, eyewitnesses have been testifying about the resurrection of Jesus Christ."

How did the king respond? Agrippa saw himself as the great king, a pious friend of Caesar and of Rome. Though he ruled a very little country, he was swollen with pride and intellectual arrogance. As a result, he did not believe in the Scriptures. But Agrippa was also a savvy politician; therefore, he would neither deny nor confirm Paul's message publicly. Instead, he retorted, "Do you think that in such a short time you can persuade me to be a Christian?" (Acts 26:28). He was saying, "Don't you realize how powerful and intellectually sophisticated I am?"

We see the loving heart of the great apostle in Paul's answer: "Short time or long—I pray God that not only you but all who are listening to me today may become what I am, except for these chains" (Acts 26:29). Tragically, neither Agrippa nor anyone with him responded to Paul's message in faith. Even today, in hell's torment, they are seized with bitter regret.

Have you responded in faith to the gospel? If not, you will soon join King Agrippa, Festus, the rich man of Luke 16, and every other fool who ever lived; and one day, you will stand before God in judgment and enter into everlasting misery. May you, instead, repent and believe, and enjoy eternal life!

You deserted the Rock, who fathered you; you forgot the God who gave you birth. —Deuteronomy 32:18

ow did Israel respond to God's lovingkindness? Inexplicably, they turned to despicable idolatry. In Deuteronomy 32 we read, "Jeshurun grew fat and kicked" (v. 15). Jeshurun is a pet name for Israel that means "straight one." Because the Lord is righteous, his children should also be righteous. Here *Jeshurun* is used in reproach, because those who were supposed to be righteous had instead become corrupt, foolish, and unfaithful. They had gladly received the gifts God gave them, but instead of paying the tribute of heartfelt worship to their covenant Lord, they now served the Baals.

The Holy Spirit is speaking here of the problem of materialism. One of the worst trials for a Christian is not poverty, sickness, loneliness, or persecution, but prosperity. Martin Luther said, "A full stomach does not promote piety, for it stands secure and neglects God." Material prosperity is extremely dangerous, for it tends to produce the spirit of Laodiceanism. The Lord told the church of Laodicea, "You say, 'I am rich; I have acquired wealth and do not need a thing.' But you do not realize that you are wretched, pitiful, poor, blind and naked" (Rev. 3:17).

Prosperity often blinds us to spiritual realities and tends to produce independence and self-sufficiency. We then kick God out of our lives and treat his worship with contempt. We become too busy for prayer and the study of God's word. We have so many other things to do: to eat and drink, to marry and give in marriage, to buy and sell, to plant and harvest, to take vacations and recuperate from vacations.

Prosperity also causes many Christians to neglect daily devotions. If we do not have much, we will get up early in the morning to pray and seek the Lord. But when we have plenty, we tend to fall into the mindset, "Why do I need to read the Bible? Everything is going well; why do I need to pray?"

This is the deadening effect of prosperity, especially on those who yearn for it. So instead of praying for more money, I hope we will pray, "O God, please keep me from experiencing prosperity if it turns me away from you. Instead, I thank you for the trials you provide me, for they keep me close to my God."

O Lᴏʀᴅ, you have searched me and you know me. —Psalm 139:1

salm 139 introduces us to the infinite, personal God who is self-existent and who sees and knows every act, word, and thought of every person who has ever lived. If God were not omniscient, there could not be any final, just judgment. Such a judgment requires perfect, exhaustive knowledge of everything you and I have done.

"You are familiar with all my ways" (v. 3). Not even one way is unknown to him. He sees all things in one glance, and knows all things immediately, without research. "Before a word is on my tongue, you know it completely, O Lᴏʀᴅ" (v. 4). He knows when we tell truth, and when we lie. The Father is truth, the Son is truth, and the Holy Spirit is called the Spirit of truth. God cannot lie. What he promises, he performs; what he threatens, he will surely bring to pass.

The Bible is replete with examples of those in the covenant community who thought they could lead a secret life and hide something from God. Though Achan and his entire family saw God's mighty power in the destruction of Jericho, they agreed to hide the spoils under their tent in defiance of God's directive. Ananias and Sapphira, despite living in the days of the Pentecostal outpouring, lied to the face of the apostle Peter. In each case, these offenders suffered an immediate, horrifying judgment. Everything is uncovered and laid bare before the eyes of him to whom we must give account (Heb. 4:13).

May the Lord help us to read his word with fear and trembling so that we will have a true understanding of his greatness, glory, wonder, holiness, and omniscience. When we truly understand the God with whom we have to do, we will be careful to obey.

What about you? Have you been lying? Did you break your covenant commitments? Are you tempted to change your mind? Think carefully; God cannot be fooled. May God give us the fear of the Lord, which is the beginning of wisdom, so that we might say with the psalmist, "Search me, O God, and know my heart. See if there is any offensive way in me, and lead me in the way everlasting" (vv. 23–24).

In the beginning was the Word, and the Word was with God, and the Word was God. —John 1:1

he most important question a man can ask is, "Who is Jesus Christ?" In other words, who is this who was born a helpless babe in a lowly manger? Who is this who later said, "The Son of Man has no place to lay his head"? Who is this who was crucified under Pontius Pilate? Most people, when they hear of Jesus, reject his claim to deity and so come under his judgment. But others, a minority, will fall down in humility, faith, and repentance, and exclaim, "My Lord and my God!"

Who is Jesus Christ? In John 1:1 we read, "In the beginning was the Word." "In the beginning" points not to the beginning of creation but to timeless eternity; it speaks about the Son's eternal preexistence. He was before the creation of the universe.

Jesus himself spoke about his eternity when he prayed, "And now, Father, glorify me in your presence with the glory I had with you before the world began" (John 17:5). The helpless, manger-born baby is from eternity. There was no time when he was not.

Jesus is not only eternal, but he is also the eternal Word. What is the purpose of words? It is to express one's thoughts and reveal them to others. So we understand from John's statement that Jesus Christ is the one who reveals God to us. Without him, we can never truly know God.

Jesus Christ is the Word of God personalized. Psalm 33:6 says, "By the word of the LORD were the heavens made," and in Revelation 19:13 we read, "He is dressed in a robe dipped in blood, and his name is the Word of God." This Word reveals God's thoughts and character to us.

Jesus is also the Word who became flesh (John 1:14). Without abandoning or reducing his deity, God the Son took upon himself human nature in body and soul. He became incarnate so that as our representative he might fully obey God and procure salvation for all who believe in him.

John concludes verse 14 by exclaiming, "We beheld his glory." No one perceives Christ's glory unless his eyes have been opened by new birth. Have you beheld the glory of God in the face of Christ? Look today in faith and live!

May 29

Everyone brings out the choice wine first and then the cheaper wine after the guests have had too much to drink; but you have saved the best till now. —John 2:10

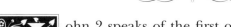

ohn 2 speaks of the first of the many miracles Jesus performed that proved he was more than a mere man. At this wedding in Cana, when there was no wine, he created it. He is the unique God/man, Christ the Lord, who alone can solve every problem we face, whether the problem of no wine, or the more serious problems of sin, death, guilt, and misery.

Whoever conducted this wedding did one thing right: he invited Jesus. Yet there was a problem: no wine. We live in a fallen world with many sorrows and problems. We will all face problems we cannot solve, and any confidence and joy that resides outside of Jesus will eventually fail. Only he can miraculously provide 150 gallons of the very best wine in our hour of need. And he is not miserly; he has an abundance of grace and life for his children.

Have you invited Jesus into your life? If so, go to Jesus, as Mary did, and tell him your problem. But you must know who he is before you can go. You must acknowledge him as Lord, King, and Savior. Only then can you go to him in prayer and expect an answer. And do not be put off when he seems to delay in helping you. He is trying your faith, but he will surely rescue you in his perfect time. He says, "I will be with you always; I will never leave you nor forsake you."

Though unseen, Christ is always near his people. Storms will rise to sink our boat when we least expect them. Happy are the people who have Jesus in their boat. Cry out to him, as Peter did: "Jesus, save us! We are perishing." He will calm our storms and lead us safely to heaven. Jesus said, "I give them eternal life and they shall never perish."

Jesus, who is our well of eternal salvation, offers us the best wine. The miracle at Cana points to the life eternal that Jesus will give us as a result of his death and resurrection. He invites us to come to him in faith to receive that life. Then our vats will brim over with joy and new wine, for his grace is abundant.

Go over before the ark of the Lord your God into the middle of the Jordan.
Each of you is to take up a stone on his shoulder, according to the number
of the tribes of the Israelites, to serve as a sign among you. —Joshua 4:5–6

 n Joshua 4, God instructed Joshua to build a memorial at Gilgal to commemorate the supernatural parting of the Jordan River. What was the purpose of this memorial? First, it was a sign for the present generation. Joshua set up the twelve stones they had taken out of the Jordan as a memorial "to serve as a sign among you" (v. 6). Those who participated in this event were to benefit from this sign. There are times when Christians, though they have crossed over their Jordans, also become discouraged, fearful, and dispirited. When this happens, we must look at such memorials and believe that he who delivered us in the past will save us again.

It was also a sign for future generations. The writer continues, "In the future, when your children ask you, 'What do these stones mean?' tell them . . ." (vv. 6–7). A memorial provokes questions. Those who see it ask, "What is this?" When your children ask, you have a God-given opportunity to evangelize them. Tell them about the historical manifestation of the power of God in saving his people. Tell them, "Our God is a living God who does amazing things. Our God is the Savior, the only true God, and we must serve him only. All other gods are false; they can do nothing."

In Hebrew, the phrase "tell them" means "cause them to know for certain." When our children ask, we must make sure they know, appreciate, and experience the salvation of the Lord. We do not want to give them mere intellectual knowledge; we want them to entrust themselves to this living God who is among his people. He is the God who saves.

Finally, the memorial is a sign for all peoples on earth throughout all ages: "He did this so that all the peoples of the earth might know that the hand of the Lord is powerful" (v. 24). God purposed that in Abraham all the nations and families of the earth would be blessed. This blessing comes through the knowledge of God, and this knowledge comes through the people of God. Why do we need memorials? Because we tend to forget God and his saving deeds. Let us not forget, but go and tell others the good news that our God reigns!

I tell you the truth, a time is coming and has now come when the dead will hear the voice of the Son of God and those who hear will live.

—*John 5:25*

n John 5, we learn of two voices that all people will hear. The first voice is the call of the gospel. Someone declares to us the good news about the person and work of Jesus Christ. The voice of God comes to us through the preacher.

Jesus speaks of this first voice in verse 25. All who hear the gospel must respond to the demand for repentance and faith contained in the gospel. We will either embrace the call and surrender our lives to the Lord Jesus Christ, or we will refuse his summons and go our own way.

How we respond to the first voice will determine what will happen when we hear the second voice. Jesus explained, "A time is coming when all who are in their graves will hear his voice and come out—those who have done good will rise to live, and those who have done evil will rise to be condemned" (v. 28).

"A time is coming," according to Jesus Christ, who is the Judge. A time is irrevocably appointed for every man once to die and then face judgment. Mary Baker Eddy and Joseph Smith and every person who manufactured a religion, every person who despised the gospel, every person who said, "Not yet. I still want to sin. But I will think about it," will surely hear the voice of Jesus on that day.

The day of our death is determined. It is an important, unchangeable date. But there is also a most crucial moment in our lives when the gospel call comes to us. When it comes, we will either obey that voice or reject it. And based on that decision, our life will end either in eternal bliss or in eternal misery. "Multitudes who sleep in the dust of the earth will awake: some to everlasting life, others to shame and everlasting contempt" (Dan. 12:7). There is no third option, and there are no exceptions.

Our personal opportunity to respond to the first voice in this life will soon come to an end. Now is the day of salvation. Have you heard the voice of the Son of Man? Have you repented and believed on him? If you have, you will welcome with joy the voice to come.

JUNE 1

Now Jericho was tightly shut up because of the Israelites. . . . Then the
Lord said to Joshua, "See, I have delivered Jericho into your hands."
—Joshua 6:1–2

n Joshua 6, Joshua was facing a seemingly insur-
mountable problem: How could the fortified city of
Jericho with its great walls be defeated? Of course,
Joshua could have thought of various strategies based
on carnal wisdom. He might have consulted his generals and
received counsel, such as, "You could use a ladder or build a ramp
up to the top of the wall," or, "You could always try a long siege, or
use subterfuge to get inside."

But Christians are commanded, "Trust in the Lord with all your
heart and lean not on your own understanding" (Prov. 3:5). We
are not to solve problems by relying on our own understanding.
We must look to God, for he alone is the way. The personal God
communicates with his people and he will tell us how to solve
every problem.

What is the way of the Lord? In Isaiah 55:8 God tells us, "My
thoughts are not your thoughts, neither are your ways my ways."
How many times have we listened to our own counsel, or sought
counsel from others, but not from God! The way of God seems
foolish to the natural man. But for us who believe, it is the power
of God unto salvation.

What was God's command to Joshua? "March around the city
during the seven days of the Feast of Unleavened Bread." God's
perfect plan did not involve any ladder, battering ram, tunnel,
siege, or subterfuge. The people of God were to just walk around
the city. It may sound like nonsense to us, but it was the word of
the Lord. And when God's people believe and act on his word in
every detail, they shall have complete victory.

The Christian life includes conflict against sin, Satan, and
the world. We also must listen carefully to our Commander's
instructions, for this is the Lord's war, not ours. Yes, we are called
to fight, but it is the Lord who will give us the victory. He is the
Warrior/Savior who will never leave us nor forsake us. Faith means
obedience to God's will to the minutest detail. Faith trusts God's
promises. Faith obeys God's commands exactly, immediately, and
with great delight. Faith is the victory that overcomes the world.

Joshua read all the words of the law—the blessings and the curses—just as it is written in the Book of the Law. —Joshua 8:34

s Christians, we reject the evolutionary view of reality and its moral relativism. We believe the Bible is the very word of God, and that God's authoritative words are the constitution of the church today, even as they were in the Old Testament. In fact, the first constitutional convention took place not in AD 1787, but around 1400 BC, as recorded in the eighth chapter of Joshua.

The law of the covenant Lord was the constitution of God's theocratic kingdom. The Lord instructed Joshua through Moses to write all the words of this law on whitewashed stone pillars that stood about six to eight feet high. Not only did Joshua write the law on the stone pillars for the people to read, but he also proclaimed it publicly to them. All the Israelites assembled at Shechem and listened as the entire word of the Lord was read aloud.

By God's command, six tribes were to stand on Mount Ebal and pronounce twelve curses, as recorded in Deuteronomy 27:9–26. As the people said "Amen," they were, in effect, saying, "We accept the constitution of this theocracy. And if we fail to obey it, may God's curses fall on us." The other six tribes stood at Mount Gerizim, the mountain of blessing, probably reading the words we find in Deuteronomy 28:1–14. Again, the people said "Amen" at the reading of each blessing. By doing so, they were submitting to the word of the covenant Lord and acknowledging that they would be blessed if they obeyed it. Finally, the people promised to abide by the constitution Joshua revealed to them.

God's constitution differs from the constitution of the United States of America; the latter was written by humans in Philadelphia in 1787, while God's law, the Scripture, comes to us straight from heaven. Paul writes, "All Scripture is God-breathed and is useful for teaching, rebuking, correcting and training in righteousness, so that the man of God may be thoroughly equipped for every good work" (2 Tim. 3:16–17).

This is why we do not practice "alternative" worship in God's church. We declare God's authoritative word, the constitution of God's church. Covenant people still delight in the law of their Lord, and as we obey it, we shall go from blessing to blessing.

The one who sent me is with me; he has not left me alone, for I always do what pleases him. —John 8:29

n John 8, Jesus declared, "The one who sent me is with me." He was speaking of his greatest joy, the communion with the Father that he knew from all eternity. What greater comfort can we enjoy than communion with the Father? We are created for that very purpose.

Jesus also testified, "He has not left me alone." Then he gave the reason: "for I always do what pleases him." Obedience brings communion. If we are born of God, we will obey God. We will seek the will of God, and do the will of God without negotiation or argument. We will find our joy in doing his will and experiencing his divine approbation.

The fear, guilt, and shame of sin disrupts fellowship with God and one another. But Christianity solves the problem of human alienation by bringing a sinner into right relationship with the Father. Jesus Christ came so that, by his life, death, and resurrection, we can experience the same fellowship with the Father that he himself enjoys.

What are we desiring and seeking? What are we running after? Are we still imagining that the things of this world will bring us true satisfaction? It is sad and tragic when we run after everything but God. When we do so, we are committing the same error that millions of people in the world commit. In Matthew 6, Jesus said that the pagans run after "these things," but we are to seek first the kingdom of God—the kingdom of righteousness, peace, and joy in the Holy Spirit.

We must care about one thing above all else—having fellowship with the Father. Obedience is necessary for this fellowship. An obedient Christian is never lonely. Jesus himself promised, "If anyone loves me, he will obey my teaching. My Father will love him, and we will . . . make our home with him" (John 14:23).

Except at the cross of Calvary, when he bore our sins as our substitute, Jesus was never alone. And if we are truly his younger brothers, we will emulate him. Pleasing the Father will be our singular purpose and goal. And when we walk in this way, we will be richly satisfied. "You will fill me with joy in your presence, with eternal pleasures at your right hand" (Ps. 16:11).

157

"Go," he told him, "wash in the Pool of Siloam." —John 9:7

 ohn 9 speaks about Jesus healing the man born blind. Let us look closely at the command that Jesus gave to this man: "Go, wash in the Pool of Siloam" (v. 7). Notice first, that this command was specific. When God speaks to us, he expects obedience, so he makes his commands very clear. Jesus was telling him to go to the pool on the southern part of Jerusalem and wash—not just in any pool, not just in any body of water—but specifically in this particular pool called Siloam.

When a professor gives an assignment, he is specific. He does not want his students to go and read books that they choose. No, he tells them what to read and what assignments to do. The Holy Spirit is also very specific. The word of God is very specific. When God speaks to us, he speaks with clarity. We hear that still, small voice speaking to us: "This is the way, walk ye in it." God is not a God of darkness, but of revelation.

This command was also simple. Jesus Christ did what was most difficult—he came down from heaven and died on the cross for our sins. The man's part was so simple—he was to go and wash in the waters of Siloam. In Isaiah, the gently flowing waters of Siloam stand for the power of the God of Israel (Isa. 8:6). In other words, we are to turn away from self and look to God for salvation. Believe on the Lord Jesus Christ and you shall be saved.

This command was also personal. The man himself had to go; not his mother, father, or neighbor. He had to wash in the pool that Jesus has specified.

Finally, this command required immediate obedience. When the word of God comes to us, we dare not say, "I'll think about it and decide later." No, Jesus Christ requires obedience now. Postponement is the same as not acting.

What was the result of the man's obedience to Jesus' command? Hear his testimony: "Jesus told me to go to Siloam and wash. So I went, I washed, and I came back seeing." May God help us to respond to the specific, simple, personal commands of God in the same way. If we do, we too shall be saved.

For it was the Lord himself who hardened their hearts to wage war
against Israel, so that he might destroy them totally. —Joshua 11:20

 omans 11:22 says, "Consider therefore the kindness
and sternness of God." This is a comfort as well as a
warning to us. Our God is a moral God; he is light,
and in him there is no darkness at all. This moral God
punishes sin in history and beyond.

The Canaanites heard the reports of how Joshua and the
people of Israel were advancing through Canaan. When Rahab
heard the gospel, she repented, and she and her entire family
were saved. When the Gibeonites heard, they surrendered and
were saved from certain death. Yet although the southern and
northern confederations heard the same report, they would not
surrender. Why? The Lord had hardened their hearts so that he
might destroy them.

This is a sobering thought. When a person stubbornly hardens
his heart, God then hardens it even more until he destroys that
person. That is the severity of God. Pharaoh hardened his heart,
and he was killed. All those who harden their hearts are eventually
destroyed. That is why we must examine our own hearts.

God said to Joshua, "I will hand all of them over to Israel,
slain" (Josh. 11:6). I am sure such warfare would not be popular
today. But God alone is sovereign; he does what he pleases, and all
that he does is just. He does everything for his own manifest glory,
and he receives glory in his judgment as well as in his salvation.

The Lord himself did this—the infinite, personal, self-existing,
self-sufficient, almighty covenant God. It was not just Joshua, but
the Lord who threw these mocking, confident, mighty people
into panic and confusion. The Lord himself put to the sword
those who heard but hardened their hearts. Joshua was simply a
delegated authority; those who defied him were, in fact, defying
the Lord. All who oppose God will experience his severity both
here and hereafter.

Surely the Lord is the great warrior. He himself will wage war
against everyone who stubbornly refuses to repent, and he will
win. We need to rid our minds of all wrong theology and return to
the reality of the Scriptures. We must fear God, understanding his
severity as well as his kindness.

JUNE 6

Trust in the LORD with all your heart and lean not on your own understanding; in all your ways acknowledge him, and he will make your paths straight. —Proverbs 3:5–6

roverbs 3:5–6 speaks about spiritual counseling, which means applying God's word to every aspect of our lives and to every situation in our lives. If we are Christians, then our lives will be regulated by the word of God in its entirety. In everything, God has something to say—whom to marry, what job to accept, where to live, what to buy. All of life must be brought under the divine counsel of God's word. Biblical counseling is thus putting into the minds of people the relevant word of God so that they may hear and do it. All authentic Christians will live their lives by God's word.

The counselor himself must be a true born-again Christian and thoroughly trained in the word of God. Moreover, the counselor must be living a biblical life of obedience to God. He must also be a Holy Spirit-filled person, so that he will be confident, bold, unafraid, and no respecter of persons. He is speaking the truth with God-given authority, so what he declares should be asserted with conviction.

The counselee must also be born of God. If the counselee is not born again, then the counselor should first speak the gospel to that person and command the individual to repent and trust in Jesus Christ alone to be saved. Thus, their relationship initially should be one of evangelism.

The Christian counselee ought to be seeking to know the word of God in order to do it, for that is what a disciple does. He trusts in the Lord with all his heart and refuses to lean on his own understanding. Our own understanding, our own unaided reason, is opposed to the will of God as made known in the Bible, and leads to death. A Christian must say, "No, I don't trust my own unaided, fallen reason; I want God's word to tell me how to live."

Thus, the proper way to come for counsel is: "I have abandoned my own ideas, my own plans, and my own purposes. I want to hear what God has to say, and I will do it no matter what it costs me, because I am a Christian. I understand that God's words will make my paths straight and lead me to life."

JUNE 7

They came to Philip, who was from Bethsaida in Galilee, with a request.
"Sir," they said, "we would like to see Jesus." —John 12:21

 n John 12, we read about some Greeks who were in Jerusalem for the Feast of Passover. They were among the many people, Jews as well as Gentiles, from throughout the Roman Empire who had come to Jerusalem to celebrate the Passover festival and worship at the temple.

No doubt they had also heard many reports about Jesus, including the recent news that he had raised Lazarus of Bethany from the dead. Accordingly, they came to one of Jesus' disciples, Philip, with a request: "Sir, we have a great desire to see Jesus."

Though they were not Jews, these God-fearing Greeks wanted to see Jesus. They approached Philip, probably because he was from Bethsaida, which bordered their own Gentile towns, and because Philip was probably bilingual and spoke the Greek language. When Philip heard the request of the Greeks, he went to another apostle, Andrew, and together they took the inquiry of these Gentiles to Jesus.

The apostle John presents Philip as a person like us—of just average intelligence and not much of a problem-solver. It was Philip who would say to Jesus, "Lord, show us the Father and that will be enough for us." What was Jesus' response? Jesus mildly rebuked Philip, saying, "Don't you know me, Philip, even after I have been among you such a long time? Anyone who has seen me has seen the Father" (John 14:9). Nevertheless, I am glad that Jesus deliberately chose Philip, for it gives us hope. Philip was certainly a Mr. Ordinary, but the Lord Jesus Christ chose him, Mr. Ordinary, as his apostle. Let me assure you, God delights to do great things through ordinary people. He chooses the nobodies of the world and makes them into somebodies for his own purpose and glory.

What is God's purpose for us? There are Greeks in our time crying out, "We would like to meet with Jesus, the friend of sinners and publicans." They are crying out to us, who are the Philips and Andrews of this world—average, ordinary Christians, disciples of Christ. But though we are ordinary and average, God has given us a profound mission: As the light of the world, we have an obligation to bring these Gentiles to meet their Savior.

JUNE 8

At the end of your life you will groan, when your flesh and body are spent. —Proverbs 5:11

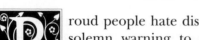

Proud people hate discipline. Proverbs 5 gives a most solemn warning to all who remain stubborn and refuse correction. Nursing homes are filled with such people, and at three o'clock in the morning you can hear their groaning, their pain, and their misery—not only physical, but psychological—because they wasted the years God gave them. They are looking back with anguish and regret, and they cannot sleep.

As we grow older, we will all look back. We will ask ourselves, "How did I do in my life?" And if we are not careful to lead a godly life now, we too shall groan, "I should have listened to my father and mother, to my teachers, to my pastor. I should have worked harder. I should have eaten less. I should not have wasted my money and my time. I should have loved God more wholeheartedly." We thought we had more important things to do. We thought we knew better. But we cannot go back; it is finished now.

A life consumed by the pleasures of sin is a wasted life, a spent life. It is a life used up in the service of the devil rather than in the service of Christ. It is a life that results in great loss and anticipates certain judgment and condemnation when Christ returns. It is a life of regret. The most profound and irremediable regret, however, is that experienced by the rebellious in hell. They will be looking back for all eternity with an unspeakable anguish that shall never be extinguished.

Today, though, you are still among the living. Therefore I exhort you, listen to instruction. Study the word of God, and do what God tells you. Honor your parents. Work hard. If you have been wasting your life in sin, repent now! Today you can escape folly. "Now is the accepted time, now is the day of salvation."

In the service of Christ, there is no regret; we are filled with his joy now and forever. "I am happy in the service of the King." Let us, therefore, redeem the time we have been given by serving God in our generation. It is indeed a glorious thing to be spent, if we are spent in the cause of Christ.

You may ask me for anything in my name, and I will do it. —John 14:14

n John's gospel we find the phrase "in my name" seven times (John 14:13, 14, 26; 15:16; 16:23, 24, 26). We are to pray in the name of Jesus Christ only. Every prayer not prayed in his name will not be answered by our heavenly Father.

What does it mean to pray "in my name"? First, we must come as Christians, as those who have believed on the name of Jesus Christ and entrusted themselves to him in loving, self-abandoning faith. We must come before God the Father in the name of our mediator kinsman/redeemer, who is also our sinless, sympathizing high priest, and in whom alone salvation is to be found. In spite of all the religions and cults proliferating today, the truth is, "Salvation is found in no one else, for there is no other name under heaven given to men by which we must be saved" (Acts 4:12).

But God does not hear the prayer of a sinning Christian. "In Jesus' name" is more than an appellation or formula. We must live in accordance with the person and work of Christ. We cannot come into the presence of God if we are not living holy lives.

To pray in the name of Jesus is to pray as Jesus himself prayed: "Not my will but thine be done." We should not pray for anything the Son himself would not pray for. To pray in his name thus means to pray by his express authority and in agreement with the Holy Scriptures. Our prayer should not be outside of his name, his revelation, and his will as revealed in the Bible.

We must pray according to God's plan and purpose. What is God's plan for us until Jesus Christ returns? It is the evangelization of the world and the building up of his church by making disciples and teaching them to obey God. A prayer to God the Father in the name of Jesus Christ for the fulfillment of this purpose will surely be answered.

What an amazing privilege we have been granted! May we therefore pray to God with boldness and confidence, in the name of Jesus, having had our robes washed and made white in the blood of the Lamb, our Lord and Savior Jesus Christ.

Remain in me, and I will remain in you. No branch can bear fruit by itself; it must remain in the vine. —John 15:4

biding is the secret to fruit bearing. In fact, in John 15, the word "fruit" appears eight times and "abide" or "remain" about ten times. Do you want to produce more fruit in your Christian life? You must abide in Christ. God does not want us to be independent, for independence results only in barrenness.

Some people say they are Christians but do not go to church. They have no connections. They are just doing their own thing, and, as a consequence, their lives are barren and fruitless. Their Christianity is in name only, and they do not glorify God.

"Abide" is a command given to those who are truly united with Christ. Only Christians can abide. Abiding means dependence on Christ, and it has both an active and a passive component.

Abiding is active in this sense: we are to live our daily lives in such a way that we receive the grace we need from God's throne of grace. What are some of the means of grace? Prayerful, regular, obedient study of God's word is of first importance. Jesus taught his disciples that blessing comes "if you abide in me and my words abide in you" (v. 7). Regular prayer and worship, both private and corporate, is also essential. Sitting under the preached word and listening to the counsel of godly brothers and sisters are further means of grace for us. Finally, we ought to fellowship with God's people regularly.

In another sense, the call to abide in Christ requires us to be passive. We abide in Christ so that we can do what God wants us to do through his enabling strength. Abiding in this sense is ceasing from our own efforts. Those who are self-confident will look to themselves for their competence; only those who are weak and tired will abide.

Spiritual vitality and fruitfulness are the result of such abiding. And we will discover the truth of the paradox that when we are weak, then we are strong, for God's strength is made complete in our weakness (2 Cor. 12:9–10). We come to God in weakness, and he pours into us his strength. That is what the Christian life is all about: He is the vine; we are the branches. And he enables us to bear much fruit that will last to the glory of God.

JUNE 11

Now this is eternal life: that they may know you, the only true God, and
Jesus Christ, whom you have sent. —John 17:3

n Jesus Christ's high priestly prayer in John 17, eternal life is defined in a new way—as the knowledge of the only true God, and Jesus Christ his Son. There are various kinds of knowledge; we must therefore be careful to understand what Jesus means by his statement in verse 3. There is knowledge in the sense of awareness. Many people have a foggy notion of God, Jesus, and the Bible, but that is not eternal life. Through general revelation, people have a certain knowledge of God as they behold his creation. As they defy God by sinning, they have an awareness of him in the depths of their being, in their consciences, but that does not mean they are saved. Mere awareness does not save anybody; it simply leaves them guilty and without excuse.

There is another kind of knowledge called information. Unbelieving theologians, for example, are quite able to talk about the Bible, but that does not mean that they are born again. Information alone will not make anyone a Christian. There are hundreds of theologians throughout the world who are not saved.

Then there is the knowledge known as experience. When we see the Grand Canyon, we are overwhelmed by its spectacular grandeur and beauty, and praise its awesome Creator. We may well experience something profound and moving as we gaze upon it, but that is not the same as knowing God. It is not eternal life.

Finally, there is real, relational, saving knowledge of the true and only God. Such knowledge occurs only where the Holy Spirit is at work in our souls. It results in a personal encounter with God in which, because of his holiness, we become aware of our sin and turn to him for forgiveness and salvation. We cry out, "Help me, O Lord! Save me! Rescue me from darkness and bring me into your marvelous light."

We see this throughout the Scriptures—consider the examples of Isaiah (Isa. 6), Peter (Luke 5), or John (Rev. 1). Saving knowledge of God necessarily includes a profound knowledge of our lostness, need, alienation, and sinfulness. Thanks be to God, when we cry out, "Have mercy on me, a sinner!" he receives us and forgives our sin. This is true knowledge of God. This is eternal life.

Tell the Israelites to designate the cities of refuge . . . so that anyone who kills a person accidentally and unintentionally may flee there and find protection from the avenger of blood. —Joshua 20:2–3

oshua 20 speaks about the cities of refuge. Provision was made in Old Testament Israel for sparing the life of one who had killed a person accidentally, without premeditation. The avenger of blood, the nearest male relative of the victim, would typically pursue the perpetrator with the intent to exact vengeance, and he would not necessarily differentiate between intentional and unintentional killing. So God required Israel to set apart six cities of refuge to which one who unintentionally killed another could flee and be safe.

These cities were to be centrally located and built on high places so they could be easily seen and accessed by all. Their gates were always unlocked. God told Moses to build roads so that people could reach them safely.

The cities of refuge were given by the Israelites to the Levites who served God, and were stocked with all provisions necessary for the refugees. When the refugee reached the city, he had to stop at the gates and present his case to the court of elders. After a preliminary hearing, he would be given conditional asylum. Then the authorities were required to establish the circumstances of the killing. If the killing was proven by the testimonies of two or more witnesses to be unintentional, the refugee was permitted to stay in the city until the death of the high priest.

These cities of refuge point to Jesus Christ, who is the true city of refuge to which every sinner can flee and be safe, not from physical death, but from eternal death. All can find refuge in him—not only those who have sinned unintentionally, but also those who have sinned intentionally.

No longer do we need to run to a sacred geographical city to be saved. We need only look to the cross and cry out to the risen Christ. The Bible guarantees that all who call upon the name of the Lord will be saved. As we look to Jesus and entrust ourselves to him, we shall be saved from the justice, wrath, and condemnation that pursue us. And just as the refugees found adequate provision in their cities of refuge, we too will find more than sufficient provision in Jesus Christ. He is our eternal dwelling place.

JUNE 13

Finally Pilate handed him over to them to be crucified. —John 19:16

Anyone with a logical mind will have a problem with this statement found in John 19:16. Here is a completely innocent man, and yet he is being handed over to be crucified. Not only so, but the Scriptures elsewhere make clear that this was done by the determinate counsel and foreordination of God. It was both God's eternal purpose and man's culpable action. These two seemingly irreconcilable truths converged in the most important event in human history: The innocent Jesus was handed over by Pilate to the mob to be crucified.

The Roman soldiers now took charge, for it was their duty to crucify Jesus. Carrying his own cross, Jesus went out to the place of the Skull, and "here they crucified him" (v. 18). No detailed description is given in any of the gospels. The evangelists do not try to manipulate our emotions by describing the details of crucifixion. It is simply stated that the soldiers crucified him. They took hold of the eternal Son of God, who had taken on human nature, and nailed him to the cross.

We must never forget that this handing over of the Lord Jesus to crucifixion, the piercing of his hands and feet, was prophesied long ago. Psalm 22 is one of the key passages that speaks about the suffering of the promised Messiah. We can imagine that as Jesus walked to the hill of Calvary, he was meditating on this psalm written one thousand years earlier.

Psalm 22 speaks of being surrounded by dogs, bulls, and roaring lions—people who by their brutish behavior had sunk to the level of beasts. A band of evil men encircled him and, as we read in the psalm, "They have pierced my hands and my feet" (Ps. 22:16). Crucifixion was not the way of execution for the Jewish people, and yet a thousand years before the death of Christ, it was prophesied. On Good Friday, this word of God received its gory fulfillment.

As we reflect on Calvary, what great comfort we have knowing that our salvation was planned long ago by our sovereign God. And what great gratitude should be ours when we consider the price Jesus paid that we might be redeemed. Jesus, the innocent Lamb of God, was handed over to death for our sins.

JUNE 14

But if you turn away and ally yourselves with the survivors of these nations that remain among you . . . then you may be sure that the LORD your God will no longer drive out these nations before you. —Joshua 23:12–13

n both the Old and New Testaments, God commands his people to separate themselves from the pagan world. We are not to conform to the pattern of this world, for we are the light of the world. So in Joshua 23, Joshua told the people, "Do not associate with these nations that remain among you; do not invoke the names of their gods or swear by them." That would be idolatry. God had left some of the nations in the land to test his people, to see whether they would demonstrate their love for him by serving and worshiping him only.

In verses 12–13, Joshua went on to issue a strong warning to the Israelites, a divine threat of covenant sanctions that the people would, in fact, experience in subsequent years. Consider, for example, the case of King Solomon. He rejected the biblical mandate to be separate and holy; instead, he became fascinated with pagan women. What was the outcome? His kingdom was torn in two. We must be careful not to associate with paganism, whether the outright paganism of the world, or the more subtle variety found in many of today's evangelical churches, where the emphasis is on entertainment and affluence rather than the word of God.

In Numbers 23:9, we find Balaam, though himself a pagan, declaring this truth about God's people: "I see a people who live apart and do not consider themselves one of the nations." This is divine separation. Christians are to be in the world but not of the world.

In 2 Corinthians 6:14–18, the apostle Paul exhorts the church, "Do not be yoked together with unbelievers." This applies to unbelievers in the world as well as unbelievers in the church. Then he asks, "For what do righteousness and wickedness have in common?" What is the expected answer? Nothing! "What fellowship can light have with darkness?" None! "Therefore come out from them and be separate, says the Lord. Touch no unclean thing, and I will receive you." In all generations, God's people are to be separate, holy unto their covenant Lord. "Be ye holy, for I am holy," says the Lord.

JUNE 15

But if serving the LORD seems undesirable to you, then choose for yourselves this day whom you will serve. —Joshua 24:15

e must decide this day whom we should serve, just as the people of Israel did in Joshua 24. Do not be deceived—not to choose is to decide in favor of idols, in favor of false gods, in favor of the devil, in favor of a sinful lifestyle that leads to self-destruction. We must be careful to choose correctly, because our choice will have lasting consequences, whether blessing or curse, both here and hereafter. This is an abiding principle in the history of redemption, found in both the Old and New Testaments.

Our choices affect not only this temporal life; the decisions we make now will determine whether we enter into eternal life or eternal damnation. It is that serious. As thinking, rational beings, we must make wise, informed decisions. We must know who the Lord is and who the devil is, and we must decide between the two. It is either God or the devil. There is no third way. It should not be difficult to choose between the devil and the Sovereign Lord, Creator, Redeemer, and Eternal Judge of all the earth. What have false gods ever done for us? What is the historical prologue of the devil? Simply one loss after another.

The devil uses the lure of sin to deceive and destroy his victims. Sin does nothing to build us up. It ruins us physically, emotionally, economically, and spiritually. It says alluringly, "If it feels good, do it!" And like a fish swallowing the bait, we are caught and destroyed.

Joshua, however, chose the Lord once for all while he was in Egypt, after hearing Moses proclaim the good news that God was going to redeem his people. In like manner, every true Christian makes such a once-for-all choice the moment he savingly trusts in Jesus Christ.

Joshua also chose God moment by moment. That must be true of us as well. We have to choose daily to do the will of God over against the will of the devil. Joshua chose to follow the Lord wholeheartedly all his life. He loved the Lord and served him, never murmuring and always obeying. What a blessing to reach old age and still be able to say along with this hero of the faith, "As for me and my household, we will serve the Lord!"

You say, "I am rich; I have acquired wealth and do not need a thing."
But you do not realize that you are wretched, pitiful, poor, blind and
naked. —Revelation 3:17

s the sovereign, omniscient Lord walks among the
churches, he sees right through every person. In
Revelation 2 and 3, he uses the expression "I know"
ten times. Our God never judges by mere outward
appearances. His eyes are like blazing fire. He looks into our
hearts, sees the reality, and speaks truth.

In Revelation 3:15, the Lord brings reality to the church of
Laodicea, saying, "I know your deeds." It is like the evaluation
given to King Belshazzar in Daniel 5:27: "You have been weighed
on the scales and found wanting."

True saving faith always involves self-abnegation and utter
dependence on Jesus. But the wealthy Laodiceans thought,
"We don't need anything." In fact, the city was so rich that after
experiencing an earthquake in AD 60, the citizens refused to
accept the large sum of money Rome sent to help them, choosing
instead to rebuild the city by themselves. This was their attitude:
"We don't depend on anyone."

This attitude infected their church as well. Jesus quotes them
as saying, "I am rich," speaking of their material wealth. Then,
tellingly, they said, "I do not need a thing," meaning "I don't really
need Jesus Christ." This church was behaving like the fool of Luke
12, who said to himself, "I am rich; I will eat, drink, and enjoy the
good life for a long time."

The Laodiceans, clearly, were completely ignorant of spiritual
reality. What was the truth? We see it in the Lord's rebuke. He
condemned them and called them pitiful, blind, wretched beggars.

Self-esteem is a lie. The opinion these people had of themselves
was one hundred percent wrong. So the Lord counseled them,
"Buy from me." Jesus alone has what we need, which is forgiveness,
righteousness and salvation. We cannot buy it from anyone else.
In Isaiah 55:1 he says, "Come, all you who are thirsty, come to the
waters; and you who have no money, come, buy and eat." Yes, we
are wretched, pitiable, poor, blind, and naked, and this salvation
is costly. In fact, it is priceless; no one can purchase it. Praise be
to God that the gift of God is eternal life in Christ Jesus our Lord.

You are worthy to take the scroll and to open its seals, because you were slain, and with your blood you purchased men for God. . . . You have made them to be a kingdom and priests to serve our God, and they will reign on the earth. —Revelation 5:9–10

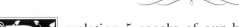

evelation 5 speaks of our kinsman/redeemer, Jesus Christ, who redeemed us and set us free forever from our slavery to sin and Satan by paying a ransom. Mark 10:45 tells us, "The Son of Man did not come to be served, but to serve, and to give his life as a ransom for many." Sin no longer has dominion over us; the devil cannot harm us. We have been set free!

What was the ransom price paid for our release? Peter tells us: "For you know that it was not with perishable things such as silver or gold that you were redeemed from the empty way of life handed down to you from your forefathers, but with the precious blood of Christ" (1 Pet. 1:18–19). Paul said the same thing to the elders of the church of Ephesus: "Be shepherds of the church of God, which he bought with his own blood" (Acts 20:28).

What was the purpose behind this purchase? We are told, "With your blood you purchased men for God" (v. 9). God did not redeem us so that we can be autonomous and unaccountable. No, we have been purchased for God, meaning we belong to God, and we are to obey him because we are his inheritance and portion. We are a peculiar people, a people of God's own possession (1 Pet. 2:9). The Lord has redeemed us so that we may serve him, our new master, with great delight forever. Paul understood this and explained to the church at Corinth: "Do you not know that your body is a temple of the Holy Spirit, who is in you, whom you have received from God? You are not your own; you were bought at a price. Therefore honor God with your body" (1 Cor. 6:19–20).

We are told these people were purchased "from every tribe and language and people and nation." Notice, Jesus did not purchase all men without exception, but he did purchase people from all nations and backgrounds without distinction. The church is an international body, without national, political, cultural, or racial distinction. Jesus Christ accomplished redemption for all those given to him by the Father to save, and they shall reign with him forever.

When he opened the fifth seal, I saw under the altar the souls of those who had been slain because of the word of God and the testimony they had maintained. —Revelation 6:9

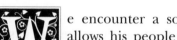

e encounter a sobering fact in Revelation 6: God allows his people to be killed. We ought not to be surprised, though. Jesus himself spelled out the cost of discipleship very clearly: "Any of you who does not give up everything he has cannot be my disciple" (Luke 14:33). Every time the gospel of the Lord Jesus Christ is shared, the evangelist should honestly tell his hearers, "Don't receive Jesus Christ to get away from trouble. You must take up the cross and follow him." The possibility of martyrdom is part and parcel of authentic Christian discipleship.

We read about a number of souls seen under the altar. An altar speaks of sacrifice, and these people sacrificed their lives for Christ. When that last moment came, they said, "I believe in Jesus Christ," and they paid the price by spilling their blood. They truly understood the gospel. Paul himself spoke along these lines: "For I am already being poured out like a drink offering, and the time has come for my departure" (2 Tim. 4:6). God tells us that our lives too should be poured out as a sacrifice—we are to give our entire life to God for his good and glorious purposes.

When a Christian begins to live a life committed to Jesus Christ, all hell breaks loose. The devil opposes us with all his might. The inevitable result is that we will experience the reproach of the world, be increasingly subject to persecution of various kinds, and possibly be killed for the sake of the gospel.

We must notice how these who were called to make the ultimate sacrifice for Jesus Christ address him in this passage. They cry out, "Sovereign Lord, holy and true." The word in Greek means "master" or "owner." In other words, they are saying, "You are the Lord, you own us." Do we see any bitterness here? No! They gave their lives, they spilled their blood, and yet their theology correctly justifies God—he is, and he remains, holy and true.

Undoubtedly there will be many who, in the face of persecution, will become apostate. But God has a remnant in every generation who will prove faithful and true even unto death. May God help us to be counted in that number!

The LORD turned to him and said, "Go in the strength you have and save Israel." —Judges 6:14

od has come to deliver us, to save us, to defeat our enemies, to restore us, to give us peace and eternal life. From the fullness of Jesus, we receive grace upon grace upon grace. It is he who says to us, "Come to me. Baal and Asherah or any other false god cannot help you. Your money cannot help you. Come to me. If you are weary and fed up with your sin, I will give you rest." Let us consider what he said to Gideon in Judges 6.

Gideon had been thinking about the true God of the Scriptures for some time, even though his own father had become a Baal worshiper. God came to Gideon's hole in the ground, to his dunghill, to his hell, where he was threshing wheat. And God said, "The LORD—covenant Lord, the Lord who defeated the Egyptians and the Amorites—is with you, mighty warrior. Gideon, you are a mighty warrior, not in yourself, but because I am with you. I make weak people strong. You are a smiter. You will crush your enemies because I am with you to help you."

God then allowed Gideon to ask three questions. First, he asked, "If the Lord is with us, then why do we have all these troubles?" God responded, "The Israelites failed to keep my covenant stipulations. They disobeyed me, and so I abandoned them. But now I am again with my people."

Then Gideon said, "If God is with us, where are all his wonders our fathers told us about?" He was asking, "Will you again do great wonders for us in our time?" The Lord turned to him, looked straight at him to increase his faith, and said, "Go in the strength you have and save Israel. I am sending you."

Gideon concluded, "How can I save Israel? My clan is the weakest." God told him, "Gideon, the Lord is not seeking the mighty and the best; he is seeking the weakest and the least who will trust in him and obey him."

What the Lord spoke to Gideon, he is speaking to us today: "Go in the strength you have. Fight the good fight, for I, the Lord, am with you. I will strengthen you to live a victorious Christian life."

When the three hundred trumpets sounded, the LORD caused the men throughout the camp to turn on each other with their swords.

—*Judges 7:22*

e read in Judges 7 that the Lord caused the Midianite soldiers to turn on each other. We may conclude that God himself will defeat all his and our enemies. He is not simply saying, "Go and fight the Lord's battles." He is also promising us, "I will go with you and act on your behalf." Our God is around us and above us, underneath us and on either side of us.

Elsewhere the Lord promises, "I will be a wall of fire around you" (Zech. 2:5). We are reminded of the horses and chariots of fire that protected the prophet Elisha (2 Kings 6). Imagine three concentric circles. We are in the innermost one. Next to that, God himself surrounds us with his angels and his fiery chariots. Then comes the outermost circle, the enemy. It is God who is facing the enemy, not us. We may therefore go with great confidence and live the life he commands in the midst of a hostile world.

Gideon had previously asked his divine visitor, "Where is the God of miracles?" not realizing at first that the covenant Lord himself was standing before him. The God of Israel had come to save his people. As in the days of Joshua, the Lord again brought miraculous deliverance and great victory to his people.

We must add faith to this passage and conclude that God will do the same for us in our generation. He will act on our behalf. I believe and serve a God of miracles, a God of wonders, a God who does mighty and unusual things. Friends, believe God. Our God is a Warrior and a Savior. The Lord is with us when we are with him.

God wants to encourage us through the story of Gideon. He is telling us to trust in him and take courage. We are not to go back into a hole and live in fear, threshing out a little wheat, hoping no one will see us. No, get up from that hole! Move out! Fear not! Be strong! Blow the trumpets and light the torches! We too shall witness the divine defeat of the Midianites, those who oppose God's church. Therefore, let us together cry out in faith, "A sword for the Lord and for Gideon!"

*Then another sign appeared in heaven: an enormous red dragon with
seven heads and ten horns and seven crowns on his heads.*
—*Revelation 12:3*

hroughout the Bible there are certain scriptures
that "part the curtain," symbolically disclosing the
spiritual realities behind world and personal history.
We wrestle not only against flesh and blood, but also
against spiritual powers of darkness.

In Revelation 12, we read about an enormous, red dragon
appearing before a woman about to give birth. The woman
represents the church, the true Israel of God, from whom would
come the Messiah. The dragon stands for Satan, a created angel
who has declared war against God. "Red" signifies that he is a
murderer, as Jesus himself taught, who comes only to steal, kill,
and destroy (John 8:44; 10:10).

This dragon has "seven heads," which stands for completeness
of wisdom and understanding. Yet the dragon twists and perverts
the wisdom of God. The "ten horns" speak of power. Do not underestimate the power of this enormous dragon; he is more powerful
than us. Now we understand why we get angry and raise our voices
when we should not. The words we speak in anger come from the
dragon. He uses us as his instrument.

How superficial is our understanding of sin! Sin is unmitigated
evil; it is joining with the dragon in his rebellion. As such, sin is
always directed against God. David prayed, "Against thee, thee only,
have I sinned" (Ps. 51:4, KJV). When we sin, do we understand the
enormity of our actions? Sin has cosmic significance.

The "seven crowns on his heads" point to Satan's arrogation
of authority. They are not legitimate crowns. The dragon takes
unto himself that which does not belong to him. As he positions
himself before the pregnant woman, his purpose is to destroy her
male child—Jesus Christ—who is destined to sit on the throne.

Notice, however, that in spite of the persecution and
opposition that God's people experienced at the hands of their
enemies throughout the many centuries, God's great promise in
Genesis 3, "The seed of the woman shall crush the head of the
serpent," was nevertheless fulfilled. Jesus crushed the very head of
the serpent, triumphing over him by the cross.

A king's rage is like the roar of a lion, but his favor is like dew on the grass. —Proverbs 19:12

odern men are all too often like neutered lions, with claws removed and vocal cords cut out. It is pathetic to see modern men—passive, walking five paces behind. A father should be king in his home.

Marriage is for adults, not children. If you are a husband and father, then it is your responsibility, and yours alone, to provide for your family. This is a biblical mandate.

But there is another responsibility given to the father, which is to rule. A father is to govern. Just providing for his family is not enough. It is sad to see a father feminized and made into an object that simply provides: "Give me, give me, give me." And the wife and the children treat the man with utter contempt. That is not the biblical model.

Proverbs 19:12 compares a leader with a lion. A lion is not the largest animal in the forest, but it rules. It roars. It governs. It demands respect, and it is respected. If you are a father, when you speak, someone should listen and someone must do what you command, because you are in charge. Yes, the father is to provide, but he is also to govern. He is to rule. And when he speaks, all the people under his authority must listen and comply.

Unlike the common Western worldview, in the biblical model the man should roar once in a while. Anger is a proper emotion for a ruler. A father may also smile and do many kind things. But there are times when his face, voice, and tone must change. He must become angry against evil. And proper respect must be accorded to him.

Jesus Christ, who is both Savior and Lord, is our example. He is both the Lamb of God and the Lion of Judah. And no one can be saved without making the good confession, "Jesus is Lord." That is the lion aspect of Jesus. Jesus rules and reigns. He is the sovereign Lord of the universe.

As duly authorized delegated authorities, fathers must also rule their families. Children should not be wild and disobedient. This is the standard of the Scriptures. If your child does not come the first time you call, you are not a lion. You did not roar. So repent, and begin ruling for Jesus Christ.

Then I looked, and there before me was the Lamb, standing on Mount Zion, and with him 144,000 who had his name and his Father's name written on their foreheads. —Revelation 14:1

n Revelation 14, we are given an anticipatory vision that promises us that the future of the church is a glorious one. While the fury of the beast is surely going to be poured out upon those who refuse to worship the antichrist, we may rest assured that God will take care of his people. The vision in this chapter is given for the comfort and hope of God's people.

We first learned of the 144,000 in Revelation 7; there we read that they shall be sealed before God executes his judgment. Whether this number represents only Jews or includes the whole church, we can agree on the fact that they are God's people. Revelation 14 gives us the assurance that every one of these 144,000 shall be saved. Not even one will be missing—God saves everyone whom he has predestinated before the very foundation of the world.

God will never pour out his wrath upon his elect. That is settled. There is no condemnation for those who are in Christ Jesus. But that does not mean that we will not experience the animosity of the devil and his followers. Throughout the centuries, the people of God have indeed been hated, persecuted, and even martyred for their faith.

Let us understand, however, the final destiny of the redeemed people of God. Even at a time when the wrath of the dragon, the antichrist, and the false prophet is being poured out on Christians, the church will not fall apart and disappear. We can take great comfort in the fact that Jesus Christ will have a church for his own possession. Nothing in all creation can frustrate God's eternal purpose. God will take care of his bride.

Notice, people are going to be divided into two camps based on what is written on their foreheads. Every unbeliever is going to be seduced by the antichrist and the false prophet, under the inspiration of the dragon, and he shall receive the mark of the beast. Those who by mercy belong to their Redeemer God, however, shall wear a different mark—the names of Jesus Christ and the Father. May we bear his name faithfully till the end.

Then they gathered the kings together to the place that in Hebrew is called Armageddon. —Revelation 16:16

he book of Revelation will not make any sense unless we believe first in the book of Genesis. Genesis is the foundation for the rest of the Bible, including Revelation. In Genesis 3, we are given God's explanation for the fundamental cause of the world's problems—sin. Here we witness the fall of our first parents; their sin brought God's wrath and curse upon all subsequent generations. Consequently, when we look around, we see sickness, death, war, and man's enmity against man, which fundamentally is enmity against Almighty God.

In Genesis 3, we also encounter the serpent. In Revelation 12:9 he is called the ancient serpent. He is the archenemy of God, and he stirs up hatred in the hearts of human beings against their Creator. All through biblical history we see this evil at work.

This Satanic enmity was finally given full vent at the cross of Calvary. Jesus Christ, who did no harm, was crucified. The ancient serpent animated the hearts of those who cried, "Crucify him, crucify him!" Both Jews and Gentiles killed the Lord of glory. But they could not succeed in destroying our resurrected Lord. Instead, we are told in Hebrews 2:14 that Jesus destroyed the serpent through his death, just as Genesis 3 promised.

Though Satan has been defeated, he continues to be active for now. In fact, he is very active in the book of Revelation. And he is going to engineer a final assault, a last battle, against the Lord Almighty at Armageddon. In Revelation 16, we read that the spirits of demons will go out to the kings of the entire world to gather them for battle on that great day (v. 14).

Chapter 19 will speak more fully about that war. There we will read that the Lord Jesus will come on a white horse with justice, to judge and make war. This is not the meek, all-loving Jesus that liberal ministers tell us about. We must have the right view of Jesus Christ. He does proclaim forgiveness of sins through his ministers, but he also opposes all evil. And he will tread the winepress of the fury of the wrath of God. He is coming again—coming to judge and to conquer all who oppose him.

Train a child in the way he should go, and when he is old he will not turn from it. —Proverbs 22:6

n Proverbs 22 we are told that we must train our children. In other words, our children must become experienced in, or accustomed to, a certain way of life. We are to train them to be experienced in godliness, experienced in God's word, experienced in worship, experienced in Sabbath-keeping, and experienced in hearing and doing.

This is a command, not a suggestion. "Train a child!" It is a condition to be fulfilled by parents. Childhood is a teachable age, and so we must seize this opportunity. We are not called to teach political correctness or psychology; we are to instruct them in God's word. We are to train them to form godly habits. This involves constant and consistent teaching and attention. It includes both theory and practice.

We are careful to train our dogs so that they will be well behaved in the house. Why, then, are we not more serious about training a creature of eternity in godliness? We teach our children to use the toilet, to read and write, and to ride a bicycle. How much more must we lead them in God's ways. Do not withhold biblical instruction, for it alone can open the way to heaven, to eternity, to righteousness, to salvation, to forgiveness of sins. Train them for many years. Training is not a one-day event. Train them until good habits are formed.

We are told to train a child "in the way he should go." Children do not naturally go the way of God. In fact, the word "way" is often used in Proverbs to mean an evil way: the way of sinners, the way of evil, the way of darkness. But this book also speaks about the good way: the way of peace, the way of wisdom, the way of life, the way of the Lord, and the way of righteousness. And when we come to the New Testament, we are told that this good way is Jesus Christ.

Ultimately there are only two ways: the evil way or the good way, the broad way or the narrow way. God counsels us to train our children from infancy to go in God's way of righteousness. He will help us to lead our children in the good way, the way of Jesus, the narrow way that leads to life.

Terrified at her torment, they will stand far off and cry: "Woe! Woe, O great city, O Babylon, city of power! In one hour your doom has come!"
—*Revelation 18:10*

he seventeenth and eighteenth chapters of Revelation concern Babylon and its final destruction. "Babylon" stands not only for a city, but for all worldly resistance to God, for any and every manifestation of godless culture throughout all ages. It thus represents Sodom, Gomorrah, Rome, and every nation that rejects the living and true God.

We are reminded of Egypt of old, whose king once asked, "Who is the LORD, that I should obey him?" People throughout the world are still uttering such words of defiance against the living God. But the book of Revelation assures us that Jesus Christ is going to come again from heaven for the grand finale, when he will manifest his sovereign judgment against every Babylon that defies the reality of the living God, the King of kings and Lord of lords.

And it is not just kingdoms that God opposes; he is against every arrogant man, woman, or child who refuses to bow the knee to his Creator, Sustainer, and Ruler. These chapters make it very clear that God knows every individual and family who attempts to live a life apart from acknowledging and worshipping the triune God. The thrice-holy God cannot and shall not let such treason stand.

How is it that puny man can be so arrogant? According to the text, Babylon was noted for riches and luxury. We read, "The kings of the earth committed adultery with her, and the merchants of the earth grew rich from her excessive luxuries." There is something about great wealth that deceives the heart. The apostle Paul warns against trusting in "uncertain riches." We must be extremely careful: when wealth increases, there is a real danger of trusting in it and bowing down before it while abandoning the living God.

Ultimately, Babylon in its entirety is worldliness. It is trying to find pleasure and joy apart from God. It is saying in our heart, "There is no God." It is folly and, finally, eternal misery. Therefore, come out from Babylon. If it is in any way affecting you, come out now! The Sovereign Lord says, "Be ye separate and I will receive you." Then you shall rejoice with great joy at Christ's second coming. Come, Lord Jesus!

Having put him to sleep on her lap, she called a man to shave off the seven braids of his hair, and so began to subdue him. —Judges 16:19

hen believers play with sin, they are putting their lives in jeopardy. They are behaving like a moth that is attracted to the light of a campfire. If you, as a believer in Jesus Christ, are toying with sin, I warn you: you are engaging in an extremely dangerous action.

Consider the example of Samson, found in Judges 16. He grew up as a Nazirite—a separated one, devoted to God. The Spirit of God came upon him, and he was used to bring deliverance to his people. But notice: "Some time later, he fell in love with a woman in the Valley of Sorek whose name was Delilah" (v. 4). With this, Samson violated God's plain teaching. An Israelite was not supposed to marry a non-Israelite, an unbeliever. But Samson did not pay attention; he went crazy in his head. He threw the Bible out. No one could reason with him.

Samson increasingly indulged his lusts—the lust of the flesh and lust of the eyes. And he increasingly played games with God's power. As he persisted in sin, he grew weaker and weaker. Finally, he revealed the secret of his power to his enemy.

"[Delilah] called, 'Samson, the Philistines are upon you!'" (v. 20). But Samson did not realize his strength was gone. This is what will happen to those who indulge in sin repeatedly, over against the severe warnings of the Holy Spirit, the Holy Scriptures, and the holy church. People stubbornly turn their backs on God and his Scriptures and his church, and then one day they wake up to discover that their wings are singed. They are rendered weak and realize they have been made slaves to the devil, who comes only to steal, kill, and destroy.

Do not think that you can sin and serve God at the same time. It never works. You may fool others, but you cannot fool God; in due time you will be found out. God has a way of exposing our sins in a most painful manner. We engage in a cover-up but it will be proclaimed from the housetops. And it suddenly hits you that you are blinded and shackled. The Spirit of God has left.

Let us be warned. Stay away from Philistine territory. Stay away from Delilah. Heed the prohibitions of the Bible. Fear God and depart from evil.

*The sea gave up the dead that were in it, and death and Hades gave up
the dead that were in them, and each person was judged according to
what he had done. —Revelation 20:13*

hat will be judged on the day of final judgment that we
read about in Revelation 20? All our thoughts, words,
and deeds done while in the body (see Matt. 25:31–46;
2 Cor. 5:10). Did we live our lives in the name of
and for the glory of Jesus Christ? That is the criterion on which
judgment will be based. As finite creatures, our responsibility is
not to indulge ourselves, but to worship our Creator and do his
will. Every word, deed, and motive will be judged by God's perfect,
unchangeable standard.

Who will be judged on the day of final judgment? All people,
including believers in Jesus Christ, will be judged by this same
standard. You may ask, "But isn't salvation by grace through faith?
Why, then, are believers going to stand before the judgment seat
of Christ? Are they not justified by grace through faith and not by
the works of the law?"

What is the answer to these important questions? Believers
must appear before the judgment seat of Christ because this
judgment will reveal whether their faith was genuine, saving faith,
or the false, demonic faith of mere mental assent that is popular in
many churches today. Salvation is by grace through faith, but our
salvation is proved by obedience in good works. Thus, in the same
chapter where Paul wrote, "By grace you have been saved, through
faith," he also said, "For we are God's workmanship, created in
Christ Jesus to do good works, which God prepared in advance for
us to do" (Eph. 2:8, 10). Saving faith in Jesus Christ always issues
in our delightful submission to God's will. Judgment by works,
therefore, will prove whether we had phony or saving faith.

Every man, woman, and child who has ever lived will either be
justified or condemned at the judgment day. And there will be no
possibility of appeal. The Lord Jesus Christ will say to those on his
right, "Come, take your inheritance. You are justified because you
trusted in the gospel and you lived your life in obedience to me."
Then he will say to those on his left, "Depart from me, you who are
cursed. You are condemned because you did not keep my law nor
did you repent and believe on my name."

JUNE 29

Nothing impure will ever enter it, nor will anyone who does what is shameful or deceitful, but only those whose names are written in the Lamb's book of life. —Revelation 21:27

esus promised us that the world will hate us. "If the world hates you," he told his disciples, "keep in mind that it hated me first. If you belonged to the world, it would love you as its own. As it is, you do not belong to the world, but I have chosen you out of the world. That is why the world hates you" (John 15:18–19). We are not of the world; we do not share its philosophies and values. Therefore, do not be surprised when the world opposes you—you no longer belong to it!

But, thank God, we are part of something much greater. The last two chapters of Revelation tell us that though we are outsiders in the eyes of the world, we are inside the kingdom of God. We read in Revelation 22:14, "Blessed are those who wash their robes, that they may have the right to the tree of life and may go through the gates into the city." We may go into the city of God, where there is everlasting fullness of joy, because we belong. Not only so, but we are also told that many of those who consider themselves to be "insiders" now will be outside then: "Outside are the dogs, those who practice magic arts, the sexually immoral, the murderers, the idolaters and everyone who loves and practices falsehood" (Rev. 22:15).

There is an outside and an inside to the city of God, and all of God's elect throughout all ages are inside. In fact, in one sense we are already inside the city, for every believer is "in Christ." And nothing in all the world will be able to separate us from this love of God that is in Christ Jesus our Lord. We may be hated, slandered, and despised by the world, but our God will never leave us nor forsake us.

There is coming a new heaven and a new earth to be populated by a new people—the people of God. We will not be strangers there. Every tear will be wiped away, and God triune will dwell with us and we with him forever and ever. Brothers and sisters, this is our future—joy unspeakable and full of glory.

Let him who does wrong continue to do wrong; let him who is vile continue to be vile; let him who does right continue to do right; and let him who is holy continue to be holy. —Revelation 22:11

n Revelation 22, the last chapter in the Bible, the angel instructs John, "Do not seal up the words of the prophecy of this book, because the time is near." This is a word for everyone—the time is near! Only the fool thinks he has plenty of time left. God is not obligated to let us live many years. If we live one day more, it is by the sheer mercy of God. The time is near for Jesus to return or for us to die. The time is near.

In verse 11, we encounter a perplexing exhortation: "Let him who does wrong continue to do wrong." That does not sound right. We plead with people to do right, but here we discern an entirely different tone. God is saying, "Do you like evil? Then go ahead and keep doing it." God, who is the King of kings, never begs. God, the only Sovereign Lord, commands the old and the young, men and women, people of all nations, rich and poor, educated and uneducated. He commands all people everywhere to repent.

If someone responds to God's summons with the arrogant retort, "I don't want to repent," he will say, "Fine; continue to do wrong and be vile." That means he has handed that person over. He has locked him up and thrown away the key. He will be given no more sobering words. Three times in the book of Romans this phrase appears: "God gave them over." God gives stubborn rebels over to their own depravity, rebellion, and wickedness. If you are sinning again and again, then be very afraid—you have been abandoned.

Thanks be to God, this is not the only word that we read in this passage. People are divided into two groups. Some are told to continue to do evil, but those belonging to the Lord are told, "Let him who does right continue to do right; and let him who is holy continue to be holy." That is the word for God's redeemed people. Jesus died on the cross for this one purpose: "to redeem us from lawlessness and to purify for himself a people that are his very own, eager to do what is good" (Titus 2:14). Therefore, as those who belong to him, let us be faithful unto death.

July 1

He who conceals his sins does not prosper. —Proverbs 28:13

rue confession of faith is always accompanied by confession of sin. As a Christian declares his faith in Jesus Christ, he will also necessarily admit his sin and guilt before God.

Due to our sinful nature, the first thing we instinctively want to do after we sin is to conceal it. King David did this prior to feeling God's heavy hand upon him. But God helped him to change, and David declared, "Then I acknowledged my sin to you and did not cover up my iniquity. I said, 'I will confess my transgressions to the LORD,' and you forgave the guilt of my sin" (Ps. 32:5).

Concealing is the opposite of confession. But Proverbs 28:13 tells us, "He who conceals his sins does not prosper." Such a person will remain a failure; he can never succeed. Are you concealing your sin? If so, you will not prosper.

Concealing sin finally leads to death, as Joshua 7 illustrates. Achan was an Israelite who clearly knew God's will, but he disregarded it. When he saw a beautiful Babylonian garment and some silver and gold in Jericho, he coveted them, took them, hid them, and refused to confess. No one, however, can conceal anything from God's sight. Achan was exposed by God's intervention, and his unwilling confession did not result in mercy. Rather, when Achan's guilt was exposed, the Israelites stoned him to death in administration of divine justice.

Willing confession, born of the Holy Spirit's convicting work in the soul, is the prelude to and condition for forgiveness. Such confession always involves forsaking and renouncing our sins. We cannot come to God and continue to be greedy or a liar or a thief or a homosexual or an adulterer. True repentance means turning away from evil and turning to God.

The Bible has no Plan B that will allow us to come to God while continuing in sin. That is a false gospel. We must forsake all sin. When Jacob went to Bethel to worship Yahweh, he acted in accordance with this principle. He instructed his household, "Get rid of all your idols," and they left them behind (Gen. 35:2).

Therefore, what should you do? Confess your sins and prosper. Confess your sins and enjoy divine liberation from all shackles. Confess your sins and live!

At that moment heaven was opened, and he saw the Spirit of God descending like a dove and lighting on him. —Matthew 3:16

n Matthew 3, we read about the baptism of Jesus. Have you ever wondered why Jesus was baptized by John the Baptist? Why would the sinless Son of God have to go into the desert to be baptized by one who was baptizing people for the forgiveness of their sins?

Jesus submitted to John's baptism in order to fulfill God's righteous requirements. He was the true Israelite who would, as our representative, fulfill all righteousness and obey all God's laws perfectly. This One, who was without sin, identified with sinners and became our substitute, the head of a glorious new humanity.

By receiving John's baptism, Jesus was also announcing that the Messiah would soon be baptized with a baptism of suffering, which would take away the sin of the world. His baptism was thus pointing to the violent death of the cross. Jesus knew from the outset that he came to die. Now he was publicly declaring to the Father and to the world that he was in complete submission to the will of God.

John's baptism of Jesus marked the beginning of Jesus' messianic journey to the cross, where he would suffer the pains of hell on behalf of his people. As he prayed, the Holy Spirit came down in the visible form of a dove. In order to fully complete this most difficult task, Jesus would need the Holy Spirit to come upon him without measure, strengthening, encouraging, and guiding him in his human nature.

After his baptism, Jesus received consolation and comfort from the first Person of the Trinity, God the Father. After the descent of the Holy Spirit, the voice of the Father came from heaven, saying, "This is my Son, whom I love; with him I am well pleased."

The baptism of Jesus reassures us that salvation is the work of the Trinity. All three Persons of the Godhead are involved in our salvation. The Son assumed the role of a suffering servant. Within three years he would say from the cross, "It is finished," indicating that his work of redemption was complete. The Holy Spirit, who descended upon Jesus, strengthened him and guided him for his mission. And the Father gave his audible approval to his Son, his servant, the one in whom his plan for our salvation would prosper.

You are the salt of the earth. —Matthew 5:13

y this brief statement in Matthew 5, "You are the salt of the earth," Jesus was warning his disciples to avoid two deadly errors. First, he was insisting that Christians not forsake the world and go into monasteries. Why? Just as salt cannot function as a preservative for meat unless it is rubbed into it, so also Christians are to be in the world so that the world may benefit by their holy lives.

Second, he was saying that Christians must avoid the opposite error of being one with the world and embracing its values and ways. Why? Because the ways of the world are evil. We must be as different from the world as salted meat is from putrid meat. We must be in the world but not of the world, so that the world may be helped by us. We must be different and must glory in that difference.

These warnings are very relevant to us today. I once visited China and talked with university professors there. They were materialists and working very hard to gain the same wealth and consumer goods as Americans. Sadly, today's church members are all too often doing the same thing. Many modern evangelicals have discovered materialism. In fact, many preachers, rather than looking forward to a heaven paved with gold, want their gold and goodies now. But when they preach such a message, they are denying our distinctiveness as the salt of the earth.

When Jesus told his lowly disciples, "You alone are the salt of the earth," this was a high compliment from the lips of the Sovereign Lord of the universe. This statement gives every Christian great dignity and self-esteem. I feel sorry for those who try to be like the world in speech, dress, value, and thought. By trying to conform to the pattern of this world, they are declaring that they are darkness, that they are rotting, that they are not Christians.

If you are a true Christian, you are different from this fallen world. You once were dead in your sins, but now you have been delivered by the power of God and made alive by Jesus Christ. Therefore, let us live as salt for the benefit of this rotting and rotten world.

Be careful not to do your "acts of righteousness" before men, to be seen by them. If you do, you will have no reward from your Father in heaven.
—*Matthew 6:1*

atthew 6 speaks about hypocrisy—not that of unbelievers, but the religious hypocrisy of those in the church. What is the nature of a hypocrite? A hypocrite is a man-pleaser, which is really to say that a hypocrite is a self-pleaser. He is a narcissist who loves, worships, and adores himself. A hypocrite feigns piety. He will perform religious works, such as almsgiving, prayer, and fasting, but they are done to bring glory to himself, not Christ.

The Greek word for hypocrite means "actor." Such a person helps the poor, for example, not because he loves them, but because he wants to be seen by others as a great and generous benefactor. His purpose is to be seen, recognized, and praised by men. He is an egoist who loves only himself.

A hypocrite has no God-consciousness and no regard for God; his life is not regulated by the knowledge of God in any way. Therefore, he is not interested in the heavenly Father's approbation. As a man of this world, the hypocrite seeks the gratification of other people's applause. But Jesus warns hypocrites in this text: "You will not receive any reward from God." The most a hypocrite can receive is the praise of men. And in the end, this is what Jesus will tell every hypocrite: "I never knew you. Away from me, you evildoers!" (Matt. 7:21–23).

What hope is there for a hypocrite? Let me assure you, God loves hypocrites even today. How can I say that? The day of judgment has not yet come. John 3:16 tells us, "Whosoever believes on [Christ] shall not perish but have everlasting life," and I am certain hypocrites are included in that "whosoever."

No man can do God-pleasing acts of righteousness from his heart unless he has been born of God. Only through Jesus Christ can we be delivered from self-centeredness and self-glorification, and begin to glory in Christ and glorify him.

If you realize that you are a hypocrite, I urge you to repent and forsake your sins this day. God will receive you, and you will discover that he gives his children power to live a holy life, a life of righteousness, from a renewed heart.

Not everyone who says to me, "Lord, Lord," will enter the kingdom of heaven, but only he who does the will of my Father who is in heaven.
—Matthew 7:21

atthew 7:21–23 is found at the end of the Sermon on the Mount. These verses constitute one of the most dreadful and terrifying statements to come from the lips of Jesus. An eternal curse is placed, not upon wicked pagans, but upon professors of Christianity. Here the Lord pronounces a sentence of final doom upon all those who all their lives thought they were Christians, but were not.

These phony believers were very confident of easy entry into the kingdom of heaven. They said the right things and engaged in many religious activities. They seemed to have great assurance of their salvation while they lived, and even at the moment of their death. They possessed no doubt that the Judge would welcome them into everlasting happiness. Yet Jesus says that they will not enter.

This is a clear warning to all professing Christians that mere orthodoxy, the confession, "Jesus is Lord," is not enough. Even demons acknowledge that Jesus is Lord, the Holy One of God, and the true God. But there is one thing that demons will not and cannot do. They refuse to submit to God and obey him.

Our conduct, therefore, must match our confession. If we truly have relationship with our heavenly Father, that relationship will produce good works pleasing to him. Those who have been born of God and who have been graciously given the divine righteousness of God, will live righteously before God by the power of the Holy Spirit. Such imputed and imparted righteousness is required for entrance into the kingdom of God. Obedience will not get a person to heaven, but at the same time, no one enters heaven without obedience—Spirit-wrought, Spirit-produced righteousness.

This passage strongly admonishes each of us who call ourselves Christians to make our calling and election sure. We must examine ourselves in the light of Jesus' teaching to see whether we are genuine Christians. If we are true believers, then, on the day of final judgment, we will hear Jesus Christ say, "Come, you who are blessed by my Father; take your inheritance, the kingdom prepared for you since the creation of the world" (Matt. 25:34).

JULY 6

In bitterness of soul Hannah wept much and prayed to the Lord.
—1 Samuel 1:10

n 1 Samuel 1, we read that Elkanah regularly took his whole family to Shiloh to worship, probably to observe the Feast of Tabernacles, the festival celebrating God's care over Israel and his blessings upon a man's crops, cattle, and family. Hannah, being barren, did not have much to celebrate, while her fertile rival, Peninnah, would mock her to her face.

Hannah's distress was so great that, no matter what her husband did, he could not comfort her. But one year, while the family was at Shiloh for worship, Hannah was guided by the Holy Spirit to get up and go to the tabernacle. She was guided to pour out her heart in prayer to the living God of Israel. She began to realize that prayer is power, that prayer prevails, and that prayer is effectual. She told herself, "I know God will hear my prayer and help me when no human being can do so."

Knowing that God was able to open her womb, Hannah prayed to the Lord of hosts. She was not praying to herself, as the Pharisee of Luke 18 did. Hannah prayed to the God of Israel, the God of infinite resources, the God who is beyond compare, the God who is almighty. Hannah believed that God alone was able to help her. She had a real need, so she prayed earnestly and specifically: "O LORD Almighty, if you would only look upon your servant's misery and remember me, and not forget your servant but give her a son" (v. 11).

God heard the cry of Hannah's heart and caused the high priest Eli to pronounce a blessing upon her. After Hannah left the house of the Lord, she lived all her life in the great comfort of the divine benediction she had received. She went home, soon became pregnant, and gave birth to a son. She called the boy Samuel, which can mean, "God hears."

What about you? Are you needy? Are you in trouble? Are you in deep distress, as Hannah was? I counsel you to follow her example. Pour out your soul in fervent prayer to God. Pray with fasting, pray in faith, pray with passion and boldness, pray with perseverance, pray specifically, and pray with thanksgiving, as Hannah did, saying, "My heart rejoices in the LORD."

190

JULY 7

Neither do men pour new wine into old wineskins. If they do, the skins will burst . . . and the wineskins will be ruined. No, they pour the new wine into new wineskins, and both are preserved. —Matthew 9:17

he members of Jesus' audience were very familiar with the use of dried goatskins to store liquids. They also knew that an old wineskin eventually loses its suppleness and expandability and can no longer safely store new, fermenting wine. In our passage, Jesus utilized this well-known fact to speak to the stubbornness of the Judaism of his day. He was, in effect, rebuking the Jews for being hardened in their ways, unwilling to change in response to the demands of the gospel. Instead, the Pharisees expected Jesus to accommodate himself to their religious system.

We, too, can be brittle and hard—we have our own complex of habits. We each have an "empty way of life" handed down to us by our parents and grandparents. Each of us has been trained for many years, and, as a result, we have habits that stubbornly resist change. This is precisely why most people reject the good news of the gospel. They hate Christianity because it will not stamp its approval on them. It calls sin "sin." It insists that sinners abandon their evil ways.

Jesus is teaching us in this parable that the kingdom of God, the gospel, the new wine, cannot be poured into a hardened, brittle complex of habits, views and ideas. Kingdom life is vigorous, powerful, dynamic. It demands radical change in our lives. We don't change the gospel. We don't change the kingdom of God. We don't change the Holy Ghost. The Holy Ghost is committed to changing us to be conformed to the image of Jesus Christ.

Who, then, is ready for the new wine of the kingdom of God? Only those who have been made new creations by the sovereign work of the Holy Spirit. He has come to make the old new. It doesn't matter what our habits have been, how dried and cracked the old wineskins are. The Holy Spirit is mighty to give us new birth and to work in us what is pleasing to him.

The new wine and the new wineskins are compatible; Jesus promised that both will be preserved. Let us therefore make our calling and election sure and then gladly embrace every change that the Word of God and the Spirit of God demand.

For I told him that I would judge his family forever; . . . his sons made themselves contemptible, and he failed to restrain them. —1 Samuel 3:13

t is not good to kick against God and his Scriptures. Fathers, are you working so hard that you neglect God's word? Or are you, like Eli, so busy luxuriating and indulging your children that you do not require them to obey you the first time? If so, you are kicking against God. And if this is true of you, you will soon discover God to be your enemy, and it will not go well for you. If you neglect God and do not honor his word, one day you will be filled with regret.

Fathers, are you functioning as a prophet in your home, representing the Prophet, Jesus Christ? Do you articulate God's word to your family and require obedience to it from them? Are you a priest, representing the High Priest, Jesus Christ to your family? Do you minister to them about salvation through Christ alone? Do you pray and intercede for them? Are you a king, representing the King of kings and Lord of lords? Do you control and restrain your children?

When we worship our children, they become Ichabods—people without glory. But when we worship God and honor him, our children become glorious. Samuel served the Lord under Eli with first-time obedience. We are told he received favor from man and God, and lived in the presence of the covenant Lord. Even though everyone else was living in darkness and apostasy, Samuel enjoyed great communion with the living God, and his fame spread from Dan to Beersheba.

The first verse of 1 Samuel 3 states, "In those days the word of the LORD was rare." The chapter concludes, however, by saying, "The LORD continued to appear at Shiloh, and there he revealed himself to Samuel through his word." The word became plentiful once again.

May we soberly examine our ways. Do we want to enjoy God's favor? If so, let us revere the word of God and the God of the word. May we be delivered from self-indulgence, from gluttony, from the love of this world, and from laziness. May we become people of the Book and practice true, biblical family values, so that we and our children will bring glory to God and, in the process, become glorious ourselves.

At that time Jesus said, "I praise you, Father, Lord of heaven and earth, because you have hidden these things from the wise and learned, and revealed them to little children." —Matthew 11:25

n Matthew 11, we read that Jesus did many mighty miracles in Korazin, Bethsaida, and Capernaum. He taught and healed the people. He performed wonders, revealing to them that he is the Son of God. But they refused to repent and believe in him.

Therefore, Jesus solemnly warned those who heard his preaching and witnessed his deeds that they would be judged more severely than the Sodomites and Tyrians. In other words, those who hear the gospel and refuse to repent and trust in Jesus will face greater judgment. It is a serious matter when people come to the church and refuse to repent and believe on God's Son, whom God has given for the world's salvation.

Though most people in Korazin, Bethsaida, and Capernaum would not repent, God's chosen few did, and their repentance gave Jesus great joy. Accordingly, he thanked his Father. Yet his reasoning may at first be difficult for us to understand. Jesus said, "I praise you, Father, because you have hidden these things from the wise and learned."

Jesus was thanking his Father because he has hidden his salvation from the smart-alecks of the world. That is my translation of "the wise and learned." The self-sufficient have no need for Jesus Christ and treat him with utter contempt. So in God's eternal plan and purpose, he keeps his salvation from them.

God, in his sovereignty and infinite wisdom, hides the message of the gospel from the self-righteous and arrogant, who think they have everything and pretend to be strong. Those who preach the gospel should not be surprised or deflated, therefore, if their listeners refuse to repent. Jesus' surprising statement is recorded in this chapter so that we may be comforted when people oppose our message and reject the offer of salvation.

By divine ordination, the gospel is the fragrance of life to some and the smell of death to others. The little children—those sinners who have been humbled and who acknowledge that they need a Savior—will be blessed. But the proud will remain under a curse. It is mysterious to us, but it is the truth. It is God's good pleasure.

July 10

It was a long time, twenty years in all, that the ark remained at Kiriath Jearim, and all the people of Israel mourned and sought after the LORD.
—*1 Samuel 7:2*

hen God's people become apostate, he abandons them to their own devices, that they might reap the fruit of their sin. In 1 Samuel 7, God had abandoned his people to misery, defeat, confusion, degradation, and oppression. What was the reason for their condition? It was their refusal to keep God's covenant.

How, then, could they get back to the living God? First, they had to recognize their true condition. After twenty years, the people of Israel were finally fed up with their apostasy and the resulting oppression they were experiencing. They'd had it! Let me ask you: Are you fed up with your life of sin, your life of defeat, your life of powerlessness, confusion, and misery? Not everyone will answer, "Yes." There are some worms who thrive in the sewer. But if God has chosen us to be his people, then he will cause us to become disgusted, and we will long for God and begin to seek him.

Has it been twenty years for you? Are you finally fed up with your sin, or do you still want a little more? Young man, young woman, old man, old woman, you must make up your mind today. As the prodigal son grew tired of his miserable condition and began to long for his father's house, so you also must grow sick of your sin. You must come to your senses and realize that sin has brought you not happiness but, rather, great misery.

You must own your sin and openly confess, as the Israelites did, "We have sinned against the Lord." You must also return to the Lord in wholehearted repentance, rid yourself of all idols and every darling sin, and recommit yourself to serve God only. There is no both/and in Christianity. Either we serve God or we serve the devil. Halfhearted worship of the true God is wholehearted worship of idols.

It is not God's intent that we remain in the misery of our own creation. I hope we will realize our folly and long for God as the Israelites did. The way that leads away from God is littered with sorrow and pain. To seek happiness without God is to find only wretchedness and confusion. Happiness is to know, worship, and serve the Lord exclusively.

July 11

Remember your Creator in the days of your youth. —Ecclesiastes 12:1

veryone reading this passage today is surely going to die. And the Bible solemnly affirms that in the end there are only two ways to leave this world. In John 8:21–24, Jesus warns against dying in one's sins; in 1 Thessalonians 4:14, the apostle Paul speaks about falling asleep in Jesus. We thus have a choice: we can either die in our sins or we can die in Jesus Christ.

Ecclesiastes 12 is an Old Testament passage that addresses this all-important subject of death. The book of Ecclesiastes contains the philosophical and theological reflections of an old man. The author was a son of David and king of Jerusalem—probably Solomon—whose life was largely meaningless because he did not rely on God and live in obedience to his word. The old man wrote this letter, not primarily to those who are old and about to die, but to those who are young, so that they can live well throughout all of life. It is God's tract for the conversion of young intellectuals, wherein he confronts them with their comfortable, self-flattering illusions and requires them to face honestly the instability and meaninglessness of a self-centered life.

Solomon had discovered through his own experiences that a life not centered on God is only frustration. Not only so, but he also warned, "God will bring every deed into judgment" (v. 14). Many centuries later, Jesus himself would ask, "What does it profit a man if he gains the whole world but loses his soul?"

To die well, then, we must live well. But what does it mean to live well? The author of Ecclesiastes concludes, "Fear God and keep his commandments, for this is the whole duty of man." God now commands everyone to repent and believe in his Son. Therefore, to live well is to live by faith in Jesus Christ. A meaningful life is a life in which one looks to God as the ultimate standard and point of reference. Life's *summum bonum* is to glorify God and to enjoy him forever. To view personal happiness as life's greatest good is sheer folly. We are truly happy only when we have surrendered to Jesus Christ and know that we will fall asleep in him.

As evening approached, the disciples came to him and said, "This is a remote place, and it's already getting late. Send the crowds away, so they can go to the villages and buy themselves some food." —Matthew 14:15

here are two ways people try to solve problems. First is the way of the natural man. We begin by sizing up the problem. In Matthew 14, we read that there were five thousand men plus women and children, so we would take that fact into our accounting. Next, we notice it is a desolate, solitary place and there are no shops. Third, we look at our purses and determine that we have no money. Next, we look at the time— it is gone. So our conclusion, if we are Jesus's disciples, is that we cannot feed the crowd. We will say, "Jesus, you need to send these people away hungry. Let them go while there is still some daylight left. You gave us this problem to solve, we looked at everything, and this is our conclusion: There is no solution here."

This is the way people most often try to address their issues: they calculate and reason and take everything into account except God, who is with them in the person of Jesus Christ. This represents the height of unbelief. Yet this problem-solving method is common even among Christians who believe in the Bible and go to church. Remember the ten spies who came to Moses after spying the Promised Land? They reported, "It is a good land; it flows with milk and honey. But we cannot go in and defeat the people because they are stronger than we are. Compared to them, we are grasshoppers." These spies surveyed and calculated and came to a seemingly logical conclusion. But unbelieving human reason always fails because it leaves out the infinite, almighty, omniscient Creator and Sustainer of the universe.

This is our failing too. That is why we are often anxious, fearful, angry, and frustrated. And so the disciples counseled Jesus, "With our resources we cannot feed them—no one can. And we want to point out that it is late. So, please, send them away."

People are supposed to come to Jesus for solutions, but here the disciples wanted the crowd to go away. They failed because of unbelief. It is only when we have faith that we see Christ the Lord ruling and reigning. Let us bring our five loaves and two fish to him. Then we can watch him feed the five thousand with them.

The woman came and knelt before him. "Lord, help me!" she said.
            —Matthew 15:25

hat does authentic, saving faith look like? In Matthew 15, the Canaanite woman gives us a beautiful portrait. She came through the trial of her faith successfully. No one could get her to stop asking Jesus for help. She kept on crying out and worshiping. Despite the initial "No," she believed Jesus would help her. First, then, faith's mouth cannot be stopped; it ever cries out to the Lord.

Second, authentic faith agrees with the word of God that says we are sinners dead in trespasses and sin. In other words, it wholeheartedly embraces the declaration that we are dogs, Canaanites, unrighteous, filthy, lost, miserable, and wretched. Real faith says, "That's exactly right. That's a description of me." Those who are pretenders will be offended, get angry, and go away.

If we will not acknowledge that we are totally lost and depraved sinners in our minds, emotions, and wills, then Jesus cannot help us. Why? He is in the business of raising only the dead. He saves only sinners. The man who proudly clothes himself with his own righteousness will never receive any blessing from Jesus Christ.

Third, faith argues and reasons. But we must make sure our arguments are biblically sound. In Mark 7, we learn that Jesus had said to the woman, "The children must first be fed." And this woman reasoned by faith that "first" means there will be a second. Jesus did not say, "I will never help you." There was hope.

The woman agreed that she was a dog, but pointed out that even a dog must be fed. And she must have noticed that Jesus did not use the Greek word for wild dogs, but the word for pet dogs who lived in the house and played with the children. While their owners ate their meal, these pet dogs were allowed to lick up what was spilled under the table.

So she said in all humility, "I don't need a whole loaf. All I need is a crumb." A crumb from the hand of Christ is more than sufficient to meet our every need. Yet he never gives us just a crumb. In response to our living, saving faith, he gives us himself. This woman had such faith, and Jesus healed her daughter.

This is my Son, whom I love; with him I am well pleased. Listen to him!
—Matthew 17:5

ust before Jesus' transfiguration, Peter had told Jesus, "You are the Christ, the Son of the living God" (Matt. 16:16). This revelation was given to Peter by God the Father. In response to Peter's confession, Jesus taught his disciples that he was soon going to Jerusalem to suffer many things, be killed, and on the third day be raised to life again. All of this had been eternally ordained by God, and Jesus knew it was God's will for him.

Peter, however, could not bear the thought of a suffering Messiah. In rebellion against God's plan, he rebuked Jesus for speaking about his death. Jesus, in turn, reproved Peter severely and said his disciples must deny themselves, take up the cross daily, and follow him to death, losing their lives in order to gain them when he returns in power and great glory.

So in Matthew 17, Jesus did something to encourage his disciples. He took Peter, James, and John to a high mountain and gave them a preview of the glory that was to follow his suffering on the cross. There, for a brief time, Jesus' body shone with the light and resplendence of his heavenly divinity.

Once again, Peter spoke without thought: "Lord, it is good for us to be here" (v. 4). He preferred basking in the glory of God on the mountaintop to going down to Jerusalem with Jesus and resuming a life which, in time, would lead also to his own death. So God commanded him, "Listen to my Son!"

The disciples had to learn that glory comes after death, not before. Hebrews 12:2 says, "Let us fix our eyes on Jesus, the author and perfecter of our faith, who for the joy set before him endured the cross, scorning its shame, and sat down at the right hand of the throne of God." The transfiguration gave to Jesus and to the disciples, and also to us now, a foretaste of the joy and glory that awaits those who obey God.

This understanding of the transfiguration helped the disciples face the hardships of the days ahead. And it is this understanding of the glory that is to come which ought to motivate us also to persevere as we take up our cross and follow Christ.

July 15

*"You acted foolishly," Samuel said. "You have not kept the command the
LORD your God gave you." —1 Samuel 13:13*

od tests our faith by the criterion of obedience.
Samuel had given King Saul clear instructions: "Go
down to Gilgal. I will surely come to you and offer the
sacrifices. But you must wait seven days until I come"
(1 Sam. 10:8). This was a test designed by Jehovah, the Lord of
lords, to see whether Saul would look to God alone.

Saul waited as long as he thought reasonable, but Samuel did
not come. In 1 Samuel 13, we read that on the seventh day, Saul
arrogated to himself the power of the priesthood. He reasoned
that it was surely the time for sacrifice, even though Samuel had
not yet come, so he offered it himself. The moment he finished,
Samuel arrived (v. 10).

Saul offered a self-justifying explanation for his lack of
obedience, shifting the blame to Samuel (vv. 11–12). He falsely
accused the prophet of not coming at the set time. Was God
impressed with Saul's excuses? Not at all. Samuel told the king,
"You acted foolishly." This had been a test. Saul should have kept
Samuel's words in his mind, loving and obeying them, no matter
what. He should have fully relied on Samuel's word that he would
surely come and offer sacrifices after seven days.

What was Saul's problem? He was looking at everything except
the clear word of the Lord that came through Samuel. He saw
everything around him except God. Yes, Saul was facing three
thousand chariots, six thousand charioteers, and countless enemy
soldiers. That is a scary prospect unless one looks to God, who
created the entire universe by the word of his power.

Have you been adjusting and reinterpreting God's word? Was
there a time when the word of God gripped you and shook you,
but now nothing happens, despite your going to meeting after
meeting? If so, you must tremble and humble yourself before God.
If you do not, the time will soon come when you will be abandoned
to the wilderness of human ideas, human psychology, and human
philosophies, and they will rule over you and your family.

May God have mercy on us and help us to turn to him. May we
cherish and embrace his word, hold fast to his statutes, and run to
obey them every time.

July 16

When they received it, they began to grumble against the landowner.
—Matthew 20:11

re we characterized by thankfulness? This parable in Matthew 20 about the workers in God's vineyard challenges us to examine our hearts and see whether we are prone to thanksgiving or grumbling. We will be grumblers if we view ourselves as those who work hard in our own strength, and think that God therefore owes us something, especially something more than others receive.

Those in the parable who were hired first had worked all day, and they became angry when those who were hired last received the same reward. What are we to learn from this parable? Jesus was first concerned to teach his disciples that salvation is by grace, and that serving is by grace. No one serves God unless he or she is saved, and we can do nothing to merit our salvation. If one is a Christian, he or she has been saved by grace on the basis of what God has done in Christ, not on the basis of what that person has earned. All that we are, and all that we do by way of good works, is the result of grace and mercy. We need to appreciate that grace.

Those who grumbled forgot not only about grace, but also about the duty of a Christian. Jesus taught this principle in Luke 17:7–10, where he spoke about an owner of a field who had a servant. The slave worked in the field all day, but when he came home, his master did not thank him. The slave was still expected to cook and feed his master. And when he had done all, his attitude, Jesus said, should have been, "I am an unworthy servant; I have only done my duty."

We also are unworthy slaves. And as slaves we should be saying, "Thank God for making us *his* slaves! We were once slaves of Satan, who hated us. He wanted to destroy us. Praise God that we have been made the slaves of Jesus Christ! We are glad that we have life, so that we are in his household and have food to eat. We are glad to have the great honor of serving our good Master." That is what we will say when we recognize and appreciate God's grace to us.

July 17

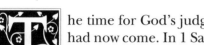

*I am grieved that I have made Saul king, because he has turned away
from me and has not carried out my instructions.* —*1 Samuel 15:11*

The time for God's judgment to fall on the Amalekites
had now come. In 1 Samuel 15, the Lord commanded
Saul, "Go, attack the Amalekites and totally destroy
everything that belongs to them" (v. 3). Then he gave
specific instructions so there would be no misunderstanding.
God clearly reveals to us what he expects us to do. He does not
mumble. He speaks with clarity and authority. So we read, "Do not
spare them; put to death men and women, children and infants,
cattle and sheep, camels and donkeys."

Did Saul obey the Lord Almighty this time? No! Rebellious
Saul did his own will, not God's. He did not act as a servant of the
Lord, but, instead, did what he pleased. He edited the word of
God, adding to it and subtracting from it. So he killed the worthless
animals and spared the best. Most significantly, he spared Agag,
the king of the Amalekites, although the Lord Almighty had
specifically said, "Spare them not!" Saul could not be trusted with
a mission. He would not function as God's servant. He would not
submit to the will of his King, the Lord Almighty.

What did God say about Saul's disobedience? "I am grieved."
The Lord knows when we are turning away from his word and
refusing to carry out his instructions, even though we attempt
to justify ourselves by insisting, "I obeyed the Lord." Such
disobedience grieves him.

Paul writes, "Do not grieve the Holy Spirit of God, with whom you
were sealed for the day of redemption" (Eph. 4:30). Some people
are depressed and miserable because they have grieved the Lord.
We cannot grieve the Holy Spirit and be happy at the same time.
God told Cain, "Why are you angry? Why is your face downcast?
If you do what is right, will you not be accepted?" (Gen. 4:6–7).
We cannot do evil and expect to be full of joy. If the Holy Spirit
is grieved, we will be depressed, and we will not be free of that
depression until we truly repent and do what is right in God's sight.

Because Saul rejected the word of the Lord, God rejected him.
Such is the destiny of all who will not be governed by the Lord and
his word.

Come, let us go up to the mountain of the LORD, to the house of the God of Jacob. He will teach us his ways, so that we may walk in his paths.
—Isaiah 2:3

he peace that Jesus inaugurated at his first coming will continue even after his return, when he will begin his millennial reign. The millennium will be a time of greater peace than earth has ever experienced. Isaiah 2 tells us that in those last days, Mount Zion will be established and raised high. All nations will come to Zion and be subject to the Messiah's rule and instruction.

Why will the nations stream to the mountain of the Lord in the last days? These Gentiles desire to learn God's ways. They hunger and thirst after righteousness. They desire to be taught truth. They recognize that Jesus alone is the way, the truth, and the life. For years, they lived in dissipation, deception, materialism, and self-worship. But now, sick and tired of all the lies of human philosophies, they want the truth that is found only in Jesus.

But why are they studying doctrine (i.e., God's ways)? Is it because of mere intellectual curiosity? No. We oppose all forms of dead orthodoxy. The Christian's purpose for learning doctrine is to put it into practice. There is a vital link between doctrine and life that must not be broken. Thus we read, "He will teach us his ways, *so that we may walk in his paths.*" Authentic knowledge of doctrine always leads to God-pleasing ethics.

This insistence is not popular in today's churches. Most subscribe to a "Don't ask, don't tell" philosophy. But we cannot be satisfied with orthodox doctrine alone; ministers also have to ask church members how they are living. Suppose a man refuses to work, but lives off his wife. It is biblical to come to him and say, "No, you must support your wife. If you don't, you are worse than an unbeliever" (1 Tim. 5:8).

True disciples desire to obey their Master. They want to hear and do. True converts are marked by obedience to the truth. Accordingly, if you do not obey the doctrines of Jesus, you are not a Christian. All your profession is mere self-deception. A true Christian is known by how he lives. He is the light of the world and the salt of the earth. He has been called out of darkness so that he may walk in the light of the Lord.

*Those who are left in Zion, who remain in Jerusalem, will be called holy,
all who are recorded among the living in Jerusalem. —Isaiah 4:3*

saiah 4 speaks about Zion, the holy city of God. The
term "city of God" refers not to infrastructure and
physical buildings, but to the people of God. Isaiah
paints a grand and glorious picture of every true
believer in Jesus Christ.

The Bible clearly teaches that God has a people of his own,
chosen from before eternity in accordance with his eternal
counsel. They are described in Isaiah 4 as escapees, survivors, the
remnant, those who are left in Zion, those who survived the divine
judgment. The word "remnant" tells us that the vast majority of
people are not included in this category called "God's people."
Only a few will be saved.

Paul speaks about the chosen people of God in Romans 11:5:
"So too, at the present time there is a remnant chosen by grace."
What is grace? Some say it is unmerited favor, which is true. But
we can go further: Grace is giving heaven to those who merited
hell. The people Isaiah speaks about were chosen for salvation
through God's divine mercy alone.

These chosen people have been recorded in God's book of
life by God himself before the creation of the world. Some people
think that when a person receives Christ, God will turn a page
in his book and write that person's name in. No, his salvation
has been decreed from eternity past. And if your name has been
written in God's book of life, you will fully repent of your sins and
trust in Jesus Christ.

In Revelation 21, we find the apostle John's description of
what is awaiting every person who has trusted in Christ, who has
been justified, who has been called holy, whose name has been
written in the book of life:

> I saw the Holy City, the new Jerusalem, coming down out of
> heaven from God, prepared as a bride beautifully dressed for
> her husband. And I heard a loud voice from the throne saying,
> "Now the dwelling of God is with men, and he will live with
> them. . . . He will wipe every tear from their eyes. There will be
> no more death or mourning or crying or pain, for the old order
> of things has passed away." (Rev. 21:2–4)

This gospel of the kingdom will be preached in the whole world as a testimony to all nations, and then the end will come. —Matthew 24:14

n Matthew 24, Jesus revealed to his disciples that his second coming at the end of the age would not take place at the same time as the destruction of the temple, but later on, at a time that no man knows. Then Jesus gave a preview of all that would happen between the time of his ascension and the time of his coming again. During this period, Jesus said there would be global evangelism.

We must understand that the preaching of the true gospel brings about persecution, and therefore many will not preach it. Yet in this chapter we are told that in the midst of this great persecution, pain, trouble, flogging, and killing, God will raise up people to declare that Jesus is the Christ, the Savior of the world. Not only must the gospel first be preached, but there is also a promise here: it *will* be preached. The Sovereign Lord will raise up authentic Christians in each generation who are filled with the Spirit of God to preach the gospel with power.

The Holy Spirit will make Christ's disciples bold and articulate, and they will not fear death. Satan cannot shut the mouths of God's people. The Holy Spirit will open their mouths and they will prophesy, in keeping with Jesus' great commission:

> All authority in heaven and on earth has been given to me. Therefore go and make disciples of all nations, baptizing them in the name of the Father and of the Son and of the Holy Spirit, and teaching them to obey everything I have commanded you. (Matt. 28:18–20)

Jesus promised that, in spite of false prophets, false Christs, wars, famine, pestilence, earthquakes, persecution, hatred, apostasy, and the killing of Christians, the gospel must and will be preached to all nations. It is his gospel. He is the Sovereign Lord, and his will shall be done. God's servants will cry out, "Repent and believe on the Lord Jesus Christ and you shall be saved."

That is what is happening, even today, throughout the earth. Let us, therefore, be filled with the Holy Spirit and, impelled by the love of Christ, faithfully declare to an unbelieving, dying world: "Be reconciled to God."

July 21

*The virgins who were ready went in with him to the wedding banquet.
And the door was shut. —Matthew 25:10*

The parable of the ten virgins in Matthew 25 speaks about our need to be ready to meet Christ when he comes. No one knows the day or hour when this will happen. He will come suddenly, when no one expects it, like a thief in the night. Therefore, it is vital that we be prepared for his return.

It is not easy to distinguish the foolish virgins from the wise ones in this parable, for there are many similarities. All are virgins, all have torches, all sleep, and all awaken. They all trim their torches when they hear the cry in the middle of the night. They all intend to be in the procession and to feast with the bridegroom.

In the same way, in the visible church there are professing Christians who look like true believers. Such professors confess Christ, carry Bibles, join the church, worship regularly, give money, and perform various religious duties. Yet the truth is, they are not true believers. They lack one essential ingredient.

The crucial missing ingredient is oil, which represents the work of the Holy Spirit in the life of a believer. This work results in sanctification, by which we increasingly hate sin and increasingly love and do the will of God.

Preparation for Christ's second coming does not consist in a life of passive watching and waiting. Wise virgins are effectual and productive in their knowledge of the Lord Jesus Christ. They daily search the Scriptures to know and do God's will. They are not engrossed in this world, but are always thinking about the world to come. While others are eating, drinking, and relaxing, they are ever engaged in loving and serving God.

The foolish virgins never gave any forethought to their need for oil. Spiritually asleep, they enjoyed a false security. At their moment of need, they sought to borrow from the others, but they could not. We cannot borrow a relationship with Christ from someone else. Salvation is personal, based on a vital relationship with Jesus Christ that is lived out day by day. On the last day, when the door is shut, it will be too late; but right now, the door is still open. I urge you to prepare today to meet your God.

If you do not stand firm in your faith, you will not stand at all.
—*Isaiah 7:9*

lthough Ahaz was a son of David, he was wicked, and in the course of time God brought big trouble to him (Isa. 7). This trial openly revealed Ahaz' unbelief; we are told that his heart was shaken "as the trees of the forest are shaken by the wind." Trouble will come to us too. It may not come today or tomorrow, but in due time God will test us as well.

Troubles are part of our lives because we live in a fallen world. But Christianity is very realistic. It does not say suffering is mere illusion, as some religions do. We will experience real troubles, and the foundation of our lives may be shaken. We may hear from the doctor that our child has a serious illness, or the banker will tell us that he will not give us the loan. There may be floods, fires, earthquakes, or accidents. And all of us will experience a final shaking when we realize we must die.

In what or in whom do you put your trust when such troubles come? A natural disaster reveals a building's structural flaws; in the same way, trials reveal the nature of our faith. Despite what we profess, what we really trust in will be revealed when big troubles come. For instance, when serious calamities beset Job, he refused to curse God and die, though this is what his wife urged.

Because he was wicked, Ahaz could only shake and tremble. He sought no answer from God's prophets and he refused to pray. When the shaking comes, many people who call themselves Christians will not and cannot pray because they have never prayed before in their lives. Such people do not trust in God at all.

I hope we will not be glib when we consider where we are placing our hope and trust. When times are good, our foundation seems to make little difference. But when times are bad, it makes all the difference. We must think about these things now so that we will not rely on creation, but in the God of creation. Everyone trusts someone or something. We must savingly trust, not in our wives or husbands or children or money or houses or country, but in God alone.

July 23

So Judas threw the money into the temple and left. Then he went away and hanged himself. —Matthew 27:5

 n Matthew 27:1–10, we read about Judas the materialist. Judas was an apostle who had walked closely with Jesus Christ for three years—learning of him, witnessing his miracles, and enjoying great fellowship with the Son of God and his disciples. What a remarkable privilege for Judas to be so closely associated with God incarnate! But, being an unrepentant materialist at heart, Judas was not changed in any way by his close association with the Savior. During the time he walked with Christ as an apostle, Judas never stopped looking for power, position, and, above all, lots of money. He loved this present world more than he loved Jesus, and, eventually, he betrayed and abandoned the Son of God for what he thought would be his own gain.

A materialist is concerned with living a life of maximum pleasure and obtaining the means to achieve it. His motto? "Let us eat, drink, and be merry, for tomorrow we will die." A materialist may affirm some theoretical faith in God, but, in practice, he lives as if there is no God.

Sadly, many who even affirm Christian creeds live as materialists. Jesus warned against such thinking: "Do not store up for yourselves treasures on earth, where moth and rust destroy, and where thieves break in and steal" (Matt. 6:19); "No one can serve two masters. Either he will hate the one and love the other, or he will be devoted to the one and despise the other. You cannot serve both God and Money" (Matt. 6:24).

We must take warning and guard our hearts. If you have put your hope in money or in any other material thing, I urge you to repent truly while there is still time. Judas' repentance, "I have sinned," was false. It was a confession made without godly sorrow, without turning to God in faith, without asking for forgiveness of his sins. And so Judas, who wanted to gain all, lost all. He lost his money, his ministry, and his life. He was so close to heaven and eternal life, so close to the Savior, so close to experiencing hope and joy in Christ, but he missed it all. Instead, he went and hanged himself and entered an eternity of torment.

For to us a child is born, to us a son is given, and the government will be on his shoulders. And he will be called Wonderful Counselor, Mighty God, Everlasting Father, Prince of Peace. —Isaiah 9:6

ho is the infant whose birth we celebrate at Christmas? Of first importance, he is God/man. The incarnation of Christ is the conjunction in one person of all that belongs to the Godhead and all that belongs to manhood, yet without sin. In Isaiah 9 we are told that he will be called Wonderful Counselor. In the Hebrew it reads, "He is Wonder." Jesus Christ is the greatest wonder imaginable because his very person is wonder. As the God/man he is unique; there is no one else like him.

In ancient times, kings had counselors. But this One does not need any such advisor. He is the Counselor who carries out all things according to the counsel of his own will. What he plans, he fulfills. The people of the world foolishly seek the counsel of mediums, spiritists, and "experts" who mutter nonsense (Isa. 8:19). But God has given us the counsel of his Son in the Bible.

This promised Son is the Mighty God, *El-Gibbor. El* means God and *Gibbor* means warrior. Jesus Christ is mighty in battle. He said to his disciples, "In this world you will have trouble. But take heart! I have overcome the world" (John 16:33). Jesus Christ is Mighty God. Do you confess him as such? Has he conquered you?

This God/man is also called Everlasting Father, Father of eternity. "Everlasting" points to his deity and "Father" to his humanity. Jesus Christ is father to us eternally. As does an earthly father, so also Jesus Christ cares for us, forgives us, instructs us, provides for us, and loves us everlastingly.

This One is the Prince who brings peace, not by negotiation, but by the conquest of all his enemies. The world cannot give us peace. But the Prince of Peace extends peace to us like a river through the cross of Calvary. Because Christ died for our sins, he now offers peace to those who submit to his government.

May God deliver us from sentimentalism and worldly philosophies! May we recognize that this child, this son, this divine gift whose birthday we celebrate at Christmas, is Mighty God, the great King and only Savior of the world. Then we will be able to rejoice with joy unspeakable and full of glory.

Make known among the nations what he has done. —*Isaiah 12:4*

saiah 12 speaks about proclaiming to the nations what God has done. The good news of God's salvation can never be contained. If we are containing it, we do not have it.

The Jordan River continually flows into the Dead Sea, but there is no outflow. As a result, the water in the Dead Sea is contained, and there is no life. In the same way, if we refuse to share the gospel, we have no salvation, because salvation is life. The gospel is the good news about the mighty deeds God has done. And we are commanded to make the gospel known among the nations. "Make known" assumes that there are unbelievers who remain ignorant of the gospel. God has chosen his elect to be saved, but they can only learn about Jesus when the good news flows out of us.

The greatest deed God ever did was to send his own Son to die for our salvation. It is a sin to contain this good news. Isaiah 12:5 says, "Sing to the LORD, for he has done glorious things; let this be known to all the world." We must share the gospel by telling of God's mighty deeds. Celebration of salvation leads to evangelism. I saw this when I was growing up. No matter who came to our house, my mother would speak to them about Jesus Christ and him crucified.

What about you? Is your mouth sealed? Do you pray, "Bless us four and no more"? Do you say, "I have my job and my house, and my family is saved. Isn't that enough?" No! We must share the gospel, passing it on to others as of first importance (1 Cor. 15:3). Declare it among the nations! We do not have to travel to faraway destinations; we can meet people from all over the world right where we live. Tell them of the mighty deeds of God. Tell them that Christ died, Christ was buried, Christ was raised, Christ was seen, Christ ascended, Christ is seated, Christ is King, and that Christ is coming again to judge the living and the dead. Tell them about the kingdom of God, the greatest reality in the universe. Share all these truths with them, for it is through people like us that God spreads the fragrance of the gospel everywhere.

For the word of God is living and active. Sharper than any double-edged sword, it penetrates even to dividing soul and spirit, joints and marrow; it judges the thoughts and attitudes of the heart. —Hebrews 4:12

ebrews 4 tells us that the word of God judges. *Kritikos* is the Greek word used, from which we derive the words "critic" and "criticize." Not only does the word of God probe our hearts, discerning our feelings, thoughts, and motivations, but it also criticizes and judges us with a judgment that is always true and final.

As creatures, we are to hear and do God's perfect will. But because we are fallen, we arrogantly sit in judgment of God and his everlasting word. Man has long been in the business of judging the word of God and rejecting it as foolishness. But man's judgment of God and his word will not stand. It is God's judgment of man that will prevail. "For it is written: 'I will destroy the wisdom of the wise; the intelligence of the intelligent I will frustrate.' Where is the wise man? Where is the scholar? Where is the philosopher of this age? Has not God made foolish the wisdom of the world?" (1 Cor. 1:19–20).

God's word is our judge. Jesus says, "There is a judge for the one who rejects me and does not accept my words; that very word which I spoke will condemn him at the last day" (John 12:48). Every word God has spoken to us, whether from the pulpit or from the Bible, will judge us on the last day.

Nothing is more inaccessible than the emotions, intentions, and motives concealed in the depths of man's depraved heart. We all have an innate tendency to circumvent truth when confronted with our sin. But God's word exposes our hearts, just as the prophet Samuel exposed the wicked heart of Saul and the prophet Nathan exposed the wickedness of David. A sinner hates such truth. He chooses instead to believe that he, somehow, will not have to face God in judgment. He sits in his Jericho, thinking that he is protected by impenetrable high walls. But, in a flash, by the power of God, his protection will disappear.

We must understand that the word of God judges us, and we will do well to pay attention to it. May we submit to its teaching, rebuke, correction and training. May we stand under God's word and be saved, for all who stand over it shall be destroyed.

July 27

You are slow to learn. —Hebrews 5:11

he recurring theme of the book of Hebrews is the high priesthood of Jesus Christ after the order of Melchizedek. But the church of the Hebrews, about thirty years old when this epistle was written, was not intellectually equipped to understand this doctrine and live out its vital implications. This truth demands muscular, not mushy, Christianity. It requires that we be adult Christians, not ones who prefer to remain in infancy. Hebrews 5 and 6 address this issue.

The Hebrews were not growing intellectually, because a mature knowledge of Christianity demanded that they forsake Judaism with its laws, covenant, and high priesthood, and follow Jesus Christ as the perfect high priest. It demanded continued suffering for the gospel, and they had grown tired of being persecuted. They wanted a religion that entertained them, a religion of escape and little thought. They were not getting ready to go to heaven; they just wanted to live comfortably in the here and now.

These church members were in danger of abandoning the true gospel, which includes suffering and high spiritual discipline, in order to embrace a false gospel of peace, health, and affluence. They wanted to return to a second childhood in which they would be taken care of and not have to assume any responsibilities, especially the responsibility of evangelizing and making disciples.

This is the reality in many churches today. Many welcome the notion that now is the time to enjoy life, not to suffer for Christ. They are not interested in learning serious doctrine. They have no delight in regular, methodical, painstaking Bible study. Thus, they lack the ability to discern and make correct decisions. They refuse to grow up and produce fruit; they remain spiritual infants.

The writer to the Hebrews had already warned his readers several times: "We must pay more careful attention. . . . Do not harden your hearts. . . . See to it that none of you has a sinful, unbelieving heart that turns away from the living God" (Heb. 2:1; 3:8, 12). Now he takes time to further admonish them about their spiritual inertia, mental laziness, and regression into childhood. These temptations are the all-too-common enemies of muscular Christianity that we in our generation must also recognize and oppose in the power of the Holy Spirit.

JULY 28

So Saul and his three sons and his armor-bearer and all his men died together that same day. —1 Samuel 31:6

ove yourself to death!" This saying summarizes the life of King Saul. It describes the way of the arrogant and unregenerate, those who do not believe God and who will not do his will. It is speaking about the person who says, "I want to do what I want, when I want, how I want. Who are you to tell me what to do?" It is an apt description of the culture in which we find ourselves—the culture of autonomy and self-love.

In Saul's thinking, the greatest commandment was, "Love yourself with all your heart, with all your soul, and with all your mind." He tried to use God and religion to promote his own power and glory. He chose to affirm rather than to deny himself. He chose his own kingdom and glory rather than seeking first the kingdom of God. He was self-centered rather than God-centered, pursuing worldly fame and ambition. He wanted to gain the whole world even though it cost him his soul.

Saul tried to gain his life, and he lost everything. The Bible tells us that the Holy Spirit departed from him, and that God became his enemy. He lost the word of God, he lost communion with God, he lost the kingdom, he lost his children, and he lost his mind. The final tragic consequence of Saul's self-love was death for him and his family, as we read in 1 Samuel 31.

The life of Saul is a warning to all in the church today. It is a warning especially to those who call themselves Christians but who are not truly born again. Saul stands for unregenerate "Christians" who do not obey God, who treat his word with contempt, and who do not persevere. Ultimately, such people cannot and will not live for the glory of God; in due time they will fall away from the faith.

I hope that all of us will deny ourselves, take up the cross daily, and follow the Son of God, Jesus Christ, by whose death we live now and forever. If we surrender ourselves to Christ, we will surely live. I pray that none of us will imitate the sad, tragic life of Saul, who wanted to be number one, but ended up dead last.

I will put my laws in their minds and write them on their hearts. I will be their God, and they will be my people. —Hebrews 8:10

he law given on Mount Sinai was written on stones, not human hearts. Man's problem, however, is that he is a sinner; thus he hates God's law from the heart and his mind rejects it, exchanging truth for a lie. He loves evil and chooses evil.

We read about the total depravity of man in Jeremiah 17:9: "The heart is deceitful above all things, and desperately wicked: who can know it?" (KJV). Jesus located sin not outside but inside fallen human nature: "From within, out of men's hearts, come evil thoughts . . . arrogance and folly" (Mark 7:21–22).

Our problem, therefore, is not fundamentally external or environmental. Our problem is internal rottenness. The only solution is a new heart, a new mind, a new will, and new affections. We need nothing less than to be regenerated by the Holy Spirit— spiritual resurrection, the life of God placed in the soul of man. This is not superficial, decisional salvation, but a salvation in which God writes his law in our hearts.

God's marvelous work of raising his people from spiritual death is prophesied in Ezekiel 11:19–20: "I will give them an undivided heart and put a new spirit in them; I will remove from them their heart of stone and give them a heart of flesh. Then they will follow my decrees and be careful to keep my laws."

When we are regenerated, we naturally begin to delight in God's laws from the heart and we will obey them on a daily basis. We will eagerly study God's law with our renewed minds and we will gladly choose to obey it with our sanctified wills. True salvation does not mean we get rid of God's law and become antinomian. There is nothing wrong with the law. In fact, the law is the transcript of God's nature, to which Christians are being conformed.

When God saves us, he implants his law in our hearts, that we may know and love it, as we read in Hebrews 8. And in obeying it, we honor God himself. Once we were not able, but now he himself has given us a new heart, a new nature, a new spirit, and new power to obey.

July 30

And let us consider how we may spur one another on toward love and good deeds. —Hebrews 10:24

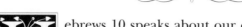

Hebrews 10 speaks about our obligation to each other as members of Christ's church. We must never forget that, as Christians, we are children of God the Father by adoption, and brothers and sisters in Christ. We are living stones being built by Jesus Christ himself into a spiritual house, which is the church, the family of God, the body of Christ. We are placed in relationship to God and to every other elect believer in the community. Autonomy is gone. No longer lonely and alienated, we now belong to God's family through a bond more vital than any natural human relationship. As a result, we gladly live a life of covenant love.

The church is not a club, a gathering of autonomous beings, each doing his own thing. We are a family; therefore, we love one another and are responsible for one another's welfare. We are not independent, but rather interdependent. Just as the body has eyes, ears, hands, legs, and so on, so we who are the body of Christ are many members with shared responsibilities for one another. We minister to others, and they minister to us. You are needed and I am needed in the glorious body of Christ.

As the body of Christ, we are under the headship of Christ, who commands us, "As I have loved you, so you must love one another" (John 13:34). Loving one another is not optional. It is not something we do only when we feel like it. We must always be willing and ready to lay down our lives for the benefit of our brothers and sisters. We no longer do things out of selfish ambition or vain conceit, but in humility consider others better than ourselves.

The Western world emphasizes individualism and unfettered freedom, but not so the church of Christ. We are not like Cain, who asked, "Am I my brother's keeper?" We *are* our brother's keepers, by divine ordination. As members of Christ's body, we love one another, submit to one another, serve one another, and bear one another's burdens. We rejoice with one another, weep with one another, and speak the truth in love to one another. And considering others better than ourselves, we lay down our lives for the people of God, all to the glory of God.

July 31

Others were tortured and refused to be released, so that they might gain a better resurrection. —Hebrews 11:35

ebrews 11:34 says that by faith God's people escaped the edge of the sword, while verse 37 says that by that same faith some were put to death by the sword. There is, however, no contradiction. As believers, we live by faith and we die by faith. We may experience God's miraculous deliverance from troubles, or we may die a martyr's death. We must come to understand and embrace Christ's teaching that includes our suffering.

This particular passage provides extremely important balance for our lives. The thrust of much modern evangelism is that by receiving Jesus into our hearts, we can not only avoid hell and go to heaven, but we can also avoid pain and enjoy health, wealth, and fame in this life. Such notions are false, and those who preach them are false teachers.

Hebrews 11 reinforces the truth that in God's sovereign plan, Christians do suffer and may even become destitute and homeless. In fact, Christians are destined to suffer more than others because of their confession of Christ. Jesus said, "If the world hates you, keep in mind that it hated me first. . . . In fact, a time is coming when anyone who kills you will think he is offering a service to God" (John 15:18; 16:2).

In God's perfect will, he may save us from a given trouble, or he may not. Jesus demanded that Christians deny themselves, take up their crosses daily, and follow him. In other words, we must come and die so that we may live forever. Jesus did not say he would give us trouble-free and prosperous lives in the here and now. He did promise, "I give them eternal life, and they shall never perish" (John 10:28).

"Faith is being sure of what we hope for and certain of what we do not see" (Heb. 11:1). Faith means that we can clearly see the invisible things of God. And when we do so, this present, visible world will lose its charm. Through faith, we are enabled to forfeit life itself, if necessary, to gain the better world to come. Faith is the response of all who are conscious of their own nothingness; therefore, in absolute trust we rely totally on God. Faith is the victory that overcomes the world.

August 1

The Lord's anger burned against Uzzah because of his irreverent act;
therefore God struck him down and he died there beside the ark of God.
                                                          —2 Samuel 6:7

 hen David first decided to bring the ark to Zion, he consulted with all Israel and made a plan. In 2 Samuel 6, we read that they went together in a great procession to Kiriath Jearim, about eight and a half miles from Zion, took the ark from Abinadab's house, put it on a new cart pulled by oxen, and assigned Uzzah to walk behind the ark to keep an eye on it. Everyone was worshiping with all his might, singing, shouting, and rejoicing before God in great celebration.

But this was not acceptable worship. In fact, it was confused worship. God could not bless this worship because David and his people were not worshiping according to the Holy Scriptures. They may have been zealous, but they acted without knowledge.

At one point in the procession, the oxen stumbled and the ark of the Lord began to fall off the cart. When Uzzah reached out and took hold of the ark, God became angry at Uzzah's irreverent act, and Uzzah instantly died before the Lord. What irony! Uzzah had come to worship; instead, he died. Rather than blessing, his worship resulted in judgment because he had not acted in keeping with God's constitution.

Why had this joyful day ended in such tragedy? David once had been a man of prayer, but in this very important matter of bringing the ark to Zion, he and the other leaders failed to consult with God. Not only did David neglect to pray, but he also neglected to study the word of God so that he could discover the will of God. It was David's duty as Israel's deputy king to always have a copy of God's word in his possession so that he might live in accordance with it.

Afterwards, in his desire to know the cause of God's anger, David took his old copy of the Scriptures, dusted it off, and started reading it very diligently. At the same time, he began to pray earnestly. In time, God showed him from his word the prescribed way.

We must always keep in mind that, as Christians, our guide is the Scriptures, not culture, modernism, philosophy, psychology, paganism, or worldliness. We must never imitate the world, but remain faithful to our constitution—the Bible.

You will keep in perfect peace him whose mind is steadfast, because he trusts in you. —Isaiah 26:3

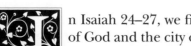

n Isaiah 24–27, we find the tale of two cities—the city of God and the city of man. Every citizen of the city of God is entitled to enjoy *shalom,* "great peace," even in the midst of great disturbance. Why will such a person not be disturbed? It is because God himself will remove the cause of disturbance. Elsewhere Isaiah says concerning the Messiah, "The punishment that brought us peace was upon him, and by his wounds we are healed" (Isa. 53:5). Jesus Christ suffered the wrath of God that was due us. When God forgives our sins, they are totally blotted out and we are clothed in the perfect righteousness of Christ. As a result, we have peace with God.

In Romans 5:1, the apostle Paul writes, "Therefore, since we have been justified through faith, we have peace with God through our Lord Jesus Christ." And in Philippians 4:6–7 Paul begins, "Do not be anxious about anything. . . ." Anything! If you are a citizen of the city of this world, you will be anxious about everything. In fact, you have no reason to be confident or at peace about anything. But Paul writes, "Do not be anxious about anything, but in everything, by prayer and petition, with thanksgiving, present your requests to God. And the peace of God, which transcends all understanding, will guard your hearts and your minds in Christ Jesus." All who dwell in the city of God can experience peace when everything else is crumbling all around.

Have you experienced this peace? It is the inheritance of every city-dweller whose mind is stayed on the Lord. Is your mind fixed on Christ, or is it stayed on your money, your position, your children, or your possessions? When our eyes are not focused on the Lord, the Rock of Ages, we forfeit this rest.

Isaiah 26:4 goes on to say, "Trust in the LORD forever, for the LORD, the LORD, is the Rock eternal." We must fix our eyes on Jesus. And as we trust in him, the Prince of Peace who accomplished peace for us on the cross, we shall find that our Rock is strong to bear us up and shelter us from every storm. We will together enjoy his shalom inside the glorious city of God.

David asked, "Is there anyone still left of the house of Saul to whom I can show kindness for Jonathan's sake?" —2 Samuel 9:1

 hat does Mephibosheth mean? In Hebrew, *bosheth* means "shame," so I believe it means "big shame." Mephibosheth represents all sinners who are redeemed. We must therefore give special attention to 2 Samuel 9 because it speaks of the redemption of God's people.

Mephibosheth deserved death. His grandfather Saul was an unregenerate who refused to obey God's command and sought his own glory instead. After David ascended to the throne, it would have been proper and just for him to kill all the descendants of his rival Saul, as kings normally did in those days. As a direct descendant of Saul, Mephibosheth son of Jonathan knew and acknowledged that he was liable to being killed. He later said as much to King David after Absalom's rebellion: "All my grandfather's descendants deserved nothing but death from my lord the king" (2 Sam. 19:28).

But David had made a covenant with Jonathan, and he wanted to honor it. After being established by God as the undisputed king of Israel, David expressed his desire to show kindness to any living descendant of his mortal enemy Saul. And so we find the amazing language seen in verse one above.

That invitation is still going out even this day wherever the gospel is preached. It is the invitation of the great King, who, rather than showing justice, chooses to show kindness to his enemies. What is the invitation? "Come unto me; I will give you rest." This is what the gospel is all about. We are all, by nature, Mephibosheths—sinners, people of great shame, enemies of God and deserving of his wrath. But God in mercy sends out his great gospel invitation, and we are saved. Why? "For God so loved the world that he gave his one and only Son, that whoever believes in him shall not perish but have everlasting life" (John 3:16).

This is the great theme of this chapter: God's covenant mercy shown to the Mephibosheths of the world. The great King, of his own initiative, shows his kindness, grace, and unfailing mercy, not to well-deserving, or even ill-deserving people, but to his hell-deserving shameful enemies. And, like Mephibosheth, we are given a place at the banqueting table of the great King.

Like newborn babies, crave pure spiritual milk, so that by it you may grow up in your salvation. —1 Peter 2:2

ur heavenly Father, who gives us new birth, also desires that we grow up. To do so, we need a proper diet. Junk food may be tasty, but it is harmful and destructive to our health. As unbelievers, we ate spiritually unhealthy food, but now God insists that we eat that which will make us grow in grace and in the knowledge of Jesus Christ. First Peter 2 tells us that we need to become mature so that, having learned to deny ourselves, we can love God and the people of God deeply from our hearts.

"Pure spiritual milk" stands for the word of God. First Peter 1:23 says, "For you have been born again . . . through the living and enduring word of God." God's word not only gives us new birth, but it is also the living and abiding word. It nourishes us continually that we may grow to the full stature of Christ.

We must therefore listen to God's word carefully, so that we will not remain as infants, never maturing in God. Consider this: There is beauty in an infant, but when a twenty-year-old person has not grown up, it is ugly and shameful. If you want to grow up in God and your salvation, you need to listen attentively every time God's word is spoken.

We are to crave the word "like newborn babies." What does this mean? Healthy newborns desire to eat eagerly and frequently, day and night. Every time they wake up, they are voracious. The psalmist said, "My soul thirsts for God, for the living God" (Ps. 42:2). Such thirsting is a sign that a person is born from above.

God's word is essential to us. When Jesus was tempted by Satan to make bread out of stone, he quoted Deuteronomy 8:3: "Man shall not live on bread alone, but on every word that comes from the mouth of the LORD." We must daily take in the word of God. It alone is the well balanced, nourishing spiritual food God has provided for us. As believers, we are called to understand it, meditate upon it, add faith to it, and do what it says.

Then David said to Nathan, "I have sinned against the Lord." Nathan replied, "The Lord has taken away your sin. You are not going to die."
—2 Samuel 12:13

ave you ever lied? If you are honest, you will admit that you have. But have you ever wondered why you lie? Most often it is to hide sin. Man is continually trying to somehow cover up his sin. Such attempts are not new. David tried to cover up his sins of adultery and murder, but he too failed and was brought to confess his sin by Nathan the prophet, as we read in 2 Samuel 12.

In Psalm 139, David asks, "Where can I flee from your presence?" We must realize that when we sin, we are sinning in the sight of an omniscient God. That is why all our attempts to cover up our sin will fail. In due time, the fig leaves we cover ourselves with will shrivel.

Since all our attempts to cover up are guaranteed to fail, God himself had to make a way to spare us from his judgment. Can a just and holy God ignore our sin? No. God does not ignore sin, but he has provided us with a divine covering for our guilt. Leviticus 16 describes the way of salvation given by God for his people. Once a year the high priest was to enter the Most Holy Place, bringing with him the blood of a freshly killed goat. God was present above the cover of the ark, looking down on it and the two tablets of the law, contained within the ark, which represented man's sin and guilt. God is angry because of sin, which is man's transgression of that law. But once a year, on behalf of the people, the high priest would come and sprinkle the blood of the sin offering upon the lid of the ark. Then, when God looked down, what would he see? Blood—the blood of the innocent substitute.

This Day of Atonement foreshadowed the sacrifice of Jesus Christ for our sins. We read in Hebrews 9:12, "[Jesus] entered the Most Holy Place once for all by his own blood, having obtained eternal redemption." God himself covers the believer's sins by the blood of his Son, our Lord and Savior Jesus Christ, shed on the cross. And so Nathan, on behalf of God, could tell David, "The Lord has taken away your sin. You will not die." Praise God for his great mercy!

AUGUST 6

Tell us pleasant things, prophesy illusions . . . stop confronting us with the Holy One of Israel! —Isaiah 30:10–11

In Isaiah 30, the Israelites demanded that the prophet Isaiah adjust his message to suit their interests and desires. They wanted to hear only smooth and pleasant things. As a minister of the gospel, I am called to bring you good news. But before I can prophesy good things, I must declare the bad. Before the promise of the gospel can be proclaimed, the terror of the law must be preached.

What, then, are some of these unpleasant things we must preach? First, we must say that in the beginning, after God created the heavens and the earth, Adam and Eve sinned against God. There was a fall that affected the whole universe, and, as a result of the Fall, we are all now born sinners.

We must say that not only are we born sinful, but that we also practice sin daily. We are by nature dead in trespasses and sins. We are guilty before God Almighty, and the wrath of God is being revealed from heaven against all the ungodliness and unrighteousness of men. The Bible says it is appointed for man once to die and then comes the judgment. There is a final judgment and eternal death in hell awaiting every unrepentant sinner.

False ministers preach a different gospel. They say exactly what people want to hear. They base their messages on polling results because they want to be popular and make more money. They choose to preach pleasant things that will please their audiences. Rather than rebuking, correcting, and training in righteousness, they speak instead of self-esteem and moral relativism.

True ministers, however, refuse to preach according to poll data. They refuse to pursue popularity; rather, they endeavor to be faithful ambassadors of Christ. They preach about the narrow way, the path of obedience and faith that alone leads to eternal life. Because they confront people with the holy God, they are often hated, persecuted, slandered, and sometimes killed. But when a sinner comes to such a true prophet, he will be told the truth about his deadly rebellion against God and shown the way of perfect salvation in Jesus Christ. He will hear the divine words, "In repentance and rest is your salvation, in quietness and trust is your strength" (v. 15).

There will be false teachers among you. —2 Peter 2:1

odly pastors—the true prophets of God in today's churches—hear the word of God and declare it to their people. They are committed to the infallibility and the authority of Scripture and they therefore study the Bible with great care and prayer. They know that these are the words of life, and so they preach with all passion, clarity, and divine unction. Such pastors are God's gift to the church.

But just as it did in the apostle Peter's day, the church today must contend with many dangerous, deceitful pastors who are false prophets. These self-called men teach "destructive heresies," ideas they have developed in their imaginations, stories they have concocted. Not only so, but they also typically espouse antinomianism—"the error of lawless men" (2 Pet. 3:17).

Not surprisingly, these false prophets are very popular in the world today. Peter foresaw that "many will follow their shameful ways." Nominal Christians like to be flattered. They enjoy worship services full of humor, designed to entertain but never convict the audience. Their end, though, will be swift destruction.

How can we keep ourselves from the baneful influence of false preachers? First, we must diligently and daily use the means of grace available to the children of God. We have to study the word of God and regularly sit under biblically faithful preaching. We must pray earnestly. We ought to enjoy deep fellowship with serious Christians.

Second, we must be on the lookout for the heretical teaching that promises freedom, but, in fact, leads to slavery to depravity. Those who preach a "feel good" gospel—one that abandons discipline and self-control—may grow a large church, but it will be a synagogue of Satan.

Finally, many false pastors can be recognized by their greed; one of their chief goals is to lift money from your pocket. To this end, they tell stories and make fantastic promises to manipulate the gullible and naïve. The apostle Paul explicitly warns against those "who have been robbed of the truth and who think that godliness is a means to financial gain" (1 Tim. 6:5).

May God help us to discern and repudiate the false gospels and false preachers of our day!

August 8

He is the atoning sacrifice for our sins. —1 John 2:2

hat is the goal of the Christian life? To live as Jesus did. That means we must try not to commit any sin; our goal is nothing less than perfection. A Christian is always moving toward perfection, which we will arrive at when our Lord Jesus Christ comes again.

If a Christian commits a sin, however, he is not to despair. We have an advocate in heaven, Jesus Christ, the Righteous One. His advocacy is totally effective because it is based on the cross of Calvary—his atoning sacrifice in our behalf. The phrase "atoning sacrifice" in 1 John 2:2 in the New International Version is an interpretation, not a translation. The Greek word is translated correctly in the King James Version as "propitiation." But what exactly is propitiation?

There are a number of words that the Bible uses to describe our salvation. One is redemption, which comes to us from the world of commerce—buying and selling. The second word is justification, which comes to us from the world of law and the courts. Then there is propitiation, which comes from the sacrificial system found in the ancient religious world.

In the Greek, the word "propitiate" means to appease, to placate, to avert, or to turn aside the wrath of an offended person by means of a sacrifice. Four aspects are involved in propitiation: first, there is an offended deity; second, an offending sinner; third, the offense committed; and fourth, the sacrifice which removes the offense and causes the offended person to be gracious to the one who offended him. Propitiation is directed toward God to turn away his wrath, which is revealed against our offense, so that he may be gracious to us.

Never think that God is unwilling to forgive sinners. He is so willing that he himself planned and provided a propitiatory sacrifice in our behalf by sending his own Son as the only adequate propitiation that could turn away his wrath and cause him to be favorable toward us.

We needed a substitute who is infinite and perfect, both righteous man and holy God. God gave us such a One who is both the priest and the victim—the Lord Jesus Christ. He alone is the acceptable propitiation for our sins.

And a highway will be there; it will be called the Way of Holiness.
—Isaiah 35:8

he Bible tells us plainly that there are only two possible roads upon which to travel in life. One is straight and narrow and leads to eternal life; the other is broad and winding, leading away from God to eternal destruction.

How many people travel on the broad way! Some may even claim to be Christians, but it makes no difference. Our claims mean nothing unless God claims us as his own. Each of us has to travel on one road or the other, and in due course we each will arrive at the final, eternal destination we have chosen.

How does Isaiah describe the highway to heaven in Isaiah 35? We read, first, "a highway will be there." This means that this highway is not of human origin, design, or construction. It is designed by God from all eternity and built by him at the highest possible cost—the precious blood of Christ. And it is God himself who places us on the highway leading to his city.

This highway is the only way out of the city of sin to the city of God. It is the way out of Egypt through the wilderness to the land flowing with milk and honey.

This highway is called, "the Way of Holiness." It is designed and built by the thrice-holy God. It is a *high* way, meaning it rises above the muck and mire of this world. Those who travel on it are called saints—holy ones. Such people set their affections on things above, not on things below.

This highway is safe. No lion is on it to tear us apart. Yes, we will hear Satan's roaring, but do not fear: We can overcome him by faith in the Lion of Judah, who destroyed the devil by his death on the cross.

This highway to heaven is a person—the Lord Jesus Christ himself, who said, "I am the way and the truth and the life. No one comes to the Father except through me" (John 14:6). There is no other way to God.

Finally, this highway leads to glory. When we arrive at our journey's end, we will be with God forever, celebrating the never-ending festival of salvation and worshipping the King of righteousness in all his beauty.

Anyone who does not believe God has made him out to be a liar.
—1 John 5:10

rust in human testimony is foundational to the continuance of society. How can a husband live with his wife unless he trusts her? How can the courts function without relying on the statements of witnesses?

People trust the words of others daily. But God's testimony, as we read in 1 John 5, is greater. It is greater in terms of its validity—he is the infinite, personal God who knows all things and who cannot lie. It is greater in terms of its authority—he is the King of kings and Lord of lords. Accordingly, we who are his rational, moral creatures are to trust him implicitly, believe his testimony, and obey him in all things.

God speaks infallibly about all areas of life, but his most important testimony concerns his Son, Jesus Christ, the only Savior of the world. God loves sinners; therefore, he has revealed to sinful men the only way to be saved from his just wrath. What mercy and condescension!

Yet the vast majority of people throughout the world do not believe God's testimony, especially God's witness of his Son. They will not take him at his word. All unbelievers make the triune God out to be a liar. This false accusation is as old as the Fall. The people in Noah's day treated his warnings with ridicule and contempt. Lot's family did not really believe that they must flee the coming destruction. The vast majority of the Israelites did not trust in God's promise to safely bring them into the Promised Land.

This is what the heretics of John's day did also. They refused to acknowledge that Jesus was the Christ, the Son of God. They rejected the biblical teaching that Jesus was crucified for sinners on the cross. They trusted in their own ideas rather than God's gracious words of life. Man today makes the same fatal mistake.

God's testimony is specific and exclusive: Salvation is found in Jesus Christ alone; he alone grants us eternal life. Do you believe this, or have you made God out to be a liar? May God help us all to trust him implicitly and to entrust ourselves to him who is eternal life. Believe on the Lord Jesus Christ, and you shall be saved.

AUGUST 11

O my son Absalom! My son, my son Absalom! If only I had died instead of you. —2 Samuel 18:33

econd Samuel 18 is not only about a rebellious son, but it also concerns a rebellious father—King David. His own son had become his enemy, pursuing him with intent to kill, yet David wept uncontrollably when he heard the news of his death. It was a cry of foolish sentimentality, an irrational emotional response. It was worldly sorrow, not godly sorrow.

What provoked such a reaction? David had begun to realize that, though he was a superb warrior and king, he was an utter failure as a father. His own sin had contributed to his children's moral delinquency. He remembered the words of the prophet Nathan, "The sword will never depart from your house."

David had indulged his sons instead of disciplining them. He should have known better, for it was his duty to have a copy of the Bible, read it daily, and be governed by it. This word of God gives us plentiful instruction on how to discipline our children. But the king would not teach, train, rebuke, or punish his own children. Instead, every son was given an estate, a large house, and servants. And every one ended up disobeying and despising God. Thus did David enable his children's wickedness.

Why did David not discipline his sons? When parents practice sin, they lose the moral authority to discipline. When Amnon raped Tamar, David was furious. But he never brought him to justice, for he himself had committed adultery. When Absalom murdered Amnon, David shielded him, for he himself had murdered Uriah.

We all have a destiny. We are going to experience either joy or sorrow, based on whether or not we lived a Bible-centered life and raised our children in the fear and admonition of the Lord. At the end of our lives, we will either rejoice in our children's salvation, or mourn over their perdition.

We must examine ourselves in light of David's life. Are we walking in the way of righteousness and training our children to honor God in all of life? Are we teaching them the word of God so that it permeates their entire worldview? Or are they open to the charge of being wild and disobedient? May God keep us from becoming a father like David.

AUGUST 12

I your servant know that I have sinned. —2 Samuel 19:20

himei was a wealthy and important man, a relative of the deceased King Saul; consequently, he hated King David. When he had the opportunity, he called down curses upon the king and showered him with dirt as he fled Jerusalem (2 Sam. 16:5–14). This was a capital offense; the book of Deuteronomy commands, "Do not blaspheme God or curse the ruler of the people." Shimei, however, paid no heed, for he was convinced that David would soon be destroyed.

In God's grace, David prevailed against his rebellious son, and in 2 Samuel 19 we see him returning to Jerusalem. Note the alacrity and show that Shimei demonstrated to pay honor to the restored king. He knew he deserved to be killed and so he came, not alone, but at the head of a one thousand-person retinue. He fell down on his face and called David, "My lord." He confessed, "I have sinned" and even used the biblical language of repentance and mercy: "Do not count my sins against me."

The question we must ask is this: Was this biblical repentance, or phony repentance? I have had people cry profusely in my presence and I sometimes have mistaken it for godly sorrow. Genuine repentance results not only in tears, but also in turning from every sin and turning to God in faith. This is what, in due time, we see lacking in Shimei's life.

David did discern that Shimei's repentance was phony, and he later directed his son Solomon to "bring his gray head down to the grave in blood." Solomon tested Shimei's repentance by the one standard that matters—obedience. Shimei agreed to the king's terms and complied for a season. Eventually, though, he violated his word, thinking that his sin would never be brought to Solomon's attention. In this he was mistaken, and he paid for his sins with his life (1 Kings 2:9, 36–46).

We must think seriously about the issue of true and false repentance. David sinned grievously, but his confession was genuine, from the heart, and he went on to live the rest of his life for God. Shimei never experienced godly sorrow or sincere hatred of sin; he simply wanted to avoid punishment with lip service. May God grant us the evangelical grace of true repentance and faith.

"Do not be afraid, O worm Jacob, O little Israel, for I myself will help you," declares the LORD, your Redeemer, the Holy One of Israel.
—Isaiah 41:14

he Bible's wisdom and the world's are at loggerheads. The world celebrates the "self-made man," whereas Jesus taught that "the first shall be last and the last first." The world views the proud, self-confident man as successful, but the Bible says that God opposes him and will bring him down. It is the way of humility that, paradoxically, leads upward. The man who has been humbled by God has been set on the pathway of blessing.

Old Testament Israel is an object lesson. In Isaiah's day, she had grown proud. When Israel failed to repent, the Lord subjected her to severe chastisements, even Babylonian captivity. In Isaiah 41, we discover Israel's consequent self-evaluation: "O worm Jacob, O little Israel." She had come to her senses and humbled herself, and she was now ready to receive God's mercies. Therefore God could speak words of comfort: "Do not be afraid; I myself will help you."

Dear Christian, have you ever felt like a worm, about to be crushed? Do you feel insignificant, as though God has rejected you? The truth is, God has not rejected you nor can he do so. God is here to help the poor and needy. He does not help those who are arrogant and self-reliant, who think they are competent to save themselves. But he promises to strengthen all who acknowledge their weaknesses and failures before the sovereign Savior.

God promises to transform weak worms into powerful threshing sledges, capable of overcoming all obstacles. Jesus told his disciples, "You will receive power when the Holy Spirit comes on you" (Acts 1:8). When we are filled with the Holy Spirit, we can resist the devil, and he will flee from us.

God says to us, "Fear not! I am your God. In all the concerns of life I will be with you to strengthen you, help you, and uphold you. I will hold your right hand and make you strong." Yes, we must acknowledge our own weakness and inability, but let us not despair. Let us instead rejoice in the Lord and glory in the Holy One of Israel. Let us declare along with Paul, "I delight in my weaknesses . . . for when I am weak, then I am strong" (2 Cor. 12:10).

The LORD said, "It is on account of Saul and his blood-stained house; it is because he put the Gibeonites to death." —2 Samuel 21:1

he three-year drought experienced by David and Israel in 2 Samuel 21 had an explanation; nothing happens by accident in God's universe. No one, though, gave the lack of rain much thought in the first year. Nor did David seek the Lord in the second year. Often, we do not really pray until we are in great distress. Now, in the third year, famine set in, and David finally inquired of the Lord. He was told, "This is happening because of Saul's sin."

Many years earlier, Joshua had made a treaty with the Gibeonites (Josh. 9). Though the decision was ill-advised, it had been made by invoking the name of God. Therefore, the Gibeonites were given a perpetual promise that could not be violated by Israel.

Saul, however, paid no heed to this treaty; in alleged zeal for God, he struck down the Gibeonites. In this he brought great dishonor to the name of the eternal God, who cannot break his word. Yet afterwards, for twenty-five years, the Lord appeared to take no notice. How many times have we sinned and nothing appears to happen in response! We therefore tend to think that we can violate God's laws with impunity. This chapter teaches us not to draw such wrong conclusions.

Every time we sin, God is dishonored, and God will defend his honor and glory. He often does not punish sinners immediately. But in due time, God will repay, and their foot shall slip (Deut. 32:35). Note, too, that though Saul was the one who had sinned, he was not the only one to suffer the consequences; his sons and grandsons paid a terrible price as well. This should inspire every parent to fear the Lord and shun evil.

God must punish every sin. If he failed to do so, he himself would be guilty of injustice. Is there, then, any hope for the sinner? Yes! Every sin must be punished, either in the sinner, or in Jesus Christ. If we place our trust in Jesus, repenting of our sins and believing on his name, our sins will be forgiven forever. And though we may subsequently sin, our heavenly Father will chastise us, sometimes even severely, but he will keep his promise—he will bring us safely to heaven.

When you pass through the waters, I will be with you. —Isaiah 43:2

 here do you turn when fear arises in your heart? Do you turn to psychology and pills, to family and friends? Or do you turn to Christ of the Scriptures, who triumphed over death in our behalf? Even believers sometimes try to calm their fears by human means rather than through Christ who, by his atoning death, has set us free from all fears.

Isaiah 43 begins, "But now, this is what the LORD says. . . ." "But now." God is speaking something new, and I hope we will pay attention to it. What is the Lord saying? "Fear not!" We find these words twice in the first seven verses. They are spoken from the heart of God to our hearts. God's promises to Israel cannot fail. In spite of their persistent disobedience, arrogance, and idolatry, God will save his people.

The covenant Lord promises to be with us forever. God is transcendent, but he is also Immanuel, God with us. The ascended Christ poured out the Holy Spirit on his church at Pentecost, and God the Holy Spirit will never leave us nor forsake us.

The truth is, we all must experience trials. Jesus himself promised, "In this world you will have trouble. But take heart! I have overcome the world" (John 16:33). The floodwaters destroyed the Egyptians, but God saved his people. The fire destroyed Sodom, but God saved his people. God will be with us in our floods, in our rivers, and in our flames. Count on it. Our spouses may not be there, our children may not be there, our friends may not be there, but God will be there. As he was with Joseph in Egypt, with Daniel in the lion's den, and with Paul in prison, so he will be with us.

Paul once declared, "At my first defense, no one came to my support, but everyone deserted me. . . . But the Lord stood at my side and gave me strength" (2 Tim. 4:16–17). No flood, no fire, no trial can ever separate us from our God and Christ.

If you are fearful and anxious, the Lord is speaking to you today: "Fear not, for I have redeemed you; I have summoned you by name, you are mine."

Then the people began to plead with Jesus to leave their region. —Mark 5:17

here are three prayers in Mark 5. First is the prayer of the demons. These demons were at enmity with God and hated him. But every demon and devil is under God's sovereign control. Therefore, after acknowledging Jesus as Son of the Most High God, they pleaded with him that the time had not yet come to throw them into the Abyss. They begged him to send them into the pigs instead.

The second prayer was that of the materialists, the citizens of the region. After seeing the miraculous deliverance of the demoniac, the herdsmen told the owners of the pigs, "Sirs, there is a man named Jesus who just came over in a boat, and the demonized man went out to him. Jesus spoke a word, and the demoniac was transformed. He is even now sitting down, clothed, and in his right mind. But something else happened: when the demons came out of the man, they went into the pigs, and they all ran into the lake and were lost."

These materialists went to Jesus and declared, "Jesus, we love pigs, and we understand that you destroy pigs, so we want you to go away and leave us alone. Jesus, we love our life of ease, pleasure and luxury. We don't care about our souls. We prefer pigs!" At their own request, the Savior left them.

The third prayer was that of the demoniac who had been saved by grace. Jesus saved and transformed this man. He filled him with the Holy Spirit and peace. And so he also prayed, asking if he could stay with Jesus.

This man wanted to be with Jesus. Why? So that he could learn from him, express his gratitude to him, and serve and worship him all of life. He understood that Jesus was not just a man, but God and Lord. And he realized that Jesus had come all the way from heaven to seek and save him; he wanted to spend the rest of his life with his Savior.

I pray that we will not be like the Gadarenes, preoccupied only with the material things in life. Rather, let our prayer be like that of the former demoniac: "Lord, I am not interested in pigs. I am interested in you. I love you and want to be with you forever."

I will not sacrifice to the LORD my God burnt offerings that cost me nothing. —2 Samuel 24:24

 heap worship—worship that does not cost us anything—is the result of our failure to understand God and his grace. Cheap worship is the worship of idols— gods that cannot show infinite mercy. When our appreciation of salvation is true and deep, then our worship will be passionate and costly.

In 2 Samuel 24, we see King David coming to the threshing floor of Araunah in response to the prophet Gad's directive. Though David had sinned greatly in the matter of the census, he had confessed his sins. The Lord would now show him covenant mercy. The king realized the magnitude of this unmerited kindness and how great a salvation God had provided; therefore, when Araunah offered to give him the threshing floor for free, David adamantly refused. He would not sacrifice to his gracious Lord an offering that cost him nothing.

Authentic spiritual worship is costly, for it demands nothing less than the entirety of our being surrendered in worship to our great God and Savior Jesus Christ. We see such adoration in the twelfth chapter of John's gospel. There Mary, the sister of Lazarus, gladly anointed Jesus with costly perfume, a gift that must have cost her entire life savings. Mary understood mercy!

The apostle Paul taught the same truth in Romans, "In view of God's mercies, offer your bodies as living sacrifices, holy and pleasing to God" (Rom. 12:1). In the first eleven chapters, Paul exposited the gospel indicatives—the mercies of God in Christ. In Romans 12, he issues an imperative in light of what God has done for us. This mandate is more all-encompassing than David's payment of silver and gold. We are called to offer *ourselves* to our Lord—our bodies, minds, wills, and affections.

If we have difficulty adoring and obeying Christ, our comprehension of the salvation and mercies we have received is defective. David was spared at the threshing floor, and Isaac was spared on that same mount centuries before. But the Son of God was not spared. We must once again look at the cross where God showed us mercy and spared us from eternal hell. Then we will leap at the opportunity to worship him with all our being.

Even to your old age and gray hairs I am he, I am he who will sustain
you. I have made you and I will carry you; I will sustain you and I will
rescue you. —Isaiah 46:4

 ll gods of the nations are idols and lies, for they are
merely the creation of fallen man. These idols always
fail their worshipers, especially when crisis strikes.
Who, then, can help miserable and weary sinners? The
answer is given in Isaiah 46. If you are thirsty, if you are hungry, if
you are weary, if you are depressed, if you are unsaved, wake up and
pay attention. "Listen to me!" God says to his elect remnant, his
chosen ones. "Away from all idols! Away from creature worship!"

In verse 4, God says, "I am he"; in other words, "I AM THAT I
AM." He alone is the changeless, self-consistent, non-contingent,
self-existent, self-dependent, covenant-keeping God. Then he
says, "I myself made you." In the Hebrew text, the emphasis is on
the pronouns: "I myself made you—not idols, not Bel, not Nebo,
nor an angel. I myself!"

Only the God of the Scriptures can bear our burdens and help
us in our time of need. He alone saves us. He alone is the great
I AM—the glorious, uncreated, infinite, personal God. He alone is
the Lord; there is no other. The God of the Scriptures transcends
creation and time, and directs history to his desired end. He alone
can predict, dictate, and bring to pass his plan, and no one can
prevent him from doing what he pleases. He upholds us by the
power of his outstretched arm; in him, we live and move and have
our being.

Have no fear! The eternal I AM, the triune God, created us and
cares for us. Not only did he sustain us in the womb and in our
infancy, but he also sustained us in our childhood, through our
teenage years, and into adulthood. And he promises to help us even
to our old age and gray hairs. What a commitment God has made to
us! He is the God of all tenses—he helped us in the past, he helps
us in the present, and he will help us in the future. He is our God,
who was and is and is to come. He loved us before the creation of
the world, he loves us now, and he will love us for eternity.

You know in your heart all the wrong you did to my father David. Now the LORD will repay you for your wrongdoing. —1 Kings 2:44

he first two chapters of 1 Kings speak about judgment; here we see King Solomon executing judgment on several individuals in accordance with the will of his father David. This foreshadows the divine, inescapable, final judgment that will be accomplished by Jesus Christ.

The old and dying David had come to realize his failure to rule in righteousness in several cases. For example, the king had failed to discipline his sons and had reaped the whirlwind with regard to Amnon, Absalom, and Adonijah. He also had lost his moral authority over Joab in the case of Uriah the Hittite; therefore, he never brought the guilty general to justice. As a result, it was now left to Solomon to see that God's righteous will was done in the nation.

In each case, the offender had concluded that he could get away with opposing the increasingly weak David and his young son Solomon. And in each case the sinner's day of reckoning came suddenly, without warning. The rebellious Adonijah was summarily executed after violating his oath of submission. The arrogant priest Abiathar was removed from the priesthood, fulfilling the word of God spoken to Eli years before (1 Sam. 2:30–33). The murderous Joab was dragged from the horns of the altar and cut down without mercy. And Shimei, who had become complacent when shown mercy, in due time received capital punishment.

Every sin is a personal assault on God's glory. It is requisite, therefore, for God to punish defiant sinners and vindicate his glory. He will do so in a final judgment—a judgment that is necessary, universal, and inescapable. There will be a day of reckoning for every one of us—a climactic day of judgment at the end of history.

Like Adonijah, Abiathar, Joab, and Shimei, we too are conspirators and rebels by birth. We come into the world as enemies of God. Yet the Sovereign Lord offers salvation to us on the basis of submission to him. This is still the day of grace, when all guilty sinners can come in sincerity and faith and plead for pardon. If we will bow the knee to Jesus Christ now and confess him as Lord, we need not dread the day of reckoning that is coming.

I asked your disciples to drive out the spirit, but they could not. —*Mark 9:18*

n Mark 9, we read of a father who brought his demonized son to Jesus for healing, but when he arrived,
Jesus was not there. Turning to the disciples, he asked
them to heal the boy. They tried, but failed. Only
when Jesus returned from the Mount of Transfiguration was the
demon cast out.

This afflicted boy is a symbol of the modern world in need.
Even today there are those who are God's elect who need to hear
the gospel and be delivered from their bondage through the
instrumentality of the church.

The disciples symbolize today's church. Just as Jesus was not
there when the demonized boy was brought for help, so too, Jesus
is not physically present with us now. And just as the disciples
found themselves unable to solve the problem, so too today's
church—both corporately and individually—finds herself largely
incompetent, impotent, and frustrated, despite the fact that the
church has been given authority and power by Jesus Christ himself.

We see this investiture of authority and power in Mark 3:15 and
Mark 6:7. Jesus did not ask the disciples to do something that they
could not accomplish. And he has not commanded the church
to be his witness without empowering her for that purpose. He
desires us to minister healing to a dying world. This mandate is
not optional, and it is not directed solely for ministers. Every one
of us has been given a charge to be the light and salt of the earth.

There are people in the world who need to be delivered, who
need to be helped, who need the church to show them the way of
the Lord. Why has she so often failed in this mission? First, she has
forgotten her Lord's commission and has become preoccupied
with the pursuit of personal peace and affluence. How sad it is to
see the world tormented like the demonized boy, and the church
more interested in her own well-being. Not only so, but the church
also neglects prayer, relying instead on her own strength. The
disciples failed to pray and failed to help the boy.

I pray that we will come out of our self-confidence, and in
great humility depend upon God moment by moment in prayer.

When he heard that it was Jesus of Nazareth, he began to shout, "Jesus, Son of David, have mercy on me!" —Mark 10:47

artimaeus, though a poor, blind beggar, had a keen sense of hearing and an inquiring mind. In Mark 10, we read that he wanted to know why there was great commotion one day. He was told that Jesus of Nazareth was passing by. This is the gospel.

Bartimaeus must have heard of Jesus and the miracles he had performed—enabling the lame to walk, curing the lepers, raising the dead, and giving sight to the blind. Moreover, he must have known that these reports signaled the arrival of the day of the Messiah, a day for which every devout Jew longed. Most importantly, Bartimaeus had received spiritual illumination—regeneration—through the Holy Spirit. He now understood that Jesus of Nazareth is the Lord, the Son of David, the Savior.

As a result, this beggar cried out to Jesus in persevering, passionate faith, "Lord, Son of David, have mercy on me!" He knew well that he was a poor, undeserving, powerless outcast, yet he did not stop. He heard the crowd all around rebuking him and insisting that he be quiet, yet he would not be deterred. True faith will not be discouraged by any obstacles or opponents of grace. True faith has no "Plan B." True faith says, "Today is my appointed time, this is my day of salvation, now is the Year of Jubilee!"

The Bible says that Jesus stopped. Miracle of miracles! In response to the humble cry of this miserable beggar, the Lord of the universe stood still. God loves sinners, and he hears their cries. The crowd that had recently rebuked him now told Bartimaeus, "Take courage! Jesus is calling for you!" When Jesus calls us with an effectual call, it is good news. We can rejoice, for salvation has come to us.

When he summons us, our response should be the same as this beggar's. With alacrity, he threw his outer garment aside and ran to the Savior; he made every effort to enter through the narrow gate. When asked what he desired, he uttered a very specific, heartfelt prayer of faith: "I want to see." And, having been healed, he, with great thanksgiving and gratitude, followed Jesus along the road.

Jesus is passing by us today. May God help us to cry out, "Lord, have mercy on me!"

The LORD has laid on him the iniquity of us all. —Isaiah 53:6

 saiah 53 is the heart of the great prophecy of Isaiah, and the heart of chapter 53 consists in verses 4–6. Everything we need is offered in this passage: peace, healing, righteousness, justification, forgiveness of sins, and eternal life.

What does a sinner say when he looks upon the Suffering Servant? Isaiah tells us, "He was despised and rejected by men" (v. 3). When people looked at Jesus on the cross, many drew the wrong conclusion. They said, "Jesus is a great sinner. He is a blasphemer, under God's curse; that is why he is being crucified. He is suffering and dying for the guilt of his own most horrible sins, for his own transgressions of God's law."

How completely different is God the Father's estimation of his Servant! The suffering he experienced was unique and is not to be interpreted in an ordinary way. To understand the person and work of this Servant correctly, we need the Father's perspective given to us in the Bible. Accordingly, in this chapter we are given divine revelation regarding the suffering of the Servant. Contrary to the common explanation, this One was not suffering because of his own sins. He was innocent.

Verse 3 says this Servant was "a man of sorrows, and familiar with suffering." Why did he suffer? We are given the reason in verse 4: "He took up our infirmities and carried our sorrows." Christ suffered because of our sins. We sinned; he suffered. We deserved death; he died in our place.

Isaiah 53:4–6 thus constitutes the good confession of the believer, who has grasped the gospel truth. Because God's truth has been revealed to us objectively in the Scriptures, and subjectively in our hearts through the regenerative work of the Holy Spirit, we no longer consider the Messiah a sinful man who deserved to be crucified, nor view him as a big zero. We now stand at the foot of the cross, adoring the One who was punished in our stead, the One who suffered the eternal consequences of our sin. We now realize that the Suffering Servant is Immanuel, the Son of God, Mighty God, the Everlasting Father, the Prince of Peace. He is the atonement, the Redeemer of his people, the divinely given mediator and substitute. Hallelujah!

She, out of her poverty, put in everything—all she had to live on.
—Mark 12:44

he poor widow of Mark 12 teaches us about the grace of giving—how to give in a way that pleases the Lord. The scene is the court of women outside the Jewish temple, where thirteen large trumpet-shaped receptacles for money had been placed. Jesus sat down opposite the place where the offerings were deposited; he made it his business on that occasion to observe what the people gave. He had the right to do so, for he is the King of kings and Lord of lords. We must not think that giving is an appendix to worship; it is a vital part, and Jesus notices our giving today as well.

The woman whom Jesus commended found herself at the lowest rung of the society of those days. She had no husband to support her, no Social Security check or welfare payment, no retirement account—nothing. And yet she came and put all she had to live on (two nickels in our currency) into the offering box for God's temple. She was laying up for herself treasures in heaven.

A common excuse some Christians employ is, "But I don't make much, I am just a student." They say this, though they will get haircuts, go out to dinner, take vacations, and even own cellphones. But the poor widow teaches us that the poor are not exempt from giving. In fact, God's work is generally done not by the rich but by the poor. Our attitude ought to be, "I want to give first to God."

In 2 Corinthians 8, we read about the Macedonian churches who urgently pleaded with the apostle Paul for the privilege of giving to their fellow Christians. There too we see the grace of giving: "Out of the most severe trial, their overflowing joy and their extreme poverty welled up in rich generosity" (2 Cor. 8:2).

Brothers and sisters, we are the losers when we plead inability to give. In truth, we cannot afford not to give. And when the Lord of the church sees that we are giving willingly and sacrificially, he will not only take notice, but he will also bless us with great joy and delight in him. May God increase our faith, so that we can be a generous people, to his glory.

Come, all you who are thirsty, come to the waters; and you who have no money, come, buy and eat! —Isaiah 55:1

 saiah 55 is the Lord's invitation to a great feast. As poor, needy, sinful people, we can never find satisfaction in this world for our spiritual hunger and thirst. But God has prepared a banquet to satisfy our spiritual needs. He invites us to come and eat freely of his spiritual delicacies and to drink from the living water made available through the death and resurrection of his Son, Jesus Christ.

Who are the invitees to this great feast? They are those who thirst, not after gold, but after the true and living God. They are those who say with the psalmist, "As the deer pants for streams of water, so my soul pants for you, O God" (Ps. 42:1). If you hunger and thirst for righteousness, you are invited to this feast.

The invitees are also those without money. Isaiah presents us with a paradox: the feast is priceless, yet it must be purchased. The psalmist also tells us that the cost of redemption is beyond our ability to pay: "No man can redeem the life of another or give to God a ransom for him—the ransom for a life is costly, no payment is ever enough—that he should live on forever and not see decay" (Ps. 49:7–9).

The invitation comes, nevertheless, to bankrupt sinners: "You who have no money, come, buy and eat!" How can this be? This feast of salvation that is prepared for hungry, thirsty sinners, is paid for by another. First Peter 1:18–19 tells us who paid that price: "For you know that it was not with perishable things such as silver or gold that you were redeemed from the empty way of life handed down to you from your forefathers, but with the precious blood of Christ, a lamb without blemish or defect." The price for our redemption was the life of the Suffering Servant of Isaiah 53.

Not only are the poor and thirsty invited to the feast, but in verse 7 we are told that the wicked are also welcome. Everyone is invited who comes in true repentance, willing to forsake sin and turn to God. On such people, God will have mercy.

Are you a sinner? Then you are invited to God's great feast!

This is what the LORD says: "Maintain justice and do what is right, for my salvation is close at hand and my righteousness will soon be revealed." —Isaiah 56:1

s the people of God who have bound ourselves to him through repentance and faith, how then should we live? What is our present responsibility as we wait for the second coming of Christ and the fullness of salvation? In Isaiah 56, the Sovereign Lord tells us, "Maintain justice and do righteousness" (v. 1). Then he says, "Blessed is the man who does this" (v. 2). Thus, as we are waiting, we must love, serve, and obey God. Our responsibility is to live holy lives and shine as lights in this dark world. As we do, we shall discover that happiness is obedience.

Blessed is the man who honors the covenant Lord by keeping God's covenant by God's grace. Blessed means happy, so we could say, "Happy is the man who obeys God." True joy comes to us through obedience to the Lord. Isaiah is saying that the happy man is a holy man, and the happy woman is a holy woman. If you are not happy, you must examine yourself and see whether you are serving God or yourself. A self-centered person is miserable. I counsel such people to look upward and outward, that is, to serve God and God's people. Then you too will experience true happiness.

Those who become servants of the Lord, who commit themselves to love the Lord and serve him only, will surely be blessed by the Lord. Those who try to make themselves kings shall be brought down to shame, while those who make themselves his servants will be honored as kings in due time. That is the way God works. He humbles the arrogant and lifts up the humble. Do you desire to be happy? Then serve the Lord only. There is no other way to experience everlasting joy.

As we wait for the Lord's coming, it is God's will that we live a life pleasing to him. We are to shine as the light of the world, so that men may see our good deeds and praise our Father in heaven. We must keep on doing the will of God daily. This is the formula for true happiness. And, in time, we will be brought to Mount Zion for the incomparable experience of communing with God forever.

"There is no peace," says my God, "for the wicked." —Isaiah 57:21

od promises peace for the contrite. The life of the wicked is one of misery, worry, fear, and judgment. But those who walk uprightly will enjoy great peace. The choice is up to us: peace or anxiety, life or death. In Isaiah 57, the prophet sets before us the way of peace. If you are a wicked person, I pray you will listen, because God in mercy is offering you a way out.

Verse 14 tells us that God is preparing a way for his people to come to him: "Build up, build up, prepare the road! Remove the obstacles out of the way of my people." We need a way to God so that we can experience the great peace, joy, and life that he has for us. But we are hindered by sin, guilt, and unrighteousness. How can guilty sinners approach a holy God? Thanks be to God, God himself has prepared the way for us. It is the way of the Suffering Servant, revealed in Isaiah 53. Through him our way is made smooth—all hindrances and stumbling blocks are removed.

Who is this way? The Lord Jesus Christ himself declared, "I am the way and the truth and the life" (John 14:6). Hebrews 10:19–22 says, "Therefore, brothers, since we have confidence to enter the Most Holy Place by the blood of Jesus, by a new and living way opened for us through the curtain, that is, his body . . . let us draw near to God." Through his life and work, Jesus prepared the way for us to come to God. So he bids us: Come in joy! Come in confidence! Come in peace!

Isaiah 57:15 says, "For this is what the high and lofty One says: 'I live in a high and holy place, but also with him who is contrite and lowly in spirit, to revive the spirit of the lowly and to revive the heart of the contrite.'" God does not dwell with everyone. He abides only with people of a certain character—those who are brokenhearted, crushed, and humble, those who repent of their sins. He will not dwell with arrogant idol worshipers. If we would enjoy his peace and presence, let the wicked forsake his way and the evil man his thoughts; let us turn to the Lord, and he will have mercy on us!

We look for light, but all is darkness; for brightness, but we walk in deep shadows. —Isaiah 59:9

ave you ever complained to God, asking him why he has not answered your prayers? Have you ever questioned why he has not delivered, healed, or blessed you? Isaiah 59 speaks about such a complaint lodged by the people of Israel. God's people had concluded that their covenant Lord was to blame for the lack of an answer. They asked, "Why does God not come speedily to our aid every time we call on him? Why does salvation wait? Why is deliverance far away?" These are valid questions, and we find the answers in Isaiah's prophecy.

First, we must realize that it is not due to any lack in God that we do not experience deliverance. In Isaiah 50:2, God asked his people, "Was my arm too short to ransom you? Do I lack the strength to rescue you?" God himself answers these rhetorical questions in Isaiah 59:1: "Surely the arm of the LORD is not too short to save, nor his ear too dull to hear."

Why, then, does God not always rush to the aid of his people? He says in Isaiah 59:2, "Your iniquities have separated you from your God; your sins have hidden his face from you, so that he will not hear." In the Hebrew Bible, the word "iniquities" appears five times in Isaiah 59. God is not the one to blame for our lack of deliverance. It is we who have created the wall of separation between ourselves and God. The fault lies with us.

As long as we shift blame to God and to others, as long as we refuse to repent and confess our sins, and as long as we refuse to say, "Have mercy upon me, the sinner," we will not experience God's salvation. But beginning in verse 12, the focus suddenly shifts. Now we hear the people of God confessing their sins. There is no more blame-shifting, no more accusing God. The first-person pronouns "we," "our," and "us" appear many times in this section. The elect people of God finally agree that, rather than being the problem, God is their only solution. And then we are given the good news: "The Redeemer will come to Zion, to those in Jacob who repent of their sins" (v. 20).

AUGUST 28

As Solomon grew old, his wives turned his heart after other gods, and his heart was not fully devoted to the LORD his God. —1 Kings 11:4

ing Solomon ought to have loved the Lord God wholeheartedly for the unparalleled favors he had received. God had twice appeared to him personally, given him surpassing wisdom, and chose him to build the magnificent temple in Jerusalem. In fact, God himself gave Solomon the name *Jedidiah*, which means, "Loved by the Lord" (2 Sam. 12:25). But that is not what happened. Instead, the king was unfaithful to his covenant Lord, as we read in 1 Kings 11.

How can one start out so greatly favored of God and yet wind up like a pagan? The rebuke given by the risen Lord to the church of Ephesus provides the answer: "You have forsaken your first love" (Rev. 2:4). This forsaking is subtle, gradual, and not noticeable at first. It can happen in a marriage, and it can happen in our walk with Christ. Over time, our love cools and our heart wanders.

Solomon started well, but over a long life marked by prosperity and success, he eventually became Israel's first pluralist. He abandoned covenant exclusivity and embraced the principle of "both/and"—the worship of other gods along with Jehovah, the great God. He continued to pay lip service to the Lord, but his heart was drawn away to idols—Chemosh, Molech, and Ashtoreth—who would let him sin.

The king's downward spiral was the reason for, and the result of, his holding fast in love to many foreign women. In doing so, he vetoed and nullified God's explicit word given to Israel's kings in Deuteronomy 17. Here is a man who not only had a copy of the Scriptures, but actually added to the canon under the Spirit's leading. Yet he came to a place where the Bible no longer meant anything to him. Instead of being transformed by the continual renewing of his mind by God's word, he became a cultural conformist, a multiculturalist, a syncretist, a large-hearted open-minded man who "loved" everybody, except the Lord his God.

We read that Solomon's defection angered God, so the Lord raised up enemies to oppose Solomon and bring him to his senses. Yet we do not hear of Solomon ever repenting and returning to Jehovah with wholehearted devotion. We must take warning, lest we too in time wander from our first love and never return.

But Rehoboam rejected the advice the elders gave him and consulted the young men who had grown up with him and were serving him.

—1 Kings 12:8

n 1 Kings 12, the young king Rehoboam was faced with a major crisis: ten of the twelve Israelite tribes threatened to rebel and break away from his kingdom. Surely Rehoboam needed divine wisdom to avoid a national catastrophe.

The king was not without the necessary resources. He knew that the king of Israel was commanded to study God's word and seek the Lord in prayer, as his father Solomon had done in his youth. Yet Rehoboam failed to do this. Instead, he leaned onto his own understanding, and the country suffered a devastating loss—permanent partition.

It appears the king approached his decision with a self-confidence born out of arrogance and pride. Rehoboam came to the elders with his mind already made up, and when their counsel crossed his will, he found younger men who would pamper his ego and rubberstamp his plans.

There also were well-known prophets in the land at that time, such as Ahijah, the prophet of Shiloh, and Shemaiah, the man of God. These men were God's gifts to the nation to give godly guidance to the leaders responsible for the people's welfare. Yet we do not see Rehoboam inquiring of these prophets of God.

Most importantly, we do not read that Rehoboam sought counsel from the covenant Lord through earnest prayer and serious study of the Scriptures. The king's disregard for the Bible should not surprise us, for we read in the parallel account, "After Rehoboam's position as king was established . . . he and all Israel with him abandoned the law of the LORD" (2 Chron. 12:1).

We all will face important decisions that will impact our family's and our church's welfare. If we do not want to repeat King Rehoboam's grievous mistakes, we must begin by walking in humility and holiness. Then we must earnestly seek the Lord with prayer and fasting, asking for wisdom. Finally, after we have wrestled in honest prayer, we must come to the men of God who have the word of God and accept their counsel so that we may go forward with the assurance that our decision is of God.

But where sin increased, grace increased all the more, so that, just as sin reigned in death, so also grace might reign through righteousness to bring eternal life through Jesus Christ our Lord. —Romans 5:20–21

e learn in Romans 5 that both sin and death reign as kings. But, thanks be to God, grace also reigns. And God's grace is not just equal in power to sin and death; it is infinitely greater. There is no equal ultimacy of evil and good. Grace reigns forever over sin and death.

The grace of God in Jesus Christ comes to take us, not to where Adam stood before his fall, but beyond—to sit at the right hand of Christ himself. Grace comes to our hell and takes us to heaven itself. This is the power of grace. This power is called the grace of God (v. 15); the grace of our Lord Jesus Christ (v. 15); abounding grace (v. 17); and even super-abounding grace (v. 20). It is amazing grace, triumphant and full of glorious, incomparable, and unsearchable riches (Eph. 2:5–8).

Grace takes the initiative to save us. It gives us the free gift of righteousness, which is our greatest need. By nature, we are unrighteous sinners, condemned to death. We do not need human righteousness; we need divine righteousness. So divine grace flows to us from eternity past through the covenant of redemption, in which the Father planned our salvation, the Son agreed to accomplish our redemption, and the Spirit of God agreed to apply this redemption to every elect sinner.

The apostle Peter speaks of this grace in his first epistle: "[Christ] was chosen before the creation of the world, but was revealed in these last times for your sake" (1 Pet. 1:20). Paul likewise writes, "This grace was given us in Christ Jesus before the beginning of time, but it has now been revealed through the appearing of our Savior, Christ Jesus, who . . . brought life and immortality to light through the gospel" (2 Tim. 1:9–10).

This triumphant grace is irresistible. It fights, even with God's own people and wins by defeating our rebellion, stubbornness, and wickedness. It saves the most wicked of sinners, like Saul of Tarsus, the self-righteous Pharisee, conquering him and transforming him into a battle-scarred veteran of the cross.

Grace has triumphed for us too! Let us live in its superabundance and give God the glory through our Lord Jesus Christ.

In the same way, count yourselves dead to sin but alive to God in Christ Jesus. —Romans 6:11

he first imperative in the entire book of Romans is found in Romans 6:11. We are exhorted here to reckon, to regard, to keep in mind the reality of our position as Christians. The Greek term is a bookkeeping word used to deal with mathematical realities, not wishful thinking. It is, as F. F. Bruce said, not a game of "Let's pretend."[1] Sound thinking is the first step toward living a holy life.

This verse exhorts us to regard the truth, remember the truth, and act in line with the truth that we are dead to the old king, sin, and alive to our new King, Jesus. Paul is not asking us to die to sin; he is pointing us to the reality that we are already dead to it.

Paul is telling us that what is true of Jesus, our representative and mediator, is true of us by virtue of our union with him. When Christ died, he died to sin. Therefore, when we believed in Christ by God's own supernatural enablement, we died with him to sin. Thus, we are finished with sin; it has no more claim on us and no dominion over us. It is not that sin is dead, but that we are dead to it.

Not only so, but we are also alive to God in Christ Jesus. When Christ rose from the dead, we in him also rose from the dead; in him, we have experienced spiritual resurrection. In him, we are alive forevermore and shall never die spiritually again. What is true of Jesus is true of us.

Thus, we must know and count on the reality of our new status in Christ. We must tell sin, "I am no longer under your control; I have been set free! You can yell all you want, but I will not obey you. I refuse to think and act as your slave. I have a new master, the risen Lord Jesus Christ."

Now we have a choice that we did not have before. Yes, sin still dwells in our body and will be with us until we die, but we have been set free from its dominion. We can say "No" to sin's demands and make it stick.

---

1 F. F. Bruce, Romans, *Tyndale New Testament Commentaries* (Grand Rapids: Eerdmans, 1999), p. 132.

My servants will sing out of the joy of their hearts, but you will cry out from anguish of heart and wail in brokenness of spirit. —Isaiah 65:14

hen God's people were in Egypt, God made a distinction between them and the servants of Pharaoh. There was light in Goshen, but darkness everywhere else; there was life in Goshen, but death in the rest of Egypt. In Isaiah 65, the prophet tells us that God is once again going to make a distinction. He will differentiate his servants from Satan's; for God's, there will be eternal blessings, but for Satan's, eternal curses.

The vast majority of people will not be saved. But in every generation, God saves a remnant, the elect, his servants. In this chapter, God is saying to the wicked, "My servants will be given a new name, but your name will be accursed. My servants will be blessed, but you will be put to death. My servants will forget all their troubles, but you will remember all of yours. My servants will dwell in the new heaven and the new earth, where there will be no more weeping, sorrow, or tears, no more loneliness, death, or parting, where there will be total security and total peace, and, finally, no more enmity. My servants will enjoy life with me, eating, drinking, rejoicing, and having eternal fellowship with me."

Who, then, are the servants of God? They are those who confess with their mouths that the risen Jesus is Lord. They are those who gladly do what is right. They are those who pray, "Thy will be done on earth as it is in heaven." They are the covenant-keepers.

We must always keep in mind the eternal destinies that await every individual: eternal life with God in heaven or eternal death away from God in hell. There is a way of life and a way of death. I pray that we will not attempt to create our own reality, for the religion of our depraved imagination will only lead to destruction. It is the religion of the broad way, the way of hunger, thirst, shame, wailing, and brokenness of spirit forevermore. By contrast, the way of Jesus is the way of obedience, forgiveness, and salvation. It is the way of righteousness, peace, and joy in the Holy Spirit. It is the way of God's servants; they and they only shall be blessed.

This is the one I esteem: he who is humble and contrite in spirit, and trembles at my word. —Isaiah 66:2

hat we do in this life matters for eternity. Our lives here will soon end, and then we will enter into an eternity of life or an eternity of death. Our destiny is based on our relationship, or lack thereof, with the Lord Jesus Christ. Yes, we may live here seventy years, or by reason of strength, eighty. But compared to eternity, our time on earth is short. The question that we each must face is this: Will I spend my eternity in heaven or in hell? The answer depends on whether we are blessed or cursed by God. I pray that we will strive to belong to the company of the blessed.

In Isaiah 66:2, the Lord himself identifies who his blessed people are. The word for esteem means "to look upon with favor." God looks upon these people as his treasure and loves them as his bride. The desire of God is nothing less than to dwell in the hearts of his people.

God necessarily opposes the arrogant, but he dwells with the humble and contrite. "Contrite in spirit" means "crippled in spirit." It speaks about one who acknowledges his sin and cries out to God to have mercy on him. Such a person mourns before God, hungering and thirsting for God's righteousness. He is like Jacob, who, having been crippled by the angel, had to lean on God. Jacob cried out to God, and God blessed him, renaming him Israel (Gen. 32:24–29).

Our verse says that God esteems the one who "trembles at his word." Do you tremble at God's word? Are you anxious to hear and do God's will? Is obedience to God's word your chief interest and delight? Or are you like King Saul, who adjusted God's command to fit his own agenda and received this rebuke from Samuel: "Does the LORD delight in burnt offerings and sacrifices as much as in obeying the voice of the LORD? To obey is better than sacrifice" (1 Sam. 15:22).

There are only two peoples and two destinies. What then should you do? You must choose, not your own way, but the way of God as revealed in the Scriptures. Walk with him in the way of humility, the way of trembling, the way of blessing that leads to eternal life.

She went away and did as Elijah told her. —1 Kings 17:15

idows in the Old Testament age were poorest of the poor. There was no Social Security to help them, and they were easily exploited by the society. The widow of Zarephath (1 Kings 17) was also very poor. Yet she was chosen by God to be saved. Thus, Elijah, the prophet who left Ahab and Jezebel in judgment, was sent to this widow by divine commission. Elijah asked her for some water and some bread. She replied that she was going to prepare two silver-dollar-sized cakes with the last of her flour and oil, one for her son and one for herself. They would eat their last little meal together and then die.

The condition of this widow is the miserable condition of all Adam's descendants. All have sinned and come short of the glory of God. The widow was dying, and her son was dying. But God sent his prophet all the way to Zarephath, to this widow and her son, not to conduct their funeral but to bless them with life eternal.

But first the widow must believe and obey the prophet. So Elijah told her, "First make a cake and bring it to me." Then he gave them the gospel: "For this is what the LORD, the God of Israel, says: 'The jar of flour will not be used up and the jug of oil will not run dry until the day the LORD gives rain on the land'" (v. 14). The widow did believe and obey, and she and her son were saved from death.

The God who saves us also demands all from us. He demands, "Love the Lord your God with all your heart, all your soul, all your mind, and all your strength." He demands, "Seek ye first the kingdom of God and his righteousness, and all these things shall be added unto you."

Elijah told the widow, "I know your situation, that you are about to die. But God has sent me to tell you that you shall not die; you shall live. He is giving you life as a gift." The God of Elijah offers the same gift to us today. Trust and obey him. Give all to him. Offer him the sacrifice of a broken spirit and a contrite heart, and you will be saved.

"I have not made trouble for Israel," Elijah replied. "But you and your father's family have. You have abandoned the LORD's commands."
—*1 Kings 18:18*

here are two ways in which a person can be a troublemaker. One is by sinning against the Lord. In that sense, everyone who sins joins Satan, the ultimate troublemaker. So if you are sinning, I want you to know that you are in league with Satan. You make trouble for yourself, your family, your church, and your society.

But some in the church are considered troublemakers in another sense. If you are a father who leads your family in the way of the Lord, your children may look upon you as a troublemaker, because you bring trouble to their consciences. Ministers of the gospel are labeled troublemakers because they give no peace to a sinner. They declare the truth, and rebels do not like it.

In truth, none of us likes to be told to repent. None of us likes to be reminded of the Holy God's sovereign demand upon our lives. We think, "That preacher goes too far! He wants to tell me how to raise my children and how to order my life. He preaches the word and commands me to repent. I am sick of him!" King Ahab was no exception. He did not appreciate Elijah preaching against his flagrant idolatry. He called him "the troubler of Israel."

But Elijah declared to Ahab, "I am not the troubler of Israel in the sense you think I am. I am not responsible for this severe drought afflicting the nation. I have not committed a crime against the state. But you and your father's family have. You have abandoned the Lord's commands in the Bible and have followed the Baals. For this sin, God has cursed you and your nation. Not I, King Ahab, but you, are the real troubler of Israel."

Behind all of fallen humanity, there is Satan, who is the evil troublemaker. He comes to steal, kill and destroy. He deceives us into thinking, "My father is the troublemaker, my pastor is the troublemaker, and, above all, God is the troublemaker." No! The real troublemakers are those who follow Satan's ways. But praise be to God, Christ has come and defeated Satan, sin, hell and death. He is the Savior. And if you believe his gospel, you will be saved.

Accept him whose faith is weak, without passing judgment on disputable matters. —Romans 14:1

 omans 14 speaks about life in the family of God. As God's children, how do we relate to each other in God's holy church? We come from different backgrounds, countries, cultures, and tribes. We are Jews and Gentiles. We eat different foods. Yet we all are children of the heavenly Father who loves us with an everlasting love. We all live by the grace of God, which enables us to abound in good works.

Here Paul is commanding the strong believers to receive the weak believer—one who is not convinced that the gospel gives him the freedom to eat meat, especially meat offered to idols and sold in the market. The weak Christian is not sure that the ceremonial laws have been abrogated. The strong are not to force him to eat meat and thus violate his conscience and cause him to sin. The strong are commanded to take the initiative and go out of their way to receive their weak brothers. They are to do so enthusiastically, not just receiving them into the church through baptism and then treating them as second-class citizens. The strong are to accept and receive the weak believers unconditionally, without reservation. They are to welcome them heartily into their inner circle, and into their hearts with warmth, kindness, and genuine love.

When it came to the truth of salvation, justification by faith, Paul refused to compromise. He boldly declared that we are justified by grace alone through the righteousness of Christ alone freely imputed to us. Christ took all our sins upon himself, and his death is our atonement. He gave us his perfect, divine righteousness, and so we are justified. We need not fulfill any law to justify ourselves by a legal righteousness of our own.

But Paul did compromise in *adiaphora*—in disputable matters that make no difference in regard to salvation. The kingdom of God is not a matter of eating and drinking (Rom. 14:17). So weak vegetarians are in God's kingdom, and strong non-vegetarians are also in God's kingdom. It is not a sin to be a vegetarian. We all belong to God's one family and must love one another. And in this way we prove our salvation by living a life of love.

I commend to you our sister Phoebe, a servant of the church in Cenchrea.
—Romans 16:1

n Romans 16, Paul recommends Phoebe to the Christians in Rome as "our sister" and "a servant of the church" and asks that they "receive her in the Lord." Though she was a sister in the Lord, Phoebe was also a Gentile. There should not have been any discrimination in God's church, but there was, even in the apostolic church. In Acts 6:1, we read that the poor Jewish widows who spoke Greek were not given food because they were not Hebraic Jews. This was sin. So Paul wanted to avoid that.

We must make every effort to maintain the unity of the Spirit through the bond of peace. Why? Because there is only one body, one Spirit, one hope, one Lord, one faith, one baptism, and one God and Father of all (Eph. 4:3–6). We are all fellow citizens with God's people and members of God's household (Eph. 2:19). The Gentiles are heirs together with Israel, members together of one body, and sharers together in the promise in Christ Jesus (Eph. 3:6).

We are therefore to love one another deeply. Weak vegetarians are to love the strong meat-eating believers. Gentile saints are to love Jewish saints. We are to receive one another as Christ received us in order to bring praise to God (Rom. 15:7). We are to welcome each other into our hearts, into our homes, and to our tables. The saints were to receive Phoebe, for whom Christ died, for the Lord's sake because she, like them, was united with Christ. She was a member of Christ, a member of the body of Christ, a member of the family of God. And a family takes care of its own.

Paul also says they were to receive her in a way "worthy of the saints." Not only was Phoebe a sister and a servant, but she was also a saint. Mary the mother of Christ was a saint, and so are all of us. We were once ungodly sinners, enemies of God, under God's wrath. But God made us all saints by a divine miracle. So Paul exhorts the saints in Rome to give Phoebe a welcome worthy of one who had traveled eight hundred miles to deliver the precious gospel contained in Paul's letter. Let us likewise welcome, love, and serve the saints.

The message of the cross is foolishness to those who are perishing.
—*1 Corinthians 1:18*

n 1 Corinthians 1, Paul exposes the estimation of unbelievers, whether Jews or Gentiles, of God's gospel of salvation. The apostle calls this gospel "the message of the cross." The arrogant, unbelieving intellectuals of every age consider this message to be foolishness.

The apostle goes on to describe these mockers as "those who are perishing." One way to discern who is under God's judgment is to see how that person esteems the gospel. The Bible calls damned all who refuse to believe the gospel and who treat Jesus' person and work as nonsense. It matters not how educated, wealthy, or influential a person is; if he scoffs at the gospel message, he is perishing and shall perish eternally.

God responds to all who refuse him: "I will destroy the wisdom of the wise" (v. 19). He is warning every unbelieving philosopher, scientist, and scholar of this world. The Sovereign Lord has a plan to turn the tables and make foolish the wisdom of this world. He challenges the proud and arrogant: "Come on. Where are you? Make your appearance before me!" And we know the final outcome: Every knee shall bow and every tongue confess that Jesus Christ is Lord, to the glory of God the Father (Phil. 2:10–11).

Moreover, God has chosen to save the "foolish"—those who are not wise, not influential, not of noble birth—to shame those who are wise in their own eyes. No flesh shall boast before him; God alone will be exalted on that day.

Let us therefore give up our intellectual pride and arrogance, and humbly accept "the foolishness of what was preached," which is the message of the cross. As Paul says later in this same epistle, "If any one of you thinks he is wise by the standards of this age, he should become a 'fool' so that he may become wise" (1 Cor. 3:18).

The Scriptures declare, "God so loved the world that he gave his only begotten Son that whosoever believes on him should not perish but have everlasting life" (John 3:16). If you persist in your unbelief, the wrath of God abides upon you, and you shall not see life. If, however, you turn to God in humble repentance and faith, you will not perish, but enjoy eternal life here and hereafter.

If anyone destroys God's temple, God will destroy him.
—*1 Corinthians 3:17*

n 1 Corinthians 3, Paul put the following question to the church at Corinth: "Don't you know that you yourselves are God's temple and that God's Spirit lives in you?" (v. 16). The Corinthian church was nothing less than the Holy Place, the Holy of Holies, the temple of God.

Like the Corinthians, we also ought not to be ignorant. We should understand that the local church, which is constructed of individual, born-again men and women who are united with Christ, is the living temple of God. And not only so, but the Spirit of God also dwells in that temple. Just as the glory of God, the *shekinah,* dwelt in the Holy of Holies, so also the Holy Spirit of God is present in power in the local church.

The church is not a social club where we can come and go as we please, where we can gossip or act destructively, or where we can do whatever we want regardless of others. If anyone behaves in this manner, he is opposing not only the pastor or the elders, but, ultimately, the Head of the church, the Lord Jesus Christ himself. If anyone dares to harm or destroy that which belongs to God, the Lord will, in turn, destroy him.

Are you a church-builder or a church-wrecker? There are wrecking companies that are hired to come with cranes and large balls to strike down old buildings. Some people treat the local church in the same manner: they function as wrecking balls.

If you are tempted to be a wrecker, receive this warning: God, who dwells in his church as the *shekinah* glory, will destroy any person who dares to defile her. And we should have nothing to do with anyone who would harm the church, for our God is a zealous and jealous God. He will protect his blood-bought people.

Let us be careful: God's temple is holy, and we are that temple. Each local church that preaches the gospel is the church of Jesus Christ in which the Spirit of God dwells. Let us resolve to be church builders—encouraging one another, instructing one another, correcting one another, and building one another up— so that our church may grow in both grace and numbers, and may glorify God.

Is it because there is no God in Israel that you are going off to consult Baal-Zebub, the god of Ekron? —2 Kings 1:3

hen Ahab died in 853 BC, his son Ahaziah became king. I have no doubt that King Ahaziah knew that Jehovah is the true God. I am sure he was present with his father on Mount Carmel when Elijah challenged the false god Baal and demonstrated the power of the true God. Yet King Ahaziah refused to submit to the great Jehovah. He was stubborn and rebellious. The way of Baal worship seemed good to him. Why? He hated Jehovah, the God of justice, the God of holiness. He knew that Jehovah hates sin, but Baal loves it. Ahaziah knew that Jehovah requires repentance, but Baal allows man to be arrogant.

Amazingly, the God of Israel was patient with this king. He gave Ahaziah many opportunities to humble himself and return to the true worship of the great king, the covenant God, Jehovah.

We read in 2 Kings 1 that after Ahaziah became king, Moab rebelled against Israel (v. 1). Since the days of David, Moab had been subject to Israel, but the Moabites soon realized that Ahaziah was a weak king. So they rebelled against Israel, causing great political humiliation for Ahaziah. Who was behind this humiliation? God. This was God's plan to help Ahaziah humble himself.

Did political trouble cause Ahaziah to repent and call upon Jehovah? No. So God dealt with Ahaziah in a different way. This time he gave him economic trouble. In 2 Chronicles 20:35–37 we read that Ahaziah entered into a ship-building venture with Jehoshaphat, king of Judah. These two kings expended a large amount of money to build their ships. No doubt they were counting on a great return on their investment. But they lost everything.

Did Ahaziah repent as a result of this economic disaster? No. So God dealt with Ahaziah in a third way, a personal way, by touching his health. In 2 Kings 1:2, we read, "Now Ahaziah had fallen through the lattice of his upper room in Samaria and injured himself."

Sadly, even then Ahaziah would not consult the true and living God, the infinite, eternal, unchanging God—the patient God who alone is able to redeem a sinner. Ahaziah's actions proved where his trust really lay. He would not submit to the God of Israel, and he perished in his stubbornness.

The body is not meant for sexual immorality, but for the Lord.
—1 Corinthians 6:13

he believer's body is for the Lord's service, not fornication, and if we are using our bodies for the Lord, he promises to take care of them and save them. But this promise is conditional—we must walk in holiness if we want the assurance of his provision. What we do with our bodies matters, for they are permanent, redeemed at the high cost of the death of Christ. Our bodies are the temple of the Holy Spirit (1 Cor. 6).

Every Christian's body belongs to a new owner. Before we were redeemed, we could only serve our old master, Satan. We had no choice in the matter. When we were unbelievers, we thought we were our own bosses. But, in fact, every unbeliever does exactly what Satan wants him to do.

Our old master was a cruel tyrant. The Lord Jesus says Satan comes only to steal, kill, and destroy. But now we have been redeemed by our new owner, who became our master when we confessed, "Jesus is Lord." We are now his slaves who do his will.

As slaves of Christ, we have no rights, as the apostle states: "You are not your own; you were bought at a price" (v. 20). Recall the slogan of the Corinthians: "Everything is permissible for me" (v. 12). Here Paul brings the whole discussion to an end. He invalidates this saying because, as slaves, we have no rights. Praise God, though, our new Master is gracious. He loves us, saves us, and always has our best interest at heart. I would rather be submitted to Jesus Christ than to Satan.

Imagine what would happen if young Christian men and women dedicated themselves to live for Jesus Christ and to honor God with their bodies. Imagine a young person making a decision today to consecrate his or her life, saying, "I want to live a holy life for God." What blessings that person would reap! Such people would be filled with wisdom and would make God-honoring choices in all that they do. They would give the treasure of virginity to the spouses they marry. The Spirit of the living God would dwell in them with power, and they would know the joy of living in a victorious, God-pleasing way throughout all of life.

Those who use the things of the world [should live] as if not engrossed in them. For this world in its present form is passing away.
—1 Corinthians 7:31

he world in its present form is passing away and will soon be gone forever. Thanks be to God, though we are in this world, we are not of this world; we are of the world to come. We are of God, and we belong to the kingdom of God. Every person who is regenerated by the Holy Spirit is enabled to see and enter into the kingdom of God, which is described as righteousness, peace, and joy in the Holy Spirit.

In 1 Corinthians 7, Paul writes that those who buy something should do so "as if it were not theirs to keep" (v. 30). Some have misinterpreted this to mean that owning private property is forbidden. But this is wrong thinking. Neither is Paul advocating divorce, celibacy, stoicism, or asceticism. Marrying, buying, selling, building, eating, drinking—these are all necessary and proper aspects of human life. So we have to ask the question: What is the apostle teaching?

Paul is telling us that we should not seek all these things as of first priority, as though this world is the final and most important reality. It is engrossment in these things that is prohibited in this chapter. God opposes such hungering, thirsting, and pursuing. Jesus said that "the pagans run after all these things" (Matt. 6:32). This is what unbelievers seek with all their heart. This is what they worship. They believe, "If I could only possess more things, then I could arrive at happiness." It is this idolatrous mindset that God is so adamantly opposing.

We must study diligently and work hard so that we can make money. But that money is not finally ours; it is entrusted to us to use for God's purposes. All of us should examine our lives and ask whether we love God more than anything else in the world. We must love him more than our jobs, our money, our families, and even our own lives. We ought to develop a deep relationship with God now so that when we are called to heaven we will go eagerly and with great joy. We should be able to say, "I know someone already in heaven. He is the Lord Jesus Christ. I know him, because I have been walking closely with him in this world."

Go, wash yourself seven times in the Jordan . . . and you will be cleansed.
—2 Kings 5:10

he Lord of Israel will never heal an arrogant sinner who thinks he is better than others. In God's view, there is only one class of sinners: the worst class. Whether publican or Pharisee, the Jewish Saul or the Syrian leper Naaman, every sinner must repent and believe in Jesus Christ. No proud sinner will ever be saved unless he first humbles himself and trusts in Christ alone.

In 2 Kings 5, we read that Naaman came to Elisha with his own view of salvation. Asserting that he was a "first-class" sinner, he thought he should come through a different gate than others. He wanted a more dignified gospel, not the gospel of the cross. No, Naaman. You must surrender totally to God's way of salvation.

God had to humble the arrogant Naaman. So instead of sending Elisha personally to greet him, he sent Elisha's servant Gehazi with the following message: "Mr. Naaman, it is clear that you are a leper. Here is the cure for your leprosy. Go down to the Jordan River—not to the rivers of Damascus, which you think have cleaner water—immerse yourself in the Jordan seven times, and you will be healed."

Naaman was offended because Elisha did not give him preferential treatment. In fact, he almost missed his healing because of his pride. His wise servants, though, persuaded him to heed the prophet's counsel. And so he humbled himself, went to the Jordan, and stripped off his regalia, displaying his leprosy for all to see. He immersed himself in the muddy waters of the Jordan seven times, according to the word of the man of God. Where there is obedience, there is faith. Where there is faith, there is obedience. And as he obeyed, Naaman was cured of his leprosy.

If we seek salvation our own way, whether in materialism, philosophy, science, good deeds, or in any other religion, we will not find it. Jesus Christ alone is Savior. "Salvation is found in no one else, for there is no other name under heaven given to men by which we must be saved" (Acts 4:12).

I urge you, do not be offended by the gospel and die in your sins. Follow Naaman into the river Jordan. Call upon the name of the Lord, and be washed clean.

"Don't be afraid," the prophet answered. "Those who are with us are more than those who are with them." —2 Kings 6:16

aints of God, your heavenly Father is speaking to you through this passage in 2 Kings 6. What are you afraid of? Going to school? A new job? The uncertainties of today's economic or political situation? I hope you will identify what you are afraid of. Then listen carefully to what God is saying to you: Don't be afraid!

God's heavenly army surrounds his people. Remember how one angel of God destroyed one hundred and eighty-five thousand mighty soldiers of the army of Sennacherib and brought victory to King Hezekiah (2 Kings 19:35)? God's people are always surrounded by his holy angels.

Not only so, but we are also kept in the hand of Christ and in the hand of the Father. Who can snatch us out of his mighty hand? We are precious to him. We are his portion and inheritance, having been redeemed by the precious blood of Christ. God spared us from eternal destruction by not sparing his own Son.

May God, therefore, open our spiritual eyes to see reality, just as he opened the eyes of the servant of Elisha so that he could see the hills full of horses and chariots of fire surrounding him. We are not naïve or ignorant; we know that we have enemies because we preach the true gospel. The devil and demons hate us. The world hates us. False brothers and false churches hate us. Just as the Arameans wanted to arrest Elisha and his servant, so our enemies want to destroy all true pastors and true churches. But remember: We are held by Jesus Christ in his right hand.

So fear not, saints of God! Because God and his angels are with us, we are invincible. No one can destroy us, for, in order to do so, our enemies must destroy God. Yes, God may permit us to be killed when our work on earth is done. But death itself is a servant of God, for it opens the door of heaven to us. To live is Christ and to die is gain. To be absent from the body is to be present with the Lord, which is much better. So do not be afraid. Perfect love casts out all fear. Be filled with God's Spirit and live an overcoming life.

Love never fails. —1 Corinthians 13:8

irst Corinthians 13 paints a picture of true love, the love that proceeds from God himself. True love never fails. Why is that? It is the love of God shed abroad in our hearts. It is not man's intermittent and occasional love. God's Spirit has shed abroad his love into our hearts; therefore, it never fades or falters.

True love abides forever because love is truth. "Truth," in Hebrew, means that which abides. And we are told to speak the truth and to practice the truth. I have no respect for so-called Christians who affirm their love, only to later change their minds. What is the difference between them and the people of the world? Nothing! But God is love and God is truth.

True love communicates; thus, God communicates. He does not have to speak to us, for who are we? We are nothing and less than nothing; we are fallen human beings. Yet God loves sinners, so he gave us a Bible. The Bible is God's communication, his love letter, to us. And in the Bible, God tells us how much he loves us in Christ. The Bible speaks of Jesus Christ—his life and death for our eternal salvation.

Love communicates. If you do not speak to your spouse or your parents, you have a problem. If you love, then you will talk about what is going on in your life.

True love also communes. A loving husband does not say, "You live in California and I will live in New York." Love comes together and communes and fellowships with the other. Married people are supposed to live together, not independently to promote their own careers.

God loved us and sent his Son to come and dwell with us. The Word became flesh and dwelt among us, and we beheld his glory (John 1:14). When Jesus ascended into heaven, he sent the Holy Spirit to dwell with us and be in us. God loves us and has come down to fellowship with us. He shall never leave us nor forsake us.

Finally, true love sacrifices. In other words, love dies for the benefit of another. Love is not always trying to get a better deal. Love gives. Love sacrifices. Love lays down its life for another. May God increase our love for him and for one another.

But Christ has indeed been raised from the dead, the firstfruits of those who have fallen asleep. —1 Corinthians 15:20

I n 1 Corinthians 15, notice the phrase, "fallen asleep." It teaches us that God's people who have died will wake again. At the sound of the last trumpet, they will rise up with bodies that are imperishable, immortal, and glorious—bodies that are transformed by the mighty power of God.

Christ is called the firstfruits of those who have died. Firstfruits is first discussed in Leviticus 23, when the people of God were instructed to bring a sheaf from the first ripe grain to the temple and offer it to God, thereby dedicating the whole harvest to him. The firstfruits were a guarantee and pledge that an abundant harvest would be coming. Jesus Christ is the firstfruits, the firstborn from the dead (Acts 26:23). He is the guarantee and pledge of our own coming resurrection, and we are the harvest.

Herein we see the grand purpose and order of God: Christ as the firstfruits was raised from the dead. Then, at his second coming, those who belong to him will be raised up also. In John 6, Jesus himself promised his disciples four times, "I will raise them up on the last day." In Adam, all died, but in Christ, all believers are made alive. Jesus said, "Because I live, you also will live" (John 14:19). He is risen and now lives. Therefore, we also are alive now spiritually. And we will be granted glorious resurrection bodies when he comes again.

The purpose of redemption is to bring us to God. Jesus is the resurrection and the life for us. If you believe in him, Jesus Christ lives in you by his Holy Spirit. And the same Spirit who raised Christ from the dead will also give life to your mortal body. When he has raised us from the dead with bodies like unto his own, the Lord Jesus Christ will bring us with all glory into the presence of the Father to live with him forever. Our present union with Christ guarantees that we will also be raised up with him on the last day.

Jesus Christ is surely coming again for those who belong to him. We are savingly united to Christ by faith alone in the gospel alone. If you do not belong to him, I urge you to trust him now. Then death will also be your entrance into everlasting glory.

You are to destroy the house of Ahab your master, and I will avenge the blood of my servants the prophets . . . shed by Jezebel. —2 Kings 9:7

econd Kings 9 reminds us in a graphic way that the Lord our God is the Lord of history. In fact, history is simply the unfolding of his sovereign plan, which no man can thwart. Our God is almighty, omniscient, and everywhere present. He knows the end from the beginning, because he controls the end from the beginning.

In order to grasp the significance of this chapter, we must first remember what God told his prophet Elijah in 1 Kings 19. After his great victory on Mount Carmel, Elijah became afraid of Jezebel's threats and ran for his life. Sitting under a broom tree in the desert, the prophet said he wanted to die. He felt as if he was the only one left who loved and served Yahweh. God responded to him in a still small voice: "Elijah, I remain the sovereign covenant Lord of my people, and I have a plan whereby my justice and holiness shall be vindicated in due time. You are to quit running away and return to anoint three people whom I will use to carry out my purposes—Hazael, Jehu, and Elisha."

Elijah obeyed the word of the Lord and found Elisha son of Shaphat. He then commissioned Elisha to anoint Hazael and Jehu. It took several years to reach fruition, but God's purpose was ultimately realized. In 2 Kings 8, Elisha told Hazael that he would become the next king of Aram, and God used this pagan ruler to punish his unfaithful people in the northern kingdom of Israel. Now, in 2 Kings 9, we witness the anointing of Jehu son of Jehoshaphat at Elisha's word.

Jezebel, the vile widow of King Ahab, must have thought that she would get away with all the evil she had perpetrated in the northern kingdom. She had murdered many of the Lord's prophets (1 Kings 18:4), yet had never been brought to account. Elijah himself ran when she threatened his life.

God may choose not to intervene when his prophets are killed, for to die is gain if we fall asleep in faith. But we can also be certain that God's universe is moral; no one gets away with sin. "In due time their foot will slip" (Deut. 32:35). With great zeal, Jehu executed God's vengeance on Ahab's entire household in accordance with the word of the sovereign Lord of history.

Unlike so many, we do not peddle the word of God for profit.
—*2 Corinthians 2:17*

n 2 Corinthians 2:17, the apostle Paul gets to the heart of the distinction between true and false ministers of the gospel. Sadly, the majority of ministers in today's churches are false. These pastors, such as those who propound liberalism and liberation theology, the health and wealth gospel, the word-faith cult, shallow evangelicalism, and the celebrity-star-pastor cults, all reject the absolute authority of the Bible. They do not have the mind of Christ and therefore cannot understand the gospel. They add to, subtract from, and misinterpret the Scripture. They are incompetent to interpret the Bible because they are not born again and indwelt by the Spirit of God.

These false ministers use all sorts of secret and shameful methods to promote their anti-gospel of easy believism and cheap grace. They oppose the true gospel at every turn through their lies. They peddle the word of God and corrupt it to deceive the gullible, make money, and become famous in the eyes of the world. They do not worship Jesus Christ; they worship and serve money and power. By soothing, smooth words, they pick the pockets of those who crowd into their churches to be entertained. These self-called ministers tell stories and jokes to make people laugh. They preach themselves. They are star performers, not servants of Christ. And those who are non-elect will go to watch them perform.

Paul reassures the church that he and his fellow workers, however, are not like that. "On the contrary, in Christ we speak before God with sincerity, like men sent from God." True ministers are called and commissioned by God himself. Having been called and sent by God, they preach with divine authority. Paul was clear, direct, and straightforward. He was not a crook. He preached what people needed to hear. He did not preach for financial gain, nor did he have any secret, selfish, shameful agenda. He preached for the salvation of the lost. He preached Jesus Christ as Lord.

Christ is with all true ministers, to defend them and support them. When such pastors speak, Christ himself is speaking. And if anyone rejects their gospel, he is rejecting Christ. Let us therefore thank God for faithful ministers, and let us hear and obey their preaching, for our blessing.

Now the Lord is the Spirit, and where the Spirit of the Lord is, there is freedom. —2 Corinthians 3:17

ord" means king, sovereign, one who has absolute authority over his subjects. The Old Testament speaks of God the Father as Lord. The New Testament speaks about Jesus Christ as Lord. But the Bible also tells us that the Holy Spirit is Lord. Our view of the lordship of God is therefore triune. All three Persons of the Godhead exercise lordship.

The Holy Spirit is a person, and when he comes to indwell us, he exercises lordship. He is not a servant. He is not a mere helper. Yes, he does comfort, counsel, and guide; but he is first and foremost, Lord. And so he has complete, total, absolute authority in our lives. He can tell us which way to go, what to do, what to say, and what to think. He convicts us of sin, righteousness, and judgment.

We are told in 2 Corinthians 3 that "the Lord is the Spirit" and that "where the Spirit of the Lord is, there is freedom." The latter phrase can be translated, "*where the Spirit is Lord.*" When the Spirit is recognized by the believer as Lord, the believer will enjoy wonderful freedom.

We must not distort freedom to mean disorder, confusion, doing our own thing. Rather, the text is speaking of the marvelous freedom that a Christian has not to sin. He who sins is a slave to sin. But if we live in the light of the fact that the Spirit is Lord, and render him obedience, we experience the freedom to do righteousness with joy. If the Son sets us free, we shall be free indeed.

Obedience by the power of the Spirit is not misery. As unbelievers, we were selfish and self-centered. Now, by God's grace, we serve others. We are set free to sing, to pray, and to witness. The Holy Spirit has broken the chains that bound us and has granted us liberty. What condition must we meet for this freedom? We must recognize the Spirit's lordship in our lives.

How do we recognize the Holy Spirit's lordship? By obeying him. It is not enough to sing, "He is Lord." Nothing will prove the lordship of the Holy Spirit in our lives except when we obey him from our hearts. When we do so, we will enjoy the glorious liberty of the children of God.

God made him who had no sin to be sin for us, so that in him we might become the righteousness of God. —2 Corinthians 5:21

he salvation we have in Jesus Christ is a real accounting miracle. The Greek word *logizomai* means "to impute, to put into the account of another, to credit someone with." The word is used about forty times in the New Testament. Paul often employs this accounting term to describe the salvation process because we all have an account with God. The problem is, we have only liabilities in our account. This should not surprise us. The Bible teaches that we are sinners in Adam who are born in sin and who daily commit sin against the holy God. Thus, we need God's miracle of divine accounting, of non-imputation, of not counting our sins against us.

In 2 Corinthians 5, we find one of the most important New Testament passages that discuss the non-imputation of sin. By nature, God and man are enemies, God being the offended party and man the offender. But God took initiative to bring about reconciliation between himself and man through his Son, Jesus Christ. In verse 19, Paul writes, "God was reconciling the world to himself in Christ, not counting men's sins against them." This is the wonder of divine mercy.

But there is more to this accounting miracle. We read in verse 21, "God made him who had no sin to be sin for us, so that in him we might become the righteousness of God." In other words, he who knew no sin, the Lord Jesus Christ, was made sin, meaning not a sinner or a sin offering, but a sin-bearer for us. Jesus was intrinsically and extrinsically impeccable. Yet in God's perfect plan of salvation, our sin was imputed to him, put into his account.

Not only was our sin credited to Jesus' account, but his righteousness was also credited to our account. Because of this miracle of double imputation, the man who is in Christ has the full righteousness of Christ in his asset column and no liabilities. This is the glorious gospel presented in this chapter. As Christians, we are in Christ; thus, when we stand before God, we have absolutely no sin, no guilt, no judgment, and no condemnation. As Paul writes in Romans 8:1, "Therefore, there is now no condemnation to those who are in Christ Jesus."

But if they had stood in my council, they would have proclaimed my words to my people. —Jeremiah 23:22

eremiah 23 is given to us as a warning against false shepherds and lying prophets. If you are a person steeped in the Holy Scriptures, you will not listen to every prophet who prophesies; the Scriptures themselves tell you not to. There should be a spiritual antenna within you that perceives danger and says, "Warning! Pay no attention!" We are careful to turn the television off because of perversion and violence. But, ultimately, the most damaging thing in the world is lying prophets delivering false messages. The world is filled with traps and snares, but the most serious danger to a Christian is a heretical pastor. Religious television programs that invade our homes and that are full of spiritual adultery, that will not confront us about our sin and God's wrath, that will not say, "Repent for the kingdom of heaven is at hand"—these programs can bring great trouble to our souls.

In Jeremiah 23, God is warning the remnant, the true church, to not listen to lying pastors, because they fill us with false hopes. They ignore repentance. They promise to heal all our diseases. They say that our income will be increased as long as we give them money. What animates them is money and pleasure. And as long as we support them, they will prophesy good things for us.

But the hopes they engender are false and will ultimately disappoint, for those who make these promises are speaking not from God but from their own subjectivity. They are not true pastors. They are not interested in serious study of the Scriptures in the original languages. They do not stand on the shoulders of Luther, Calvin, and Edwards. Rather, they are enamored of their own dreams and visions. The Lord is explicit in this chapter—these men have not stood in the council of God. Such pastors and prophets are self-called men; God has not sent them.

In contrast, a God-called, God-sent pastor understands that he has no authority to teach or preach anything other than the Bible. He is not afraid to confront and correct, because he does not prophesy for profit. He studies hard and practices what he preaches, that he might feed his people with the pure, life-giving word of God. May God bless his people with such pastors!

And God is mighty to make all grace abound to you, so that in all things at all times, having all that you need, you will abound in every good work. —2 Corinthians 9:8

ur God is mighty. In 2 Corinthians 9, we read that he is mighty to give us grace—amazing, unmerited divine favor, divine ability. Not only so, but God also gives his people grace in abundance. We need this grace each new day, for we are his workmanship, created in Christ Jesus for the purpose of daily doing the good works he has prepared for us to do (Eph. 2:10). We are able to do God's will only by God's amazing grace.

This grace is described as "all sorts of grace." It is grace to wash the dishes, grace to take care of your elderly parents, grace to raise your children in the fear and admonition of the Lord, grace to go to work and do the best job, grace to love your wife, grace for you to submit to your husband and respect him with joy. In other words, God gives us grace for every aspect of our lives—grace to live and grace to die.

God is mighty to abound grace "to you," the believer, his child. In fact, you should expect to receive God's grace. If you are a Christian, and you prayed and asked God for grace, it will come to you in accordance with his promise. This is a promise God makes to every true Christian.

God is mighty to make all grace abound to us "in all things." This reminds us of Paul's statement in Romans 8:28: "In all things God works for the good of those who love him." God's grace abounds to us in all of the various circumstances of life, whether we are experiencing pain or pleasure, joy or sorrow.

God's grace empowers us "at all times." It is not that once in a while it works. The analogy is what Jesus said: "I am the vine; you are the branches." The flow is continuous from the vine to the branch, so that we can bring forth fruit, more fruit, and much fruit. In God's grace, we have "all sufficiency"—we need nothing more. God gives us what it takes, and more than what it takes, to live life in a way that is pleasing to him.

What is God's purpose in sending this mighty effusion of grace toward us? Simply put, that we may do the will of God with joy, with pleasure, as an expression of thanksgiving to God for saving us.

Such men are false apostles, deceitful workmen, masquerading as apostles of Christ. —2 Corinthians 11:13

true pastor refuses to speak nonsense. He refuses to speak a different gospel or a different Jesus, in order to attract more people. Sadly, the hidden agenda of many modern evangelicals involves precisely this—a new gospel, a new way of "doing religion." Paul addressed this problem in 2 Corinthians 11.

The first and chief point of attack is always against authority, specifically the authority and inspiration of the Bible. Now, these evangelicals do not stand up in the church and openly declare the Bible to be the work of men. No, they masquerade and deceive. How, then, can we recognize a church that no longer believes in the authority of the Bible? Simply observe the lives of its people and see whether they obey the Scripture. Note whether they live disciplined lives, lives governed by the Scriptures and the Holy Spirit.

Knock down the authority of God's word and we are left with pluralism—the idea that all religions ultimately lead to the same God. This is the message some "Christian" leaders have communicated to the Muslim world. "We believe that there are other ways of salvation. Let's all just get along. We'll preach Jesus; you preach Mohammed." For them, to say that salvation is through Jesus Christ alone is narrow-minded and intolerant.

Knock down the authority of God's word, and we are left with humanistic worship that includes discussions, dancing, rock music, drama, and so on. Humanistic worship means anthropocentric worship. It means catering to people's desires for entertainment and an emotional high. It is no longer preaching the gospel, the herald proclaiming the news of the king with authority. Instead, it makes its appeal to people's emotions and felt needs.

Knock down the authority of God's word, and we are left with selfism, that says, "I am God, and my subjective feelings are the final authority." Selfists reject the language of sin, repentance, hell, and judgment. Instead, they embrace a different gospel, a different Jesus, a false religion that will lead them to hell.

Let us reject false teachers with their false gospel. Let us, instead, proclaim, *"Sola Scriptura!"* and be governed by the Scripture alone in all matters of faith and life.

The LORD removed them from his presence. —2 Kings 17:23

he Bible alone is the word of God; thus, it alone determines our doctrine and ethics. It does not matter what the Supreme Court or the president of the United States says; we must do what God says.

God's insistence on holiness and discipline for his people is found throughout the Bible. Accordingly, despite the cultural norm of "toleration," the Lord demands that his church expel unrepentant heretics from her membership to the sphere of the devil. She must do so without prejudice, putting out very powerful members as well as those who are not. If church members will not repent, after having received due warnings, they must be put out.

The church must do so to maintain her purity. Yet we should understand that it is Christ himself who is ultimately acting through the church. It is not finally the pastor's church but Christ's church, and he will discipline, whether the pastor does so or not. He does so because he insists on having a radiant bride, not a dirty one filled with immorality, adultery, fornication, homosexuality, lying, and cheating.

Second Kings 17 gives us a striking Old Testament example of this principle of excommunication. Three times we are told that the covenant Lord himself thrust his people from his presence. Despite multiple warnings from the prophets and seers, the Israelites remained stiff-necked and would not give up their fascination with sin, idolatry, and the customs of the surrounding nations. As a result, God's righteous anger was provoked and he carried out his threatenings. Exile from the Promised Land ensued.

We serve the same living and true God today, and we also are under covenantal obligations to depart from evil and fear the Lord. I pray that we will fear and tremble, if we are members of God's holy church. He sees everything we do. He sees us sinning. He even sees our inward thoughts and motivations. Let us learn from the Israelites' tragic conclusion. May God help us to submit to the Lord's work of sanctification and humbly accept the ministry we receive from church leaders, so that we may become a radiant bride for Christ, without stain or wrinkle, made holy by the Lord himself.

Hezekiah trusted in the LORD, the God of Israel. —2 Kings 18:5

 ing Ahaz was an unbeliever; he refused to put his trust in Jehovah. Ahaz preferred to be a vassal to the Assyrian king than to the Lord his God. Thus, he brought the kingdom of Judah to near ruin (see 2 Kings 16; Isaiah 7). Yet God in mercy gave him a son, Hezekiah, whose name means "God is my salvation." By God's miracle, the son of a wicked king became a great believer in Yahweh. In 2 Kings 18, we read that Hezekiah "did what was right in the eyes of the LORD" (v. 3).

In verse 7, we read something very significant about Hezekiah: "He rebelled against the king of Assyria and did not serve him." In this, Hezekiah is a type of every true Christian. Everyone comes into the world a sinner serving Satan. Satan is the great overlord, the god of this age. But a born-again Christian is given divine power to say "No" to Satan, ungodliness, and worldly passions. In other words, the Christian has sworn his allegiance to the Lord Jesus Christ and refuses to serve the devil any longer. We say "No" to Satan and "Yes" to Christ with all our heart, soul, mind, and strength.

Satan and all the hosts of hell will bitterly oppose us because we have been redeemed. But if we serve God as Hezekiah did, the Lord will give us victory over all our enemies. Sennacherib with his fearsome army came to make war against Hezekiah, engaging first in psychological warfare. He threatened, "Do not let the god you depend on deceive you" (2 Kings 19:10). But Hezekiah knew his God; therefore, he refused to give way to doubt or fear.

Hezekiah strengthened his people and exhorted them also to not be afraid or discouraged. His counsel was not the product of glib optimism, but was based on certain fact: "There is a greater power with us than with him" (2 Chron. 32:7). This was tremendous understanding. Sennacherib was the greatest king of that age; yet, Hezekiah knew that Jehovah is the King of kings and Lord of lords.

When we face crises in our life, we must react as Hezekiah did. If we fully place our trust in God, we can enjoy the same comfort, strength, and victory that Hezekiah experienced.

"For I know the plans I have for you," declares the LORD, "plans to prosper you and not to harm you, plans to give you a hope and a future."
—*Jeremiah 29:11*

If you want to hear genuinely good news, to whom should you look? Look to God. God has a plan for you and for me and for all his elect. It is a plan for prosperity, a plan of hope.

We all have an interest in knowing what the future holds for us. Here the covenant Lord promises that our future is bright. We serve a God who is a person, who thinks, plans, and speaks. In Jeremiah 29, he tells us, "I know the plan I have for you, for I devised that plan and will surely bring it to pass." What amazing love, that God would take a personal interest in us!

I do not have to worry about understanding every detail of God's decrees. In fact, I do not even know what tomorrow will bring. But I do know the One who has planned tomorrow from all eternity, and I know that he is working all things together for my good. I can live in peace and joy no matter my circumstances, for I know that God has an unchangeable plan to bring me to glory. He has already taken care of my sin, misery, and confusion at the cross.

Hallelujah! It does not matter what has happened in the past, or even what is taking place now. God himself says we have a future. Not only so, but we can also rest in the confidence that our covenant children will inherit this blessing. The Bible promises that all Christians are destined to glory, to prosperity, to a hope that will not disappoint. Let us then believe God and not look at our circumstances or listen to the devil.

But notice, this passage also says that we must be patient. There is always a cross before a crown. In the Israelites' case, seventy years had to pass before God would bring them back to their land from captivity. We may be tempted to say, "Seventy years is too long; we want our bright future now!" But God may answer, "I have placed you in captivity because of your sin. Now is the time to reflect, repent, and be rid of all your idols. Return to the true and living God, and in his perfect time you will be lifted up."

I have loved you with an everlasting love; I have drawn you with loving-kindness. I will build you up again and you will be rebuilt.
—Jeremiah 31:3–4

n Jeremiah 31, God's people were in deep trouble, exiled and in captivity. Their captors mocked them, telling them to sing the songs of Zion. All seemed lost. But then, through the prophet Jeremiah, came God's comforting word to his people: "My love for you is eternal, everlasting, unbreakable, never-ending. I know you are a ruined city, but I will rebuild you." He is the architect and the builder. And he does not speak idle words.

God's eternal, electing love is the foundation for all that he does for us and in us. Each of us must understand and appreciate this marvelous truth. We may say, "O God, I am a wretched, miserable, filthy sinner." Yet he will respond, "Yes, I fully understand that. It is no surprise to me. But know this—I have loved you with an everlasting love; I have drawn you with loving-kindness. I will redeem you, and I will make you pure."

In this chapter, God was looking on his people—his sinful, wasted, destroyed people. Yet because of his everlasting love, he was promising to rebuild them. "God is not a man, that he should lie, nor a son of man, that he should change his mind" (Num. 23:19). I want you to apply it, boys and girls, men and women, old and young. God is speaking to you. He sees you in your sin; yet he is saying to you, "I will rebuild you." He has saved us, he is saving us, and he will save us and bring us safely to heaven.

We cannot fathom this divine love, but we must take God at his word and receive his comfort in our souls. No matter what our problems are, no matter how much we have sinned in the past, God is not going to abandon us. "How great is the love the Father has lavished on us, that we should be called children of God! And that is what we are!" (1 John 3:1). We are children of God.

What will we do if we understand Jeremiah's word for his people? "Again you will take up your tambourines and go out to dance with the joyful" (v. 4). Let me tell you, if we believe in this gospel, we will rejoice greatly and praise God's glorious name.

SEPTEMBER 27

When the king heard the words of the Book of the Law, he tore his robes.
—2 Kings 22:11

osiah means "the Lord has helped." His grandfather Manasseh was the most wicked king in the history of Judah and Israel, and his father Amon was wicked too. Yet, in God's mercy, Josiah became the most godly of all the kings. We must recognize God's grace to the house of David. Though the grandfather and father were evil, there came a little boy, eight years of age, who was absolutely different (2 Kings 22).

Josiah was totally committed to God, though he was completely surrounded by filth and idolatry of every kind, not just in the streets of Jerusalem, but inside the temple itself. Josiah was loyal to the Lord of the covenant at the time of the greatest apostasy in the history of Israel.

This ought to give us great hope. Today's culture is wicked also, but we can still be faithful to our covenant Lord. We can be the light of the world. A true Christian can and must live a life that shines brightly in the darkness all around.

Just see what one young person can do when he gives himself totally to the service of the Lord! Josiah did not even have a Bible at first, yet God drew him and gave him a hatred for sin, wickedness, and idolatry. In response, the king sought the Lord, crying out, "O God, give me guidance. Give me help." And God heard his plea.

As the temple was being cleansed and repaired, in God's providence a discovery was made—there was a Book. We ought to pay close attention to the king's response when the contents of this book were read to him. He was still a young man, in his early twenties. Yet see his reaction to God's words! Josiah humbled himself and tore his clothes. He responded with a heartfelt repentance that moved heaven.

Is that what you do when you hear the word of God? Do you exhibit true repentance? Have you wept and humbled yourself before him? Have you confessed your sins and cried out, "O God, have mercy upon me!" We must pray today, "Lord, break down my stony heart. Give me a heart of flesh. Help me to humble myself before you and weep as this king did."

275

I keep asking that the God of our Lord Jesus Christ, the glorious Father,
may give you the Spirit of wisdom and revelation, so that you may know
him better. —Ephesians 1:17

s believers, we are privileged to experience an ongoing restoration of our spiritual sight. Some people say, "I know I'm saved because I remember twenty-five years ago I went forward one day." No! If we have truly been born again, God will continue to open our eyes daily so that we will have greater and greater spiritual vision and knowledge of eternal realities. We read about this in Ephesians 1.

God saved the Ephesians—they were chosen, predestinated, and redeemed. Their sins were forgiven, they were adopted into the very family of God, and they had been sealed with the Holy Spirit of promise. Yet in Ephesians 1:16–19, we find the apostle Paul praying that God would again enlighten these people so that they might come into a greater understanding of him.

Every time we come before God, whether in prayer, worship, or Bible reading, we must ask him, "O God, open my eyes! As I read the Scriptures, may I understand what they are saying, that I may know you—not just know about you, but that I may know you, confide in you, trust in you, lean on you, and rest on you."

The Greek word for knowledge means "to have accurate, personal, experimental, intimate knowledge." Many people know God only as the demons know him, believing in certain propositional truths regarding God and his character. In fact, there is no great difference between the intellectual orthodoxies of many people and those of demons. But knowing about God is not the same as knowing God. We must know God as a son knows his father, as a wife knows her husband, as a friend knows a friend. This is just what Jesus taught in his high priestly prayer: "Now this is eternal life: that they may know you, the only true God, and Jesus Christ, whom you have sent" (John 17:3).

When the Spirit of God opens our eyes, we will flourish in personal, intimate, vital knowledge of God the Father and God the Son. I pray that God will remove from our eyes the spiritual cataracts of worldliness, pride, love of pleasure, and trust in temporal things, so that we may see the ultimate reality of God— his infinite power and great salvation.

To him be glory in the church and in Christ Jesus throughout all generations, for ever and ever! Amen. —Ephesians 3:21

od planned to reveal his glory through the church even before the creation of the world. In Ephesians 1:12, Paul made the amazing declaration that the church of Jesus Christ is "for the praise of his glory." What does this statement tell us? That God is fascinated with his church. God's plan is to dwell with the members of his church for all eternity, and the fulfillment of this plan is the meaning of all history.

Historians find no meaning in history. Philosophers find no meaning in history. Hegel said, "History teaches us that history teaches us nothing." "Meaningless, meaningless, meaningless," said the Preacher long ago, in reference to the unbeliever's view. Yet throughout history God has been creating a most beautiful creation—the church, the body of Christ. The Lord Jesus Christ and his church alone give meaning to all history.

There is no meaning in history unless we find our meaning in the One who came into history in the midpoint of time. Jesus came to redeem the church at the cost of his precious blood, and without him there is no church. The Bible tells us that Christ loved the church from before the foundation of the world and gave himself for her. We were enemies of God and of one another. But through the miracle of Christ's death on the cross, we are now enabled to love God and one another. We who have been called into the church of Christ are becoming a radiant church, the bride of Christ, the most beautiful temple ever built—a temple built, not by man but by God, for God to dwell in.

Christians are always on display to show forth God's glory and splendor. We are God's new creation; he is committed to making us sparkling, radiant, and glorious. His purpose is that his manifold wisdom should be made known to the universe through his church, as we read in Ephesians 3. The more glorious the church is, the greater his glory will be. Let us then be aware of the dignity that God has conferred upon us. And let us then be careful how we behave. We are God's people and God is for us. Let us rejoice in that truth and live to glorify him!

Be filled with the Spirit. —Ephesians 5:18

hat does it mean to be filled with the Holy Spirit? It is to be under his controlling influence. Suppose, for example, that a young lady is so fascinated with a young man that she is always speaking about him. We can say that she is "filled" with him, because out of the abundance of the heart the mouth speaks. Whatever wholly takes possession of our intellect, will, and emotion is said to fill it. To be filled with the Holy Spirit, therefore, is to be controlled by the infinite Third Person of the Trinity.

Being filled with the Spirit is to be led and energized by the Holy Spirit. The Greek word for "fill" can be used to describe the wind filling the sail of a ship to move it along. The ship is energized and directed by that wind-filled sail. In the same way, a person who is filled with the Spirit joyfully keeps in step with the Spirit. We do not turn to the right or to the left. We are ruled and directed by the Spirit, not by our emotions. And by the Spirit, we put to death the misdeeds of the body (Rom. 8).

To be filled with the Holy Spirit is to obey the Holy Scriptures, because the Holy Spirit directs us through the Scriptures, which he authored. To be Spirit-filled is to obey Jesus Christ, whom we confess as Lord and who dwells in us.

Being filled with the Holy Spirit is the normal state of the Christian life; it is the condition in which every Christian is to live. As saints in whom the Holy Spirit dwells, being filled with the Spirit is a condition we can fulfill. And when the Holy Spirit controls us, we will do what is right; we will do the will of God.

An unbeliever, by stark contrast, is controlled not by the Holy Spirit but by an evil spirit, as we read in Ephesians 2:2. Never think an unbeliever is free to do what he likes. He is completely controlled by a spirit and does exactly what that spirit wants him to do. An unbeliever may glory in his "freedom," "independence," and "individualism," but it is all false. Freedom is found in Jesus Christ alone.

Obey the LORD by doing what I tell you. Then it will go well with you, and your life will be spared. —Jeremiah 38:20b

ing Zedekiah was a double-minded man. He listened to Jeremiah, but he never acted in faith on Jeremiah's message. He never obeyed. We read, "Neither he nor his attendants nor the people of the land paid any attention to the words the LORD had spoken through Jeremiah the prophet" (Jer. 37:2). We are living at a time when it is considered a shame to obey anyone. We are deceived into thinking that autonomy is the way to go. But there is no true autonomy. We either obey God or the devil; there is no third way.

Zedekiah went to Jeremiah frequently to hear a word from God, and God's prophet would give him God's word. He said over and over again, "Zedekiah, go out. Surrender to the king of Babylon. If you do so, you will live, your family will live, and the city will not be destroyed." That remained the message: Surrender and live. God will never bow down to us; we must bow down to him.

Nevertheless, Zedekiah thought that God would eventually relent and grant him his wish. But the Bible says God cannot change, and therefore his word does not change. Some people hope that I will change and preach a different message. It will never happen. I will preach the old-time gospel that saves you.

Zedekiah's final meeting with Jeremiah is recorded in Jeremiah 38. Had the word of God changed for the king? No! Jeremiah declared, "This is what the LORD God Almighty, the God of Israel, says: 'If you surrender to Babylon, your life will be spared and this city will not be burned down; your family will live'" (v. 17).

The message today is the same: Surrender to the Lord Jesus Christ and you and your household will be saved. Sadly, like Zedekiah, the vast majority of the people of the world refuse to believe this gospel. They think God is a joke. But our God rules the heavens and the earth.

If you do not want to listen to what the Bible and a godly pastor has to say, you will meet Zedekiah's end. He thought he could escape God's word and save himself without surrendering. It did not happen. Zedekiah's sons were slaughtered before his eyes and he was taken in chains to Babylon. I urge you today to surrender and live.

But the Babylonian army pursued them and overtook Zedekiah in the plains of Jericho. —Jeremiah 39:5

any types of people come to a pastor for counsel. Some come because they perceive it to be a duty. Suppose a boy wants to date a girl, but her father says that he must first speak with their pastor. That young man goes, not because he wants to hear a word from God, but because it is the father's expectation. He has no genuine heart or interest in listening to the pastor. In fact, he would rather do without.

Others come deceptively, with a hidden agenda. Such counselees come ostensibly for help, but their real intent is to get the pastor to speak, so that they can twist the pastor's words and use them later against him. Remember the Jews who came to Jesus and asked, "Should we pay taxes to Caesar or not?" They wanted to trap and trip Jesus. This can also happen to ministers.

Some people come for counsel with some true interest, but they leave disappointed. They listen to what God's will is, but they deem it too costly. They come honestly, but they discover that the gospel is the most expensive thing in the world, and they are not ready to pay the price.

But thanks be to God, some people do come in sincerity and truth, ready to hear and do the word of God as spoken by the man of God, no matter the cost.

Jeremiah 39 describes King Zedekiah's final outcome. His father Josiah had been a good king, and Zedekiah could have gone the way of his father, loving the word of God, responding to the word of God, and obeying the counsel of the man of God. He and his family could have lived a blessed, happy life if he had but respected and obeyed Jeremiah, God's prophet.

Did Zedekiah listen to Jeremiah's counsel? Not at all! The events of Jeremiah 39 could have been avoided had Zedekiah listened. But he did not, and the Babylonians captured his children and killed them in his presence. Then they gouged out his eyes. The last thing he saw was his children being killed, one after another.

Not to listen to the counsel of God from the man of God is terrible, destructive, and damning. Let us resolve to receive God's counsel and be blessed.

I have learned the secret of being content in any and every situation, whether well fed or hungry, whether living in plenty or in want. I can do everything through him who gives me strength. —Philippians 4:12–13

aul's condition when he wrote Philippians 4 was worse than that of a slave. A slave had some freedom of movement, but Paul was in prison, chained to soldiers on his left and right. How, then, could he say he was content? Here is the secret: If heaven is where God is, then this prison was heaven to Paul, because the Lord was with him. This is the key to it all. Paul could choose to look at his chains and the prison and the darkness, or he could look to God, who was with him. The Lord who appeared to him and apprehended him on the road to Damascus never forsook him.

The apostle wrote elsewhere that at his first trial, though all his friends deserted him, the Lord stood with him and gave him strength (2 Tim. 4:16–17). So the secret to Christian contentment is not a thing but a person—God himself. Paul could honestly say, "To me to live is Christ" and "I no longer live, but Christ lives in me." That is the key to true happiness.

The apostle had not always been like this; the Lord had to teach him through the school of fiery wilderness experiences. Just read 2 Corinthians 1, 4, 6, 11, and 12. These chapters recount many of Paul's trials. He learned his lessons well enough to be content whatever his circumstances.

Paul was taught by the Lord himself to be happy and to rejoice at all times. Whether demoted or promoted, sick or healthy, poor or rich, despised or praised, hungry or filled, lonely or surrounded by friends, shipwrecked or safe on land, Paul rejoiced in God his Savior.

Paul learned he could have deep peace in his soul in the midst of suffering. He learned he could pray instead of murmuring, and sing instead of sulking. Thus, when he was stripped, severely beaten, and thrown into an inner jail cell in the city of Philippi, he began to pray and sing hymns at midnight. Paul was the branch and Christ was the vine. We too are able to do all things—to live for him and die for him—through Jesus Christ, who continuously imparts his divine strength to us.

October 4

When Jeremiah finished telling the people all the words of the LORD their God—everything the LORD had sent him to tell them . . . all the arrogant men said to Jeremiah, "You are lying! The LORD our God has not sent you to say, 'You must not go to Egypt to settle there.'" —Jeremiah 43:1–2

he Bible says, "Trust in the LORD with all your heart and lean not unto your own understanding; in all your ways acknowledge him, and he will direct your paths" (Prov. 3:5–6). Our God speaks to us and guides us in his will. The God of the Bible is a God of revelation. He reveals himself to us through creation, conscience, Christ, and the canon of Scripture. He is always speaking to those who want to hear.

But we often have our own little ideas, our own pet schemes. This is arrogance. As a result, we want the prophet to change the word from God to suit our preferences. This is exactly what took place in Jeremiah 43.

What happened to these nice people—these seemingly pliable, obedient, loving people? They agreed, in the presence of God and and each other, to obey God's counsel, and then they changed their minds. Additionally, they also turned around and blamed the man of God who had preached the truth to them.

The people said, "Jeremiah, please speak to us. Please counsel us." And he told them, "Stay. Don't worry about Nebuchadnezzar or Babylon or their army. All the armies of the world are under God. Lean not unto your own understanding." But they retorted, "Babylon is coming; Babylon is going to kill us." No, nothing like that was going to happen. The Lord had promised them, "I am the Sovereign Lord of the universe. You stay, you plant, you harvest, and I will see to it that you will prosper. I will take care of you." That is what the Bible guarantees: "Believe on the Lord Jesus Christ and you will be saved." We must take God at his word.

Inexplicably, the Israelites did not believe God. Instead, they treated him with contempt. As a result, many of them would soon be killed in Egypt; it literally happened in 567 BC.

Let us revere God and respond to him with obedience, so that we may receive a blessing. He is God, who tells us the end from the beginning. Let us not trust in ourselves, but let us live by faith in our covenant Lord and his infallible word.

For in Christ all the fullness of the Deity lives in bodily form.
—Colossians 2:9

omplete divine power dwells in Jesus, the incarnate Son of God. Deity in its fullness—not merely divine attributes or certain qualities of divinity that come and go—permanently dwells in the Son, as Paul tells us in Colossians 2.

The knowledge of this great fact ought to strengthen and encourage us, because we are Christ's body, and we "have been given fullness in Christ" (v. 10). The more we discover about the glorious head of the body—Jesus Christ—the happier we are.

The Bible teaches us that we are married to Christ. What did we bring to this marriage? Only sin and liabilities. We had nothing—no assets whatsoever. But we came in humility, we came in repentance, we came just as we were, without one plea. Now, having been united to Christ by faith, all the fullness of God flows into us, because we are vitally connected to our heavenly Husband. We are told in John 1:16 that from his fullness we all have received grace upon grace. He is the richest One, the greatest One, the mightiest One, the infinite One, the immortal One, the almighty One—and all his assets flow to us. We receive grace upon grace every day and for every moment of our lives from the all-glorious Son.

When we study the universe and the sun, we discover that the sun is slowly running down—its energy supply will one day be exhausted. But that is not true of Christ. His is an inexhaustible fullness. No power in the world is able to rob him of this fullness of Deity, for he is King of kings and Lord of lords, supreme, sovereign, unassailable. In Jesus we cohere and consist. Therefore there is no reason for us to worry or be anxious about anything. We need simply to look to him in the morning and evening and whenever we need grace, for our King delights to grant us all-sufficient strength. We dare not look to ourselves.

One day the Son shall present us to himself and to his Father completely holy and without any trace of sin or blemish. By the power of his might we will be made perfect, glorious saints. To Jesus be the glory!

And whatever you do, whether in word or deed, do it all in the name of the Lord Jesus, giving thanks to God the Father through him.
—*Colossians 3:17*

he chief principle of conduct for a Christian is that he must do all things for the glory of God. We cannot do so, however, unless we do all things in the name of the Lord Jesus. This is impossible until we have been given the authority to act in his name.

Saul of Tarsus was a persecutor of Christianity until the day he was apprehended by Jesus Christ on the road to Damascus. God's purpose for Saul was "to carry my name before the Gentiles" (Acts 9:15). A Christian is one who, from the moment of his new birth, is given the greatest gift in all the world—the name of Jesus. He is authorized to represent him, to speak in behalf of him, and to act in behalf of him. We read in John 1:12 that God gives to all who receive Jesus the authority to be a child of God.

What does it mean, then, to do all things "in the name of the Lord Jesus," as Paul instructs in Colossians 3? It means that I must recognize that Jesus is my Lord, having full legal authority and power over my entire life. I am not my own; I am the servant of the Lord Jesus Christ, who is my Redeemer and who gave his own life to redeem me from the slavery and thralldom of the devil. Therefore, every aspect of my life—intellectual, emotional, ethical, vocational, political, church, and family—is governed by his lordship. I cannot have my own plan. I must seek out God's plan for my life, and do it with all my heart, mind, soul, and strength.

If you and I have come under the influence of the mighty Holy Spirit and experienced new birth, we will consider it the greatest blessing ever given to us by God that we are in Jesus Christ—and we can now live all of life in his glorious name. We must never consider the name of Jesus to be nothing. He is King of kings and Lord of lords; he has been exalted and has been given a name that is above every name. May we never treat the name of Jesus Christ with contempt! It is the greatest gift we can receive.

We loved you so much that we were delighted to share with you not only the gospel of God but our lives as well. —1 Thessalonians 2:8

n Thessalonica, Paul had been called a fraud by his Jewish opponents. In 1 Thessalonians 2, he defends the integrity of his God-given ministry to the Thessalonian believers. In doing so, he also gives us a clear picture of how ministers should take care of their flocks.

In verse 11 Paul writes, "You know that we dealt with each of you as a father deals with his own children." His ministry was personal, to "each of you," not a detached, "don't bother me" ministry, or an "I will come Sunday morning and say something, and you are to give me the money" ministry. He treated the Thessalonian believers as his own children. He was a father to them—one who trained them, taught them, and told them how to live.

Ministers must measure themselves by these standards: "Do I care for others, especially the people of God, as my own children? Am I a father to them? Do I nurture them and train them, encouraging, comforting, and urging them to live lives worthy of God? Are they dear to me?"

There are many churches today where immorality is practiced, and no one cares because the pastors themselves have committed immorality. The "Don't ask, don't tell" philosophy reigns. Such churches are open to all types of immoral people. "Come on in," they say, "just pay the money!" But that is not the model presented here by the apostle. He opposed immorality. He denounced disorder. And he insisted that the impenitent be excommunicated. Holy living was lovingly demanded.

The way of Jesus is the way of holiness. The way of Jesus is the way of obedience. The way of Jesus is the way of order. He himself said, "Deny yourself," which means that every Christian must deny the broad way of sin and autonomy. The church consists of holy people who believe the gospel and live the gospel. A God-called pastor cannot teach differently. He cannot let someone live by his or her own rules. The narrow way is the way of Jesus, and it alone leads to heaven. The minister who loves you will encourage, comfort, and urge you in this way, that you might safely reach heaven's shores and be welcomed into eternal glory.

Finally, brothers, we instructed you how to live in order to please God.
—1 Thessalonians 4:1

hat is the Bible's purpose? It is to show us how to live in a way that pleases God. The goal of all gospel preaching and teaching is given in 1 Thessalonians 4:1. The right way to live is taught in the Bible alone. Therefore we must have a voracious appetite for God's word. We must be steeped in this Book, which codifies the will of God. We must attend a Bible-preaching church, where we will hear from the pulpit what pleases God. We will never be taught that in any other place.

Life becomes simple when we ask ourselves this question: What is the will of God for me today? The answer will emerge instantly when we ask with sincerity and earnestness. Confusion arises when we are interested in pleasing ourselves or in pleasing another person. But these difficulties will evaporate the moment we commit ourselves to pleasing our Lord. To know the will of God and to do it is the very essence of Christianity.

To please ourselves or to please God—that is a decision we face every moment of every day. To please ourselves results in fights, clamor, misery, unhappiness, bitterness, envy, jealousy, and division. Look at children—they so often are self-centered, unwilling to share. Look at a married couple. What is the reason for quarrels? Each person is focusing on getting what he or she wants.

But when we honor God, he will honor us. When we please God, he will be pleased with us, and we will go on to enjoy the greatest thrill possible for a creature. There is no greater joy in the world than the joy we have knowing that God is pleased with us because we sought his will and did it, irrespective of difficulty or suffering.

This is my challenge to you: Are you going to live to please God or to please yourself? The purpose of the Christian life is not to set forth certain wants and desires that God must grant us. No, the purpose of our lives is to discover the will of God and then do it, so that divine approbation may fill our souls. Therefore, always and in every circumstance, we need only to ask one question: What will please our Lord and Savior? And then we must do it.

He will punish those who do not know God and do not obey the gospel of our Lord Jesus. —2 Thessalonians 1:8

 favorite hymn correctly says, "Trust and obey, for there's no other way to be happy in Jesus." If we do not obey, we are not trusting. We are fakes. We are practicing lies. We are embracing a theology that permits us to sin.

Is it possible to savingly believe in God, in Jesus Christ, without loving him and obeying him? The answer is indisputably "No!" And yet modern evangelicalism has come to teach that we can. A growing number of evangelicals are antinomian. Their Jesus is the incarnation of a false, pantheistic god, one who is both good and evil. The God we serve, the true and living God, is not one who embraces both righteousness and sin. He alone is holy. He commands, "Be holy, because I am holy." He saves sinners in order to make us holy, and everyone whom God saves will indeed be conformed to the image of his Son.

We are told in 1 Corinthians 13 that faith, hope, and love abide. Where there is authentic faith, there is authentic love and authentic hope. And where love is, there is obedience. Jesus himself said, "If you love me, keep my commandments." Conversely, where there is no obedience, there is no love and thus, no true faith.

In both epistles to the Thessalonians, the apostle Paul makes clear that authentic, saving faith must produce good works. He writes, "We continually remember . . . your work produced by faith" (1 Thess. 1:3). He later prays "that God may fulfill every act prompted by your faith" (2 Thess. 1:11).

Dead faith does not produce good works. James the Lord's brother warns us that faith without obedience is dead, demonic, and damning. He writes, "Do not merely listen to the word, and so deceive yourselves. Do what it says" (Jas. 1:22). Faith that is devoid of obedience is serious, demonic deception.

In 2 Thessalonians 2, Paul explicitly tells the Thessalonians that the Lord Jesus will punish those who do not obey his gospel. Orthodoxy alone will not save us. We must do what God is speaking in his orthodox doctrine. May God help us to embrace his description of the church: "Everyone who confesses the name of the Lord must turn away from wickedness" (2 Tim. 2:19).

*"In those days, at that time," declares the L*ORD*, "search will be made for Israel's guilt, but there will be none, and for the sins of Judah, but none will be found, for I will forgive the remnant I spare." —Jeremiah 50:20*

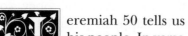

eremiah 50 tells us that God has an eternal plan for his people. In verse 19 he promises, "I will bring Israel back to his own pasture and he will graze on Carmel and Bashan." God has a plan of restoration for you and me so that we can feed on rich pasture once again. This rich pasture, as far as I am concerned, is feeding on Christ, the living bread. There is no other pasture for a believer than Jesus Christ himself. He is the Good Shepherd and he is the pasture.

God scattered his people across the nations because of their sins. But now through his prophet, he promises that his people will graze and be satisfied. This is pointing to nothing less than salvation in Jesus Christ. What a great promise for you and me! Yet, this promise is not for everyone. It is only for those whom he will spare, his elect remnant.

We read in verse 20, "In those days, at that time, search will be made for Israel's guilt, but there will be none." Inexplicably, this search will be completely unsuccessful. We do not know who will do the searching, but the one who has a right to find out our guilt and punish us is the Lord God. Yet here is a search in which God fails. Praise God! Here is one time where failure is success, because in the eternal plan of God, he has decided to do away with our sin and our guilt in such a way that no one, not even he himself, will find it.

Jesus Christ paid for all of our sins on the cross. He defeated sin by receiving in himself the punishment that was due us. So let a search be done. Let heaven search. Let man search. Yes, let even the devil search. Let them search in heaven, on earth, and under the earth. Let them search, for our God has solved our sin and guilt problem in such a way it shall never be found. Hallelujah! This is good news of great joy; this is the gospel of Jesus Christ. This means we will never be punished. And this means we must live a life of gratitude to God for his great mercy.

The ark of God remained with the family of Obed-Edom in his house for three months, and the LORD blessed his household and everything he had.
—1 Chronicles 13:14

f your pastor came to live with your family as a visitor for a month, I guarantee that you would change your lifestyle. You would be more disciplined and more careful how you lived with your spouse, because you would have a heightened sense of decency and decorum. You would not leave your dirty clothes on the floor or your dirty dishes in the sink. You would not argue with one another. You would have morning and evening devotions, because you respect that pastor who has come to live with you.

Now, forget about that pastor, and think about God himself coming to live with you. This is what happened to the family of Obed-Edom. Oftentimes we do not fear God as much as we fear other people. Why do we clean our house when someone comes to visit? The truth is, if we feared God as we ought, then we would change how we live. Our God is an awesome God!

In the parallel passage, we read that this awesome God struck down Uzzah "because of his irreverent act" of touching the ark (2 Sam. 6:7). At first, David was angry; then he became afraid. That is exactly what the awesome God wanted. King David, as an Israelite, was not allowed to behave like a pagan and bring the ark back in a pagan way. God disciplines his people when they fail to act in accordance with his revelation.

What did the king do? He did not dare to move the ark to Jerusalem, because he was afraid and unsure. Instead, he took it to the house of Obed-Edom the Gittite. Now, imagine that Obed-Edom is told by the king that the ark, which just killed Uzzah, was being brought to his house. What sobriety and concern must have filled Obed-Edom's household for those three months.

Yet Obed-Edom and his family feared the Lord and were very careful to do what was right in his sight. We do not read of any further judgment. Instead, we read, "The LORD blessed his household and everything he had" (v. 14).

The awesome God has come to live with us in the person of the mighty Holy Spirit. Let us fear him, respect him, and obey him as Obed-Edom did. Then we too shall receive everlasting blessing.

The Spirit clearly says that in later times some will abandon the faith and follow deceiving spirits and things taught by demons. —1 Timothy 4:1

uch of what is shown on religious television around the world today presents a perversion of the gospel and is taken straight from Western countries. Its message is how to get wealthy and healthy and be successful in this life—nothing more. Hell, judgment, the wrath of God, and repentance of sin are never mentioned. This false gospel is now broadcast everywhere, seven days a week. Yet it is not the gospel that saves. It is a different, counterfeit, toxic gospel that damns.

In 1 Timothy 4, we learn that the Holy Spirit expressly revealed to Paul that there would be false prophets peddling false gospels. Jesus told his disciples, "Follow me." But these false prophets will abandon the Lord Jesus Christ and his gospel and follow demonic spirits.

Demons are still active in the world today. And just as was true in the days of Christ, these fallen angels can influence and control people now. As a result, false prophets teach, and gullible people believe doctrines of demons. In verse 2, we read that the consciences of such people are seared, cauterized; they have lost all moral discernment.

How can we recognize false teachers in the church? Let me assure you, they will not come to us and say, "I am a false prophet, a messenger of Satan." No, Jesus said they will come as wolves in sheep's clothing (Matt. 7:15). By smooth talk and flattery they deceive those who are naïve and mentally empty (Rom. 16:18). They seduce the unstable—those who do not pray, who do not read the Bible carefully, and who do not hear the word of God preached regularly. That is why I must warn you: If you are not studying and applying the Scriptures daily, you are at great risk.

I pray that we will have Holy Spirit discernment and be able to distinguish between the real Jesus and a false one, between the real gospel and a false gospel, between a real minister of the gospel and a false prophet, and between the doctrines of the apostles and the doctrines of demons. There can be no more serious distinctions. We have only one life, and what we believe and do now matters for eternity.

*It was because you, the Levites, did not bring it up the first time that the
LORD our God broke out in anger against us. We did not inquire of him
about how to do it in the prescribed way.* —1 Chronicles 15:13

e read in 1 Chronicles 13 of King David's good intent
to bring the ark back to Jerusalem. The way he went
about it, however, conformed to the Philistine culture,
not the Bible. God therefore became angry and struck
down Uzzah.

At first, David was angry and fearful. Then he came to his
senses and meditated on what had gone wrong. He turned to the
Bible, and the Holy Spirit opened his eyes. The king summoned
the priests, saying, "It was because you, the Levites, did not bring it
up the first time that the LORD our God broke out in anger against
us." How do you like that? If we insist on doing our own thing, the
Lord will break out in anger. We may become ill or lose our money.
Our business may not prosper. God has a way of dealing with our
insubordination. Then David confessed, "We did not inquire of
him about how to do it in the prescribed way." If we want blessing,
then we must live in the prescribed way laid out for us in the Bible.

There is a Book given to us from the mouth of God. It tells us
how we should live—how to repent and believe in Christ alone
for our salvation. It tells us that we should be baptized and that
we should join a church and be submitted to its leaders. Some
people say, "Oh, I don't have any pastor. I belong to the church
universal." Such people are not living in the prescribed way, and
they will not be blessed.

We must live in the prescribed way in every aspect of life.
Father, are you the head of your family? Do you govern? The Bible
calls you the head, not your wife or mother-in-law. Stand up and
rule and govern in the prescribed way. What about your work life?
How is your financial life? How is your devotional life? Everything
matters. We do not have the right to live any way we want. The
Bible is our prescription. It tells us how we should live to glorify
God and enjoy him forever.

In verse 26 we read, "God . . . helped the Levites who were
carrying the ark of the covenant of the LORD." When David brought
the ark back in the prescribed way, there was great blessing.

[God's grace] has now been revealed through the appearing of our Savior, Christ Jesus, who has destroyed death and has brought life and immortality to light through the gospel. —2 Timothy 1:10

econd Timothy 1:10 gives us a beautiful summary of Christ's work and reveals the heart of the gospel. What did Jesus do for his people? First, we read that he abolished our death by his death on the cross. Christ died in our place. Jesus said, "When a strong man, fully armed, guards his own house, his possessions are safe. But when someone stronger attacks and overpowers him, he takes away the armor in which the man trusted and divides the spoils" (Luke 11:21–22). Thank God for a stronger One, Jesus Christ, who came and bound death, Satan, and sin, and set us free.

All of sinful man's fear is centered in his fear of death. Jesus abolished death, rendering it powerless and inoperative. By Christ's death, our enemies—death, Satan, and sin—were defeated. That is why we can resist the devil in the name of Christ.

Believers will not experience eternal death, for they have been made alive in their spirits by God's gracious, effectual call. Believers need not fear even physical death, for they shall fall asleep in the Lord, not in their sins. Death for Christians is not loss but gain. They have crossed over from death to life because of the death and resurrection of Jesus Christ.

We also read that Christ has brought life and immortality to light. Jesus himself is life and immortality. He asserted, "I am the resurrection and the life" (John 11:25). We enjoy this life in increasing fullness in three stages. First, God gives eternal life to all who believe in Jesus. Union with Jesus by faith is union with life and immortality now. Second, at death our perfected spirits will enter into God's presence, where we will enjoy life with God in greater degree. There we will rest and be comforted by him. Finally, at Christ's second coming, we shall be given incorruptible and glorious bodies in which we will dwell with our triune God forever.

Jesus said, "This is life eternal: that they may know thee, the only true God, and Jesus Christ, whom thou hast sent" (John 17:3, KJV). To know God is to love him and dwell with him and his Son forever. Truly, death has been swallowed up in victory!

All Scripture is God-breathed and is useful for teaching, rebuking, correcting and training in righteousness, so that the man of God may be thoroughly equipped for every good work. —2 Timothy 3:16–17

n 2 Timothy 3, Paul tells us that all Scripture, being God-breathed, is profitable for training in right-eousness. Show me a man or woman who is sinning, and I will show you a person who has stopped reading the Bible, stopped praying, and has not listened to the word of God for some time. Yes, such a person may still come to church, but that does not mean anything. A spiritual deafness and blindness can take place over time that results in a hardened heart.

Not only does Scripture teach us truth, but it also trains us to practice truth. So not only should we hear and understand truth, but we must also do truth. Jesus taught, "Now that you know these things, you will be blessed if you do them" (John 13:17). He also said, "Everyone who hears these words of mine and puts them into practice is like a wise man who built his house on the rock" (Matt. 7:24).

Paul instructs, "He who has been stealing must steal no longer, but must work, doing something useful with his own hands, that he may have something to share with those in need" (Eph. 4:28). When a thief comes to Christ in faith, he becomes a child of God, repenting of his sins and confessing Jesus is Lord. He is now trained to stop stealing and to start obeying God's commandment by working six days a week. Not only does he provide for himself and his family, but he is also able to give to those who are needy.

The repentant thief does all this through the training of the Scripture in the Spirit's power. He knows what God's will is and he does it. Through the training of Scripture in righteousness, the former thief becomes a giver. This is true conversion. Likewise, an adulterer will become completely faithful to his wife. A liar will tell the truth. A lazy man will become highly productive. A dropout will graduate at the top of his class. A drunkard will become sober, delivered from all addiction by the mighty Holy Spirit.

Truly, God's word is profitable for this life and the life to come. Through the ministry of the mighty Holy Spirit, may we be trained by the Bible until doing the will of God becomes our habit, delight, and character.

In everything set them an example by doing what is good. In your teaching show integrity [and] seriousness. —Titus 2:7

he ultimate example of a how a man should live is, of course, the life of Jesus Christ. Paul writes, "Be imitators of God, therefore, as dearly loved children and live a life of love, just as Christ loved us and gave himself up for us as a fragrant offering and sacrifice to God" (Eph. 5:1–2). But, in fact, all believers are to live lives that others can imitate. And all delegated authorities ought to live exemplary lives, whether they are husbands, parents, pastors, employers, magistrates, Supreme Court justices, or presidents. All people are to live by the word of God, whether they are believers or unbelievers. They should not be scoundrels or liars.

In the same way, Pastor Titus was to be a model of good works and piety for his congregation. People needed to hear Titus preaching, but they also needed to see him and his family living out the gospel in all areas of their lives.

As a teacher, Titus had to be incorruptible. His motive was to be the glory of God, not self-enrichment. Titus was to tell the church what to believe and what to do from the Scriptures. So he had to show seriousness when he preached and taught. He had to do all things with dignity as an ambassador of Christ the King. He could not be a joker or an entertainer. This did not mean he should look dour and miserable. But he must be respected in the church.

A pastor must also be biblically sound in the content of his preaching. He must preach the whole counsel of God, the whole Bible. He must preach the whole truth and nothing but the truth, especially when that truth is unpopular.

Just as a pastor must be a model for others to imitate, so we also must live exemplary lives, for we are the light of the world. When people come to us desiring to see Jesus, we should invite them to see him in our holy lives and in our proclamation of the gospel. We ought to be able to say, "You want to see Jesus? Come to my house. See my children. See how we live. See how we love one another. It is all because Jesus is here with us."

Woe to us, for we have sinned! —Lamentations 5:16

amentations serves as a large, flashing red light to warn God's people who are living in the world today. When we come to this book, we must stop, not for a short while, but for a long time. We must stop, ponder, and reflect. We must examine ourselves.

In the Hebrew Bible, this book is titled *Ekah*, which means "How?" or "Alas!" It is an exclamation of grief. Each of the book's five chapters is a funeral song. So there are five dirges, five elegies. They are the product of the prophet's overwhelming sorrow at what was taking place during the destruction of Jerusalem by Babylon in 586 BC.

Just think: There was no necessity for this book. It need not have been written, if the Israelites had simply been careful to pay attention to the Lord's prophetic warnings given throughout the Old Testament, particularly in the book of Deuteronomy. When we examine Deuteronomy 28, we see that nine hundred years before Jerusalem's fall God had explicitly told his people how he would punish them if they did not live in covenant faithfulness. God does not deal with us capriciously and arbitrarily; he always has a holy and just reason when he subjects his people to his severity. God is long-suffering, but we must never abuse his grace.

The idea of the wrath of God is scoffed at today, not only throughout our nation but also in the church itself. Hell has become the butt of jokes. Most people have a foggy notion that God is ever-gracious and would never do anything terrifying. All such notions are totally false.

What shall we conclude as we read these tragic chapters? When we obstinately refuse to pay attention to the word of God and its warnings, there comes a time when the judgment of God will fall. When such judgment comes upon us, we will be utterly without comfort. We read in Lamentations 1:9 that Israel "did not consider her future." When people sin, they are oblivious to their future. But there is a future for sinners, and it will be terrible. What type of future do you want? If you want to have a future filled with peace, then fear the Lord and depart from sin.

The angel went to her and said, "Greetings, you who are highly favored!
The Lord is with you." —Luke 1:28

n Isaiah 7:14 we read, "Therefore the LORD himself will give you a sign: The virgin will be with child and will give birth to a son, and will call him Immanuel." The fulfillment of that stupendous prophecy is recorded in Luke 1 and 2. In the fullness of time, Jesus came, and the promise of Genesis 3:15—that the Seed of the woman would crush the head of the serpent—was realized.

God is faithful to all his promises; not one will ever fail. People make many promises, yet they often break them. We can trust others only with some reservation. But we can fully trust God and his promises. So God sent Gabriel in the fullness of time to the city of Nazareth to the house of the holy teenager Mary. God was preparing a body for his own Son in her womb so that, as a man, the Son might live and die to accomplish our redemption.

Gabriel came to holy Mary. Three times Luke states that she was a virgin, in fulfillment of Isaiah's prediction. He greeted her, saying, "Rejoice!" When God greets us, we can rejoice. God is taking the initiative to save us miserable sinners.

Gabriel continued: "You highly favored one" or "highly graced one." The meaning is that God chose Mary from all eternity, a choice of grace. He had shown favor to her and now he would continue to show grace to her. What grace begins, grace continues, and grace will complete. Mary was truly full of grace, a grace sufficient for all her needs, a grace that enabled her to do God's will and abound in good works.

Gabriel promised, "The Lord is with you." This was an indicative, meaning it was a present reality. God was present with Mary at that very moment. We all need God's presence, for it is useless to go anywhere without him. Gabriel was telling Mary, "The Lord is with you to provide for you, to protect you, and to solve all the problems that will come about as a result of this virginal conception. The Lord is with you to guide you every step of the way." Praise God, this is true also of us. God gives us grace upon grace.

*David said to him, "Let me have the site of your threshing floor so I can
build an altar to the LORD, that the plague on the people may be stopped."*
—*1 Chronicles 21:22*

he gift of atonement—how we can have forgiveness of
sins—is the theme of 1 Chronicles 21, and, indeed, of
the entire Bible. The basis of forgiveness is atonement,
and atonement is the gift of God.

The context of this glorious teaching is King David's sin of
pride manifested in his unauthorized counting of the fighting
men. David felt very strong and secure: "I don't need God. I have
the troops, the military might." This is what Satan incites us to
do—to be independent of God, to trust in ourselves.

We read that David later came under great conviction and said
to the Lord, "Now, I beg you, take away the guilt of your servant"
(v. 8). This is an impossible request, for we have sinned against
an infinite God. Our sin is great; it is measureless. How can it
be forgiven, unless we are punished? A just and holy God must
punish sinners.

Is there any remedy? God alone can provide the gift of
atonement. We read, "Then the angel of the LORD ordered Gad to
tell David to go up and build an altar to the LORD on the threshing
floor of Araunah the Jebusite" (v. 18). Here is the solution
provided by a merciful God. The king built the altar there on
Mount Moriah, and the Lord confirmed his acceptance of the
sacrifice by sending fire from heaven.

David concluded that this was the location where the altar
should remain and the temple should be built. But there is more to
the story. When we look back, we remember Mount Moriah as the
very place where Abraham was commanded to sacrifice to God his
only son, the son whom he loved. We know that Isaac was spared,
and the ram caught in the thicket was sacrificed in his place.

More importantly, we must also look forward to Jesus Christ,
the incarnate Son of God, to whom every Old Testament sacrifice
pointed. He lived a perfect life, and willingly went to the cross
of Calvary—on the same Mount Moriah—to die a substitutionary
death. Here is God's true gift of atonement for guilty sinners. It is
not the blood of bulls and goats that atones for our sins, but the
precious blood of Jesus.

Go now to your countrymen in exile and speak to them. Say to them, "This is what the Sovereign LORD says," whether they listen or fail to listen. —Ezekiel 3:11

zekiel was taken to Babylon around 597 BC. His name means "God hardens" or "God strengthens." God had to strengthen his prophet because the basic characteristic of the people to whom he was to prophesy was rebelliousness. God was calling Ezekiel to be his prophet to the Israelites who had been taken captive because of their longstanding refusal to obey.

Ezekiel's commission is similar to ours. If you are a believer, then this is for you: "He said to me, 'Son of man, stand up on your feet'"—this is God speaking from his throne—"'and I will speak to you.' And as he spoke, the Spirit came into me" (Ezek. 2:1–2). Every Christian is to be a prophet and a witness to Jesus Christ. To do so, we must be filled with the Holy Spirit. God has poured out his Spirit in these last days so that we can prophesy to a hostile, fallen world.

We go on to read in verse 9, "Then I looked and I saw a hand stretched out to me. In it was a scroll." This is Scripture. Do you want to be an effective witness to Jesus Christ? Then you need the Holy Scriptures as well as the Holy Spirit.

The Lord then said to Ezekiel, "Son of man, eat what is before you" (Ezek. 3:1). That means reading, studying, and meditating upon the Bible until the Scriptures are part of our being. Only then will we be qualified to speak.

What is the peculiar calling of the prophet? To be a watchman (Ezek. 3:17). A watchman is one who stands on the wall and looks for dangers. He is the one who must sound the alarm. Ezekiel sees the awesome God coming in judgment; his job is to declare to both the righteous and the wicked that this God is coming as the holy Judge.

Do you feel inadequate to witness? There is no question that you are inadequate unless you are filled with and prepared by the Spirit and the Word. Since the day of Pentecost, God has been pouring out his Spirit on his people so that they can prophesy. We, too, must be his witnesses to declare his coming judgments and his saving grace.

Jesus returned to Galilee in the power of the Spirit, and news about him spread through the whole countryside. —Luke 4:14

 n Luke 4, we read that Jesus returned to Galilee in the power of the Spirit. We, like him, are called to proclaim the gospel to a lost world. I am not speaking about the ordained ministry, but rather about the ministry that is the responsibility of every Christian. We are all called to minister in the power of the Spirit. Do you want to enter into ministry? Then you have to have power for ministry, the power of the Holy Spirit.

How can you and I receive the power we need? The power of the Holy Spirit is released to each one of us on the basis of our obedience to the Spirit of the living God. As we obey God, God's power flows into our life, so that we may do the work of ministry, which is the work of the kingdom of God. Jesus himself promised, "You will receive power when the Holy Spirit comes on you, and you will be my witnesses" (Acts 1:8). This mighty Holy Spirit is only given to those who obey him (Acts 5:32).

What was the thrust of Jesus' ministry? Luke tells us that he read from chapter 61 in the Isaianic scroll: "The Spirit of the Lord is on me . . . to proclaim the year of the Lord's favor." Here God was promising a Messiah, the Anointed One, who would come to liberate his people from the power of Satan and sin. This is the program of Jesus. Since the time of his coming in the midpoint of time, he has initiated this program, which is the proclamation of the year of the Lord's favor and grace.

Now is the accepted time, now is the day of salvation. And if the Son sets us free, we are free indeed. So when we pray for someone and that person is healed, the kingdom of God has come. When a person is ministered to by the love of Jesus through us, the kingdom of God is extended. When a person is converted to Christ, the rule of Jesus is enlarged. We all have a divine mandate to speak about Jesus to our families, our neighbors, and even our enemies. What an honor and privilege it is to minister in the power of the Spirit!

I will surely repay you for your conduct and the detestable practices among you. Then you will know that I am the LORD. —Ezekiel 7:4b

zekiel 6 and 7 speak about knowing the Lord, but not in a way that brings joy and blessing. Rather, it speaks of knowing God in terms of his judgment. When God Almighty comes with outpoured wrath, everyone, including his own people, will know it.

The prophet uses the expression, "They will know I am the LORD," over sixty times in this book. He was prophesying from Babylon about 597 BC against the Israelites. Why was the Lord angry? His people had abandoned him, the self-existing, self-sufficient Creator God, who upholds all things by the word of his power, who is holy and righteous, and who demands complete obedience. They were subscribing to a principle called "both/and"—both Jehovah and Baal. Their high places were filled with idolatry, thus violating the first commandment.

What was going to happen? God gave the answer through Ezekiel. There would be disaster, doom, and punishment. A definitive, final moment had come for the people of God. We read in Ezekiel 6:9, "Then in the nations where they have been carried captive, those who escape will remember me—how I have been grieved by their adulterous hearts, which have turned away from me, and by their eyes, which have lusted after their idols." Why must sin be punished? To demonstrate the righteousness of God. Every sin must be punished in due time, so that God may reveal to all that he is just. Now, judgment was coming to his own people.

But, praise God, this passage also says a remnant would be spared. The Sovereign Lord declares "But I will spare some. . . . They will loathe themselves for the evil they have done and for all their detestable practices" (Ezek. 6:8–9). In every generation, there are some who are spared. They will repudiate and forsake their evil, and they will remember the Lord.

God does not speak in vain. His judgments, as well as his salvation, are ultimate reality. How do you want to know the Lord? Everyone is going to know him—it is his sovereign, unchangeable determination. He will not let a single human being go on without acknowledging him. How do you want to know the Lord—in his grace, mercy, and love, or in his severity and wrath?

He said to me, "Son of man, have you seen what the elders of the house of Israel are doing, each at the shrine of his own idol? They say, 'The LORD does not see us.'" —Ezekiel 8:12

n Ezekiel 8, the prophet was prophesying to those who had been taken captive to Babylon about the hidden, sinful things that were being done in the temple at Jerusalem. It was a message of woe and destruction that would culminate in the burning of that same temple six years later.

God supernaturally gave Ezekiel a vision of what was really going on in Jerusalem. He wanted Ezekiel to understand that God would be fully justified when he destroyed the temple in 586 BC.

The people, including the religious leaders, had been secretly sinning in God's holy sanctuary. We too are tempted to do our own thing. We think no one will notice or care. The church is a place where hypocrisy can flourish because we all dress nicely and behave decently in public. We are good at clothing ourselves with piety. No one can peer into our thoughts to see what is really going on. But let me tell you: The infinite God sees us very, very clearly. Never think that God is like us, subject to time and space and other limitations. The living and true God knows us perfectly. He sees it all, for he is the transcendent One.

The prophet stated in verse 5, "In the entrance north of the gate of the altar I saw this idol of jealousy." We are reminded of Exodus 20:5, which teaches us that the omniscient God is also a jealous God; he will punish severely all those who commit adultery and idolatry. He will not tolerate a paramour, someone on the side. Jesus said the same when he warned his disciples that they could not serve both God and Mammon.

The Israelites' persistent sin aroused the covenant Lord's fierce anger; so he declared, "I will not look on them with pity or spare them" (v. 18). Here we see God's anger poured out, not upon Assyria or Babylon, but upon his own people. The book of Lamentations tells us what happened when God destroyed the temple by the Babylonian army.

God concluded, "Although they shout in my ears, I will not listen to them" (v. 18). May God help us to understand who he really is, and then serve him with holy fear.

Slaughter old men, young men and maidens, women and children, but do not touch anyone who has the mark. Begin at my sanctuary.
—*Ezekiel 9:6*

 zekiel 9 reveals both the severity and kindness of God. First, we hear him call in a thundering voice, "Bring the guards of the city here, each with a deadly weapon in his hand" (v. 1). They were to be the destroyers. Judgment was about to be poured out.

Listen carefully to Ezekiel's language: "As I listened, he said to the others, 'Follow [the man in linen] through the city and kill, without showing pity or compassion'" (v. 5). The six destroyers were to follow behind the man clothed in linen and execute all who were guilty of idolatry. Was this destruction happening in Sodom? No, Ezekiel was speaking about Jerusalem, the city of God, where God's people dwelt.

Thanks be to God, there was the man clothed in linen, perhaps a priest, with a pen and an ink bottle. God had already commissioned him to go throughout the city and look for those who grieved (v. 4). These Israelites were the remnant—those who stood for the glory of God. They were the elect, who kept covenant.

In every age, no matter how dark, there will always be people who will be faithful to the word of God. They will love God, and be grieved at the sin that prevails in their generation.

And so this man, clothed in linen, was to go before the guards and carefully examine every person in the city. Those who were covenant-keepers were to be marked on their foreheads with a visible sign, an "X" that looked like a cross. This mark was a sign of hope and divine ownership, of being spared from destruction.

This account reminds us of the Passover. When God was about to pour out his judgment on Egypt, the Israelites found salvation by marking the doorposts with the blood of the sacrificial lamb. The destroying angel spared all who had the mark.

I hope we will have a biblical view of God. He shows mercy to the humble but he judges the rebellious. There is an end to God's patience. Too many "Christians" in our day persist in worshipping idols in the church. Unless they repent, they too will experience God's severity. In every generation, judgment must begin at the sanctuary, in the house of God.

OCTOBER 25

But the seed on good soil stands for those with a noble and good heart,
who hear the word, retain it, and by persevering produce a crop.
—Luke 8:15

hat is the visible church? Not every church that calls itself Christian is part of the true visible church of Jesus Christ. A true church is one where the word of God is preached with fidelity and authority, where there is a pious and learned pastor who preaches the word, and nothing but the word, in the power of the Spirit.

Even in the local visible church of God, however, where the true gospel is preached and lived out, not every member is a true believer. Jesus' parable of the four soils in Luke 8 speaks to this difficult truth. In fact, only the fourth-soil Christians, the good-heart Christians, shall be saved.

Good-heart Christians alone will persevere to the end. Yes, they may stumble, but they will never finally fall away. They have good hearts, noble heart, new hearts given by God himself. Good-heart Christians alone are born again. They exercise genuine repentance and saving faith all of life. They hear and treasure the word of God, and produce fruit that remains for God's glory and for their everlasting blessing. They are led by the Spirit and the word. They are by faith vitally connected to Christ and to his holy church.

Good-heart Christians are not seeking money or fame; they seek Christ, who is their life. And they are willing to suffer for Christ, even martyrdom. They are even now seated with Christ in heavenly places. Their eyes are fixed on the crucified, risen, and reigning Lord Jesus Christ. This Lord is their shepherd, and they shall lack nothing.

I urge you to make your calling and election sure, as Peter exhorted us (2 Pet. 1:10). Paul likewise told us, "Examine your-selves to see whether you are in the faith" (2 Cor. 13:5). We must apply this test: Do I have the fruit of ongoing, present obedience? Jesus said, "By their fruit you will recognize them."

Test yourself. Which soil are you? You may be a member of a visible church, but are you a true believer? Can you say with Paul, "I have been crucified with Christ and I no longer live, but Christ lives in me. The life I live in the body, I live by faith in the Son of God" (Gal. 2:20)?

Then he said to them all: "If anyone would come after me, he must deny himself and take up his cross daily and follow me." —Luke 9:23

very true Christian is a disciple of Jesus. Discipleship is not some higher calling. Some people think that at first we can be just ordinary Christians, and later on we become disciples. That is not true. Christ makes this ultimate demand up front: We must love him absolutely. We must love him more than our father, mother, wife, children, brothers, sisters, and even our own lives; and we must be willing to give up everything we have. Jesus promises and guarantees eternal life in the world to come, but he demands the sacrifice of everything in this present world.

In Luke 9, Jesus said to his disciples, "Deny yourself." This denial is a voluntary act of love, and every genuine Christian will do so. To deny oneself means to once and for all refuse the demands of one's own desires. A disciple has died to sin; he counts himself "dead to sin but alive to God in Christ Jesus" (Rom. 6:11). He says, "I have been crucified with Christ and I no longer live, but Christ lives in me. The life I live in the body, I live by faith in the Son of God, who loved me and gave himself for me" (Gal. 2:20). Why do we deny ourselves? Because we love Christ, who loved us and gave himself for us. If we are Christians, Jesus Christ, our commander, "teaches us to say 'No' to ungodliness and worldly passions, and to live self-controlled, upright and godly lives in this present age" (Titus 2:12).

Not only so, but we must also voluntarily take up our cross. In Jesus' day, a criminal had no choice. He was forced to take up the crossbeam upon which he would be crucified. But because a disciple loves Jesus, he freely takes up the cross to suffer for Christ and for the gospel. A true disciple will not seek a life of ease. He understands that life in this world is not free from suffering, no matter what today's false evangelists may preach. A true disciple knows that as the world treated Christ, it will treat those who are his.

Suffering is our lot in this world; yet we can rejoice, for we have the sure hope of eternal life.

Which of these three do you think was a neighbor to the man who fell into the hands of robbers? —Luke 10:36

 he *sine qua non* of a healthy Christian life is the love of God. The first commandment directs us to love God with our whole being. Only true Christians can love God this way because only they have been given the abundance of love by the Holy Spirit. Each born-again Christian is endowed with this gift of love, and thus enabled to love God and obey him. If we give God first place in our hearts, then we will also be enabled to love one another in the way that pleases him.

Love is not just a feeling. It is action. It is self-sacrifice for the benefit of the loved one. John says, "This is how we know what love is: Jesus Christ laid down his life for us. And we ought to lay down our lives for our brothers" (1 John 3:16). The one who loves God will also necessarily love his neighbor.

In fact, the love of God is so powerful that we can love even our enemies. Are you a Christian? Do you have the love of God in your heart? If so, it does not matter how you feel about your enemy—you are commanded and therefore enabled to love him.

The parable of the Good Samaritan in Luke 10 teaches us that our neighbor is anyone who is in need, including our enemy. The Samaritan's enemy was the Jew, for Jews and Samaritans were bitter opponents. But in Jesus' parable, the Samaritan loved the Jew, who had been beaten, stripped, and left for dead by the robbers. The priest and the Levite did not love their fellow countryman, but the Samaritan did. He stopped and went to him. He bandaged him with his own clothing and poured his oil and wine onto his wounds. He lifted the Jew and put him on his donkey while he himself walked. He took him to an inn and adjusted his traveling plans in order to stay with him. He gave money to the innkeeper for the care of this Jew. He did everything to promote the health and welfare of his enemy. That is self-sacrificing love in action.

Such a demonstration of God's love in us for our neighbor, and even our enemy, is the badge of Christianity. May God help us to show such love in our own lives!

One day Jesus was praying in a certain place. When he finished, one of his disciples said to him, "Lord, teach us to pray, just as John taught his disciples." —Luke 11:1

ne day Jesus was praying in a certain place." Now, that itself is a very revealing statement. Why should Jesus pray? He is the eternal God. He is without sin. He is the second Person of the Trinity. If anyone is all-sufficient, he is. Yet we see him praying. Prayer means dependence. Prayer means we are not sufficient unto ourselves. Prayer means we cannot live without God helping us. And Jesus prayed. This ought to stand as a challenge to all of us.

Jesus' disciples often saw him praying; it was an integral part of his life. And so they said to him in Luke 11, "Lord, teach us to pray, just as John taught his disciples." And as the disciples saw Jesus praying, so also our children and others should see us praying. If Jesus prayed regularly, through the entire night sometimes, asking God to help him and give him grace and strength to minister to the weary, how much more must we.

We must confess the truth that often we do not pray as we ought. That does not mean we do not ever pray. But I think there is often a certain formality and routineness about our prayers.

May Jesus teach us to pray as he did. He used the term, *"Abba,* Father." The only one who did so was Jesus. If we study ancient Judaism, we will not find *"Abba"* ever used by anyone to address God, because he is too transcendent. But Jesus calls him with a familiar family name: Daddy. That speaks about a vital and intimate relationship.

The very mission of Jesus was to bring the transcendent God near to us. In Jesus Christ, our sin problem is solved. Now we too can have communion with God the Father, and he gives us the unspeakable privilege of calling him Daddy.

This is amazing love. Through Jesus Christ, the thrice-holy God has become our Father. Your spouse may not listen to you and your boss may close the door, but you have a heavenly Father ready to hear whatever you have to say. Whatever your needs are, pray! The greatest blessing in the world is our privilege of prayer. May we therefore join with the disciples and say to our Lord, "Teach us to pray."

You fool! This very night your life will be demanded from you.
—Luke 12:20

 esus had no time for those who sought to use him to promote their own interests. He came to reveal the Father, not to make his listeners affluent. He came to lift men's hearts to heaven. Yet in Luke 12 we read that one petitioner in the crowd remained fascinated with stuff. Like a pig, he was always looking down. He was a materialist, and, therefore, he was a fool. Jesus' disgust with the man came to expression in the ensuing parable about the rich fool.

Jesus uttered a biting condemnation of greedy materialists, who worship Mammon and are thereby guilty of idolatry. No matter what their religious profession may be, in reality they are practical atheists who are consumed with themselves and their net worth. Their goal is to make money and retire early, so they can eat, drink, and be merry. In all their thoughts there is no transcendental perspective, no room for God.

Such materialists mistakenly believe that they can even exercise control over their own destiny. Notice the rich fool's preoccupation with self and self-will: six times in three verses he says "I" or "I will." He does not think he needs to consult God because he is self-reliant and successful. He knows how to plan and solve problems. But he made just one miscalculation: he presumed upon his ability to determine the future.

God shows up at the end of the parable, not because the rich man is seeking him, but because his patience has run out. "You fool!" God says, "I gave you your life. I gave you your prosperity. But in your arrogance you rejected me, thinking your money is the answer to every problem." The rich fool is abruptly brought face to face with one problem not remediable by wealth—death.

When God comes and demands our life from us, we cannot refuse. We are reminded of Jesus' rhetorical question posed elsewhere: "What does it profit a man to gain the whole world and forfeit his soul?" Our Lord wants us instead to be rich toward God. How may we do so? First, we must believe on the Lord Jesus Christ to be saved. Then, we must store up for ourselves treasure in heaven by living a life of obedience pleasing to our Lord and Savior.

But unless you repent, you too will all perish. —Luke 13:3

 n Luke 13, Jesus was told by some in the crowd that Pilate had killed some Galileans while they were worshiping. Perhaps they had committed a serious crime against Pilate and the authority of Rome, and they mistakenly had assumed that they would be safe in Jerusalem and in the temple courts, that the law would not catch them.

The real issue in this passage, however, is that those Jews who reported this to Jesus did so with the assumption that those who had been murdered by Pilate must have been very wicked people. And they meant by implication that they themselves must be very righteous. In fact, if we study Judaism, whether it is conservative, reformed, or orthodox, we will notice that there is no conception of salvation based on genuine repentance and faith. No, the Jews thought they were already God's children.

But, notice, Jesus spoke something in reply that was absolutely unexpected. What did he say? "Do you think that these Galileans were worse sinners than all the other Galileans because they suffered this way? I tell you, no!" And then he gave a further bombshell. He looked directly at those who thought they were righteous, who assumed they had no need for a Savior, and warned, "I tell you, unless you repent, you too will all perish."

Jesus focused his attention on the most important issue in the life of these self-satisfied people. He was saying plainly that all people are sinners in need of a Savior. Not only the Gentiles, not only the Galileans, whom the Jerusalemites looked down upon, but all are sinners. Notice how quickly he directed his listeners to the issues of sin, death, and hell. He said, in effect, "You who pretend to be righteous and think you have no need for salvation, you who like to talk about theology—it is you who are in serious danger right now."

There is a real hell where all impenitent sinners shall suffer eternally. Jesus warns all self-righteous and impenitent people what awaits them. But, thank God, we can be saved if we repent and cry out to him, "Lord, have mercy on me, a sinner." Jesus came to save sinners, and only sinners, from perishing. Let us acknowledge our sins and cry out to him.

Blessed is the man who will eat at the feast in the kingdom of God.
—Luke 14:15

 am not in the least disappointed when I am not invited to holiday parties at the White House. Why? I have already been invited to the greatest party that is going to be held in this universe—the grand banquet that will be held by the Lord Jesus Christ when he returns. I have received an invitation, and have accepted it by receiving Christ Jesus as my Lord and Savior by faith. Not only so, but all of us who have accepted this invitation have already tasted of this heavenly food through the Holy Spirit, who gives us a foretaste in this life of the future joys that are surely coming.

In Luke 14, Jesus used the figure of a great banquet to explain salvation to a Pharisee. This Jew was certain that he and his fellow Pharisees would be among those who would eat at the feast in the kingdom of God. He presumed upon his heritage and his legalistic righteousness. Jesus addressed his presumption with a parable.

Jesus' parable focuses on the many ill-conceived, wicked excuses men give for not responding to the banquet invitation of the great King. All are invited by this generous King, but few say "Yes." The Pharisee himself was relying on his own righteousness. He thought he was too good to need Jesus' salvation. But the Bible clearly teaches that all have sinned and come short of the glory of God. Sinners can only enter into God's banqueting hall through the door of humility, repentance, and faith in Jesus.

What will happen to every proud Pharisee? Through the words of the king, Jesus warned, "Not one of those men will get a taste of my banquet." We read elsewhere that the subjects of the kingdom—the self-righteous Pharisees—will see many from the east and the west taking their places at God's feast with Abraham, Isaac, and Jacob. But they themselves will be thrown outside, where there will be weeping and gnashing of teeth (Matt. 8:11–12).

I have given you the invitation today, and the way to accept that invitation is simple. Look to the Lord Jesus Christ and be saved. Come to him as the lame, the blind and the deaf did—not in self-righteousness, but in all humility. And everyone who calls on the name of the Lord shall surely eat at his feast.

The younger one said to his father, "Father, give me my share of the estate." —Luke 15:12

uke 15 has been called the gospel within a gospel. It tells us of the new direction taken by a prodigal son. The gospel call to repentance is just this: the summons from God to take a new direction in life.

Jesus begins his parable saying that a man had two sons, one of whom patently hated the authority and government of his father. Blinded by the devil, this young man thought that he could be truly happy only when he got out from under the restraints of his father's home. This spoiled, rich kid wanted to go to the far country to get as far away as possible from his father. As he left his home, he burned all his bridges behind him, vowing that he would never return to his miserable town or see his terrible father again. To this boy, good was evil and evil good; light was darkness, and darkness light. To him, autonomy spelled happiness.

What about you? Do you hate your father? Do you hate your church? Do you hate the Bible? Are you just waiting to break loose of all parental influence and go to a far place to seek happiness in independence and lawlessness? If so, you are deceived and blinded like the prodigal son.

Some prodigals leave and never return. Abandoned by God, they in due course enter into eternal torment and agony. Others, if God has mercy on them, come to see through pain and loss that the way of rebellion is hard. "There is no peace," says God, "for the wicked."

God brought this prodigal to the end of his rope. "Even the hired servants have an abundance," he told himself, "while I am here perishing." This was the reality he finally faced. So he said to himself, "I will arise, go to my father, and confess my sins." He now recognized that his problem was not his father, nor his pastor, nor the church. It was his own sin. What clear thinking!

If you are seeking to cast off the restraints that God has put in your life, I counsel you not to do so. Why? Only in God's presence is there fullness of joy and pleasures forevermore.

But if a righteous man turns from his righteousness and commits sin and does the same detestable things the wicked man does, will he live? . . . Because of the unfaithfulness he is guilty of and because of the sins he has committed, he will die. —Ezekiel 18:24

zekiel 18:24 constitutes a very serious warning for those who have been in a church for many years. They may begin to think, "I have walked with God all these years. Now I can relax and begin to do what I want." And so, after thirty years of church attendance, all of a sudden that person walks out on his covenant commitments. Let me assure you, it makes no difference what you did yesterday. Present obedience is what matters, not yesterday's. Present obedience to God's commands is the proof that you are saved.

I believe that authentic salvation is impossible to lose. But I also believe that a born-again Christian will persevere in the faith to the very end. Anyone who turns from righteousness to sin and refuses to repent has not been born of God. So we teach eternal security, but we also preach present righteousness.

We should put away the widely held presumption that a person merely needs to confess, "Jesus is Lord," and that person is saved, no matter what he or she does. This is not true. Those who make such a confession and are baptized must then go on to serve the Lord Jesus Christ. Those who instead continue to live like a devil, whether lying, cheating, living in immorality, or otherwise sinning, invalidate their Christian claim. Mere profession is not sufficient. Living a righteous life is the only sure proof of salvation.

At the end of *Pilgrim's Progress,* John Bunyan writes: "Then I saw that there was a way to hell, even from the gate of heaven." He pictures a pilgrim who after many years had arrived at the very entrance to heaven, but who carelessly throws it all away in the end. We too can be in the church for thirty or forty years, calling ourselves Christians, and then commit egregious sin. We must never presume that we are temptation-proof, lie-proof, or sin-proof. We remain sinners until our dying day. We must therefore continue to be very careful how we live. We must continue to make our calling and election sure. We must enter by the narrow gate and continue on the straight path that alone leads to heaven. If you are a true believer, you will surely do so and persevere to the very end.

If my people, who are called by my name, will humble themselves and pray and seek my face and turn from their wicked ways, then will I hear from heaven and will forgive their sin and will heal their land.
—2 Chronicles 7:14

his verse contains one of the most important promises in all of Scripture. God made this wonderful promise in 2 Chronicles 7 to his people after Solomon dedicated the temple. The temple—which pointed to the substitutionary, atoning death of Christ on the cross—reminds us that Jesus' sacrifice alone permits the promise to be offered and fulfilled.

But someone may ask, "Can the God of Israel really be trusted? Can we rely upon his promises?" The resounding answer is "Yes!" We can and we must trust God. We must trust God for our healing, for our forgiveness, and for our eternal salvation. The Scriptures tell us that God is not a man that he should lie. We are told that God is light and in him there is no darkness at all. We are told that God is truth and that he is a covenant-keeping God. No matter how many promises God has made, they are all "Yes" in Christ (2 Cor. 1:20).

I do not believe, however, in an unconditional salvation. Whenever the question is put in the Bible, "What must I do to be saved?" there is always the answer, "Believe on the Lord Jesus Christ and you will saved." In other words, without repentance and faith, no one will be saved.

What were the conditions God gave Solomon? Humility, earnest prayer, and sincere repentance. This is the unchangeable will of God. Why, then, are so many people not restored and healed today? There is only one answer: They have not met the conditions given in the Scriptures. They want an unconditional salvation that does not require them to turn from sin, but there is no such thing. God saves only those who forsake their sin, and humbly cry out to him for forgiveness.

When we study the history of the kings of Judah and Israel, we notice that those who fulfilled these conditions did, in fact, receive God's blessing. They were restored, reconciled, and healed. They were saved according to the promise of God. And when we fulfill the conditions, we also will discover God's sovereign faithfulness to save us, heal us, restore us, bless us, and forgive our sins.

When he came near, Jesus asked him, "What do you want me to do for you?" "Lord, I want to see," he replied. —Luke 18:41

n Luke 18, we read that, upon hearing that Jesus was passing by, Bartimaeus began to shout, "Jesus, Son of David, have mercy on me!" This was a prayer born out of spiritual illumination, born out of the miracle of miracles—new birth. Only through regeneration by the Holy Spirit can we call Jesus the Lord, the Son of David, the King and Messiah. Neither the Pharisees nor the Sadducees nor the Herodians made this confession. In fact, they called Jesus a blasphemer. But although Bartimaeus was physically blind, when he heard about Jesus of Nazareth, his spiritual eyes were opened and he was given understanding into the person of Christ.

We read next that Jesus touched his physical eyes. What a touch of love! Jesus is the great high priest who sympathizes with us. Here was a sheep without a shepherd, and the Good Shepherd had compassion on him. Bartimaeus instantly received his sight and was filled with thanksgiving. If we are truly born of God, we will respond to our Savior as Bartimaeus did.

The life of Bartimaeus was instantly and radically changed. Once a beggar, he now became a disciple, devoting his entire life to Jesus in thanksgiving for what Jesus had done for him. This is just what every Christian will do. From the moment a person is saved, he will follow Jesus in joyful worship and obedient service, for he has been delivered from bondage to Satan, who blinded his eyes, to serve Christ, who opened them.

May God give us humility to see ourselves as we are. Whether we are young or old, rich or poor, we are like Bartimaeus—blind, poor, and miserable. But Jesus came to save sinners. He is the eternal God who is moved with love for us, and only one qualification is necessary. He will not heal the healthy, he will not save the self-righteous, but he will hear the prayer of a sinner who cries, "Lord, have mercy on me!"

Like Bartimaeus, then, let us reject the devil and others who would silence us, and let us instead call out to Jesus in faith. Let us persist, as this beggar did, saying, "This is my opportunity to cry out to Jesus, and I must continue until he answers my prayer!"

When Jesus reached the spot, he looked up and said to him, "Zacchaeus, come down immediately. I must stay at your house today." —Luke 19:5

hen Jesus stopped at the foot of a tree and looked up, he saw a man named Zacchaeus, a man despised by the Jews, yet loved and chosen by God the Father from all eternity, hiding in the branches. "Come down immediately," he commanded.

In Luke 19, we are told that this Zacchaeus had become a chief tax collector. As a result, he was hated by all the Pharisees and scribes in the district, and was made to stand with the Gentiles at a distance when he went to the temple. Zacchaeus had achieved his ambition of becoming rich, but he was not righteous, pure, or happy. He thought the pursuit of happiness was in the amassing of money, but in reality, money had made him miserable. In this miserable, unhappy state, Zacchaeus came to hear some good news, that Jesus of Nazareth—the friend of sinners and tax collectors—was passing his way. And so he ran ahead and climbed the tree.

Jesus told Zacchaeus, "I must stay at your house today." The Greek word Jesus used for "must" is *dei*, meaning that this encounter proceeded from divine necessity. In other words, from before the creation of the world, this day had been ordained by God the Father. Oh, there were many great mansions in Jericho, where all sorts of people who considered themselves to be religious and righteous lived. But Jesus did not come to any of them. He came to Zacchaeus' house, not because he needed shelter, but because Zacchaeus needed him and his salvation. Jesus is salvation. Jesus must preach the gospel to this poor, chosen sinner so that Zacchaeus might be saved.

How did Jesus know Zacchaeus' name? Jesus is the omniscient God who created Zacchaeus. He is the One who says, "Fear not, for I have redeemed you; I have summoned you by name; you are mine" (Isa. 43:1). He knows our names too, for he calls all his sheep by name (John 10:3). Never think that Jesus does not know where his lost sheep are. He knows exactly where you are. He knows your name, your problems, your misery, and where you are hiding. He knows, he seeks, and he saves all who have been given him by the Father. Not even one will be lost.

NOVEMBER 6

Give to Caesar what is Caesar's, and to God what is God's. —Luke 20:25

n Luke 20, we see the religious authorities trying to trap Jesus with a question about taxes. As Christians, we must recognize that we have dual citizenship. Every Christian belongs to a state, that is, the country in which he lives. Yet every Christian also belongs to the kingdom of heaven. Paul was a Roman citizen, but he knew that his most important loyalty was to the King of kings: "Our citizenship is in heaven. And we eagerly await a Savior from there, the Lord Jesus Christ" (Phil. 3:20).

The Lord expects us to take part in the political life of our state. Christians ought to be the best citizens in their communities. We need to be informed as to what our elected representatives are doing, and we have a God-given obligation to pay our taxes, pray for the authorities, and vote for the candidates of our choice. We should protest societal injustices and anti-Christian policies and laws, and we should attempt to persuade others from a Christian point of view. We must support policies that help the weak and downtrodden, and that promote biblical morality. We must speak against the rape of the environment, the moral degradation of our public schools, and any policies that destroy families.

We cannot forget, however, that we are also citizens of heaven. God is the one to whom we owe all worship and adoration. Jesus Christ is Lord of all the spheres, and we must render to him his due. The denarius that bore the image of Caesar belonged to Caesar. Even so, we who bear the image of God belong to God by virtue of creation and redemption. He is Lord and has absolute authority over us. No father has absolute authority over his children and no state has absolute authority over its citizens, but the authority of Christ is ultimate and comprehensive.

We must, therefore, worship God and obey him absolutely, even if it costs us our life. Jesus rejected Caesar's blasphemous claim to divine prerogatives. Jesus alone is our great high priest and the Lord of all. We cannot worship Caesar, nor can we obey him when his demands conflict with the supreme law of God in Scripture. When a Caesar becomes demonic, we must oppose him with all our God-given strength. To God alone is due worship and unquestioning obedience.

He replied: "Watch out that you are not deceived. For many will come in my name, claiming, 'I am he,' and, 'The time is near.' Do not follow them." —Luke 21:8

n Luke 21, Jesus answered two pressing questions posed by his disciples. Previously, Jesus had surprised them by telling them that Herod's temple, a most magnificent, seemingly permanent building, would be thoroughly and utterly destroyed. And so the first question the disciples asked Jesus was, "When will this happen?" Second, they asked, "What will be the sign of your coming and of the end of the age?" In one discourse the Master addressed both the proximate and the remote events. His instruction continues to be of the greatest interest and importance to all who are his disciples today.

Jesus explicitly warned his listeners that Jerusalem would soon be judged for her rejection of the Messiah: "When you see Jerusalem being surrounded by armies . . . let those in the city get out . . . for this is the time of punishment" (vv. 20–22). According to church history, as the Christians in Jerusalem saw what was about to happen, they studied Jesus' words. Those who took Jesus at his word and decided to leave the city were spared. In AD 70, the temple was burned to the ground by Rome.

We also should take Jesus at his word as we study what he taught about his future coming. What warning did Jesus give us? In verse eight we read, "Watch out that you are not deceived." The Lord prophesied that when evil increases and troubles are all about us, charismatic leaders will rise up to manipulate and deceive the gullible. This is exactly what is happening in many churches today. A false Jesus and a false gospel are promoted under the guise of entertainment and the promise of health and wealth. Those who are not word-centered will be led astray.

Jesus concluded, "Heaven and earth will pass away, but my words will never pass away." The word of God alone is sure, abiding and eternal. Every word he has spoken shall surely be fulfilled. How we should tremble before him!

What does all this mean for us? It means that we must diligently study, understand, and believe the Scriptures. They alone will anchor us, guide us, and keep us from being deceived. May God help us to believe his word, heed his solemn warning, and live.

After Rehoboam's position as king was established and he had become strong, he and all Israel with him abandoned the law of the LORD.
—*2 Chronicles 12:1*

 econd Chronicles 12 teaches us an important principle that we do well to heed as we ourselves enjoy ever-increasing prosperity. When did King Rehoboam and the Israelites abandon the law of the Lord? After they became strong.

Starting out in life, some people may feel their need for God and consequently pursue a little worship and a little piety until they are financially established. After they have a dependable paycheck, however, and have bought their "dream" house, they all of a sudden feel very proud and secure. Once, they had some humility; now, without qualms, they begin to abandon the King of kings and Lord of lords and his laws. Oh, they may not take the Bible and throw it into the garbage. But what they do is to increasingly neglect the altar of God—daily devotions, church attendance, and fellowship with the saints. In the end, the true and living God himself is forgotten.

Solomon had many other sons besides Rehoboam, so we can surmise that Rehoboam must have been pretty shrewd to maneuver his way into power. In the process, he learned to rely on his own strategies and understanding. Yet who, in fact, gave King Rehoboam his power and authority? God gave it to him as a gift. We tend to think that our strength and ingenuity is self-derived. Such an attitude is a denial of the very principle of grace. Self-satisfied, autonomous people hate the message of grace because it means that they are what they are because of God and therefore have no room to boast. Arrogating to oneself the glory due God is really to despise the God of grace. This pride is the sin that made the devil the devil. God opposes all such arrogance but gives grace to the humble.

There is another way to live. We read in Deuteronomy 8:18, "Remember the LORD your God, for it is he you gives you the ability to produce wealth, and so confirms his covenant." We who are rich in this present world are commanded not be arrogant nor to put our hope in wealth, but to put our hope in God, who richly provides us with everything (1 Tim. 6:17).

Father, forgive them, for they do not know what they are doing.
—*Luke 23:34*

n Luke 23, we find this prayer, offered for the forgiveness of Jesus' enemies. It was the first word that our Lord spoke from the cross. It was probably spoken as the nails were being driven into his hands and feet. There was no bitterness, no rancor, no malice in Jesus toward his enemies. Instead, he cried out, "Father, forgive them." Jesus was concerned about the salvation of his murderers.

Does this mean that Jesus' murderers, both Jews and Gentiles, would be forgiven of all their sins automatically by the Father? The answer is no. But it does reveal that the Father will forgive even the most terrible sin of murdering the Son of God on the basis of repentance.

After his resurrection, Jesus told his disciples, "This is what is written: The Christ will suffer and rise from the dead on the third day, and repentance and forgiveness of sins will be preached in his name to all the nations" (Luke 24:46). The apostles did exactly this on the Day of Pentecost and thereafter. Peter declared, "This man was handed over to you by God's set purpose and foreknowledge; and you, with the help of wicked men, put him to death" (Acts 2:23). Convicted of their sins, those listening cried out, "What shall we do?" In essence, they were saying, "Yes, we acknowledge that we nailed Jesus to the cross and murdered him. How then can we be saved?" Peter told them, "Repent and be baptized, every one of you, in the name of Jesus Christ for the forgiveness of your sins." Later, he spoke similarly: "Repent, and turn to God, so that your sins may be wiped out" (Acts 2:38; 3:19).

God's forgiveness is conditioned upon our repentance toward God and faith toward Jesus Christ. As Jesus prayed from the cross, he was acting as our mediator and high priest. He was making intercession for sinners in fulfillment of Isaiah 53. His prayer was not for the automatic salvation of all sinners, but for the salvation of any sinner who would repent and believe in him.

Friend, have you paid attention to this first word of Jesus from the cross? His prayer shows that God the Father will forgive any sin, no matter how terrible, of any repenting sinner who comes to Christ in faith. Let us, therefore, turn to him today and be saved.

When he had led them out to the vicinity of Bethany, he lifted up his hands and blessed them. —Luke 24:50

he gospel of Luke concludes with a glorious benediction. At the end of his forty days of post-resurrection appearances, Jesus led his disciples to the Mount of Olives. There, as the great high priest who had offered himself as the perfect, once-for-all sacrifice of atonement, he performed his last act on earth. He did what the priests in the Old Testament had done only typically before—he lifted up his hands and blessed his people. Having offered the perfect sacrifice, Jesus then pronounced blessings on the church—the blessings that are the result of his mediatorial work; the blessings of repentance and faith, of forgiveness and justification; and the blessing of the Holy Spirit.

Such a benediction was once the peculiar function of the priests in Israel after they had offered acceptable sacrifices to God. Here, however, the Great High Priest himself lifted up his hands in blessing—the blessing of God's presence and peace, the blessing of being reconciled to God. Because Christ died for our sins and was raised for our justification, the covenant curses have been removed and the covenant blessings are now ours. From his crucified hands flow benediction and salvation. As a result, God's smile is now upon us; his face is shining, and so we in turn shine. By blotting out all our sins once for all, Jesus Christ brings us, his redeemed children, unafraid into God's very presence.

These eternal blessings are found in Jesus Christ alone. "There is no other name under heaven given to men by which we must be saved" (Acts 4:12). There is no other mediator. There is no other high priest. There is no other covenant-keeper. There is no other atonement. There is no other savior except the unique God/man, Jesus Christ.

Thank God for Jesus Christ, who took care of the problem of our sin, guilt, and alienation! Not only did he bring us to the Father, but he also brought the Father to us. As a result, the Aaronic benediction is forever ours: "The LORD bless you and keep you; the LORD make his face shine upon you and be gracious to you; the LORD turn his face toward you and give you peace" (Num. 6:24–26).

The LORD is with you when you are with him. If you seek him, he will be found by you, but if you forsake him, he will forsake you.
—2 Chronicles 15:2

he words of Azariah the prophet in 2 Chronicles 15 address two groups of people: the faithful and the unfaithful. Woe to us, if we forsake our covenant Lord! God once told Eli the priest, "Those who honor me I will honor, but those who despise me will be disdained. The time is coming when I will cut short your strength" (1 Sam. 2:30–31). If we refuse to follow the Lord in covenant obedience, he will bring trouble and distress into our lives.

Think about your own life. God knows how to humble us and break down the pride of every arrogant, independent, self-centered person. He knows how to cure our backsliding. And he will use every kind of trouble at his disposal to discipline us, if we are indeed his elect. The goal of this discipline is to turn us back to him. So the prophet reminded King Asa, "In Israel's distress they turned to the LORD, the God of Israel, and sought him, and he was found by them" (2 Chron. 15:4).

There is another important lesson to be learned here: The Lord is with us when we are with him. If we seek him, he will be found by us. Jesus taught the same truth: "Ask and it will be given to you; seek and you will find; knock and the door will be opened to you. For everyone who asks receives; he who seeks finds; and to him who knocks, the door will be opened" (Matt. 7:7–8). Thanks be to God!

Azariah gave a final encouragement to Asa: "But as for you, be strong and do not give up, for your work will be rewarded" (2 Chron. 15:7). This is what God is saying to us also. Do not quit serving God, but continue to follow Christ. Work hard in the Lord's work, and your work will be rewarded. Paul exhorts us, "Therefore, my dear brothers, stand firm. Always give yourselves fully to the work of the Lord, because you know that your labor in the Lord is not in vain" (1 Cor. 15:58).

In the same way that Azariah's words strengthened Asa to continue in his reforms, so we too should take great encouragement from the Scriptures and faithfully continue to do God's will in our generation.

Then Peter said, "Silver or gold I do not have, but what I have I give you.
In the name of Jesus Christ of Nazareth, walk." —Acts 3:6

he story in Acts 3 and 4 of the healing of a congenital cripple is the story of my life and yours. This man had been looking for a handout, nothing more. Like him, we tend to think that money will solve our problems and make us happy. The truth is, a little more money cannot fundamentally help us at all. Why not? Because our problem is sin. Sin has crippled us—it has radically affected our thoughts, wills, and affections so that by nature we are arrogant, proud, and at enmity with God. Sadly, we are not interested in being rescued from our total depravity; we just want to make more money.

What was this cripple's true need? It was primarily restoration to God, and Jesus Christ alone could help him. So Peter told him, "Look at us!" Peter and John were witnesses of Christ, and this man could only come to believe in Christ by listening carefully to their gospel message. "Faith comes from hearing the message, and the message is heard through the word of Christ" (Rom. 10:17).

Peter commanded the beggar to look at him because he needed to hear what the apostles had to proclaim by the unction of the Spirit. The risen Lord Jesus Christ had purposed from all eternity to save this man who was crippled in body and soul. Therefore, as the beggar listened to the preached word of God, the Lord opened his heart to respond to the message. He came to know Jesus, the one who died for our sins and was raised for our justification. When he looked at the apostles in faith, he saw Jesus Christ, who instantly saved and healed him.

What about us? We have to confess that we ourselves have believed the heresy that money is the solution to every problem. Man's true need, just as was true for this beggar, is restoration to God in soul and body. May God help us to spend our time in his word and become so familiar with it that we can provide an answer when someone asks us about the hope that is within us. Then we can say with Spirit-given confidence, "Look at us! We have something infinitely greater than money to give you."

This is what the Sovereign LORD says: I myself will search for my sheep and look after them. —Ezekiel 34:11

 he prophet assures us in Ezekiel 34 that the sovereign, almighty, all-wise, all-compassionate God has himself promised to shepherd his sheep. We see the words, "I will," repeated throughout this passage: "I will take care of you"; "I will save you"; "I will search for you"; "I will find you"; "I will heal you." What great comfort we ought to derive from these magnificent promises of God!

Notice, he calls us "my sheep." We are God's sheep by creation, election, and redemption. The Father loves us, cares for us, saves us, and provides for us. As a shepherd, he met our greatest need by giving us to his Son, so that he might die for us and save us. Jesus is the Good Shepherd who told the Father, "Thy will be done," and laid down his life for the sheep.

God our shepherd will also meet all of our daily necessities. We are reminded of the words of the apostle Paul: "He who did not spare his own Son, but gave him up for us all—how will he not also, along with him, graciously give us all things?" (Rom. 8:32). Why, then, should we be afraid or anxious? Our heavenly Father will never fail, and neither will his Son Jesus.

Jesus said, "The Son of Man came to seek and to save what was lost" (Luke 19:10). Into every nook, crevice, and dark place, both far and near, God's Son will come to save his sheep—sheep who were born sinners, under the wrath of God, weak, scattered, afraid, wounded, sick, lost, and in slavery to sin and Satan. But thank God, Jesus came, sought, and found us. He took us home to God to enjoy the blessing of eternal redemption.

Are you part of the Father's flock? Are you Christ's sheep? Have you repented of your sins and entrusted yourself to Jesus Christ? Do you hear Christ's voice in the gospel? Do you follow him? Do you love his word? If all this is true of you, then great comfort and joy are yours, for you have eternal life and are secure forever. Jesus himself declared, "I give my sheep eternal life, and they shall never perish; no one can snatch them out of my hand" (John 10:28).

Now Jehoshaphat had great wealth and honor, and he allied himself with Ahab by marriage. —2 Chronicles 18:1

ehoshaphat evidenced love for God in the early years of his reign, but gradually he changed as he attained great wealth and honor. Such blessings do not necessarily have to weaken one's faith and defile one's conscience, but it takes much spirituality and trust in the Lord to avoid being corrupted by money and power. Tragically, Jehoshaphat was unable to retain the zeal he had when he was young and relying on God.

The king of Judah eventually allied himself with the wicked king of Israel. The Bible strictly prohibits such alliances between believers and unbelievers. Jehoshaphat was seeking a political alliance based on a marriage between his son Jehoram and the daughter of the evil Ahab. Jehoshaphat's conscience had become insensitive over time. Now he had no problem fellowshipping with wicked and unbelieving people if it was politically expedient.

Christians can also fall into the same trap when making life-changing decisions, such as whom to marry. They often look for outward beauty rather than real spiritual character. Without the Holy Spirit of God, the natural man always resorts to such criteria. Such Christians are typically not interested in receiving counsel from their parents and their pastor. Thus, they will make some of life's most important decisions based solely on their own thoughts and feelings. I say that they are headed for big trouble!

Jehoshaphat's lack of discernment and judgment continued to cripple him throughout the rest of his life. He retained a vestige of his former spirituality and was dissatisfied with the flattering counsel given to Ahab by the four hundred false prophets. But when Micaiah, the one true prophet, boldly spoke the word of the Lord, Jehoshaphat ended up ignoring it. It seems that he had enough conscience to seek the Lord's counsel, but not enough to follow it. We will only be blessed, however, if we hear and obey.

The company we keep will either encourage us to obey God or discourage us. May God grant us purity of heart and a clear conscience, and keep us from entering into ungodly alliances. May we not, like Jehoshaphat, fall from our first love and allow fame and wealth to corrupt our conscience and warp our decisions.

Those who had been scattered preached the word wherever they went.
—Acts 8:4

n God's sovereignty, all things work together for the ultimate good of his church. Even though Stephen was martyred, in Acts 8 we read that God raised up another man to take his place in spreading the gospel. Philip was a Hellenistic Christian who understood the good news that Stephen had preached—that salvation is by grace and not tied to the ritual of the temple. As a result of the persecution following Stephen's death, Philip traveled to Samaria and began to preach Christ there.

Let us be very clear about what we as Christians are called to do. We are told that those who had been scattered "preached the word." These people were preaching the objective, historical facts about Christ. We must preach God's word, not our own subjective experience. "I was blind but now I see" may be a heart-stirring testimony, but by itself it will not save anyone. Christians are to preach the word of God, especially about the person and work of Jesus Christ.

"Preach the word," Paul commanded Timothy as he neared the end of his life, and he instructed the young pastor to do so in season and out of season. He was to guard it and preach it because the gospel alone is the power of God unto salvation for everyone who believes. In other words, we are not told to preach stories or shed tears; only preaching about the person and work of Jesus Christ can save a sinner.

The chief activity of God in the world since the fall of man has been the salvation of sinners. All other historical events serve simply as background for this grand purpose. God's intent from all eternity has been to save his people from his wrath, and he is accomplishing this through the proclamation of the gospel of his Son. As we preach the gospel, others will hear it, believe it, call upon the name of the Lord, and be saved.

Preaching, therefore, is a divine necessity. And it is not just for ministers. As Christians, we all must bear witness to the gospel; this is God's plan for our lives. Knowing Christ and making him known—not becoming educated or getting married or having children—must be our primary focus in life.

Alarmed, Jehoshaphat resolved to inquire of the LORD, and he proclaimed a fast for all Judah. —2 Chronicles 20:3

hen we are afraid and troubled, we must pray—earnestly, humbly, and in repentance and faith. Great trouble requires focused, persevering prayer. In 2 Chronicles 20, we read that when trouble came, not only did Jehoshaphat determine to seek the Lord, but the people did also. What a wonderful blessing when the Spirit of the living God unites his people in seeking him! The Spirit of God guided people from throughout Judah to come to the temple to pray and fast. They came by the thousands to stand before the Lord for hours—men, women, children, and infants. They were not like modern Christians who need comfortable pews and entertainment to keep their minds occupied. Out of eagerness to seek help from the covenant Lord, these people stood and prayed.

Unlike his father Asa, Jehoshaphat remained loyal to Yahweh and refused to ask for assistance from Syria, Samaria, or Assyria. He resolved to seek help only from the covenant Lord of Israel. He brought together all the people in unity to meet with God and ask him to solve their huge problem. They needed deliverance, and they knew that only the Lord could save them. God guarantees that everyone who calls on his name in this manner will be saved.

Additionally, the Israelites showed their earnestness by fasting. It is good to fast, especially when faced with a life crisis. Too often we do not cry out to the Lord because we think, "I can handle this problem myself. Why should I bother God?" But consider the directive of the prophet Joel: "Declare a holy fast; call a sacred assembly. Summon the elders and all who live in the land to the house of the LORD your God, and cry out to the LORD" (Joel 1:14).

The prayer of Jehoshaphat was not only earnest and emotional, but it was also intelligent and biblically informed. He based his petition upon God's previous promise to help his people: "For the eyes of the LORD range throughout the earth to strengthen those whose hearts are fully committed to him" (2 Chron. 16:9). God is always watching those who trust in him, in order to deliver and guide them. When we face problems, before we go to the doctor or lawyer, we should cry out to God. He is our problem solver.

This is what the LORD, the God of your father David, says: "You have not walked in the ways of your father Jehoshaphat or of Asa king of Judah."
—2 Chronicles 21:12

hough Elijah generally ministered to the northern kingdom, on at least one occasion God commissioned him to write a letter to Jehoram, the wicked king of Judah. Undoubtedly this was not the first rebuke given to Jehoram. But how had he responded? He said, "Forget about you. I'll do what I want, how I want, when I want."

This letter from the prophet was God's final communication with Jehoram. We can draw this conclusion by the absence of any command to repent. This omission is a grievous thing. When a person reads such a letter from God, he is reading his own doom and destruction. There shall be no more mercy, no more forbearance on the part of God. There comes a time when he is finished with those who are resolutely stubborn.

This is a sobering message that we find throughout the Scriptures. "My Spirit shall not strive with man forever," was God's pronouncement before the flood (Gen. 6:3). He warned Noah's generation for one hundred and twenty years, saying, "I am going to bring floodwaters on the earth." In Noah's six hundredth year, however, God's long-suffering came to an end and the floodgates of heaven were opened.

Let us understand that God does not always punish sin immediately. As the apostle Peter writes, "God is patient with you, not wanting anyone to perish" (2 Pet. 3:9). God in his mercy warns and exhorts us again and again. But if we persistently show contempt for the riches of his patience, there will come a time when our chance to repent is over. He no longer speaks to us, and his Spirit no longer stirs us. That means the end is imminent.

Look at what happened to Jehoram. We read that Judah's enemies attacked the palace and kidnapped Jehoram's children. Then the king himself died of a painful, lingering disease. The chapter concludes, "He passed away, to no one's regret."

He who has an ear, let him hear what the Spirit is saying. Do not resist the Holy Spirit, but yield to his promptings. When he convicts you of sin, be quick to repent, confess, and forsake your sin, and you will enter into blessing.

So Peter was kept in prison, but the church was earnestly praying to God for him. —Acts 12:5

ow did the church respond to James' death and Peter's imprisonment? In this time of great trouble and confusion, the church first and foremost sought God through prayer.

Prayer was the disciples' first priority because the power of the church is in prayer. The power of the church is not the power of an army or of money or of influence. James reminds us, "The prayer of a righteous man is powerful and effective" (James 5:16). Here in Acts 12 we see the whole church uniting to pray about this serious emergency.

We are led to ask the question, "Why pray at all? Isn't God sovereign? Doesn't he do what he wants, when he wants, where he wants, and how he wants, with no effective opposition?" Or you may protest, "Isn't God omniscient? Doesn't he know everything with a perfect, infallible knowledge? Why, then, should we pray?"

What is the biblical answer to these questions? God, the Sovereign Lord of the universe who ordains his ends, also ordains the means by which those ends come to pass, and one of those means is prayer. Jesus promised, "I will do whatever you ask in my name, so that the Son may bring glory to the Father. You may ask me for anything in my name, and I will do it" (John 14:13–14).

Prayer, then, is a God-ordained means for accomplishing his will on the earth. Notice, though, that we are speaking about the prayer of a righteous man, not the prayer of a wicked man. The Bible is clear—God refuses to hear the prayer of a wicked man who conceals his sins, but promises to answer the prayer of a righteous man who pleases him.

What characterized the prayers of the church at this time of crisis—prayers that proved effectual and saved Peter's life? Our passage teaches us that the believers' prayers were publicly lifted up to God the Father in the power of the Holy Spirit. They joined together in great unity and prayed earnestly with one very specific request in mind.

Such earnest, passionate, persevering prayer says, "O God, we have no other hope, no other plan, but to pray and seek you!" This is the type of prayer that glorifies God and delivers the saints.

The two of them, sent on their way by the Holy Spirit, went down to Seleucia and sailed from there to Cyprus. —Acts 13:4

hen most so-called missionaries speak about missions today, the first thing they mention is money. Modern missionary candidates have to raise certain sums of money, so they go around from church to church, imploring, "We are going to this place to work for the Lord. Give us a love offering."

Interestingly, we do not find any mention of money in Acts 13. When the Holy Spirit truly sends us, we do not have to worry about money, because a laborer is worthy of his hire. In fact, when Jesus sent out his disciples, he specifically told them not to take any supplies with them (Matt. 10).

It is my judgment that the church of Syrian Antioch did not give any money to Barnabas and Saul when they sent them out. Paul would write later to the Thessalonians, "Surely you remember, brothers, our toil and hardship; we worked night and day in order not to be a burden to anyone while we preached the gospel of God to you" (1 Thess. 2:9; see also 1 Cor. 9:6 and Phil. 4:15–18).

This does not mean we should never help missionaries financially. But the current focus on money in modern missionary ventures is foolish. When I came from India to this city and started this work, I did not have any money and no one gave us any. But the history of this church itself proves that God will meet every need, giving us abundantly more than we can ask or imagine.

In this chapter, we read that Barnabas and Saul were sent on their way by the Holy Spirit. Not only were they sent by the church, but they were also sent by God. This is a most important point. The church may send us out, but if the Holy Spirit does not send us, we will in time fail. Conversely, when the Holy Spirit does commission us, he also will go with us, for Jesus Christ promised, "Surely I am with you always, to the very end of the age."

If we are called to be missionaries, we must not focus on money. Rather, we should live in a way that pleases the Holy Spirit. When he is with us, he will bless our ministry and take care of all our needs.

He made no distinction between us and them, for he purified their hearts by faith. —Acts 15:9

n Acts 15, we find the church elders assembled to address an important question: Must Gentiles become Jews in order to be saved? Peter told the assembly that God had chosen to give the Gentiles the gospel, and that God had accepted the Gentiles and had given them the Holy Spirit. His speech emphasized God's sovereign role in initiating and accomplishing salvation. Then he said, "God made no distinction between us and them," meaning between Jews and Gentiles. That was all a big blow to the Judaizers.

God is not concerned about whether a person is tall or small, white or black. He does not make any distinction between poor or rich, educated or uneducated, man or woman, beautiful or plain, Jew or Gentile. There is no difference, Paul says in Romans 3. All have sinned, all must be saved by faith in the gospel, and all who do believe are one in Christ Jesus. That is a tough concept to swallow for people who are suffused with a superiority complex.

In fact, God has never paid any attention to externalities. In ancient Israel, Samuel was about to anoint the oldest, tallest son of Jesse as king, but God said, "No, he's not the one. I look at the heart, not outward things" (1 Sam. 16). With God there has never been racism such as that practiced by man.

Peter went on to explain to his Jewish audience, "God purified their hearts by faith." Man's problem is not an external one; his problem is inside—his corrupt, twisted, unclean human heart. The Jewish people considered the Gentiles to be unclean and claimed that only the Jews were pure when, in fact, they were just as corrupt as the Gentiles. There is only one who can truly clean us up, and that one is God himself. The blood of Jesus Christ cleanses our hearts when we place our faith in him.

At the glorious conclusion of Peter's sermon, he boldly affirmed the doctrine of grace: "We believe it is through the grace of our Lord Jesus that we are saved, just as they are" (v. 11). May God help us to embrace this gospel of grace and embrace all our brothers and sisters who share in the same grace of God.

When Amaziah returned from slaughtering the Edomites, he brought back the gods of the people of Seir. —2 Chronicles 25:14

ing Amaziah's behavior in 2 Chronicles 25 displays the height of impiety and stupidity. Though the idols of Edom did not spare the Edomites from being defeated by Amaziah, this foolish king collected the very same idols and brought them back to Jerusalem to set up as his own gods. People today also like a "both/and" theology. They say they are not refusing to worship Jesus Christ, but they also want to make room for every other god. Such worship is an abomination in God's sight.

The anger of the Lord burned against Amaziah. Yet he graciously sent a prophet to him with the following question, "Why do you consult this people's gods which could not save their own people from your hands?" The Bible is divine revelation and it is logic. What was Amaziah's response? While the prophet was still speaking the king interrupted, "Have we appointed you an advisor to the king? Stop! Why be struck down?" This was a total rejection of the gospel of salvation, the gospel of freedom, the gospel of healing.

God in his grace continues to send prophets who are bold and unafraid. We are reminded of Robert Bruce, one of the great heroes of the church in sixteenth- and seventeenth-century Scotland. This great man of God was more revered in Scotland than the king himself. Once the king was in attendance while Bruce was in the pulpit. He noisily mocked the minister while he preached. When the minister would stop, the king would stop; Bruce would start again and the king would resume talking. The third time, Bruce said, "The Lion of Judah is roaring; let all petty kings keep silent." The king, who could have had Bruce executed with a command, was publicly and fearlessly rebuked.

What happened to the petty king Amaziah? In due time, God destroyed him because he did not heed the prophet's counsel. Though Amaziah fled all the way to Lachish, a fortified city, an assassin was sent there to kill him. It is time that we feared God and stopped playing games. Never trifle with a holy God, nor mock his delegated authorities. The Lord is in his holy temple; let all the earth be silent.

One night the Lord spoke to Paul in a vision: "Do not be afraid; keep on speaking, do not be silent." —Acts 18:9

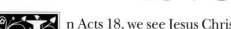

n Acts 18, we see Jesus Christ himself giving comfort to Paul while he was experiencing persecution in Corinth. Remember what he said in his great commission to his disciples? "Surely I am with you always, to the very end of the age" (Matt. 28:20). Jesus was with his disciples when the church was in its infancy, and he is with us now, to help, comfort, strengthen, protect, and enlighten those who serve him.

No doubt the unrelenting persecution Paul experienced at the hands of the Jews caused him to wonder what would happen next. By now he knew well the response he could anticipate as he continued to proclaim the gospel. Usually when he arrived in a new city and began to preach, many people would believe. Then opposition by unbelieving Jews and Gentiles would begin to grow, and Paul would be driven out.

Now, in Corinth, Paul was once again beginning to encounter serious opposition to his ministry. As a result, he may have been somewhat lonely, afraid, and depressed. He may have even been tempted to stop preaching the gospel and start speaking something that would be more palatable to his enemies. He may have wondered if he should just leave town now and go somewhere else.

Even though Paul was an apostle, he was undoubtedly affected by the severe trials he faced. Never think that ministers are not tempted to waver when they experience trouble. It simply is not true. Pastors are just like anyone else—they are subject to fear, anxiety, weakness, discouragement, and despair. But that is not all that was true about Paul. In his distress, he started to pray.

As Paul prayed and waited on God, God gave him a vision to encourage him. The first exhortation Christ gave Paul was, "Do not be afraid." Paul, the mighty apostle, was full of fear, so the Lord had to tell him, "Stop fearing!"

The second word the Lord spoke to Paul was, "Keep on speaking." Why should we keep on declaring the gospel? Because the only way of salvation appointed by God is through the preaching of the gospel by his Spirit-filled servants. Our speaking is absolutely vital to the salvation of a lost world. May God help us, therefore, to keep on declaring the glorious gospel of Christ.

And the name of the city from that time on will be: THE LORD IS THERE.
—*Ezekiel 48:35*

zekiel 48 speaks about the new city of God and the new temple of God. In the final verse, we are told about the ultimate blessing bestowed upon this new city and new temple. What is the ultimate blessing? *Yahweh-Shammah*—the Lord is there. A city without God is under a curse. A nation without God has no blessing. But in a blessed city, the Lord is there—not as an ornament, not as a statue, not as a pillar, but as one who lives, rules, reigns, defends, and saves.

I believe that there is going to be a future, visible reign of God in this world, where God will rule and reign over all the nations from his throne in Jerusalem. But this scripture receives one fulfillment even now—we, his church, are God's city, and we are his holy temple (1 Cor. 3:16, 6:19; Rev. 21). What makes a temple is God's presence.

If God is with us, there is no need to fear. Why should we worry? Why should we be discouraged? Why should we be confused? The transcendent, most holy, infinite, personal God in Jesus Christ has promised to be with us until the end of the ages. He is with us as God, King, Savior, Physician, Shepherd, and Healer. He meets our every need. We can thus join with the psalmist and say, "The Lord is my shepherd; I shall lack nothing."

Think of the blessing that accompanies God's being present in your home. He is there to help you, bless you, heal you, instruct you, defend you, and protect you. Your home becomes part of the kingdom of God. And what is the kingdom of God? Righteousness, peace, and joy in the Holy Spirit.

"The Lord is there" is true for his people even today. We must therefore rejoice and rest in the fact that God is with us in our homes, workplaces, and schools. The implications are obvious and profound. If you are one who loves autonomy, arrogance, and sin, you will hate and suppress this truth. But if you are a lover of God, you will find this divine constant to be your greatest delight.

But Daniel resolved not to defile himself with the royal food and wine.
—*Daniel 1:8*

e live today in Babylon, which stands for the corrupt culture surrounding us. As Christians who have been made new creations, we are not to conform to this culture, but to live holy, separated lives, standing up for God and the Bible. We learn how to do so by studying the lives of the four Hebrew men introduced to us in Daniel 1. We must dare to be a Daniel in our Babylon.

Daniel, Hananiah, Mishael, and Azariah lived for the glory of God in the midst of a corrupt alien culture. They were about fifteen years old when they were taken by King Nebuchadnezzar from Judah to Babylon. Though they grew up at a time of extreme apostasy in Judah, their parents were godly and had trained them to be God-fearing, Bible-centered, and holy.

The king tried to reeducate Daniel and his companions in Babylon's paganism and idolatry, hoping that they, like so many others, would soon forget their country, their Bible, their temple, their God, and their customs. He wanted them to become well-adjusted, nice pagans, so he gave them pagan names linked to pagan gods and began to educate them in pagan literature and pagan ways at the University of Babylon. But these teenagers refused to compromise. They remained holy even in Babylon.

Sadly, we find ourselves living in the very same situation in which these four young Hebrew men lived. We too must live holy lives, glorifying our God triune who alone is sovereign. As trees who have been made good (Matt. 12:33), we must produce good fruit, whether we are planted in Jerusalem, Babylon, or the United States. As God's children, we are to shine as stars in this crooked and perverse generation, holding forth the word of life.

God always has a remnant who will serve him. They are a minority, but they will stand for God's truth and for holiness. Although Nebuchadnezzar changed the names of these Hebrew youths, he could not change their nature. They remained non-conformists, people with spiritual backbones, counter-culturalists. They were truly the light of the world and the salt of the earth. And as a result of their witness, the Babylonian king eventually praised the God of Israel as the only sovereign God.

Some of the disciples from Caesarea accompanied us and brought us to the home of Mnason, where we were to stay. —Acts 21:16

n Acts 21, we read about Paul and his companions going to the house of Mnason in Jerusalem. It is quite probable that Mnason's home was a house church, because the church of Jerusalem had become very large by this time. In fact, James told Paul that there were literally thousands of Jews who had believed the gospel. There were possibly some ten to fifteen thousand Christians who met in various homes throughout the city. Paul and his traveling companions received warm hospitality from Mnason and his family, and I am sure they enjoyed sweet fellowship.

The church is where we get a foretaste of that great Sabbath rest awaiting us. It is a place of rest, refreshment, and fellowship with God's people. Even the mighty apostle Paul needed love and encouragement from other Christians. In fact, whenever he came to a city he would look for the local congregation so that he could enjoy fellowship with the believers there. He needed strength to face the certain trials that he knew awaited him in Jerusalem. And so in Troas, Miletus, Phoenicia, Ptolemais, and Caesarea, whether staying one day or one week, Paul sought out the company of the saints.

We too must thank God for our brothers and sisters—believers from all languages, races, and cultures—who are the faithful people of God. We all have the same heavenly Father and the same Redeemer, our Lord Jesus Christ. Let us be thankful for the forgiveness, love, hope, and faith we receive in the church. Let us also be ready to give back—to pray for one another, to help one another, to strengthen one another, to counsel one another, and to spur one another on toward love and good deeds, so that we all may be strengthened in the Lord and in our most holy faith.

May God help us to appreciate the privilege of belonging to his church. May we consider it our highest joy to gather together each Sunday with our brothers and sisters, to share communion with God and with one another. May we cherish the proclamation of God's holy word. When we come as Paul did, with troubles and trials awaiting us, God will encourage us through his word and his people, and enable us to live victorious Christian lives.

Suddenly the fingers of a human hand appeared and wrote on the plaster of the wall, near the lampstand in the royal palace. —Daniel 5:5

elshazzar was a perverted playboy king. He never accomplished anything in life; rather, he lived in dissipation. But the true God was watching him and weighing his actions. Why? Just as sin is not static, God is not static either. He is an active God, and in due course he carries out his judgments. He acted in the great flood of Noah's time and in the destruction of Sodom and Gomorrah. He acted in the defeat of Egypt when Moses led the Israelites out, and through Joshua in the defeat of the Canaanites when their iniquity was full.

The true and living God is an acting God, and there is an end to his patience. So he brought about the overthrow of Babylon as he promised. At the peak of revelry, as the partygoers drank from the goblets that had been taken from the temple of Jehovah, Jehovah himself suddenly contributed something to the party—the fingers of a human hand appeared and wrote a message from heaven on the plaster of the lighted wall. The wall was covered with all sorts of lies, but now, for the first time, truth was recorded. Immediately the partyers' revelry turned to stunned silence. Reality had come. The celebration was over.

The face of the king grew pale. His knees gave way and he fell face down. There was no more drinking, carousing, or mocking. The one-time revelers became dumbfounded, frozen with fright. They had not thought about an end to this party. In fact, they had never thought about an end to anything in life. They assumed Babylon, like their carousing, would go on forever. They were surprised by hell.

There is an end to God's patience for all the wicked. Jesus himself warned of this in the parable of the rich fool: "God said to him, 'You fool! This very night your life will be demanded from you. Then who will get what you have prepared for yourself?' This is how it will be with anyone who stores up things for himself but is not rich towards God." May we take heed and not love the world, for the world and its desires are passing away. Let us be faithful in serving God, knowing that the man who does the will of God will live forever.

Then Paul made his defense: "I have done nothing wrong against the law of the Jews or against the temple or against Caesar." —Acts 25:8

n Acts 25, we find the apostle Paul behind bars, wrongly imprisoned for over two years, praying every day, and yet having seen nothing happen. What possible comfort could Paul have in such circumstances? The Bible is filled with divine answers to this question, answers we ourselves must take to heart when we go through hard times.

First, we know that authentic Christians will be persecuted by the world. Suffering is our lot, but the Lord will be with us in the midst of any and all persecution.

Second, we are immortal until our work is done. When Jesus appeared to Paul, he told him in essence, "I have a job for you to do in Rome, and no one will destroy you" (Acts 23:11).

Third, the Bible teaches that all things work for the good of those who love Christ (Rom. 8:28). As Paul sat in the prison of Jerusalem, I am sure he remembered the words he himself had written and received great comfort from them.

Fourth, God ordains troubles to work character in the lives of his people. Paul himself wrote, "We also rejoice in our sufferings, because we know that suffering produces perseverance; perseverance, character; and character, hope" (Rom. 5:3–4). The more we suffer, the more patient and godly we become, and the more we will hope, not in the world, but in Jesus' return.

Fifth, God's power is made perfect in our weakness. Elsewhere we learn that Paul prayed three times for God to remove the thorn in his side, but nothing happened. Finally God told him, "My grace is sufficient for you, for my power is made perfect in weakness" (2 Cor. 12:9).

Sixth, God is with us. When Paul spoke about those who had abandoned him, he added, "But the Lord stood at my side" (2 Tim. 4:17). We know that he will never leave us nor forsake us.

Finally, God is sovereign over all. He is in control of all things, both large and small. Nothing happens outside of his will. And this sovereign God is committed to accomplishing the salvation of his people.

May God minister the truth of his word to us as we are called to endure hardship.

Be strong and courageous. Do not be afraid or discouraged because of the king of Assyria and the vast army with him, for there is a greater power with us than with him. —2 Chronicles 32:7

n response to the threat of Sennacherib recorded in 2 Chronicles 32, King Hezekiah exhorted the people to trust in their covenant-keeping God. Such biblical trust does not negate reality. We must face facts as they are. Assyria had a brutal, fierce army of vast numbers of soldiers and chariots. The reality was that the greatest military might of the time was coming against little Judah. Yet Hezekiah commanded his people, "Do not be afraid or discouraged."

How could Hezekiah make this demand? He took into account the greater, unseen reality of God and the forces of heaven. He reminded the people, "There is a greater power with us than with him" (v. 7). We too must remember and take to heart the greatest fact of all, that the living and true God is with us. And he is greater than any earthly king.

Hezekiah's prayer, found in the parallel account in 2 Kings 19, is filled with biblically informed statements of fact that encouraged all who joined with him in seeking the Lord for deliverance. The king adored Israel's God, the one true God, who is infinitely greater than anything in his creation. He took great comfort in knowing that this God had chosen Israel for himself as his inheritance. Nor was Yahweh an absent God, but rather an immanent One who dwells with his people. The Lord of Hosts could therefore be relied upon to defend his covenant community.

In light of these grand indicatives, the king's imperatives directed to his subjects made perfect sense: "Be strong, be courageous, be not afraid, be not discouraged!" In fact, throughout the Bible we are commanded to be strong—not in ourselves and our own righteousness, but in the Lord. The catechism tells us that he restrains and conquers all his and our enemies.

Let us follow Hezekiah's example and look to our God and Savior when our enemies rise up to attack us. God is in control, and he will always take care of his people, no matter how great a problem we face. He is with us to help us, deliver us, heal us, forgive our sins, encourage us, make us strong, and enable us to stand firm. Greater is he who is in us than he who is in the world.

Last night an angel of the God whose I am and whom I serve stood beside me and said, "Do not be afraid, Paul. You must stand trial before Caesar; and God has graciously given you the lives of all who sail with you." —Acts 27:23–24

he events of Paul's voyage to Rome as recorded in Acts 27 witness to the fact that God's servants are invincible and indestructible until their God-ordained work on earth is done. We know that when God appointed Paul to be an apostle, he also promised to rescue him from all his enemies (Acts 26:17). Satan and all hell might try to stop him— every spiritual force of evil in the heavenly realms—but nothing can thwart God's divine decree. It was God's will from all eternity that Paul go to Rome, and that plan would be accomplished.

God had graciously revealed this plan to Paul when he was arrested in Jerusalem. The Lord Jesus Christ appeared to Paul in the night, saying, "Take courage! As you have testified about me in Jerusalem, so also you must give witness to me in Rome" (Acts 23:11). In the Greek, we find the word *dei*, which means "you must." The word signifies divine ordination, divine decree. In other words, God was telling Paul, "I have decreed it; it is my purpose and plan that you witness about me in Rome, and nothing will successfully thwart this intention of mine for you."

On the way to Rome, a great storm arose. What was the apostle doing during this storm? Praying earnestly. In response, God again gave him a message of great comfort. Though the storm would continue, God promised Paul that not only would he be safe, but also all who were sailing with him. What was Paul's response to this promise? "I have faith in God that it will happen just as he told me" (v. 25).

We each must understand this truth and apply it to our own lives. In our life's journey, there will be times when we experience contrary winds and sudden storms. There are times, as Jesus himself promised, when the rain will come down, the streams will rise, and the winds will beat against us. When we are buffeted by the storms of life, we must remember one thing: God is with us in our storms. He never tells us to go out on our own; rather, he tells us to follow him who is always leading us, him who promised, "I will be with you always, even unto the end of the ages."

Therefore I will block her path with thornbushes; I will wall her in so that she cannot find her way. —Hosea 2:6

he book of Hosea tells the story of God's love—a love that will not let us go; a love that will cure our backsliding; a love that in covenant faithfulness will betroth us to God again in righteousness, justice, faithfulness, and compassion.

Because of God's great love, his people who are walking in obedience normally enjoy a hedge of protection around them. Even Satan understands that God puts such a hedge in place. Satan said of Job, "Have you not put a hedge around him and his household and everything he has? You have blessed the work of his hands" (Job 1:10). When we love and obey God and come to him when he calls, he promises to be a wall of fire around us. But when we become stubborn and refuse to respond to him, he changes his hedge of protection into a hedge of thorns that will hurt us at every step.

Because of his great love, the Lord God thus becomes the divine blocker when necessary. He builds a hedge of thorns around us to inflict discomfort, and he knows just how much pain is necessary to bring about our restoration. We may try to wiggle out of God's plan, but we will continue to bump into this thorny hedge. In the process, we become scratched and bruised and experience distress of every kind—spiritual, physical, psychological, social, and economic—until we repent and return to him.

If God has decided from all eternity to save us and make us holy, he will surely bring it to pass. He knows how to do it and he is able to do it. Our all-wise, almighty God will sanctify us in spite of our sin, stubbornness, wandering, and backsliding. Did you say that you no longer want to obey God? If he has chosen you from all eternity, he will do whatever it takes to change your mind and you will come willingly.

Let us not, however, misuse or misunderstand this great truth. God does bring his elect people back to him, but any sin and rebellion in us will necessarily result in regrettable, lifelong consequences. The way of the wicked is hard; what we sow, that we will reap. The way of first-time obedience is the way of wisdom.

Through him all things were made; without him nothing was made that has been made. —John 1:3

he gospel of John does not open with the words, "In the beginning were the dinosaurs." He does not say, "In the beginning was man," or "In the beginning was matter." Rather, he asserts, "In the beginning was the Word." Jesus Christ, the Word, created all things, visible and invisible, animate and inanimate, angels and men. All things were created by him and for him, and he is the heir of all things. Jesus Christ was before all things, and all things hold together in him. He created them, not out of preexisting matter, but *ex nihilo*, out of nothing.

Not only did Christ create all living creatures, but he also sustains them moment by moment. Look around at the world and at yourself. Jesus Christ is the one who has given us being and it is he who is upholding us at this very moment. By his will every bird flies, and by his will every human dies to face him as Judge.

Notice the breadth and profundity of John's statement in John 1:3. Herein he denies that matter is eternal. He denies that creation proceeded from preexisting matter, or that a creature can exist independently of its Creator. He denies pantheism—the worldview that believes that creation is God itself. And he rejects the deification of nature.

John goes on to say, "In him was life." The word "life" is used here in its broadest sense to speak of all life, whether physical or spiritual. Created life cannot exist without Jesus Christ. The true origin of all life is not chemicals but Christ. There is intelligent design to the universe, and the Designer is Jesus Christ.

Most importantly, Jesus alone gives us eternal life. In his first epistle, John writes, "That which was from the beginning, which we have heard, which we have seen with our eyes . . . this we proclaim concerning the Word of life. The life appeared; we have seen it and testify to it, and we proclaim to you the eternal life, which was with the Father and has appeared to us" (1 John 1:1–2). Jesus himself proclaimed, "I give them eternal life, and they shall never perish" (John 10:28). In him is life, in him alone is life, and in him alone is eternal life.

But they mocked God's messengers, despised his words and scoffed at his prophets until the wrath of the LORD was aroused. —2 Chronicles 36:16

econd Chronicles describes the catastrophic events that shook Judah in 586 BC. Nebuchadnezzar came to Judah because his vassal, King Zedekiah, had rebelled against him. Zedekiah broke the terms of the covenant, against the counsel of the prophet Jeremiah, who had repeatedly told the king, "Don't do that. This is the plan of God." But this little fellow Zedekiah stubbornly chose to rebel against the mighty empire of Babylon.

I say "little fellow" because this term is an apt description of us in relation to the sovereign, eternal God. Every time we disobey, we are rebelling against God's rule and reign in our life. In fact, the biblical concept of covenant is this: we are nothings, yet we are given an opportunity to be saved by the Great Sovereign and enjoy life. The condition, however, is total surrender. His absolute sovereignty demands our absolute submission if we would be saved. If we remain stubborn, we shall experience our Sovereign's anger.

Zedekiah refused to be subject to King Nebuchadnezzar. He was warned again and again by Jeremiah of the consequences of his action, and in due time Nebuchadnezzar arrived. I am sure Zedekiah had deceived himself into thinking that Nebuchadnezzar would not really bother to come. But he did, and he breached the wall and destroyed the temple.

What happened to Zedekiah and Judah should serve as a serious warning to us, because this is the way God responds to those who will not submit to him. Zedekiah's problem was not primarily that he did not submit to Nebuchadnezzar. His problem was that he would not submit to God.

Why did God use Nebuchadnezzar to punish Judah? It is true that God's people had sinned, but that is not the final reason. Ultimately, they experienced the outpoured wrath of Nebuchadnezzar because they would not receive God's offers of mercy. The final reason for a rebel's destruction is always his refusal to receive God's mercy based on repentance. God sends pastors with his word of mercy to rebels, yet most reject the divine offer of reconciliation. Thus, judgment shall surely follow. Let us, therefore, take heed and accept God's gracious terms of peace.

In the first year of Cyrus king of Persia, in order to fulfill the word of the LORD spoken by Jeremiah, the LORD moved the heart of Cyrus king of Persia to make a proclamation throughout his realm. —Ezra 1:1

nly God can foretell the future, because only he is sovereign over his creation. The Lord who makes promises also fulfills them in his perfect timing. He does so by means of his sovereign control over the day-to-day affairs of history. In the book of Ezra, we find the Lord God acting through what may look to us to be the ordinary processes of history. We read about these seemingly routine historical events, and yet God, unseen, is at work. Modern man tends to despise history, but God is the Lord of history who guides it to his saving purpose.

The Lord who had promised liberation for his people through the prophets Isaiah and Jeremiah seventy years earlier was now fulfilling that word by taking the initiative to stir and move the heart of King Cyrus of Persia. The Lord God, who works all things according the counsel of his own will, was at work in the mind, will, and emotions of the king, so that he issued his decree in 538 BC.

We read in Proverbs 21:1, "The king's heart is in the hand of the LORD; he directs it like a watercourse wherever he pleases." When God stirs our hearts, we will do as he has decreed, whether we love him or not. The word translated as "moved" means "made hot." God moved Cyrus by controlling his thinking, changing his attitude, and inspiring him to act in a focused manner to accomplish God's eternal purposes.

Cyrus thus became an instrument in God's hands. Yet the king was acting on his own volition. When God stirs our hearts, we will know what to do and we ourselves will want to carry it out. God's providence thus involves a kind of effectual calling. When God stirs us up, we will become so highly motivated that we will not stop until we finish the job. God works through human beings—believers and unbelievers—to accomplish his preordained plan to save his people.

The sovereign God of history stirs, moves, inspires, guides, and leads all people everywhere to carry out his decretive will. In his wisdom, he governs all his creatures and all their actions. What a mighty God we serve!

Yet a time is coming and has now come when the true worshipers will worship the Father in spirit and truth. —John 4:23

n John 4, Jesus disclosed an amazing truth: The infinite, triune God, who does not need of any of his creatures, is nevertheless seeking authentic worshipers who will worship him in spirit and in truth. Moreover, he has been seeking such worshipers since the fall of man. Why does God himself have to take the initiative? The reason is that it is utterly impossible for a sinner to seek and worship his Creator unless God first makes him able to do so.

In this chapter we see the Father seeking and saving the Samaritan woman by sending his Son to her. This same God is even now seeking to deliver sinners from the slavery of creature worship so that they might know and worship him.

The word *worship* appears ten times in this passage. What is true worship? The Greek word means to bend down, to kiss, or to prostrate oneself. It speaks about the worshiper bowing low before the great One. It means to honor and respect a person of great worth and to demonstrate that reverence in the way we approach him.

We find this kind of reverence accorded to Jesus throughout the New Testament. When the Magi from the East came to see the baby Jesus, the text says they bowed down and worshiped him (Matt. 2). When the blind man healed by Jesus learned who Jesus really was, he declared, "Lord, I believe," and worshiped him (John 9).

Just as no one can truly believe in the Lord without also worshiping him, so no one can truly worship him without first believing, and no one can believe without knowing who he is. Belief in Jesus, therefore, requires that we first recognize his greatness. We must understand that he is not a mere man, but very God and very man, the Sovereign Lord of the universe.

This is just what Jesus did for the Samaritan woman and her neighbors—he revealed his greatness to them. First, she exclaimed, "Come, see a man who told me everything I ever did. Could he be the Christ?" Then, at the Samaritans' request, Jesus spent two more days with them, and many more became true worshipers, saying, "We know that this man really is the Savior of the world."

Return, O Israel, to the LORD your God. —Hosea 14:1

od has diagnosed our condition as human beings and the diagnosis is not good. It runs completely contrary to the common notion of "I'm okay, you're okay." That self-assessment, though a popular one, is tragically false. Our true state of affairs is that we are by nature enemies of God.

We have another problem as well: we cannot heal ourselves of the wickedness and sin within us. There is no self-salvation. But God, in his grace and mercy, offers us a divine prescription to deal with our problem, and we must pay attention to it. It is given in Hosea 14:1: "Return, O Israel, to the LORD your God."

The Hebrew word for "return" means to return unconditionally, with a repentance that is total, complete, and authentic. We cannot take one or two steps in God's direction and think we are returning satisfactorily. We must come all the way back to the Lord our God, whom we abandoned.

We must return to God because he alone has exclusive rights of ownership over us. He is the great Sovereign, and we are his vassals. Like Hosea's wife, Gomer, we became unfaithful rebels (Hosea 9:1). But now God is inviting us to return to him.

How do we return to God? First, we must realize the heinousness of our rebellion, as described by the prophet Samuel: "Rebellion is like the sin of divination, and arrogance like the evil of idolatry" (1 Sam. 15:23). We must acknowledge our sins—our idolatry, our covetousness, our sexual sin, our gluttony, our greed, our lying, our deceit, our autonomy, our insubordination. We must agree with God's diagnosis: "Your sins have been your downfall!" (Hosea 14:1) and accept full personal responsibility for our wickedness.

Hosea 14:2 provides further counsel: "Take words with you and return to the LORD." What kind of words should we take before God? "Forgive all our sins." We have to confess our sins specifically and forsake them completely before God will heal us. And, finally, we must plead, "Receive us graciously." If we come to God depending on our works, God will condemn us. Salvation is based on God's love, grace, and mercy alone. It is undeserved, and we receive it by faith in Jesus Christ alone.

"Even now," declares the LORD, "return to me with all your heart."
—*Joel 2:12*

 have wonderful news for you this morning: God's invitation to come out of our distress and return to him still stands. God does not have to speak to us; he is not required to send any prophets to us. So if he is speaking, it means he has not forsaken us! And what is he saying to us from the prophecy of Joel? "Return to me now." It is not tomorrow; it is not at our own time. We must return to him and repent today.

God is not obligated to forgive our sins, nor does he have to heal anyone. He can justly destroy us in his righteous wrath, for we have sinned against his goodness. All of us have wandered and turned our backs on him. We have sinned against his person and glory. And, yet, by God's grace, the law of repentance still holds.

Many people, however, want to be brought into God's favor without turning from their sin. This will never happen. God would have to deny himself for that to be possible, and that he cannot do. Repentance remains the only way of enjoying favor with God, as the Lord revealed to Solomon in 2 Chronicles 7:14. This law of repentance is still operative today; it can never be abrogated. Anyone who takes hold of God's promise and repents will receive mercy, forgiveness, healing, and eternal salvation.

We must ask: What kind of repentance is demanded? God will not accept an external, superficial change. He requires heartfelt repentance. The Lord demands a total change of our mind, will, and emotion. He will not accept a mere form of godliness, nor will he accept the externalities of weeping, wailing, and rending of garments. Some people can easily weep, but tears by themselves do not equal God-given repentance.

A boy in Sunday school once gave this definition of repentance: "Repentance is feeling sorry for sins." Then a wise girl sitting next to him added, "enough to quit." This is true. Repentance is feeling sorry for sins enough to quit. And we could add to her statement: True, godly repentance is feeling sorry for sins enough to quit sinning and to start obeying God's commands gladly. Genuine repentance always results in a life of wholehearted obedience to God's moral law.

If anyone is thirsty, let him come to me and drink. —John 7:37

e all recognize when we are hungry. By the same token, if we are thirsty, we know it. In John 7, Jesus gives an invitation to all whose souls are thirsty for God. His invitation is given to those who have recognized their need for spiritual life. His invitation is given to those who are restless so that they may find their rest in God alone.

We all experience thirst, but what are we thirsting for? Are we thirsting for money, pleasure, ease, fame, or recognition? If we look deep within, we will find there is a thirst that we want satisfied. Is it a worldly thirst, or is it a spiritual thirst?

The psalmist speaks of true soul thirst: "As the deer pants for streams of water, so my soul pants for you, O God. My soul thirsts for God, for the living God" (Ps. 42:1–2). Such thirst has nothing to do with thirst for the things of this world, for fame and money.

Neither is this thirst for just any god. Just as it is true today, there were all kinds of false gods in those days. They were dead and deaf, gods that were creations of men. How tragic to be fascinated with gods that have no life!

So we ask again: What are we really thirsting for? What are we craving for? Think about it, because Jesus' marvelous invitation is given only to those who thirst for him. Are we longing for things spiritual or things material? Christ is extending his gracious invitation to those who have recognized deep within themselves a misery that nothing in this world can satisfy. In other words, this invitation, though broad, is also limited to those who have a particular felt need—a thirst for God.

May God stir our consciences and give us such a soul thirst for Jesus Christ! Nothing in the world can truly meet the deepest longing of a human being but God alone. If you are happy without Christ, may God have mercy on you. But if you are running to God's word, if you are running to him in prayer, if you are running to church to hear what God has to say, then Jesus' promise is for you: "Streams of living water will flow from within."

The LORD roars from Zion and thunders from Jerusalem; the pastures of the shepherds dry up, and the top of Carmel withers. —Amos 1:2

he kingdoms of Judah and Israel both enjoyed great prosperity in the first half of the eighth century BC. Everything was going well. They enjoyed military victories. The people became exceedingly rich, which, in turn, brought about a lifestyle and mindset that we find repeated throughout the history of nations. Judah may have continued to observe her religious traditions, but there was no heart, no piety toward God. And there was no justice in terms of societal behavior. What mattered to the people was making money and enjoying the good life, even if it meant treading upon the poor.

In Amos' time, the Israelites were building large houses and filling them with expensive furniture. At the same time, they were turning away from God and his law, and away from any kind of righteous behavior. This is also what is going on in the Western world today.

In the midst of all this, God raised up Amos, a shepherd, to prophesy in Israel. *Amos* means "burden bearer." Amos 1:2 tells us the burden of the entire prophecy: "The LORD roars from Zion."

Amos was giving an unanticipated, unaccepted warning to a decadent culture: "The Lord is roaring! Repent, or face his holy wrath." That call to repentance must have sounded strange to a people who were enjoying such a prosperous and sensuous life. Of course, even to compare God to a roaring lion would be politically incorrect in our day. Modern man, if he thinks about God at all, views him as nice and gracious, a God who is ever-forgiving and never asks questions.

The message of Amos is a rebuke to all such ideas of God. The prophet's picture of God as a roaring lion means judgment. It means the Lord committed himself to attack his own people because they abandoned him. It means he is already leaping to seize his prey.

Let us get used to this strange idea that the Lord is a Judge as well as a Savior, for that is what the Bible teaches in both the Old and New Testaments. God is roaring; he is thundering. He expects us to show holy fear and to walk humbly with him, because our God is most holy.

Go to Bethel and sin; go to Gilgal and sin yet more. —Amos 4:4

he prophet's shocking, mocking call in Amos 4 to "go to Bethel and sin" can be translated in modern language as, "Go to church and sin." "Bethel churches" are those churches where God is not worshiped and his word is not preached, where people are entertained and their felt needs are massaged, where a Jesus who is Savior but not Lord is proclaimed. Such churches teach that one can be saved while continuing in sin, so that a thief can be "saved," yet continue to steal; adulterers and fornicators can be "saved," yet continue to practice sexual immorality; drug addicts can be "saved," yet continue to sell and use drugs. Such churches actually promote sin and are destined for destruction.

Amos prophesied during the second golden age of Judah and Israel, during the reigns of Uzziah in Judah and Jeroboam II in Israel. During this time, these kings controlled almost all the territories that Israel had possessed in the days of David and Solomon. Sadly, though, material prosperity and true piety are almost always inversely related.

This is not to say that prosperity results in a diminution of worship. In fact, wealth produces a proliferation of worship places and styles. There is great religious diversity where there is money. Every desire for worship is catered to. Bethel churches flourish. During Amos' time, there were churches in Bethel, Dan, Beersheba, Gilgal, and Samaria, where people could feast, sacrifice, enjoy religious prostitution, and worship their own gods. All such worship was in opposition to the Holy One of Israel.

As in ancient Israel, the great prosperity in the Western world today has produced great sin against God. And the vast majority of churches are dedicated to bull worship. There is no presence of the holy God, no holy word, and no obedience to Jesus Christ the Lord. Worship is thriving, but it is worship that pleases people's whims and satisfies their felt needs. If we go to today's centers of bull worship, we will see many happy people—husbands, wives, teens, children. The only one who is not pleased is God. He is angry and about to pour out his judgment.

What then is the prophet's final word to all unrepentant Bethel churches? "Prepare to meet your God!"

Because the gracious hand of our God was on us, they brought us Sherebiah, a capable man. —Ezra 8:18

 hat do we need? The hand of the Lord. We need the all-sufficient grace of God. In Ezra 8:18, Ezra says, "The gracious hand of our God was on us." It is not just for the pastor. Every single person belonging to God can ask for it. We can pray, "O God, I am one of your children. May your gracious hand rest upon me." I feel sorry for the graceless man who trusts in his own wisdom and makes bad decisions that bring him to hell itself. We should pray, "O God, I don't want to go anywhere unless the hand of God is with me."

What will the hand of God accomplish for his people? First, Ezra says that God "brought us Sherebiah, a capable man." The word *Christos* can be translated "capacity." Jesus Christ was anointed by the Holy Spirit, making him capable of being a prophet, priest, and king. What the church needs today is capable men—men full of God-given ideas; men who execute those ideas, men of resolute mind. The truth is, God can make us capable.

Ezra goes on to say, "I was ashamed to ask the king for soldiers and horsemen to protect us from enemies on the road, because we had told the king, 'The gracious hand of our God is on everyone who looks to him'" (v. 22). We may recognize that we are weak, but we must not worry about it. God's enabling grace is for everyone who looks to him in dependence, saying, "O God, I am weak but you are strong. I am poor but you are rich." As a result, the hand of God will come and grip us, and that grip will give us strength. We will be encouraged so that we can say, "I can do all things through Jesus Christ who strengtheneth me."

Finally, Ezra said, "We set out . . . to go to Jerusalem. The hand of our God was on us, and he protected us from enemies and bandits along the way" (v. 31). This was nothing short of a second exodus, and God guided them each step of the way. His footprints were not seen, but the invisible God was with them. They arrived safely because the hand of the living God was on them.

Yet when he heard that Lazarus was sick, he stayed where he was two more days. —John 11:6

mericans do not like delays. When someone is one minute late, we become so unhappy and miserable that we begin to jump up and down. Do you find it hard to put up with delays? Oh, we are a spoiled people. We need to learn to pray during delays, for they are often God's appointments for us to be taught God's ways. It is better for us to go to God and discover what he is trying to tell us. We should pray, "Teach us, O God—your servants hear."

In John 11, we are told, "Jesus loved Martha and her sister and Lazarus" (v. 5). Yet, notice, when he heard that Lazarus was sick and dying, he stayed where he was for two more days. Apparently his delay was deliberate. No matter how much we jump up and down, God is not going to change his will for us. He will tarry and work in his good time.

Two days is a long time when someone is dying. It is not that Lazarus had cancer and eventually was going to die. No, Lazarus was in the final stages of death. Nevertheless, Jesus made a decision to wait, and that decision was made in concert with the Father's will. Jesus always did what he saw his Father doing. It was the will of the Father for him to stay where he was for two more days.

In verse 7 we read, "Then he said to his disciples, 'Let us go back to Judea.'" The Lord Jesus remained according to the Father's will; then he went to Bethany in accordance with that will. It was all in God's order. Jesus trusted in God; so he declared, "Let us return."

The disciples did not have such great faith. They knew they would be facing trouble, so they objected, "Rabbi, a short while ago the Jews tried to stone you!" But Jesus was not afraid or deterred; he knew that Lazarus had died so that Jesus might perform a mighty miracle to the glory of God. And so we learn the purpose of delay in Jesus' own words: "Lazarus is dead, and for your sake I am glad I was not there, so that you may believe." May God help us to trust in his timing so that we may also believe and be blessed.

They took palm branches and went out to meet him, shouting, "Hosanna! . . . Blessed is the King of Israel!" —John 12:13

n John 12, we read that Jesus Christ and his disciples set out from Galilee to go to Jerusalem for the Passover festival. But Jesus went as the Passover lamb to be slaughtered, so that he might take away the sin of the world. Jesus knew what would happen to him in Jerusalem during this Passover festival. He was sent by the Father to die on the cross—a necessary, propitiatory, substitutionary, exhaustive, penal death that would accomplish our redemption.

On this particular Sunday, he took a deliberate action designed to provoke the Jewish leaders to pass sentence on him: he chose to come into the city riding on a donkey as the promised Messiah, the Son of David.

In honor of the royal Messiah's arrival in Jerusalem, the people threw their outer garments on the donkey for Christ to sit on. They also cut palm branches, used in celebrating victories, and placed them on the road. These pilgrims cried out to the one riding on the holy donkey, "Hosanna," which means "Save us!" By this they were acknowledging that this One is the Savior.

They also proclaimed, "Blessed is the King who comes in the name of the Lord!" Not only is this One the Savior, to whom we cry, "Hosanna," but he is also Christ the Lord, the eternal King, the One who will not be destroyed by death.

On Palm Sunday, we see the pilgrims praying to Jesus and extolling him as their King. Yet, as he himself predicted, the Jewish leaders arrested him on Thursday, crucified him on Friday, and God raised him up on Sunday. Thus he fulfilled the eternal purpose of God in accomplishing our redemption, so that everyone who calls on his name will be delivered from the bondage of sin and death.

Not only should we cry out to Jesus, but we must also acknowledge him as our eternal King by surrendering to him and his sovereign rule. Antinomianism is antithetical to the gospel that speaks about Jesus as Savior and King. If we have surrendered to him, we will obey his rule. Then we will be numbered among the multitude in Revelation 7 who will rejoice forever before the Lamb, wearing white robes and holding palm branches in their hands.

December 13

The evening meal was being served, and the devil had already prompted Judas Iscariot, son of Simon, to betray Jesus. —John 13:2

ohn 13 tells of the last supper Jesus ate on this earth before his death. As he sat with his disciples in the upper room, none of his men wanted to wash the others' feet. Why? It was the job of a slave, and no one wants to be a slave. They all sat there. Yet Jesus, knowing that he was given all authority as the Lord of the universe, assumed the role of a servant. He took a towel and went about washing their feet, even the feet of Judas, his betrayer.

We know that Judas was a materialist and a thief, and that he had already entered into an agreement with the authorities to sell the Lord for thirty pieces of silver. He had become an apostate— one who stands away from God, away from God's people, away from God's truth, away from Scripture, and away from the light. Jesus knew all this about Judas. Nevertheless, he demonstrated his love for him by washing his feet.

Judas, however, instead of repenting, further hardened his heart. He gave way to Satan's promptings. What was the task Satan wanted him to do? Betray Jesus. It is still the temptation today. Satan puts all manner of wicked thoughts into our minds. That is normal for the Christian. But what are you going to do with his suggestions? If you are not alive toward God, if you are not filled with the Spirit, if you are not interested in truth, you will do exactly as he tells you.

Thoughts come to us all the time, either from the Holy Spirit or from Satan. As Christians, we are commanded to resist the devil. And we are promised that if we do so, he will flee from us. If we, however, follow the devil's promptings, our end will be same as that of Judas the apostate. He was seized with remorse, threw his money away, and went and hanged himself.

Let us, then, be people of integrity and honesty. Let us keep covenant with God and man until we all arrive safely in heaven, where there will be no more tears, no more sin, and no apostasy.

Do not let your hearts be troubled. Trust in God; trust also in me.
—John 14:1

n John 14, Jesus is speaking to his disciples on the last night before his death on the cross. His first words are, "Let not your hearts any longer be troubled." What were some of the troubles these disciples were facing? First, they were finally realizing that their Master was going to depart from them very soon, and now they must face the world on their own. For three years, no matter what the problem, they had gone to Jesus, and he had solved it. Additionally, they were perplexed. No doubt they were saying to themselves, "We know Jesus is the Messiah, but how can the Messiah die? The Messiah is supposed to come and conquer all his enemies. But now Jesus is telling us that he is going to die."

They were also ashamed because of their pride. They remembered how even in the last few days the big question amongst themselves had been, "Who is the greatest?" And they were deeply disturbed because Jesus had told them, "One of you will betray me," even though they could not imagine such a thing happening.

Jesus knew that soon he would be arrested, maltreated, and crucified. Yet he now spoke words of comfort to his disciples, and his words have provided great blessing to his church throughout the succeeding generations: "Trust in God; trust also in me."

Was Jesus merely speaking as the world does, glibly telling them that everything would be all right? No. We must remember that the source of all trouble in this world is sin. So Jesus was saying, "I know you are troubled and I know the reason for your trouble. It is sin. But I am going to take care of your problem by my death on the cross."

By bearing our sins on the cross, Jesus has taken care of our fundamental problem. Thus, he has good reason to say to us, "Keep on trusting in God and keep on trusting in me." Such words tell us that Jesus himself is God. It is true that our present existence is characterized by trouble, tears, pain, poverty, misery, persecution, and slander. This is the lot of true Christians in this world. The solution to all our troubles is trust—not self-trust, but trust in God the Father and in Jesus Christ his Son.

Woe to those who plan iniquity, to those who plot evil on their beds!
—*Micah 2:1*

he prophet Micah lived at a time of great apostasy in Samaria as well as in Judah. God's people had become much more interested in their own plans than those of their covenant Lord. How foolish his people were and often still are in this regard, for it is "the plans of the LORD [that] stand firm forever; the LORD thwarts the purposes of the peoples" (Ps. 33:10–11).

Micah 2:1 characterizes man's selfish ambitions: "Woe to those who plan iniquity, to those who plot evil on their beds!" Man is planning all the time. What is he thinking about at night on his bed? He is planning how to make another buck in the morning, by honest or dishonest means.

The Israelites who idolized money and amassed wealth by cheating and deceiving had violated the clear terms of the covenant, and so the covenant Lord was now warning them through the prophet, saying, "I too am planning something."

You see, man may plan, but God alone executes his purposes without fail. His righteous threatenings are true. So he said, "I am planning disaster against this people, from which you cannot save yourselves" (Mic. 2:3). Later, he declared, "O Daughter of Zion . . . you will go to Babylon" (Mic. 4:10). Yet his gracious promises are also sure: "O stronghold of the Daughter of Zion, the former dominion will be restored to you" (Mic. 4:8).

Let us understand then that there is a God who has foreordained whatsoever comes to pass, for his own glory. While we make our plans, he also has plans. We read in the book of Proverbs: "In his heart a man plans his course, but the LORD determines his steps" (Prov. 16:9); and, "Many are the plans in a man's heart, but it is the LORD's purpose that prevails" (Prov. 19:21).

God declares in Isaiah 30:1, "Woe to the obstinate children, to those who carry out plans that are not mine, forming an alliance, but not by my Spirit, heaping sin upon sin." May God purify our hearts and desires so that our plans will correspond to and coalesce with God's perfect plan. "For I know the plans I have for you," declares the LORD, "plans to prosper you and not to harm you, plans to give you hope and a future" (Jer. 29:11).

When Sanballat heard that we were rebuilding the wall, he became angry and was greatly incensed. —Nehemiah 4:1

hat happened when God raised up a man to rebuild Jerusalem, to restore its walls and put up its gates, to reinstitute the sacrifices, to promote divine order, to preach the word of God, and to require holy living? Enmity and opposition ensued, as recorded in Nehemiah 4.

Syncretism and diversity are popular today. The enemies of God's church are against the church's holding fast to the exclusivity of truth—that Christianity alone is true, that the Scriptures are alone true, and that proper worship is what the Scripture demands.

Most people like some spirituality and a general view of religion. What they do not like is Christianity, the Bible, and the deity of Jesus Christ, that he is Savior, King, and Judge. When we speak about the kingdom of God, most people hate it. They resent the Ten Commandments because God's law condemns their sinful lifestyles.

Nehemiah wanted to live for God and tell others how to have peace and joy in the Holy Spirit. Why, then, were Sanballat and his comrades so incensed at the reconstruction of the wall? Because they were inspired by the devil, who always opposes God. Such opposition will continue until the last day.

Sanballat sneered, "Will they restore their wall? Will they offer sacrifices?" (v. 2). The enemies of God are happy when God is not worshiped and the Bible not read. But when someone like Nehemiah is interested in bringing about kingdom order in a country, in a church, or in a home, all of a sudden there is trouble. The moment parents say to their children, "We have been living a disorderly life—watching television, not praying, not seeking God, not hearing and doing God's will. We are now going to serve Jesus Christ"—at that moment, there will be a fight.

Satan hates it when we pray. Satan does not want us to get up and go to church. Satan is angry when we turn off the television and open the Bible. Why? He does not want us to be strong in our faith and give glory to God. But Nehemiah and the Jews refused to cower before Satan's opposition, and we too must fight the good fight. Strengthened by God's grace, we must continue to stand for truth in a dark world, knowing that "our God will fight for us" (v. 20).

DECEMBER 17

But you, Bethlehem Ephrathah, though you are small among the clans of Judah, out of you will come for me one who will be ruler over Israel, whose origins are from of old, from eternity. —Micah 5:2

ethlehem of Ephrathah was the least of all the towns in the kingdom of Judah. In fact, it did not even make the list of 115 prominent locations recorded in Joshua 15:20–63. Like Nazareth, Bethlehem was lowly and generally despised by the other clans of Judah.

But God has a way of exalting the despised. So Micah's prophecy in Micah 5 speaks of the coming of the King of Israel, the Messiah, not out of mighty Jerusalem, but from the little town of Bethlehem. We read in verse 2, "But you, Bethlehem Ephrathah, though you are small"—despised, insignificant, excluded—"among the clans of Judah, out of you will come for me one who will be ruler of Israel." God puts down the arrogant and exalts the humble. He comforts the weary and encourages them to come to him. He reveals himself as Messiah to the trembling publican, but rejects the proud Pharisee.

In 1 Corinthians 1:26–29 we see clearly this principle of God at work in our own salvation: "Brothers, think of what you were when you were called. Not many of you were wise by human standards; not many were influential; not many were of noble birth. But God chose the foolish things of the world to shame the wise; God chose the weak things of the world to shame the strong. He chose the lowly things of this world and the despised things—and the things that are not—to nullify the things that are, so that no one may boast before him."

Bethlehem was the birthplace of David, and it would become the birthplace of the One who is David's son and David's Lord. And in the fourth century, Helena, mother of Constantine, would erect a church over some caves in Bethlehem, memorializing the birthplace of Jesus. This church was destroyed but later rebuilt by Justinian in the sixth century AD. The once-despised Bethlehem has now become world-famous. Today, vast multitudes of people continue to follow the Magi to Bethlehem, where Jesus was born.

So even in the chosen birthplace of the long-awaited Messiah we see a glorious theme that runs throughout the Bible: "God opposes the proud but gives grace to the humble" (1 Pet. 5:5).

When he had received the drink, Jesus said, "It is finished." With that, he bowed his head and gave up his spirit. —John 19:30

rom the cross, Jesus shouted triumphantly, *"Tetelestai!"*—"It is finished!" Jesus was not weeping; this was a shout of victory. In secular literature, *tetelestai* meant "paid in full," which I write on bills I have already paid. Our redemption price has been paid in full by the blood of Jesus Christ. The veil that separated us from God has been torn from top to bottom. *Tetelestai* is the declaration of heaven to us, the chosen of God, that our chains are broken, that we may come out of darkness and enter into the glorious sunlight of the freedom of God.

Let us understand the glorious, terrible cross, from which Christ shouted, "Paid in full." We deserved to die, but Christ died for us. We were sold under sin, but Christ bought us back by paying a sufficient ransom, which is his own precious blood. Children of God, there is no need for us to be slaves anymore. Be instantly liberated through faith in the once-for-all substitutionary sacrifice of Christ.

Our price has been paid in full. Why then do we behave as though we are still bound? That is a question we must face honestly. The answer is, because we like it. People get used to their chains. They come to me and say, "I want to change." But some of them do not really want to come into the sunshine. If they wanted to, they could do it instantly. The only thing that prevents us from walking in the glorious liberty of the children of God is ourselves.

Charles Wesley felt the glorious power of redemption and composed this song:

Long my imprisoned spirit lay fast bound in sin and nature's night;
thine eye diffused a quick'ning ray; I woke, the dungeon flamed with light.
My chains fell off, my heart was free; I rose, went forth and followed thee.
Amazing love! How can it be that thou, my God, shouldst die for me?

We may choose to take the chains and bind ourselves. But the death of Christ—his propitiatory, sacrificial death, his death of reconciliation and redemption—truly breaks every chain. Let us, therefore, live as free men, and show by our lives what Christ has done on the cross.

They still did not understand from Scripture that Jesus had to rise from the dead. —John 20:9

hat does the resurrection of Christ prove? Since this, the greatest miracle in the history of the world, predicted by Jesus himself, came to pass, then all the other claims and teachings of Jesus must also be true.

The resurrection of Christ thus verifies the authority of the Scriptures and Jesus' own words. Paul says Jesus "was raised on the third day according to the Scriptures" (1 Cor. 15:4). And we read in John's gospel: "Jesus answered [the Jews], 'Destroy this temple, and I will raise it again in three days.' . . . After he was raised from the dead, his disciples recalled what he had said. Then they believed the Scripture and the words that Jesus had spoken" (John 2:19, 22).

First and foremost, the resurrection proves Jesus true in his most important claim that he is who he declared himself to be. Jesus said, "I and the Father are one" (John 10:30), thereby claiming to be equal with eternal God. He also declared himself to be without sin (John 8:46), and that he came from heaven and would return again from heaven (Matt. 26:64).

The resurrection also certifies that Jesus accomplished a perfect atonement. By his life and death, Jesus satisfied the justice of the Father. The resurrection was God's "Amen" to Jesus' cry from the cross, "It is finished," referring to the work of atonement. The world, the flesh, the devil and his demons, and the last enemy, death, have all been destroyed by Jesus' death on the cross.

The resurrection of Christ also proves that heaven and hell are real. Jesus spoke more about hell than he did about heaven. He described it as a fiery furnace, a place of darkness where there is weeping and gnashing of teeth.

Finally, the resurrection proves that we can count on Jesus' promise to come again to judge sinners and glorify his people. He himself said, "At that time the sign of the Son of Man will appear in the sky, and all the nations of the earth will mourn. They will see the Son of Man coming on the clouds of the sky, with power and great glory" (Matt. 24:30).

May God help us to believe the Scriptures, which speak of the risen Lord Jesus Christ, that we may have life in his name.

So on the first day of the seventh month Ezra the priest brought the law before the assembly. —Nehemiah 8:2

very true revival is the result of the word of God preached, the word of God heard, the word of God believed, and the word of God obeyed. What we see in Nehemiah 8 is in accordance with what had been commanded in Deuteronomy 31:10–13: "At the end of every seven years . . . when all Israel comes to appear before the LORD your God at the place he will choose, you shall read this law before them in their hearing. Assemble the people . . . so they can listen and learn."

The Israelites came together as one man, in complete unity, in one accord. Why did they assemble? To hear the word of God. Whenever people have a hunger for God's word, we must conclude that God is at work in them. He works in us both to will and to do his good pleasure. Satan hates it when we study the Bible. He wants us to be ignorant of God and of his redeeming grace. I hope that you will examine your life and see whether you have a passionate interest, including an intellectual interest, in the revealed word of God.

We are told specifically that "all who were able to understand" gathered together. When we come to church, we ought to come to understand, not just to feel better. The priority of feeling is the culture of our time. But woe unto that person who is guided by his feelings.

The Israelites gave God's word a royal reception. In verse 3, the Hebrew text reads, "They put their ears to the word." They listened with great concentration and conviction to the word as it was preached. They wanted to understand it, because it is the liberating word. God's word is Spirit and God's word is life. God's word drives away ignorance and shows us how to live.

True revival and covenant renewal require, as of first importance, an intellectual grasp of God's normative word. Without understanding the will of God, we will not experience revival. We can come to church year after year, yet remain confused, anxious, and worried. That is because we have closed our minds to the word of God. God gave us minds so that we can think his thoughts after him; let us, therefore, fill them with God's word.

When I saw him, I fell at his feet as though dead. Then he placed his right hand on me and said: "Do not be afraid." —Revelation 1:17

n his encounter with the majestic Lord Jesus Christ in Revelation 1, the apostle John was so impressed that he fell at his feet as though dead. What did Jesus do when John's feet gave way? The risen Christ touched this one who trembled with godly fear, revived him, and spoke encouraging words to him: "Fear not!"

These words of Jesus are for all his children. Why should we not fear? The risen Christ gives us several reasons in this passage. First, he told John, "I am the First and the Last." Jehovah alone is the First and the Last (Isa. 44:6; 48:12). In other words, Jesus was declaring that he is Jehovah God. Jesus Christ is the Creator as well as the Consummator. He is not part of creation, but he was at its origin and he will be at its consummation. Our God is the eternal Lord of history. How, then, can we fear?

Then Jesus declared, "I am the Living One." This one who tells us to "Fear not!" is eternal life. He is the self-existing God who says, "I am the resurrection and the life. He who believes in me will live, even though he dies" (John 11:25). For us, death is actually gain, for it will usher us into the very presence of God.

Next, he stated, "I was dead," meaning, "I died on the cross for your salvation." Jesus Christ is our propitiation. His death accomplished atonement for the sins of the elect of the whole world so that we may be justified justly. The Lord continued, "Behold, I am alive for ever and ever!" A great and wonderful thing happened! God raised Jesus from the dead because it was impossible for death to keep its hold on him. Our Lord will never die again, and so we who are in him by faith will never truly die again, but will live forevermore. Physical death cannot destroy eternal life, which we have by vital union with Christ.

Jesus concluded, "I hold the keys of death and Hades." The devil does not hold them; the Lord Jesus Christ does. The Father has placed all things under his feet. He is the head of the church, and the controller of all things. Therefore, church, the Lord is saying to you, "Fear not!"

After this I looked, and there before me was a door standing open in heaven. And the voice I had first heard speaking to me like a trumpet said, "Come up here." —Revelation 4:1

n Revelation 4, Jesus Christ summons John to come into the throne room in heaven so that he can show him who is ruling the world and what must take place in the future. It is like being taken into the control tower of the busiest airport in the world. Our triune God alone rules the universe. No president, no king, no one else, including the devil and his demons, has ultimate control.

John was summoned to allow him to view ultimate reality and understand the central importance of the throne of God. The very first thing John saw in heaven was this throne. The word "throne" appears at least thirty-seven times in this book. God's throne is in the center of heaven, for it is the central reality of the universe.

Our universe is theocentric; by his will, God created all things, from the smallest particle to the largest star, including every living thing. He created them, he owns them, and he rules them. History is meaningless, and all searches for origins are futile, without this ultimate perspective from heaven.

In Revelation 4:5 we read, "From the throne came flashes of lightning, rumbling and peals of thunder." Do you hear his thunder? Do you see his lightning? Do you tremble when you think about this God? Psalm 2 tells us to rejoice with trembling. God is not our buddy. He is the Sovereign Lord. There is no equal ultimacy of good and evil. God's rule is the central reality, and we ignore it at our own peril.

God told John to write down this revelation and send it to the churches for their comfort. Christians must know that, although the world may hate, persecute, and kill them, such things happen only by the will of God. Additionally, physical death cannot separate them from eternal life, but only usher them into God's glorious presence.

If we are anxious and worried, Jesus is calling us to come and view the throne of God. Then we will have rest for our souls. In the Spirit we understand that, no matter what happens to us in this world, our Sovereign God is in control, and he will save us. Our God shall never forsake us, but will bring us safely home.

Then he said to Joshua, "See, I have taken away your sin, and I will put rich garments on you." —Zechariah 3:4

echariah 3 tells us how God solves our pollution problem. In 520 BC, two months after Haggai began his ministry, Zechariah also began to prophesy to the remnant of Jews in Jerusalem, encouraging them to rebuild the temple.

The setting of this prophetic vision is a courtroom, where there is the accused, the accuser, and the advocate.

Who is the accuser? He is identified here as Satan, who is standing on the right hand of Joshua the high priest, representing the prosecuting attorney, as we read in Psalm 109:6: "Appoint an evil man to oppose him; let an accuser stand at his right hand." Satan is the accuser of God's people. He comes in the middle of the night and accuses us.

The accused is Joshua the high priest, who represents the people of God. Joshua is ministering before the Lord, but he is wearing extremely filthy clothes. Satan's accusation is this: The mediatorial ministry of this high priest is unavailing because he is a sinner. Satan's logic is clear: How can a sinful high priest atone for the sins of God's people? If Joshua is unclean, his ministry cannot be effective; thus, the elect people of God are left with no atonement and no mediator. In the end, they cannot be saved.

The advocate is the angel of the Lord, who represents the Lord of Hosts, the One in control of all things. In this court, the angel of the Lord is both advocate and judge.

In the fullness of time, this advocate, the angel of the Lord, came into the world in the person of Jesus Christ. Zechariah 3:8–9 prophesies his coming: "I am going to bring my servant, the Branch . . . and I will remove the sin of this land in a single day." What was that single, momentous day? Good Friday—the day Jesus died on the cross as an atoning sacrifice for the sins of his people.

Praise God that our salvation does not depend on the high priest Joshua, or on our own filthy works of self-righteousness. Our salvation depends on this perfect, sinless Messiah who came in the fullness of time, born of a woman, born under the law, to redeem us from the law. And now we are clothed with Christ's perfect righteousness (2 Cor. 5:19, 21).

I looked again—and there before me was a flying scroll! —Zechariah 5:1

he "flying scroll" which we read about in Zechariah 5 is a covenant document. What is written on this scroll? Curses. Where did these curses come from? God's covenant. When we obey the covenant, we receive promised blessings. But when we disobey, we experience threatened curses.

The all-seeing God examines us daily on the basis of covenant. He sees our every thought, word, and deed. We may forget our sins, but he remembers, and they are written down. The flying scroll travels throughout the land, entering every house where God's people have violated his covenant.

The Lord said to Zechariah, "This is the curse going out over the whole land; for according to what it says on one side, every thief will be banished, and according to what it says on the other, everyone who swears falsely will be banished" (v. 3). God's people broke both the third and the ninth commandments—stealing, and taking God's name in vain. When we are baptized, if we are not true, we are lying. When we get married, if we are not true, we are swearing falsely. When we are received into church membership and we are not true, we are taking the Lord's name in vain. And God takes note of all of this.

We tend to think God does not see what we do, so we can do whatever we want. We convince ourselves that God routinely overlooks sin. Thus, people regularly and freely swear falsely, though God desires truth in our inner parts (Ps. 51:6). He demands sincerity and fidelity from us. If we are not walking thusly, we are deceiving others and defrauding them, and God will write down our lying and covenant-breaking on his scroll.

The flying scroll was sent by the Lord of the covenant, the Lord Almighty. It is like a big truck, full of junk, that arrives at our house and dumps its contents on our driveway. We may object, "I did not order this." But God will answer, "Yes, you did. You ordered this forty years ago. Remember what you did when you were seventeen?" We may have forgotten our sin. We may protest and even accuse God of acting unjustly. But we must accept the delivery. The Lord of the covenant does not err when he sends his flying scroll. May God help us to obey and receive his blessings.

She will give birth to a son, and you are to give him the name Jesus, because he will save his people from their sins. —Matthew 1:21

he fundamental problem of man is not political, economic, social, medical, or educational. The fundamental problem of man is sin. Sin has separated all men from God. As a result, the psalmist says, "No man can redeem the life of another or give to God a ransom for him—the ransom for a life is costly, no payment is ever enough" (Ps. 49:7–8). But he also promises, "O Israel, put your hope in the LORD, for with the LORD is unfailing love and with him is full redemption. He himself will redeem Israel from all their sins" (Ps. 130:7–8).

In the fullness of time, God fulfilled this promise by sending his Son, Jesus Christ, the God/man. This, then, is the purpose of the virgin birth of Christ—to provide us a Savior who is capable of saving his people from their sins. In Christ we have full salvation from the guilt, the power, the punishment, and the presence of sin. Thus, our sin problem is totally and comprehensively solved.

We must recognize that Jesus alone is perfect God and perfect, sinless man. Only he can give his life as a ransom for many (Matt. 20:28). While instituting the holy supper, Jesus said, "This is my blood of the covenant, which is poured out for many for the forgiveness of sins" (Matt. 26:28). There is no other way to save people from their sins except through the sinless God/man coming into the world and dying on the cross. "God made him who has no sin to be sin for us, so that in him we might become the righteousness of God" (2 Cor. 5:21).

The one who lay helpless in the cattle trough in Bethlehem is the Almighty God become flesh. He died on the cross for sinners that he may redeem his people, both Jews and Gentiles. God's covenant with Abraham was that in his offspring, Jesus Christ, all the families of the earth would be blessed. God saw man's fundamental problem, and sent a Savior, his only Son, to solve that sin problem and bring us back into joyful fellowship with him. Truly to us a child is born, to us a son is given—for our salvation and great joy!

A great and wondrous sign appeared in heaven: a woman clothed with the sun, with the moon under her feet and a crown of twelve stars on her head. —Revelation 12:1

he book of Revelation belongs to a particular type of literature called apocalyptic. In Revelation 12, we encounter highly symbolic language, which, though difficult to interpret, nevertheless describes actual events that shall surely come to pass in God's time.

A sign points to something else. Here the "great and wondrous sign" is that of a pregnant woman. This woman represents the ideal church of the Old and New Testament, the true Israel of God, the elect people of God. She represents the church corporately and individually. And by studying this woman we gain a greater understanding of who we are in the sight of God.

Notice the description given of this woman: she is "clothed with the sun." This speaks about the brilliance and glory of God's people. The world despises, persecutes, and demeans the church. It is better for us to listen to what God has to say about his church. Here the Holy Spirit describes her as clothed with glory. How wonderful it is to know what the Bridegroom is thinking about us, the bride of Christ. When the Lord looks upon his church, he sees her as if clothed with the sun. The church is glorious! May God help us to understand our worth in his eyes, and not give way to our own negativity or the demeaning evaluation of the world.

Not only that, the woman in John's vision is also standing on the moon, which points to dominion. We shall rule with Christ. And so the woman wears a crown. In this same chapter, we also see crowns on the head of the dragon. But those crowns represent arrogation of authority—Satan's attempt to take unto himself that which he does not possess. The woman's crown, though, is the victor's crown that the Lord has legally and properly conferred upon his church.

Therefore, do not believe what the world says about you. God looks upon his church and declares that she is glorious and victorious. He promises her a crown of twelve stars for her head. God shall present each of us to himself without spot or wrinkle, clothed in his glory, with exceeding joy. Let us give thanks to God that we are members of his beautiful, radiant, glorious church.

He was given power to make war against the saints and to conquer them.
—Revelation 13:7

evelation 13 puts the lie to the popular, heretical "health and wealth" gospel that proclaims, "Receive Jesus and you will enjoy a trouble-free life." Instead, we read in this chapter of a beast that in the future will be given power and authority by the dragon to persecute the people of God.

This great dragon, Satan, is the archenemy of Jesus Christ and his church. Recall that Satan came to Jesus and offered him all the kingdoms of this world in return for worship; Jesus rebuked him and stood firm in the temptation (see Matt. 4). But there is a man, here called the beast, who will say "Yes" to the dragon's proposition. He will be a great and charismatic orator who will lead the entire unbelieving world astray with his "proud words and blasphemies." He will even be worshipped by all those whose names have not been written in the Lamb's book of life. And we are told he will exercise his worldwide dominion to usher in a period of intense persecution, including martyrdom, against every authentic Christian.

The genuine gospel of Jesus Christ promises us trials, tribulations, and opposition in this world. Such persecution separates the false from the true saints of God. Undoubtedly, men will be given the opportunity to deny Jesus and be spared from the sword. Anyone who has been serving God for self-interest, health, wealth, or worldly success will be exposed as a coward on that day.

But thanks be to God, he will surely preserve his blood-bought children. He will grant them sufficient grace to look straight at their tormentors and declare, "I believe in Jesus; go ahead and kill me." They will fulfill the promise found in Revelation 12:11, "They overcame him by the blood of the Lamb and by the word of their testimony; they did not love their lives so much as to shrink from death."

Jesus made the cost of discipleship very clear: "Anyone who does not hate even his own life cannot be my disciple." We must ask ourselves the question, "Why did I receive Jesus?" May God deliver us from every wrong motive. Then may he help us to stand immovable in the day of trouble.

And I will pour out on the house of David and the inhabitants of Jerusalem a spirit of grace and supplication. —Zechariah 12:10

o man repents on his own volition. When we see people refusing to confess, we must understand that a spirit of grace and supplication, as we read in Zechariah 12, has not been poured out on them. But when we encounter someone who is repenting and weeping out of conviction of sin against the Lord, then we know that he is experiencing great spiritual favor.

If the Spirit of God is not resting upon us, we will continue to fight and argue. We will minimize our sin and excuse ourselves. Whenever people justify themselves and whitewash their sin, we can deduce that they are not blessed with the favor of the outpouring of the Spirit of grace and supplication. But when God's Spirit comes upon us, there will be profound, heartfelt confessions, and no more self-justification. This is true in all revivals. People will weep bitterly over having offended the Messiah.

True repentance is a gift that we can never manufacture. But when God pours out his Spirit, our hearts and souls will be changed. We will rejoice in humbling ourselves. We will beat upon our breasts and say, "Have mercy upon me, a sinner." We will voluntarily say to the pastor, "You don't understand the depth of my depravity. It is far worse than you imagine."

When the Spirit of God falls upon us, not only will we weep bitterly, but we will also hate and forsake sin. The Spirit's work illuminates the deep recesses of our darkness. We will examine our life in the light of his light and throw all our idols away, because our repentance is authentic, not superficial.

One of the most beautiful sights in the world is to see a sinner being convicted of sin and resolving and determining to live a holy life, because the favor of God has fallen upon that person. Indeed, both the fear of God and the love of God rests upon every penitent sinner.

May we all cry out to God: "O Lord, let there be a revival in which we experience this outpouring of a spirit of grace and a spirit of prayer." When this happens, the pastor will not have to convince or convict anyone. The Spirit of the living God himself shall convict and console.

With a mighty voice he shouted: "Fallen! Fallen is Babylon the Great!"
—Revelation 18:2

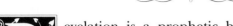

Revelation is a prophetic book—it addresses things that are future. Because there are so many symbols and visions, it is not always easy to understand what is going on. Those who claim to know the exact meaning of every aspect of this book are typically those who actually know the least.

Nevertheless, we can make certain statements with confidence regarding this prophecy. For instance, we can be absolutely sure that in the end God wins. Additionally, we know for a fact that a blessing is pronounced upon those who read this book and "take to heart what is written" (Rev. 1:3).

Revelation 17 and 18 focus on a woman, whose name is "Babylon." She is seated on the beast and represents the apostate religious system that is closely aligned with the secular powers of the world. During the Reformation period, that apostate system was identified as the Roman Catholic Church, and particularly the pope. In my judgment, however, it includes all false religious systems—even those that claim to be evangelical. Sadly, the majority of churches today do not believe that Jesus Christ is truly Lord in accordance with the revelation in the Holy Scripture.

We see in Revelation 17 that God will put it into the hearts of the antichrist, the beast, and his companions the charge to destroy this apostate religious system. God's just judgment will thus be meted out on every idolatrous or atheistic worldview—every religion and philosophy that is outside of the true faith revealed in the Holy Scripture. Revelation 19 will highlight the glorious worship service that will ensue. There shall be a victory celebration in which believers will exult in God and his righteous deeds.

Our Lord wins and will rule for all eternity. And we, the bride of Christ, will be seated with him at the wedding supper of the Lamb. In Revelation 20, we will read about our thousand-year reign with Christ (Rev. 20:6) and the final judgment for those whose names are not written in the book of life (Rev. 20:15).

Thank God that he has granted us faith to trust in his Son, who in our place experienced God's full wrath, so that we may enjoy eternal life and pleasures forevermore in his presence.

The second death has no power over them, but they will be priests of God and of Christ and will reign with him for a thousand years.
—*Revelation 20:6*

evelation 20:4–6 is a particularly crucial passage of Scripture, because nowhere else in the Bible are we explicitly told about the millennium[1]—the temporal, historical, one-thousand-year earthly reign of Jesus Christ after his second coming. It is a continuation of the present rule of Jesus Christ in heaven, but the location is shifted from heaven to this earth. During this thousand-year period, Christ and his saints shall rule on the earth while Satan is bound.

What is the purpose of Christ's millennial reign on earth? While we do not understand every reason, we do know that it will constitute a real "here and now" vindication of the cause of Christ. It will also provide tangible and convincing proof of the victory of righteousness over evil. Above all, the millennium will make manifest to the world the beneficent rule of the King, Jesus Christ—a rule which will be carried out in jutice and in peace. All judicial, legislative, and executive powers shall reside in him.

What benefit does this knowledge of the end times hold for us now? Brothers and sisters, this future is our future. Soon, we will be made like our Lord Jesus Christ, for we will see him as he is. Therefore, let us persevere, endure hardship, and be faithful to the end. Neither secularism nor sin nor sinners nor Satan nor demons nor unbelieving politicians, philosophers, or scientists will finally succeed against God. They will all wither away and die. Every opposing kingdom will fall. The kingdom of Christ will fill the earth. He will reign as King of kings and Lord of lords, and we, who have trusted in Christ, will reign with him on earth as rulers and judges for a thousand years.

If you are outside of Christ, my prayer is that the Holy Spirit will regenerate you and make you a new creation, that you may repent and believe on the Lord Jesus Christ and be justified forever. Then you too can hope in his promised, glorious coming and universal reign, which all who are eagerly waiting for him will enjoy.

---

1   Wayne Grudem, *Systematic Theology* (Grand Rapids: Inter-Varsity, 1994), 1109–1139.

"They will be mine," says the LORD Almighty, "in the day when I make up my treasured possession." —Malachi 3:17

od's great purpose for his people is to transform those who are rebels and sinners by nature into glorious jewels. We are God's treasured possession. This means we are most precious and most beautiful in his sight.

God planned to make us his jewels from all eternity, though we were not very promising material. The Bible says we are by nature wicked sinners. But God says, "I will work with them," and he does. Only God can do this, and he has purposed to do it: "For the LORD has chosen Jacob to be his own, Israel to be his treasured possession" (Ps. 135:4). The reason? Not for any value inherent in us, but simply because of God's own electing love.

In eternity past, God chose us in Christ and predestinated us to be conformed to the glorious image of his own Son. For what purpose? So that we might enjoy fellowship with him forever and that he might take delight in us.

In time, God effectually called us by the gospel of his grace: "Because of his great love for us, God, who is rich in mercy, made us alive with Christ even when we were dead in transgressions" (Eph. 2:4). Then he justified us and adopted us as his children. Now he is sanctifying us, changing us from glory to glory. Accordingly, there will be times when he puts us in his furnace and applies heat. Why? To remove the impurities from us. Just as one refines gold and silver, so God uses trials and tribulations to make us sparkling jewels, holy and blameless in his sight.

Yes, we may suffer now, but soon we shall be brought into the glorious freedom of the children of God. We may groan inwardly now as we wait eagerly for our adoption as sons, the redemption of our bodies, but we can take comfort in the thought that we are God's jewels in preparation. He bought us with the highest price imaginable—the precious blood of Christ—and we are pearls of great price in his eyes. Soon, without blemish and stain, and full of glory, we who have been prepared in advance for glory shall be brought to live in God's presence for all eternity. Hallelujah!

Daily Reading Schedule

January

1	Genesis 1	Job 1, 2	Matthew 1, 2
2	2	3	3, 4
3	3	4, 5	5
4	4	6, 7	6
5	5	8	7, 8
6	6	9, 10	9
7	7, 8	11	10
8	9, 10	12	11
9	11	13	12
10	12	14	13
11	13, 14	15	14
12	15	16, 17	15
13	16	18	16, 17
14	17	19	18
15	18	20	19
16	19	21	20
17	20	22	21
18	21	23, 24	22
19	22	25, 26	23
20	23	27	24
21	24	28	25
22	25	29	26
23	26	30	27
24	27, 28	31	28
25	29	32	Hebrews 1
26	30	33	2
27	31	34	3, 4
28	32	35	5
29	33	36	6, 7
30	34	37	8
31	35	38	9

Daily Reading Schedule

February

1	Genesis 36	Job 39	Hebrews 10
2	37	40	11
3	38	41	12, 13
4	39	42	James 1, 2
5	40	Psalms 1, 2	3–5
6	41	3, 4	1 Peter 1
7	42	5, 6	2, 3
8	43	7, 8	4, 5
9	44	9	2 Peter 1–3
10	45, 46	10	1 John 1, 2
11	47, 48	11, 12	3
12	49, 50	13	4, 5
13	Exodus 1, 2	14, 15	2 & 3 John
14	3, 4	16, 17	Jude
15	5	18	Mark 1
16	6, 7	19	2, 3
17	8	20, 21	4
18	9	22	5
19	10, 11	23, 24	6
20	12	25	7
21	13, 14	26	8
22	15	27, 28	9
23	16, 17	29	10
24	18, 19	30	11, 12
25	20, 21	31, 32	13
26	22	33, 34	14
27	23	35, 36	15, 16
28	24, 25	37, 38	Romans 1

Daily Reading Schedule

March

1	Exodus 26, 27	Psalms 39	Romans 2, 3
2	28, 29	40	4–6
3	30	41	7, 8
4	31, 32	42, 43	9, 10
5	33, 34	44	11, 12
6	35	45	13, 14
7	36, 37	46	15, 16
8	38	47, 48	1 Corinthians 1, 2
9	39	49	3, 4
10	40	50	5, 6
11	Leviticus 1, 2	51, 52	7
12	3, 4	53, 54	8, 9
13	5	55	10, 11
14	6	56	12–14
15	7	57	15
16	8, 9	58	16
17	10	59, 60	2 Corinthians 1, 2
18	11, 12	61, 62	3
19	13	63	4, 5
20	14	64	6, 7
21	15	65, 66	8, 9
22	16	67, 68	10
23	17	69	11, 12
24	18, 19	70, 71	13
25	20	72	Galatians 1, 2
26	21	73	3, 4
27	22	74	5, 6
28	23	75, 76	Ephesians 1, 2
29	24	77	3
30	25	78	4
31	26	79	5

DAILY READING SCHEDULE

APRIL

1	Leviticus 27	Psalms 80	Ephesians 6
2	Numbers 1	81	Philippians 1, 2
3	2	82	3, 4
4	3	83	Colossians 1, 2
5	4	84	3, 4
6	5	85	1 Thess. 1, 2
7	6	86	3, 4
8	7	87	5
9	8, 9	88	2 Thess. 1–3
10	10	89	1 Timothy 1, 2
11	11, 12	90	3, 4
12	13	91, 92	5, 6
13	14	93	2 Timothy 1, 2
14	15	94	3, 4
15	16	95	Titus 1–3
16	17, 18	96, 97	Philemon
17	19	98	Luke 1
18	20	99, 100	2
19	21	101, 102	3
20	22	103	4
21	23	104	5
22	24	105	6
23	25	106	7
24	26	107	8
25	27	108	9
26	28	109	10
27	29, 30	110	11
28	31	111	12
29	32	112, 113	13, 14
30	33, 34	114, 115	15, 16

DAILY READING SCHEDULE

MAY

1	Numbers 35, 36	Psalms 116	Luke 17
2	Deuteronomy 1	117, 118	18
3	2	119:1–24	19
4	3	119:25–40	20
5	4	119:41–64	21
6	5	119:65–80	22
7	6	119:81–104	23
8	7, 8	119:105–120	24
9	9	119:121–136	Acts 1, 2
10	10	119:137–160	3, 4
11	11	119:161–176	5
12	12	120	6, 7
13	13, 14	121, 122	8
14	15, 16	123, 124	9
15	17, 18	125, 126	10
16	19, 20	127, 128	11, 12
17	21	129	13
18	22	130	14, 15
19	23, 24	131	16
20	25	132	17, 18
21	26, 27	133	19
22	28	134	20
23	29	135	21, 22
24	30	136	23, 24
25	31	137	25, 26
26	32	138	27
27	33, 34	139	28
28	Joshua 1	140, 141	John 1
29	2	142, 143	2, 3
30	3, 4	144	4
31	5	145, 146	5

Daily Reading Schedule

June

1	Joshua 6	Psalms 147	John 6
2	7, 8	148	7
3	9	149, 150	8
4	10	Proverbs 1	9
5	11, 12	2	10
6	13	3	11
7	14	4	12
8	15	5	13
9	16, 17	6	14
10	18	7	15, 16
11	19	8	17
12	20, 21	9	18
13	22	10	19
14	23	11	20, 21
15	24	12	Revelation 1, 2
16	Judges 1, 2	13	3
17	3	14	4, 5
18	4, 5	15	6
19	6	16	7, 8
20	7	17	9, 10
21	8	18	11, 12
22	9	19	13
23	10	20	14, 15
24	11, 12	21	16
25	13, 14	22	17
26	15	23	18
27	16	24	19
28	17	25	20
29	18	26	21
30	19	27	22

Daily Reading Schedule

July

1	Judges 20	Proverbs 28	Matthew 1, 2
2	21	29	3, 4
3	Ruth 1	30	5
4	2, 3	31	6
5	4	Ecclesiastes 1, 2	7
6	1 Samuel 1	3, 4	8
7	2	5, 6	9
8	3	7	10
9	4, 5	8, 9	11
10	6, 7	10	12
11	8	11, 12	13
12	9	Song of Songs 1, 2	14
13	10	3, 4	15
14	11, 12	5	16, 17
15	13	6, 7	18, 19
16	14	8	20
17	15	Isaiah 1	21
18	16	2, 3	22
19	17	4	23
20	18	5	24
21	19, 20	6	25
22	21	7	26
23	22	8	27
24	23	9, 10	28
25	24, 25	11, 12	Hebrews 1, 2
26	26, 27	13	3, 4
27	28, 29	14	5, 6
28	30, 31	15, 16	7
29	2 Samuel 1, 2	17, 18	8, 9
30	3, 4	19, 20	10
31	5	21, 22	11

Daily Reading Schedule

August

1	2 Samuel 6	Isaiah 23, 24	Hebrews 12, 13
2	7	25, 26	James 1, 2
3	8, 9	27	3–5
4	10	28	1 Peter 1, 2
5	11, 12	29	3
6	13	30, 31	4, 5
7	14	32	2 Peter 1–3
8	15	33	1 John 1, 2
9	16	34, 35	3, 4
10	17	36, 37	5
11	18	38, 39	2 & 3 John
12	19	40	Jude
13	20	41	Mark 1
14	21	42	2, 3
15	22	43	4
16	23	44	5
17	24	45	6
18	1 Kings 1	46, 47	7
19	2	48	8
20	3	49	9
21	4	50, 51	10
22	5	52, 53	11
23	6	54	12
24	7	55	13
25	8	56	14
26	9	57	15, 16
27	10	58, 59	Romans 1
28	11	60, 61	2
29	12	62	3, 4
30	13	63	5
31	14	64	6

Daily Reading Schedule

September

1	1 Kings 15	Isaiah 65	Romans 7, 8
2	16	66	9, 10
3	17	Jeremiah 1, 2	11
4	18	3	12, 13
5	19	4	14, 15
6	20	5	16
7	21	6	1 Corinthians 1, 2
8	22	7	3
9	2 Kings 1, 2	8, 9	4
10	3	10	5, 6
11	4	11	7
12	5	12, 13	8, 9
13	6	14	10, 11
14	7	15	12–14
15	8	16	15
16	9	17	16
17	10	18, 19	2 Corinthians 1, 2
18	11, 12	20, 21	3
19	13	22	4, 5
20	14	23	6, 7
21	15	24	8–10
22	16	25	11, 12
23	17	26, 27	13
24	18, 19	28	Galatians 1
25	20	29, 30	2
26	21	31	3, 4
27	22	32	5, 6
28	23	33	Ephesians 1, 2
29	24, 25	34	3
30	1 Chronicles 1, 2	35, 36	4, 5

DAILY READING SCHEDULE

OCTOBER

1	1 Chronicles 3	Jeremiah 37, 38	Ephesians 6
2	4	39	Philippians 1, 2
3	5	40, 41	3, 4
4	6	42, 43	Colossians 1
5	7	44	2
6	8	45, 46	3, 4
7	9	47	1 Thessalonians 1–3
8	10	48	4, 5
9	11	49	2 Thessalonians 1
10	12	50	2, 3
11	13	51	1 Timothy 1, 2
12	14	52	3, 4
13	15	Lamentations 1	5, 6
14	16	2	2 Timothy 1, 2
15	17	3	3, 4
16	18	4	Titus 1–3
17	19	5	Philemon
18	20	Ezekiel 1	Luke 1
19	21	2	2
20	22	3	3
21	23	4, 5	4
22	24	6, 7	5
23	25	8	6
24	26	9	7
25	27	10	8
26	28	11	9
27	29	12	10
28	2 Chronicles 1	13	11
29	2	14	12
30	3	15	13
31	4	16	14

DAILY READING SCHEDULE

NOVEMBER

1	2 Chronicles 5	Ezekiel 17	Luke 15
2	6	18	16
3	7	19	17
4	8	20	18
5	9	21, 22	19
6	10	23	20
7	11	24	21
8	12	25, 26	22
9	13	27	23
10	14	28, 29	24
11	15	30, 31	Acts 1, 2
12	16	32	3, 4
13	17	33, 34	5
14	18	35	6, 7
15	19	36	8
16	20	37, 38	9
17	21	39	10
18	22	40	11, 12
19	23	41, 42	13
20	24	43	14, 15
21	25	44, 45	16
22	26	46	17, 18
23	27	47, 48	19
24	28	Daniel 1, 2	20
25	29	3, 4	21, 22
26	30	5, 6	23, 24
27	31	7, 8	25
28	32	9, 10	26
29	33	11, 12	27
30	34	Hosea 1, 2	28

Daily Reading Schedule

December

1	2 Chronicles 35	Hosea 3–5	John 1
2	36	6–8	2
3	Ezra 1	9, 10	3
4	2	11	4
5	3	12–14	5
6	4	Joel 1, 2	6
7	5	3	7
8	6	Amos 1–3	8
9	7	4, 5	9
10	8	6, 7	10
11	9	8, 9	11
12	10	Obadiah	12
13	Nehemiah 1	Jonah 1, 2	13
14	2	3, 4	14, 15
15	3	Micah 1, 2	16
16	4	3, 4	17
17	5	5–7	18
18	6	Nahum 1–3	19
19	7	Habakkuk 1–3	20
20	8	Zephaniah 1–3	21
21	9	Haggai 1, 2	Revelation 1, 2
22	10	Zechariah 1	3, 4
23	11	2, 3	5, 6
24	12	4, 5	7, 8
25	13	6, 7	9, 10
26	Esther 1	8	11, 12
27	2	9–11	13, 14
28	3, 4	12, 13	15, 16
29	5, 6	14	17, 18
30	7, 8	Malachi 1, 2	19, 20
31	9, 10	3, 4	21, 22

SCRIPTURE INDEX

Scripture	Reading Date	Preached
Genesis		
3:9	Jan. 3	1/20/2013
4:6-7	Jan. 4	1/27/2013
7:1	Jan. 7	8/6/2000
12:1-2	Jan. 10	2/17/2013
15:6	Jan. 12	2/24/2013
16:2	Jan. 13	1/20/1991
18:19	Jan. 15	8/3/1996
19:14	Jan. 16	1/31/2010
20:2	Jan. 17	3/10/2013
22:2	Jan. 19	3/10/2013
24:51	Jan. 21	4/14/2013
26:3	Jan. 23	1/29/1997
32:24	Jan. 28	9/9/1990
35:2-3	Jan. 31	12/31/1998
37:4	Feb. 2	3/17/1991
39:9	Feb. 4	7/30/2006
41:41	Feb. 6	3/19/1989
48:15-16	Feb. 11	12/31/2000
50:20	Feb. 12	2/13/2002
Exodus		
13:21	Feb. 21	5/12/1991
15:23-24	Feb. 22	3/7/2004
17:6	Feb. 23	3/5/1995
20:1	Feb. 25	3/3/2004
23:2	Feb. 27	3/1/2006
29:1	Mar. 2	3/12/2006
32:1	Mar. 4	6/7/1987
33:14	Mar. 5	6/14/1987
40:16	Mar. 10	5/28/2006
Leviticus		
9:6	Mar. 16	3/16/1994
26:3	Mar. 31	4/3/2002
27:2	April 1	4/1/1998
Numbers		
14:24	April 13	4/14/1993
16:5	April 15	4/15/2012

Scripture	Reading Date	Preached
20:12	April 18	4/20/1994
21:8	April 19	3/25/1998
22:12	April 20	5/3/1997
32:16	April 29	6/18/2010
Deuteronomy		
1:26	May 2	5/3/2000
4:29	May 5	12/3/2000
5:16	May 6	9/9/2001
6:6-7	May 7	6/26/2011
7:2	May 8	5/10/2000
17:6	May 15	5/16/2010
21:18-19	May 17	5/17/2000
27:15	May 21	5/22/2002
28:1-2	May 22	5/30/2004
29:18	May 23	5/26/2013
30:6	May 24	5/22/2005
32:18	May 26	6/19/2005
Joshua		
4:5-6	May 30	1/16/2005
6:1-2	June 1	1/23/2005
8:34	June 2	5/22/2005
11:20	June 5	3/13/2005
20:2-3	June 12	4/17/2005
23:12-13	June 14	5/1/2005
24:15	June 15	5/8/2005
Judges		
6:14	June 19	1/22/2012
7:22	June 20	1/22/2012
16:19	June 27	10/5/1997
1 Samuel		
1:10	July 6	7/22/2001
3:13	July 8	6/16/1996
7:2	July 10	7/16/2000
13:13	July 15	6/30/1996
15:11	July 17	7/23/2006
31:6	July 28	7/29/2001

Scripture	Reading Date	Preached	Scripture	Reading Date	Preached
2 Samuel			**Ezra**		
6:7	Aug. 1	8/12/2001	1:1	Dec. 3	1/13/2002
9:1	Aug. 3	8/19/2001	8:18	Dec. 10	12/12/2010
12:13	Aug. 5	8/20/2000			
18:33	Aug. 11	8/24/2003	**Nehemiah**		
19:20	Aug. 12	8/13/2003	4:1	Dec. 16	12/18/2002
21:1	Aug. 14	8/11/2004	8:2	Dec. 20	12/29/2002
24:24	Aug. 17	8/18/1991			
			Job		
1 Kings			41:1	Feb. 3	2/2/1994
2:44	Aug. 19	8/26/2001			
11:4	Aug. 28	8/30/1992	**Psalms**		
12:8	Aug. 29	10/8/1986	1:1–2	Feb. 5	10/25/1995
17:15	Sept. 3	9/11/2011	5:3	Feb. 7	11/25/1995
18:18	Sept. 4	9/7/2003	10:1	Feb. 10	12/30/1995
			15:1	Feb. 13	3/9/1996
2 Kings			18:2	Feb. 15	3/30/1996
1:3	Sept. 9	1/25/1998	19:7	Feb. 16	4/13/1996
5:10	Sept. 12	9/18/2011	21:7	Feb. 17	4/27/1996
6:16	Sept. 13	9/13/2009	22:24	Feb. 18	5/11/1996
9:7	Sept. 16	11/12/1986	23:1	Feb. 19	5/25/1996
17:23	Sept. 23	7/12/2015	30:6	Feb. 24	8/10/1996
18:5	Sept. 24	9/15/1985	34:1	Feb. 26	9/14/1996
22:11	Sept. 27	9/27/2000	37:1–5	Feb. 28	3/1/2000
			51:2	Mar. 11	4/7/1991
1 Chronicles			62:1	Mar. 18	3/19/2003
13:14	Oct. 11	10/11/1992	71:20	Mar. 24	3/24/2013
15:13	Oct. 13	10/13/2013	84:11	April 5	4/10/2005
21:22	Oct. 19	10/22/2003	90:11	April 11	6/4/2006
			110:1	April 27	6/24/2000
2 Chronicles			111:1	April 28	5/1/2002
7:14	Nov. 3	9/2/2001	130:3–4	May 18	5/23/2004
12:1	Nov. 8	7/10/1983	139:1	May 27	5/12/1999
15:2	Nov. 11	11/17/2013			
18:1	Nov. 14	11/22/1992	**Proverbs**		
20:3	Nov. 16	11/19/2006	3:5–6	June 6	10/23/2002
21:12	Nov. 17	2/10/1985	5:11	June 8	6/13/2012
25:14	Nov. 21	11/29/2009	19:12	June 22	8/26/2001
32:7	Nov. 28	12/2/2001	22:6	June 25	6/25/2006
36:16	Dec. 2	12/6/2000	28:13	July 1	2/26/2006

Scripture Index

Scripture	Reading Date	Preached
5:11	May 11	7/26/1998
7:55	May 12	8/16/1998
8:4	Nov. 15	8/23/1998
8:29	May 13	8/30/1998
9:3	May 14	9/6/1998
11:26	May 16	10/4/1998
12:5	Nov. 18	10/18/1998
13:4	Nov. 19	11/1/1998
15:9	Nov. 20	2/7/1999
16:29-30	May 19	2/21/1999
17:30	May 20	4/4/1999
18:9	Nov. 22	3/14/1999
21:16	Nov. 25	10/10/1999
25:8	Nov. 27	6/11/2000
26:27	May 25	11/5/2000
27:23-24	Nov. 29	11/12/2000

Romans

Scripture	Reading Date	Preached
3:22-23	Mar. 1	6/13/1993
5:20-21	Aug. 30	3/22/2009
6:11	Aug. 31	5/2/2004
8:13	Mar. 3	2/28/2010
13:1	Mar. 6	4/25/2004
14:1	Sept. 5	6/10/2012
15:14	Mar. 7	7/29/2012
16:1	Sept. 6	10/7/2012

1 Corinthians

Scripture	Reading Date	Preached
1:18	Sept. 7	9/20/2000
1:23-24	Mar. 8	9/29/1996
3:17	Sept. 8	9/20/1992
4:7	Mar. 9	1/30/1983
6:13	Sept. 10	10/28/2001
7:31	Sept. 11	3/12/2003
9:24	Mar. 12	10/10/2004
10:13	Mar. 13	6/22/2001
12:18	Mar. 14	7/4/1999
13:8	Sept. 14	11/11/2012
15:20	Mar. 15	4/8/2012
15:20	Sept. 15	4/20/2003

2 Corinthians

Scripture	Reading Date	Preached
1:5	Mar. 17	3/17/2013
2:17	Sept. 17	3/23/2014
3:17	Sept. 18	8/16/1986
4:8-9	Mar. 19	11/7/1999
5:21	Sept. 19	8/27/2000
7:10	Mar. 20	10/4/1992
9:8	Sept. 21	1/8/2003
9:15	Mar. 21	12/24/1995
10:4	Mar. 22	6/23/2001
11:4	Mar. 23	8/16/2009
11:13	Sept. 22	5/15/2005

Galatians

Scripture	Reading Date	Preached
1:9	Mar. 25	8/16/2009
3:24	Mar. 26	10/15/1989
6:7	Mar. 27	2/17/1999

Ephesians

Scripture	Reading Date	Preached
1:17	Sept. 28	10/1/2000
1:18-19	Mar. 28	9/14/2003
3:18	Mar. 29	9/21/2003
3:21	Sept. 29	3/19/2000
4:24	Mar. 30	7/18/2004
5:18	Sept. 30	8/29/2004

Philippians

Scripture	Reading Date	Preached
2:2	April 2	10/4/2009
4:12-13	Oct. 3	11/21/2004
4:19	April 3	1/5/2003

Colossians

Scripture	Reading Date	Preached
1:9	April 4	11/28/2010
2:9	Oct. 5	7/10/1993
3:17	Oct. 6	10/16/1994

1 Thessalonians

Scripture	Reading Date	Preached
1:7	April 6	4/20/2005
2:8	Oct. 7	4/27/2005
4:1	Oct. 8	7/20/1994

Scripture	Reading Date	Preached
4:13	April 7	4/7/1999 & 4/14/1999
5:6	April 8	2/9/1992 & 2/16/1992
2 Thessalonians		
1:8	Oct. 9	8/2/2015
3:11	April 9	6/8/1997
1 Timothy		
1:13	April 10	10/4/2000
4:1	Oct. 12	2/16/2003
6:12	April 12	8/14/1994
2 Timothy		
1:10	Oct. 14	12/19/2010
3:16-17	Oct. 15	6/28/2009
4:1	April 14	1/2/2011
Titus		
2:7	Oct. 16	4/19/2015
Philemon		
18	April 16	10/19/2003
Hebrews		
1:2	Jan. 25	10/13/1985
2:10	Jan. 26	12/1/1985
3:13	Jan. 27	12/15/1985
4:12	July 26	1/14/2007
5:11	July 27	2/4/2007
6:19	Jan. 29	1/19/1986
8:8	Jan. 30	3/11/2007
8:10	July 29	3/11/2007
10:19	Feb. 1	2/9/1986
10:24	July 30	2/17/2002
11:35	July 31	8/12/2007

Scripture	Reading Date	Preached
1 Peter		
2:2	Aug. 4	7/7/1996
5:6	Feb. 8	2/24/2002
2 Peter		
1:1	Feb. 9	1/16/1985
2:1	Aug. 7	10/3/2004
1 John		
2:2	Aug. 8	1/14/2001
5:10	Aug. 10	8/20/2006
Jude		
3	Feb. 14	4/18/2004
Revelation		
1:17	Dec. 21	8/27/2006
3:17	June 16	9/3/2006
4:1	Dec. 22	9/10/2006
5:9-10	June 17	9/17/2006
6:9	June 18	12/14/1986
12:1	Dec. 26	1/25/1987
12:3	June 21	1/25/1987
13:7	Dec. 27	2/8/1987
14:1	June 23	2/15/1987
16:16	June 24	3/17/1985
18:2	Dec. 29	7/4/1993
18:10	June 26	4/26/1987
20:6	Dec. 30	3/24/1996
20:13	June 28	6/29/2003
21:27	June 29	12/31/2006
22:11	June 30	7/1/2001

Grace and Glory Ministries

GRACE & GLORY
MINISTRIES

Grace and Glory Ministries is an extension of Grace Valley Christian Center. We are committed to the teaching of God's infallible word. It is our mission to proclaim the whole gospel to the whole world for the building up of the whole body of Christ.

For more information on the ministries of Grace Valley Christian Center, please visit:

http://www.gracevalley.org

To obtain additional copies of this book, please e-mail:

gvcc@gracevalley.org